CHILD PROTECTION IN INDIA

Child Protection in India: Assessing Multi-disciplinary Response Mechanisms offers a comprehensive exploration of the institutional, legal, and social frameworks surrounding child protection in India. Anchored in a multidisciplinary approach, the book brings together insights from law, social work, psychology, education, and public policy to examine how various systems interact in addressing the issues related to protection of children from abuse, neglect, trafficking, and exploitation.

This book is intended for researchers, academicians, legal professionals, social workers, policymakers, child rights activists, and students engaged in child welfare and protection studies. It critically analyses existing response mechanisms by stakeholders such as the Juvenile Justice Boards, Child Welfare Committees, Child Care Institutions, police, and the judiciary, and the implementation of various laws, including Juvenile Justice (Care and Protection) Act, the POCSO Act, Prohibition of Child Marriage Act, while also highlighting challenges in inter-agency coordination.

By combining chapters under four broad themes focusing on empirical research, policy review, and case studies, this volume equips readers with a nuanced understanding of the gaps and strengths in current practices and highlights of best practices around the world. The book aims to foster a rights-based and child-centric approach, encouraging collaboration across disciplines and sectors. It is a valuable resource for anyone seeking to engage meaningfully with child protection frameworks in India and to contribute to more effective, sustainable interventions.

Paromita Chattoraj is Professor of Law at the National Law University Odisha (NLUO).

CHILD PROTECTION IN INDIA

Assessing Multi-disciplinary Response Mechanisms

Edited by Paromita Chattoraj

Routledge
Taylor & Francis Group
LONDON AND NEW YORK

Designed cover image: Getty Images

First published 2026
by Routledge
4 Park Square, Milton Park, Abingdon, Oxon OX14 4RN

and by Routledge
605 Third Avenue, New York, NY 10158

Routledge is an imprint of the Taylor & Francis Group, an Informa business

British Library Cataloguing-in-Publication Data
A catalogue record for this book is available from the British Library

ISBN: 978-1-032-99995-1 (hbk)
ISBN: 978-1-032-99993-7 (pbk)
ISBN: 978-1-003-60707-6 (ebk)

DOI: 10.4324/9781003607076

Typeset in Sabon
by Apex CoVantage, LLC

For my daughters Turiya and Troyee

CONTENTS

FIGURES

TABLES

ABOUT THE EDITOR

Paromita Chattoraj is Professor of Law at the National Law University Odisha (NLUO). She graduated with an LLB (Hons) from the Department of Law, University of Calcutta, and completed her LLM, having specialization in Criminal Law, with a Gold Medal in 2004. She completed her PhD in the area of Rape Laws in 2013. She had been the recipient of an ICSSR grant in 2013–14 for data Collection in California, USA, for comparative research on Rape Investigation and Prosecution in India and the USA. She has been involved with research projects, namely, International Self-Reported Delinquency Project (ISRD-3) from 2012 to 2015; Major Research Program 2018–20 on Investigation and Trial of Rape cases in the States of WB, OD, and JH; and Research project under the special call for Vision Viksit Bharat@2047 (VVB@2047) on "Inclusive Education for Divyangjan in Odisha and Assam: Strategies for Equitable Learning and Empowerment" funded by the ICSSR. She has co-authored the book *Sexual Offences Against Children in India – Understanding the Criminal Justice Responses* by Routledge and authored other research articles in reputed international journals.

CONTRIBUTORS

Shrilekha Banerjee
PhD (pursuing), West Bengal National University of Juridical Sciences
Kolkata, India

Dr. Parimita Dash
Associate Professor at KIIT School of Law
Bhubaneswar, India

Amod Kanth
Founder and Mentor – Prayas JAC Society and Allied Organizations
Chairman – Prayas Institute of Juvenile Justice and Prayas Institute of Economic Empowerment
Founder Chairman – DCPCR/DWSSC and Former DGP
New Delhi, India

Dr. Elisha Kanungo
Assistant Professor of Law, Birla Global University
Bhubaneswar, India

Dr. Rishika Khare
Assistant Professor of Law at National Law University Odisha
Cuttack, India

Madan B. Lokur
Former Judge, Supreme Court of India, Former Judge, Supreme Court of Fiji and also Former Chief Justice of Gauhati High Court and Andhra Pradesh High Court and Former Judge of Delhi High Court
New Delhi, India

Dr. Sohini Mahapatra
Assistant Professor of Law at National Law University Odisha
Cuttack, India
Susmita Priyadarshini Mishra
Assistant Professor, KIIT School of Law
Bhubaneswar, India

Dr. Soumya Mohapatra
Assistant Professor of Sociology at KIIT School of Law
Bhubaneswar, India

Dr. Nikita Pattajoshi
Assistant Professor of Law at National Law University Odisha
Cuttack, India

Anonza Priyadarshini
Ph.D. (pursuing), Central University of South Bihar
Gaya, India

Dr. Tanaya Raha
Assistant Professor, South Calcutta Law College
Kolkata, India

Rajiv Ranjan
Assistant Professor of Law, School of Law, UPES
Dehradun, India

Dr. Rupashree Sahoo
Assistant Professor, ASBM University
Bhubaneswar, India

Dulung Sengupta
Assistant Professor of Law at the School of Law, Vellore Institute of Technology
Chennai, India

Ananya Singh
Youth Advisor to the USAID Digital Youth Council & PCYDH
India

Ayushi Srivastava
PhD Scholar, India International University of Legal Education and Research
Goa
Assistant Professor of Law at National Law University Odisha
Cuttack, India

Dr. Sonali Swetapadma
Assistant Professor, KIIT School of Law
Bhubaneshwar, India

Saumya Tripathi
LLM, National Law University Odisha
Cuttack, India

ACKNOWLEDGEMENTS

This book was conceptualized during the 9th Conference of the International Society for Child Indicators (ISCI) on the theme "Global Childhoods: Critical Perspectives Promoting Theoretical, Empirical and Policy Understandings" organized by the National Law University Odisha (NLUO) in February 2024, by Prof. Ved Kumari, the Vice Chancellor, NLUO, to be released as the "Annual Survey of Child Rights". I am deeply grateful to Prof. Ved for her invaluable insights on many aspects of child rights during the initial stage of this book and for motivating me to publish this book as a sole editor. I cannot thank Ved Mam enough, as she also encouraged me to invite contributions from two of the very prominent figures in the child rights scene in India. Justice M.B. Lokur, a Former Judge of the Supreme Court and a pioneer member of the Juvenile Justice Committee (JJC), has shared his lived experiences as a member of the JJC in his chapter, which will add immense value to this book. I thank Justice Lokur for his excellent contribution. Shri Amod Kant, who is the Founder and Mentor of Prayas Juvenile Aid Centre and Allied Organizations, which is a non-governmental organization working for children who are neglected as well as in conflict with the law since 1989, has contributed greatly to the cause of child protection in India. His chapter, highlighting the laws and policies for children in need of care and protection and the unique efforts of Prayas in providing support services, is one of the highlights of this book. I am immensely grateful to Amodji for his wonderful piece.

I also wish to thank all the other authors of this book for their contributions and multiple revisions as per the editor's comments and for being extremely patient throughout the process. A special mention for Ms. Geeti Mohapatra, who was interning under me when I received close to 40 chapters in response to the call for chapters and helped me in the screening process. I also wish to mention the support of my scholar and one of the authors, Dr. Sonali Swetapadma, during the final stages of the manuscript submission.

I wish to express my gratitude to my teachers and PhD supervisors, Prof. V.D. Sebastian and Prof. Bhavani Prasad Panda, for their unwavering faith in me. To my father, for always being there for me and keeping his blessings as my guardian angel. For my mother for giving me strength and my brother for always challenging me to test my limits. My two adolescent daughters, who think their mother can do anything, and my husband, for inspiring me to always pursue excellence. And, finally, my pranam to Ma Sharada and Swami Vivekananda and my Ishtadevata Shri Ramakrishna Paramahamsa, as it is he who is doing everything – I am but his mere instrument.

Paromita Chattoraj

ABBREVIATIONS

Abbreviation	Full Form
AFAAs	Authorized Foreign Adoption Agencies
BNS	Bharatiya Nyaya Sanhita
BNSS	Bhartiya Nagarik Suraksha Sanhita
CA	Central Authority
CARINGS	Central Adoption Resource Information & Guidance System
CAs	Central Authorities
CCI	Child Care Institution
CCL	Children in Conflict with Law
CJP	Criminal Justice Process
CNCP	Children in Need of Care and Protection
CPCR	Commissions for Protection of Child Rights
CrPC	Code of Criminal Procedure
CSO	Civil Society Organization
CWC	Child Welfare Committee
CYSA	Child and Youth Services Act (Germany)
DCP	Deputy Commissioner of Police
DCPCR	Delhi Commission for Protection of Child Rights
DCPO	District Child Protection Officer
DCPU	District Child Protection Unit
FAO	Food and Agricultural Organization
FIR	First Information Report
GOI	Government of India
ICP	Individual Care Plan
IIT	Indian Institute of Technology

IPC	Indian Penal Code
ISMW	Inter-State Migrant Workmen (Regulation of Employment and Conditions of Service) Act
IT Act	Information Technology Act 2000
JJ Act	Juvenile Justice (Care and Protection of Children) Act
JJB	Juvenile Justice Board
JJC	Juvenile Justice Committee
JJDPA	Juvenile Justice and Delinquency Prevention Act (US)
JJS	Juvenile Justice System
JSS	Jan Shikshan Sansthan
MMS	Multimedia Messaging Service
NCERT	National Council of Educational Research and Training
NCPCR	National Commission for Protection of Child Rights
NCRB	National Crime Records Bureau
NGO	Non-Governmental Organization
NIMHANS	National Institute of Mental Health and Neuro-Sciences
NORAD	Norwegian Agency for Development Cooperation
NSDC	National Skill Development Corporation
NSSO	National Sample Survey Office
OH	Observation Home
OHB	Observation Home for Boys
OJJDP	Office of Juvenile Justice and Delinquency Prevention
PCMA	Prohibition of Child Marriage Act
PIJJ	Prayas Institute of Juvenile Justice
POCSO Act	Protection of Children from Sexual Offences Act
RTE Act	Right of Children to Free and Compulsory Education Act
SAA	Specialized Adoption Agency
SARA	State Adoption Resource Agency
SCPCR	State Commission for Protection of Child Rights
SCPS	State Child Protection Societies
SH	Special Home
SJPU	Special Juvenile Police Unit
SMSA	Samagra Shiksha Abhiyan
SPSS	Sanchay Prayas Swavalamban Sansthan
UK	United Kingdom
UN	United Nations
UNCRC	United Nations Convention on the Rights of the Child
UNICEF	United Nations International Children's Emergency Fund
US	United States (of America)
YCA	Youth Courts Act (Germany)

STATUTES

Statute/Act Name

1. Bharatiya Nagarik Suraksha Sanhita (BNSS), 2023
2. Bharatiya Nyaya Sanhita (BNS), 2023
3. Child and Adolescent Labour (Prohibition and Regulation) Act, 1986/2016
4. Child, Youth and Family Services Act, 2017
5. Child Labour (Prohibition and Regulation) Act, 1986 and Amendment Act, 2016
6. Children Act, 1960
7. Children's Online Privacy Protection Act (COPPA), 1998
8. Code of Criminal Procedure (CrPC), 1973
9. Commissions for Protection of Child Rights Act, 2005
10. Constitution of India – Articles 15(3), 21-A, 24, 39(f), 14
11. Convention on the Elimination of Discrimination Against Women (CEDAW)
12. Convention on the Rights of the Child (UNCRC), 1989
13. Criminal Procedure Code, 1973
14. Digital Personal Data Protection Act, 2023
15. Factories Act, 1948
16. General Data Protection Regulation (GDPR), 2016
17. Illinois Juvenile Court Act, 1899
18. Indian Penal Code (IPC), 1860
19. Information Technology (Amendment) Act, 2008
20. Information Technology Act, 2000
21. Inter-State Migrant Workmen (Regulation of Employment and Conditions of Service) Act, 1979

22. Juvenile Justice (Care and Protection of Children) Act, 2000
23. Juvenile Justice (Care and Protection of Children) Act, 2015
24. Juvenile Justice Act, 1986
25. Juvenile Justice and Delinquency Prevention Act (JJDPA), U.S.
26. Marsy's Law (California, USA)
27. Medical Termination of Pregnancy (Amendment) Act, 2021
28. Mental Health Act, 1987
29. Mental Healthcare Act, 2017
30. Model Code on Indian Family Law, 2024 (proposed)
31. National Health Policy, 2002
32. National Mental Health Programme (NMHP)
33. National Nutrition Policy, 1993
34. National Policy on Child Labour, 1987
35. National Policy on Children, 1974
36. Odisha Child and Adolescent Labour (Prohibition and Regulation) Rules, 1994
37. Odisha Factories Rules, 1950
38. Personal Information Protection Law (China)
39. POCSO (Amendment) Act, 2019
40. Privacy Act, 1988 (Australia)
41. Prohibition of Child Marriage Act, 2006
42. Protection of Children from Sexual Offences (POCSO) Act, 2012
43. Right of Children to Free and Compulsory Education (RTE) Act, 2009
44. UN Standard Minimum Rules for the Administration of Juvenile Justice (Beijing Rules)
45. United Nations Convention on the Rights of the Child (UNCRC), 1989
46. Youth Courts Act (YCA)

INTRODUCTION

Aspects of Child Protection and Response Mechanisms

Paromita Chattoraj

Introduction

Child protection and welfare have become international issues in a globalized world. Ideas about childhood and the upbringing of children vary widely, depending upon the prevailing economic, socio-cultural, religious, and political contexts.[1] These have had dramatic effects on the way societies value children and the role acquired by the state in their protection and advancing their well-being.[2] There is a unanimous consensus among everyone that all children deserve the best possible mechanisms for the protection of their rights. Children, and especially small children, rely on adults who care for them to meet both their physical needs and their needs for security, safety, love, and a sense of[3] belonging. But children are often harmed by those whom they rely upon for protection. Occasionally, they are also killed, and more often they are injured, used for sexual gratification, or treated in ways that may not do any obvious physical harm but which have long-term emotional and psychological consequences. And then most often still they are just poorly cared for to the point that their basic needs go unmet, whether this is because their caregivers are indifferent to these needs, unable to recognize them, or simply too preoccupied with their own.[4]

Depending on the circumstances and the context, children sometimes decide certain matters for themselves, especially if they are emancipated, that is, free from parental authority and living independently. In other contexts, the parents might make decisions for a child, for example, decisions regarding medical treatment or commitment to a medical institution, and still in some other contexts, the state might make decisions on the child's behalf, as on the question of adequate parenting or even regarding medical treatment, especially in life-threatening situations.[5]

DOI: 10.4324/9781003607076-1

Children's lives are underpinned by an incoherent hotchpotch of legal principles and government policies. A rights-based approach might address at least some of their weaker aspects very effectively if the government and judiciary were prepared to utilize it more wholeheartedly. In particular, such an approach can address the problem experienced by children of being the focus of various specialized branches of law and policy, with their own distinctive character, with no coherence or similarity in objectives. By placing the differing aspects of childhood in a framework of rights rather than, for example, in a medical or education-based context, the boundaries between the various disciplines start becoming irrelevant, with a far more coherent outcome being possible.[6]

The time is right for such a change in approach, given the greatly increased level of right consciousness in the world today regarding children and their rights. The adoption of the Convention on the Rights of the Child in 1989 and its incorporation by most of the member states, including India, along with a host of legislations specifically for children, promise to guarantee an ecosystem that may be more conducive to realizing children's rights and protecting their childhood.[7]

There are different ways of approaching the idea and practice of child rights. One of the popular approaches, for example, sees the UN Convention on the Rights of the Child (UNCRC) as concerning three broad areas: provision, protection, and participation. UNICEF foregrounds what it calls the four core principles of the convention and locates these in some of the specific articles of the UNCRC:[8]

- Non-discrimination, or universality (Article 2)
- Best interests of the child (Article 3)
- Right to life survival and development (Article 6)
- Respect for the views of the child (Article 12)

The Constitution of India recognizes the special status of children through articles 23, 24, 21A, 39(e) and (f), and 45. In pursuance of the constitutional directions various laws have been enacted which covers a wide range of matters relating to children, for example, the Child Labour (Prohibition and Regulation) Act, 1986; Prohibition of Child Marriage Act, 2006; Right to Education Act 2009; Juvenile Justice Acts of 1986, 2000, and finally 2015; Commission for Protection of Child Rights; and Protection of Children from Sexual Offences (POCSO) Act 2012. Protection of children from abuse and exploitation and upholding their rights is a shared responsibility of various stakeholders for any law or policy to be effective. And, finally, it is to be noted that participation is the key, so children must be involved in decision making regarding them and must be made aware of their own rights.[9]

In this book, chapters have been brought under four broad themes. The first theme is on "Child in Need of Care and Protection and in Conflict with Law". In the Indian legal system, the juvenile justice system is covered by the Juvenile Justice (Care and Protection) Act of 2015 (JJ Act). This law in the present form has undergone considerable changes since the first law enacted as the Juvenile Justice Act 1986, after India became a signatory to the Beijing rules (United Nations Standard Minimum Rules for the Administration of Juvenile Justice adopted on 29 November 1985 by the General Assembly). Under the JJ Act anyone below the age of 18 years is recognized as a child, and the Act covers two categories of children: one who needs care and protection (neglected children) and the other category who come in conflict with the law (i.e. accused of committing an offence). The primary ideals of the law are care protection, rehabilitation, and reintegration of both categories of children. Under this theme there are four chapters as follows:

Child in Need of Care and Protection – Their Rights Deserve the First Call

This invited chapter has been authored by the Founder and Mentor of Prayas Juvenile Aid Centre and Allied Organizations and also the Chairman of Prayas Institute of Juvenile Justice and Prayas Institute of Economic Empowerment, which is a non-governmental organization working for children who are neglected as well as in conflict with law since 1989. In this chapter the author highlights the position of children in need of care and protection under the law and comes to the conclusion that children in conflict with the law are also in need of care and protection and that the rights and needs of such children are synonymous. The high point of this chapter is the section dedicated to the author's valuable experience of handling such children and the efforts made by Prayas in the rehabilitation and reintegration of the children.

Role of Higher Judiciary in Monitoring Juvenile Care Through Juvenile Justice Committees – An Insider's Perspective

This is also an invited chapter where the author shares valuable insights as the pioneering judge to be nominated for the Juvenile Justice Committee (JJC). The author, who was a former judge of the Supreme Court, had been appointed as a one-man committee to suggest improvements in the working of the homes and organization under the Juvenile Justice (Care and Protection and Children) Act, 2000 and the Juvenile Justice (Care and Protection of Children) Rules, 2007. Through this chapter the author shares firsthand experience regarding the evolution and coming into being of the JJC, the challenges faced by it, and how the various stakeholders were integrated towards the common goal of providing care and rehabilitation of the children.

Comparing the Role of Child Care Institutions in the Rehabilitation of Children in Conflict With Law in India With Global Best Practices

In this chapter, through an examination of the circumstances found in juvenile prison facilities in India and other developed countries, the author highlights the support systems and rehabilitation services open to young offenders, assessing how well they work to help them reintegrate into the community and avoid repeat offences. The chapter also throws light on the systems around the world with special reference to some of the developed countries like the US, the UK, and Germany, comparing the rights of children held in juvenile detention facilities in India along with other developed nations.

Procedural Aspects Concerning Child in Conflict With Law in the Indian Legislative Framework

In this chapter the author focuses on the handling of "children in conflict with the law" under the JJ Act due to the apparent gaps between the legally prescribed procedure and the practical implementation thereof. The chapter highlights the dilemmas faced by the courts in determining the juvenility to procedures for the transfer of cases in cases of children falling in the borderline age of 16–18 and accused of heinous or serious offences. The author analyses with "the best interests of the child" in mind, the procedural elements of circumstances when such children find themselves at odds with the law.

The second theme is on "Addressing Specific Child Vulnerabilities". Under this theme four specific situations have been discussed that tend to make the position of children especially vulnerable. In this section the chapters address the child vulnerabilities under the following chapters:

A Socio-Legal Examination of Child Marriage and Its Societal Ramifications

Child marriages are still prevalent in India, particularly in the country's rural sections and the disadvantaged sections of society. Even in today's time, when women's empowerment is one of the primary goals of the government, it is surprising to note why child marriage proponents still meet little resistance from more enlightened as well as more educated populations and why reasonable voices opposing it are suppressed. Through this chapter the authors have highlighted the factors behind the high prevalence of child marriages in India and its direct impact on the autonomy of children in matters of childbearing, education, occupation, and other pressing concerns like domestic violence and access to justice. The chapter also analyses the present legislative and policy framework for preventing child marriages and the bottlenecks that prevent the authorities.

Legal Rights of Children Born Out of Live-In Relationships

Live-in relationships challenge traditional societal norms in a tradition-bound country like India and raise complex questions regarding the recognition, legality, and social acceptance of partnerships formed outside the institution of marriage. In this chapter the author aims to discuss one such difficulty within this context, which is encountered in navigating the rights and welfare of children born out of such relationships. This chapter focuses on legal rights and protections available to such children and the potential impediments and barriers that may hinder children in live-in relationships from effectively accessing their rights and protections like birth registration, inheritance rights, parental responsibility, custody, and social benefits.

Myriads of Vulnerabilities of Distressed Child Migrants: Case Study from Odisha

Distressed migrant workers are considered to be a distinct category of vulnerable workers amongst the generally exploited larger workforce. The authors highlight in this chapter that the law in question does not deal with scenarios where a migrant worker may be a child. This chapter highlights how the socioeconomic protections contributing to the welfare and development of children remain unfulfilled due to distressed migration. Specifically, the chapter looks at four safeguards – education, working hours, employment wages, and stable living arrangements that are protected as fundamental rights under the Indian Constitution and their violations in the migrant children's destination states. The authors present findings from the data collected as part of a social mapping exercise of inter-state migrant workers in four districts of the State of Odisha (India) through a household survey, in the context of gaps existing in the law and policy framework.

Are the Children **Lacking an Exclusive Green Safeguard in India?**

In this chapter the author comprehensively discusses the different child rights, aligned with the environmental rights of the children. The chapter focuses on the UN Committee on the Rights of the Child, which has brought out the General Comment No. 26 (GC26) on the Rights of the Child and the Environment, prioritizing the climate disaster threat to the youth. A relevant elucidation of different child-based principles to amplify the scope of their environmental rights has also been provided in this chapter. The child rights-based approach is an effective weapon to overhaul the idea. The author also sheds light on children's environmental rights by focusing on youth participation and the role of NGOs.

The third theme revolves around "Protection of Children in the Online Platforms". Due to the sheer access to online platforms and the modern life being completely taken over from cradle to the grave by digital media, children cannot remain outside this storm. In the post-pandemic era, after a prolonged online mode of education for almost two years, children were exposed to the internet and social media, mostly unmonitored and without parental supervision. Even after the lockdown, however, the online activities have continued due to processes developed requiring children to continue to access electronic gadgets, internet, and social media. In this section four chapters present the pertinent issues surrounding vulnerabilities of children in the online platforms and the response mechanisms for their protection.

Balancing Protection and Participation: Children's Data, Online Privacy, and Age of Digital Consent

An immense volume of children's data is revolving in the online platforms without children having little or no say over who does what with "their" data. In this chapter, the author highlights that in the realm of the concept of "evolving capacities of the child", children, being digital natives, often have a refined understanding of the potential risks and rewards involved in the online world than the older generation. By comparative analysis of the existing frameworks under international instruments and Indian laws, the author argues that standardizing consent requirements across age groups may prove to be counterproductive to children's preparation for and participation in the digital economy. The author argues that it is crucial to move beyond chronological age as the sole determinant of the "capacity to consent" in the digital arena.

Safeguarding the Vulnerabilities of Children Relating to Cyberbullying From the Socio-Legal-Technical Dimensions in India

When it comes to the vulnerabilities of children in cyberspace, the issue of their privacy and the information pertaining to their personal lives, which they process in the virtual world, comes out as one of the major concerns. The authors in this chapter highlight the vulnerabilities specifically in cyberspace with a special focus on the issue of cyberbullying of children and the social, legal, and technological (cybersecurity technology) measures, which can be adopted for securing the interests of the children in cyberspace.

Protection of Mental Health of Children in the Digital Ecosystem

In this chapter the author discusses the *new normal* due to social distancing mandates during the post-COVID-19 period that has increased the propensity amongst most of the children to on-screen activities through various electronic devices and associated the sedentary behaviours. This translated to moderate to severe physical and mental health issues amongst the children and adolescents. This chapter focuses on the mental health problems due to prolonged sedentary behaviours and brings out the policy implications by analysing the mental health policy and relevant legislation on it in India to ensure that the rights of children are prioritized and protected.

Response of the Indian Criminal Justice System Towards Children as Vulnerable Victims of Cybercrime in the Digital Age

This chapter focuses on the offences committed against children through cyberspace in India and analyses the laws prevailing in India relating to cybercrime against children. The author highlights that in spite of legal mandates for better efficiency in handling cybercrimes against children, the rate of pendency for investigation by police, as well as the rate of pendency for trials in courts, is increasing. So, in this chapter, the author focuses on the quantitative analysis of the disposal of cybercrime cases committed against children by police and the disposal of such cases by courts to understand the responses of the criminal justice system towards children.

The fourth theme concerns "Response to Sexual Offences". Sexual abuse, exploitation, and violence against children are instances of gross human rights violations and reflect the extreme moral degradation of society. However, across the globe, such instances are frequent in spite of very stringent laws. Therefore, we are faced with a social reality that such incidents are inevitable, so it is imperative that we devise processes that help in mitigating the trauma of such child victims when they interact with the criminal justice system. Under this theme, three chapters deal with three different ideas of responding to sexual offence, out of which the last chapter takes a look at such children in their adolescence involved in sexual relations but treated as offenders due to the draconian nature of the law applicable to them. The chapters under this section are as follows:

Implementation of the Victim-Friendly Trial Procedures in Cases of Sexual Offences Against Children

In this chapter the author details the POCSO Act, 2012, designed to protect children from sexual exploitation and abuse and the victim-centric elements aimed at ensuring that the judicial process remains sensitive to the interests and rights of child victim survivors. The author presents the data collected from eight special courts designated to try POCSO cases and 61 police stations in those eight districts in the state of Odisha by way of face-to-face interview techniques. The chapter also sheds light on the victim support services in the UK, Sweden, and Canada, during the trial of child sexual abuse cases and argues for systemic changes for improved infrastructure and thorough training and effective implementation of the victim support services.

Dissecting the Conundrum of Mandatory Reporting and POCSO, 2012, in the Realm of Child Sexual Abuse

This chapter critically explores the mandatory reporting provisions under the POCSO Act, 2012, in cases of child sexual abuse, compelling professionals like teachers, medical personnel, and social workers to promptly report suspected cases to relevant authorities. Despite its gravity, a prevalent "conspiracy of silence" often envelops child sexual abuse cases, with individuals, organizations, and entire communities choosing to overlook or conceal the issue. Through this chapter the author emphasizes the societal responsibility to break this silent pact, advocating for the crucial role of reporting child sexual abuse, on the one hand, and the rights of the child and guardians, urging a conservative approach to prevent unwarranted accusations, on the other hand.

The Model for Juvenile Sexual Offenders in India: A Need for a Relook?

In this chapter the author focuses on the dichotomous situation presented by cases of sexual offences involving adolescents (within the age frame of 16–18 years) within the present legal framework where the dual laws of POCSO Act and JJ Act intersect treating the girl as a victim whereas the boy is brought under the JJ Act as the perpetrator even when the POCSO Act is a gender-neutral legislation. The present chapter looks at the model, both legal and institutional, for responding to juvenile sexual offenders, focusing on the intersectionality aspect of the JJ Act and the POCSO Act

2012. This chapter also highlights the dilemmas faced by the courts in dealing with such cases and the lack of institutional mechanisms to handle such juvenile sexual offenders, proving counterproductive to the very ideal of rehabilitation that is central to the JJ Act.

Notes

1 Penelope Welbourne & John Dixon, *La Protection et Le Bien-Être d'enfance: Culture, Politique et Pratique*, 19 European Journal of Social Work 827 (2016).
2 N. Gilbert, N. Parton, & M. Skivenes (Eds.), Child protection systems: International trends and orientations. Oxford: Oxford University Press, 2011.
3 P. Welbourne & J. Dixon (Eds.), Child protection and child welfare: A global appraisal of cultures, policy, and practice. London: Jessica Kingsley, 2013.
4 Chris Beckett, Child protection: An introduction, p.5, 2nd Ed. London: Sage, 2007.
5 Samuel M. Davis, Children's rights under the law, p.4. Oxford University Press, 2011.
6 Jane Fortin, Children's rights and the developing law, p.3. 3rd Ed. Cambridge University Press, 2009.
7 Nuzrat Parveen Khan, Child rights and the law, p.xiii, 2nd Ed. Universal Law Publishing, 2016.
8 Phil Jones & Garry Walker (Eds.), Children's rights in practice, p.6. Sage Publications, 2012.
9 Beckett, Child protection, p.xiii.

PART 1

Child in Need of Care and Protection and in Conflict With Law

1

CHILDREN IN NEED OF CARE AND PROTECTION – THEIR RIGHTS DESERVE THE FIRST CALL

Amod K. Kanth

Introduction

The children in need of care and protection (CNCP) or the children who are legally required to be looked after holistically by the stakeholders within the juvenile justice system (JJS) cover a huge segment amongst the children, who constitute nearly 40% of India's 1.42 billion population. The types of CNCP as defined under the law may range from being those found without home, settled abode, or ostensible means of subsistence or working, begging, and living on streets; residing with someone (even parents and guardians) threatening to kill, causing or creating likelihood of injury, exploitation, abuse, or neglect; children without parents and anyone to take care or protect them; and those abandoned or surrendered. The Juvenile Justice (JJ) Act, in conjunction with other legislations, such as the Child Labour (Prohibition and Regulation) Act, 2016;[1] the Commission for Protection of Child Rights (CPCR) Act, 2005;[2] the Right of Children to Free and Compulsory Education (RTE) Act, 2009;[3] and the Protection of Children from Sexual Offences (POCSO) Act, 2012,[4] among others, create a complete mechanism to fulfil the rights and needs of the CNCP, but the implementation of laws and the actual support from rescue to rehabilitation amongst the estimated 30 to 35 million of such children remains a far cry.[5]

JJS in India vis-à-vis Child Rights and International Instruments

From our experience as practitioners within the evolving JJS of India through Prayas Juvenile Aid Centre (JAC) (Society) (est. 1988) as one of the hardcore and leading organizations, with police and other segments of the system and

DOI: 10.4324/9781003607076-3

myself being the first Chairman of the Delhi Commission for Protection of Child Rights (DCPCR),[6] it is found that the 'Needs and Rights of the Children', which are synonymous, are broadly covered in the laws concerning the CNCP.[7] The Child Rights in India remained ingrained in various progressive laws relating to children, as explained hereunder, yet they remained legally undefined until we enacted the CPCR Act, 2005, giving justiciability to the United Nations Convention on the Protection of the Rights of Child (UNCRC) rights and other international instruments which India had long since ratified.[8] In our considered opinion, the fulfilment of the basic needs and rights of children (now broadly defined as the CNCP and children in conflict with law (CCL) constitutes the core of the juvenile justice and child protection systems in India.[9]

The JJS in India aligns with the UNCRC's objectives to ensure that children below 18 years are not deprived of their inherent natural rights and basic human rights, alongside the rights of children as enshrined in the UNCRC.[10] The Juvenile Justice (Care and Protection of Children) Act, 2015,[11] and the JJ Model Rules, 2016,[12] provide special status to the CNCP and CCL, a vast majority being the CNCP, whose needs and rights are crucial for their care, protection, development, rehabilitation, and social reintegration. India ratified the UNCRC in 1992, requiring the government to incorporate and enact special legislation in accordance with the same and the ratified international laws.[13]

The first formal legislation within the JJS was initiated in 1986 in accordance with the Beijing Rules, as the Juvenile Justice Act, 1986.[14] In 2014, a UN committee analysed India's periodic reports and called upon us to align our JJS comprehensively within the norms of the CRC and other applicable international standards.[15] However, due to gaps in the existing legislative framework, the Children Act of 1960[16] was reformulated as the JJ Act, 1986,[17] subsequently re-enacted as the JJ (Care and Protection of Children) Act, 2000,[18] and later further re-enacted in 2015, to facilitate necessary changes in line with requirements on the ground and to align the same with the international instruments.[19]

Evolving Positive Treatment for Children Under the Law

India's child rights legislation has thus evolved over time, focusing on the well-being and protection of children, particularly those in difficult situations as defined earlier. It may be seen that the CNCP, defined as 'neglected children' within the JJ Act 1986,[20] did not have a distinct legal treatment until recently – and, earlier, in the eyes of the law, a child was taken into the legal fold mostly as a 'wrong-doer' and not someone who required special protection. Prior to India's independence in 1947, there was no comprehensive legislation specifically addressing child welfare.[21] Post-independence, India shifted towards social welfare, including child welfare, in a holistic way. In 1950, the Constitution of India laid down principles for child protection and welfare, including Article 15(3) empowering the state to make special provisions for children and Article 39(f) mandating the state to prevent abuse and provide healthy development opportunities.[22] A plethora of laws directly or indirectly connected with the children progressively altered their legal treatment in conformity with our commitments towards the Constitution of India and towards the ratified international instruments (see Table 1.1).[23]

TABLE 1.1 Evolution of children's laws and juvenile justice system in India

1850 – Apprenticeship Act	The Apprenticeship Act of 1850 was reportedly operational to deal with children, wherein the magistrate was empowered to commit them in the age group of 10–18 years for petty offences.
1860 – Indian Penal Code	According to Section 82 of the Indian Penal Code (IPC) (now Section 20 under Bhartiya Nyaya Sanhita 2023 – BNS), children less than 7 years of age were exempted from criminal responsibility. And the children in the age group of 7 and 12 years who had not attained sufficient maturity to understand the nature and consequence of their conduct were also exempted from any criminal responsibility as per Section 83 of IPC (Section 21 of Bhartiya Nyaya Sanhita 2023 (BNS)).
1875 – Indian Majority Act	Every person domiciled in India would have attained the age of majority on completing the age of 18 years and not before.
1876/1897 – Reformatory School Act for Juvenile Delinquents	Children detained up to 18 years of age are within a clear-cut definition of juvenile. This reformatory school was enacted in the year 1876 and later modified in 1897, which was a landmark in the treatment of juvenile delinquents. This law empowered the local governments to establish reformatory schools.
1898 – CrPC	In 1898, the Criminal Procedure Code (Now Bhartiya Nagrik Suraksha Sanhita 2023) provided specialized treatment for Juvenile Offenders (Section 29B). Section 399 of the code envisaged the commitment of juvenile offenders up to the age of 15 to reformatory schools.
Indian Jail Committee (1919–20)	Separate Machinery and courts suggested for juvenile offenders through remand homes and certified schools. It was a time-tested law and a holistic step for the children in conflict with the law.
1924	The Human Rights provided and declared by the League of Nations included the rights of children as well.
1948	The Universal Declaration of Human Rights (UDHR) was adopted, and it was proclaimed that Articles 1 to 7 of the UDHR stated that all human beings are born free and equal in dignity and rights and are equal before the law. Article 25 of the UDHR specifically provides that motherhood and childhood are entitled to special care and assistance.

(*Continued*)

TABLE 1.1 (Continued)

Probation of Offenders (POB) Act 1958	An act to provide for the release of offenders on probation or after due admonition and for matters connected therewith up to 21 years. For these young offenders, their release on probation for good conduct was also provided.
Children's Act 1960	An act to provide for the care, protection, welfare, training, education, and rehabilitation of neglected or delinquent children.[24] It established children's courts, juvenile homes, and certified schools for the rehabilitation and reformation of children in conflict with the law. The act focused on the welfare of children and their best interests, with provisions for their protection from exploitation and abuse. Section 2(l) of the Children Act 1960 defined neglected children as those who are found begging, who are found without a permanent home or settled place to live, lacking any apparent means of support, or being destitute, regardless of whether the child is orphaned. It also included a child whose parent or guardian is deemed unfit or fails to provide proper care and supervision and also a child living in a brothel or with a prostitute, frequently visiting places associated with prostitution or associating with individuals leading immoral, drunken, or depraved lives.
1974 – National Policy for Children	This policy was formulated to articulate the country's commitment to children's rights and welfare. It laid down principles and guidelines for various aspects of child development, including health, education, and protection.
1986 – JJ Act	The first national legislation in the arena of juvenile justice was enacted as the Juvenile Justice Act 1986 in consonance with the Beijing Rules 1986.
JJ Act, 2000	Re-enactment of Juvenile Justice (care and protection of children) Act, 2000 – Law relating to Juvenile in Conflict with Law (JCL; now CCL) and CNCP, Care, Protection, Treatment, Rehabilitation, Social Reintegration, Adjudication, Disposition
JJ Act Amendments 2002 and 2006	The new Juvenile Justice Act (Care and Protection of Children) Act 2000, enacted by the Parliament, was further amended in 2002 and 2006 to incorporate certain changes in accordance with the International Law on Child Rights.
CPCR Act 2005	The Commissions for Protection of Child Rights (CPCR) Act, 2005, created a separate mechanism for the fulfilment of the rights of children.
2009 – Right to Free and Compulsory Education (RTE) Act	Section 2C of the RTE Act provides that children in the age group of 6 to 14 years are entitled to free and compulsory education. As per the Section 2D of RTE Act, 2009, any child belonging to scheduled caste, scheduled tribe, socially and educationally backward classes, or such other group having a disadvantage owing to social, cultural, economic, geographical, linguistic, gender, or any other factor, as may be specified by the appropriate government, by notification, are entitled to free and compulsory education up to the age of 14 years.

(Continued)

TABLE 1.1 (Continued)

2015 – JJ Act	The Juvenile Justice (Care and Protection of Children) Act 2015 was passed/re-enacted to consolidate and amend the law relating to children alleged and found to be in conflict with the law and children in need of care and protection. This act introduced the departure from treating all children, even if they have committed a crime differently under the JJS, by providing that any CCL alleged to have committed any serious or heinous offence as provided in the Act may, by determination of the Juvenile Justice Board (JJB), be tried in the children's court but like an adult under CrPC/BNSS.
2016 – JJ Model Rules	In exercise of the powers conferred by the proviso to sub-section (1) of Section 110 of the Juvenile Justice (Care and Protection of Children) Act 2015, the central government made model rules, that is, the Juvenile Justice (Care and Protection of Children) Model Rules, 2016.
2021 – Amendment in JJ Act 2015	Amendment in the Juvenile Justice (Care and Protection of Children) Act 2015, which was amended in 2021 ostensibly to facilitate and carry out necessary changes in line with the International Law, w.e.f 01.09.2022 – the Juvenile Justice (Care and Protection of Children) Amendment Act, 2021
2022 – Amendment in JJ Model Rules 2016	In exercise of the powers conferred by the proviso to sub-section (1) of section 110 of the Juvenile Justice (Care and Protection of Children) Act, 2015 (2 of 2016), the central government made amendments to the Juvenile Justice (Care and Protection of Children) Model Rules, 2016.[25]
2023 Bhartiya Nayaya Sanhita (BNS) substituting the IPC	Besides redefining the 'child' as 'any person below the age of 18 years' aligned with systems and so on, this new law creates a separate chapter V of 'offences against woman & child'. Under Section 361 (kidnapping from lawful guardianship) IPC, instead of 'Child', the expression used was 'minor' (not defined). Minors could be less than 16 years old, if male, and less than 18 years old, if female. Under BNS now, all minors are defined as children (under 18 years). The chapter separately covers offences against children, such as exposure and abandonment of children below the age of 12, 'concealment of birth' and 'secret disposal of dead body', engaging a child in committing offences, kidnapping/abduction, and skilling and buying a child for prostitution, including marital rape up to 18 years.

Dual Categorization Under JJ Act: CNCP and CCL

The JJ Act, 2015, provides for institutional and non-institutional (alternative) mechanisms for care, protection, development, rehabilitation, social reintegration, and aftercare of CNCP and CCL.

The child care institutions (CCIs) for 'children in need of care and protection' (separately for CCLs) are defined under the Juvenile Justice Act 2015, as follows: Children Home under Section 50 of JJ Act 2015; Open Shelter defined under Section 43 of JJ Act 2015 and Rule 22 of JJ Model Rules, 2016; and Specialized Adoption Agency (SAA) defined under Section 65 of JJ Act 2015.

Children's Home

As outlined in Section 50 of the JJ Act, 2015, a children's home refers to a fit facility established and maintained by any of the state governments, either directly or through voluntary organizations, CSOs, and NGOs, having a certified residential facility in each district or a group of districts. These homes are designated for the placement of CNCP, providing them with care, treatment, education, training, development, and rehabilitation. The establishment of such homes requires registration and adherence to specified standards, with the state government having the authority to designate certain children's homes as specialized facilities catering to children with special needs, based on demand.

Open Shelters

As stipulated in Section 43 of the JJ Act, 2015, and Rule 22 of the JJ Model Rules, 2016, open shelters are community-based facilities established and maintained by the state government, voluntary organizations, or NGOs having a certified residential facility. These shelters serve as short-term residential support for children in need, aiming to shield them from abuse, prevent them from living on the streets, or facilitate their transition from street life. The services offered at 'open shelters' include day care and night residential facilities and provision of basic amenities such as food, washing facilities, toilets, and other services.

Specialized Adoption Agency

Governed by Section 65 of the JJ Act, 2015, SAA refers to institutions or organizations recognized by the state government in each district. These agencies are responsible for the rehabilitation of orphaned, abandoned, or surrendered children through adoption and non-institutional care. The state government is tasked with ensuring regular inspections of SAAs, at least once a year, and taking necessary corrective actions to maintain their standards and effectiveness in child welfare.

Overlapping of CCL and CNCP

According to Section 8(3)(g) of JJ Act 2015, the Juvenile Justice Board (JJB) is empowered to transfer matters concerning CCL (i.e., such children alleged to have committed any offence) who are declared as CNCP to the Child Welfare Committee (CWC) 'at any stage'. This provision recognizes that a child may simultaneously be considered both a CCL and a CNCP, highlighting the necessity for both the CWC and the JJB to be actively involved in such cases for the rehabilitation of the children.

Section 17(2) (3) JJ Act 2015 states that if a child is found not to have committed any offence but is deemed to be in 'need of care and protection', the JJB has the authority to refer the child to the CWC along with appropriate directives.

As per Rule 9(3) of the JJ Model Rules, 2016, a child who has been exploited by militant groups or other adults for unlawful activities may be transferred to the CWC following a thorough inquiry, being recognized as a child in need of care and protection. Rule 57(2) of the JJ Model Rules, 2016, specifies that a child accused of committing an offence under Section 78 of JJ Act, which involves using a child for vending, peddling, carrying, supplying, or smuggling intoxicating liquor, narcotic drugs, or psychotropic substances, can be transferred to the CWC by the board if the child is determined to be in need of care and protection.

Legal Framework for CNCP

Child Welfare Committee

The CWC (Section 27 JJ Act) is a bench of magistrates with comprehensive, often overriding powers for all matters responsible for handling cases/matters for the care, protection, treatment, development, and rehabilitation of CNCP. It consists of a chairperson and four other members, with at least one being a woman. The CWC can admit children to licenced children's homes for protective care, treatment, education, training/skilling, development, and rehabilitation of children. Residential facilities for safe and protective stay/rehabilitation include children's homes, SAA (0–6 years), open shelters (for street and runaway children), fit institution/fit person, or referral to organizations providing non-institutional services for the prevention of abandonment/institutionalization.

The CWC can pass an order to send a child to a children's home for inquiry by a child social worker (CSW) or child welfare officer (CWO), which must be completed within four months. The CWC, separately within the framework of the JJ Act, needs assertion that as the primary 'competent authority' for the millions of CNCP across the country and thousands of them being produced every day before them by the childline, NGOs, and government agencies, this authority is the most crucial body for the children in the country.

Intersection of CNCP With Other Laws

CNCP and Child Labour (Prohibition and Regulation) Act, 1986/2016

All children dealt with within the child labour and connected laws, including those concerning child trafficking, ipso facto fall within the definition of CNCP. The 1986 Child Labour Law was substantially amended in 2016 to align the same with the RTE Act 2009, which created a legal obligation for every child from 6 to 14 years to go to school. Members of the Central Advisory Committee, Ministry of Labour and Employment, vehemently demanded that the definition of childhood be extended up to 18 years, but it was decided to bifurcate the children (6 to 14) from the adolescents (14 to 18). Nonetheless, all children or adolescents engaged in labour are also in need of care and protection. In such cases, the provisions of the JJ Act, 2015, would apply to address the comprehensive needs of the child, considering their rights, protection, and rehabilitation of the child. Section 2(14)(i) states that a CNCP is a child who is found working in contravention of the provisions of the labour laws for the time being in force or is found begging or living on the street.[26]

To trace the genesis, in response to the recommendations made by the Gurupada Swamy Committee, the Child Labour (Prohibition & Regulation) Act was enacted in 1986. This legislation aimed to curb the exploitation of children by prohibiting their employment in certain hazardous occupations and processes while also regulating working conditions in other sectors. Over time, the list of hazardous occupations and processes has been continuously expanded based on the guidance of the Child Labour Technical Advisory Committee established under the act. Subsequently, in 2016, the act underwent amendments with the introduction of the Child & Adolescent Labour (Prohibition & Regulation) Amendment Act 2016, which extended the prohibition of employment to all children below 14 years of age and imposed restrictions on the employment of adolescents aged 14 to 18 years in the scheduled hazardous occupations and processes.[27]

In *M.C. Mehta v. The State of Tamil Nadu*, the Supreme Court of India issued significant directives on the eradication of child labour on 10 December 1996.[28] The key elements of this judgement include conducting surveys to identify working children, removing children from hazardous industries and ensuring their education in suitable institutions, and imposing a contribution of Rs. 20,000 per child on the offending employers towards a welfare fund dedicated to this cause. Additionally, the judgement mandates providing employment to one adult member of the child's family or, if not feasible, requiring a contribution of Rs. 5,000 to the welfare fund by the state government. Financial aid is to be extended to families of withdrawn children from the interest earned on the corpus of Rs. 20,000 or 25,000 deposited in the welfare fund, as long as the child attends school regularly. Furthermore, the ruling regulates the working hours of adolescents engaged in non-hazardous occupations, ensuring they do not exceed six hours per day while guaranteeing at least two hours of education, with the entire educational expense borne by the respective employer. The Ministry of Labour and Employment oversees the implementation of these directives, with compliance reports submitted to the honourable court periodically based on information provided by the state/union territory governments.

CNCP and the Commission for the Protection of Child Rights Act, 2005

The CPCR Act, 2005, establishes the National CPCR at the national level and State CPCR at the state level. These commissions are responsible for ensuring the implementation and monitoring of child rights laws, policies, and programmes. Besides empowering the commissions with the legal oversight of all activities concerning the rights of the children – both CNCP and CCL, the CPCR Act creates the provision of children's courts to protect the children as victims and witnesses in crimes, in addition to dealing with the CCL beyond the jurisdiction of the JJB under the JJ Act 2015.

The CPCR Act, 2005, aims to protect and promote the rights of children. The National and State Commissions play crucial roles in formulating policies and programmes related to child protection, including those concerning CNCP, and they oversee the implementation of laws and policies related to child protection, including the provisions under the JJ Act concerning CNCP. As Chairman of DCPCR, the author had extensive experience in dealing with a couple of thousand cases of the CNCP, particularly those concerning child abuse and exploitation, and concerning the RTE Act facilitating the first-ever free enrolments of the deprived children in the private schools.

CNCP and Right to Education Act, 2009

The Right to Education (RTE) Act, 2009, under Section 3, provides free and compulsory education for all children aged 6 to 14 years in India, which is also a 'fundamental right' under Article 21 (A) of the Constitution of India. It mandates that every child has the RTE without any discrimination and aims to ensure access to quality education for all children. The RTE Act emphasizes the importance of ensuring access to education for all children, including those in vulnerable situations. The RTE Act ensures that 'children in need of care and protection (CNCP)' have the right to enrol in and attend schools without discrimination.

CNCP and POCSO Act, 2012

The POCSO Act, 2012, is a comprehensive legislation aimed at protecting children from sexual offences and ensuring their safety and well-being. The law defines various forms of sexual abuse against children and prescribes stringent punishments for the offenders. The Act also includes provisions for the 'establishment of special courts', 'procedures for reporting offenses', and the 'protection of child witnesses.

Children who are victims of sexual offences are often in need of care and protection. The CNCP framework provides mechanisms for the identification of such children and ensures that they receive appropriate care, support, and protection. The POCSO Act, 2012, provides a legal framework for addressing sexual offences against children, while the CNCP provisions under the JJ Act complement this by addressing the broader needs of children in vulnerable situations, including those who are victims of sexual abuse.[29]

Role of Other Stakeholders vis-à-vis CNCP Within the JJS

Amongst the children who come in contact with the law, namely, the victims of abuse, exploitation, and crimes, or as witnesses being dealt with in various legal fora, including the Children's courts, or as CCL and the CNCP, the last-mentioned category being the overwhelming majority. Except for the minuscule number of the CCLs, nearly 40,000 to 45,000 annually, all others practically fall in the legal jurisdiction of the JJ Act and other concomitant laws concerning children as CNCPs. The JJ Act, along with the various other laws for children, Rules, Schemes, and Programmes concerning them, becomes part of the JJS in India, which is a complex system that involves various stakeholders. They include the CWO/CSW, District Child Protection Officer (DCPO), Caregiver/House Parents, Teachers and Vocational Trainers, Health System, District Legal Services Authority, Media, Civil Society, Police, and Special Juvenile Police Unit (SJPU) under section 107 of JJ Act 2015 provides provision creation of an SJPU by State Governments/UTs for every district to coordinate Police related to children

The CWO/CSW plays a crucial role in intake, history taking, conducting enquiries, preparing reports, home visits, and individual and group counselling. The DCPO coordinates and supervises the implementation of the Integrated Child Protection Scheme (now Mission Vatsalaya (translates to childhood) in the districts and supervises all CCIs, agencies, and non-institutional care programmes run by the CWOs/NGOs. They also report to the State Child Protection Societies at the state level and the State Adoption Resource Agency (SARA) for coordinating non-institutional care, especially issues related to adoption, foster care, and sponsorship at the district level.

The staff, including the house mother/house father and others, provide care, protection, and rehabilitation of children admitted to institutions, ensuring a child-friendly environment, a sensitive and nurturing attitude towards children, proper maintenance, sanitation, hygiene, and children's participation in daily activities. Teachers and vocational trainers provide formal and non-formal education, vocational training, and teaching life skills and vocational skills.

The healthcare system, separately or integrated with government facilities, is expected to provide regular medical examinations and care to children in institutions, age verification, gynaecological examination and forensic testing, medical response and treatment in case of accidents and physical injuries, psychiatric and psychological support for psychological problems and emotional trauma, behaviour issues, and long-term treatment for children with mental illness. The District Legal Services Authority provides legal aid to children wherever necessary and legal guidance in complex matters to the CWC for the overall rehabilitation. The role of the media is extremely important within child protection services to create awareness, sensitive reporting of cases related to children, moulding of public opinion, and working towards the protection and promotion of children's rights.

Section 2(25) of the JJ Act 2015 defines and provides the childline services (or 1098, which is not integrated with the Common Emergency Number 112), a 24-hour emergency response service for 'children in crisis' (a category of CNCP), which links them to emergency support, long-term care, and rehabilitation services. Over the past 25 years, 1098-related NGO-run services became the lifeline for CNCP. But since it is now dismantled and merged with the national emergency number, as earlier, it poses a major gap and serious crisis for children and stakeholders.[30]

Section 37 of the JJ Act 2015 succinctly summarizes the intent and actions that can be taken in respect of the CNCP through the procedure adopted and orders that can be passed by the CWC. Taking into consideration its own inquiry, the social investigation reports, and the wishes of the child in case the child is sufficiently mature to take a view, the CWC is fully empowered to pass a wide range of orders. While declaring a child as CNCP, the CWC can order restoration to parents or guardians or placement of child in a fit facility like a like a children's home or adoption agency), or to a 'fit person', or 'foster care (Section 44) or sponsorship (Section 45), directing the persons or institutions/facilities regarding shelter, care, protection, rehabilitation (Education, skilling) medical, psychological support, counselling and legal aid.

Section 38 of the JJ Act 2015 outlines the process for declaring orphan, abandoned, or surrendered children legally free for adoption. If a child is orphaned or abandoned, the Committee must trace the parents or guardians and declare the child legally free within two months for children up to two years old and four months for adoption. For surrendered children, the institution where the child is placed must present the case to the Committee once the specified period is completed. The Act also addresses unique situations, such as children of mentally retarded parents, or unwanted children resulting from sexual assault. The Committee must make the final decision by at least three members and share the information with the SARA on a monthly basis about the number of legally free children for adoption and the number of pending cases to be declared as legally free.

Section 39 of the JJ Act, 2015, outlines the rehabilitation and social integration process for children, primarily guided by individual care plans. The preference is for family-based care, including restoration to family or guardian, adoption, or foster care. Siblings should be kept together in institutional or non-institutional care unless it's not in their best interest. If children cannot be placed in families, they may be temporarily or long term placed in registered institutions or with a fit person or facility. Financial support may be provided to aid reintegration into society upon leaving institutional care or special homes.

Section 40 of the JJ Act, 2015, outlines the primary objective of Children's Homes, Specialized Adoption Agencies, and open shelters: to restore and protect children deprived of their family environment. These entities must take necessary steps to restore children, either temporarily or permanently.

Restoration, Rehabilitation, and Reintegration of CNCP

Restoration, rehabilitation, and reintegration are all critical aspects of ensuring the fulfilment of rights and well-being of children, particularly those who have been involved in situations of conflict, exploitation, or abuse. While they are interconnected and often overlapping, there are distinct differences between these concepts:

1. ***Restoration***
   Restoration involves the process of returning a child to a state of well-being, dignity, and safety after experiencing harm or rights violations. It focuses on addressing the immediate needs of the child and mitigating the negative impacts of the violation or trauma. Restoration efforts may include providing medical care, psychological support, legal assistance, and temporary shelter to ensure the child's physical and emotional recovery. The goal of restoration is to alleviate the immediate harm suffered by the child and to begin the process of rebuilding their sense of security and trust.
2. ***Rehabilitation***
   Rehabilitation goes beyond restoration and involves the holistic process of addressing the underlying factors that contributed to a child's involvement in harmful situations. It aims to empower the child with the skills,

resources, and support systems necessary to reintegrate into society positively. Rehabilitation efforts may include educational programmes, vocational training, life skills development, counselling, and family reunification initiatives.

3. ***Reintegration***
   Reintegration refers to the process of reintroducing a child who has been separated from their family, community, or normal social environment back into society. It involves facilitating the child's return to a supportive and nurturing environment where they can live safely and thrive. Reintegration efforts may include family tracing and reunification.

Restoration, as delineated in Section 40 of the JJ Act, 2015, prioritizes the return and safeguarding of a child to their familial environment by Children's Homes, SAAs, or open shelters. These institutions are mandated to undertake necessary measures for the restoration and protection of children who have been temporarily or permanently separated from their families while under their care. The Committee is empowered to make decisions regarding the restoration of CNCP to their parents, guardians, or suitable individuals, following an assessment of the caregivers' capacity to provide adequate care, accompanied by appropriate directives. Regarding rehabilitation and reintegration services within institutions governed by this Act.

Section 53 emphasizes the provision of comprehensive support to facilitate the rehabilitation and reintegration of children. Such services encompass fulfilling basic needs/rights, such as, food, shelter, clothing, and medical care in accordance with prescribed standards.

All the basic rights of the children including those under the RTE Act, 2009 and need based services are to be provided to them.[31]

Rehabilitation of CNCP Under JJ Act 2015

Rehabilitation and social reintegration are essential components of child protection, and there are various methods to do it, such as individual care plans, family-based care, sponsorship, adoption, or foster care.

Adoption

Eligibility for a CNCP to be 'adopted' requires the child to be declared 'legally free' after an 'inquiry' by the CWC. The SAA must enter the child's details and photograph online within 72 hours of receiving the child, and the District Child Protection Unit must advertise the particulars and photograph of an abandoned child in a state-level newspaper within 72 hours.

Foster Care

'Foster care' is to provide a family-like environment to the child where the child lives with foster parents/family members, with preference given to families with similar cultural, tribal, and community connections. Eligible children include children aged 6–18, terminally ill, mentally ill, in jail, or victims of abuse, natural disasters, and domestic violence.

Agencies to Facilitate Adoption

Agencies to facilitate adoption include the SARA at the state level, SAA, and the Central Adoption Resource Information & Guidance System (CARINGS). The CARINGS system requires the Authorized Foreign Adoption Agency/Central Authority to register the details of parents desiring to adopt from India online and upload the duly completed Home Study Report.

Sponsorship

Sponsorship is a programme that provides additional support to families to meet their children's medical, nutritional, educational, and other needs, aiming to improve their quality of life. It can be rehabilitation or preventive, enabling children to reunite with their families in extreme deprivation or exploitation conditions. Selection criteria for sponsorship include children aged 0–18 years, in CCIs for more than six months, and families with a total income of Rs. 36,000 per annum in metro cities, Rs. 30.000 per annum in other cities, and Rs. 24,000 per annum in rural areas.

Aftercare of Children Leaving CCIs

Section 46 of the 'JJ Act 2015' provides that any child leaving CCIs after completing 18 years of age may be provided with financial support to facilitate reintegration and mainstreaming into society. Although Section 46 of the JJ Act 2015 provides for multiple services and facilities for such children (CNCP), the aftercare programme has made little headway. A programme called 'Yuva-Connect' jointly launched by Delhi Police, DCPCR, and Prayas with the support of JJB and Department of Women and Child Development, Government of National Capital Territory Delhi in 2011 deserves mention.[32]

India has a comprehensive policy and legal framework addressing children's rights and protection, but the implementation of these laws is challenging due to low priority for such children, poor allocation of funds within the given schemes, inadequate human resource capacity (poor ratio between the staff and children), and prevention and rehabilitation services. Mental and physical violence and denial of basic rights to the CNCP (& CCL) in various settings, including home, schools, CCIs under the JJ Act, and in the community, are rampant across the country despite clear legal provisions within the most progressive legislations of India.

Prayas and Children in Need of Care and Protection

Prayas (translates as an attempt or an endeavour) JAC Society (Est. 1988/ Reg. 1989) works for CNCP under the Juvenile Justice (JJ) (Care and Protection of Children) Act 2015. It began with our community-police initiatives of the Crime Branch and Railway Police, specifically the combined Missing Persons Squad and JAC, and the street children, homeless, disaster-driven, and working children-related project in the slum-resettlement colony of Jahangirpuri in North Delhi, both of which developed simultaneously. In those times, the police officers, dealing with hundreds of 'neglected children' under the JJ Act of 1986, faced a significant challenge in providing temporary care for children who had committed no offence but were homeless due to circumstances. Without protective shelters set up within the JJ Act being available, the police officers often informally accommodated these children temporarily, meeting their basic needs. This experience highlighted the urgent need for more structured, humane interventions by the police, along with other stakeholders of the evolving JJS for the CNCP and CCL under the JJ Act.

The starting point and necessity to set up an organized activity with a legal entity for Prayas came with a visit to Jahangirpuri, the aforesaid resettlement colony populated by nearly 3 lakh people – families of rag pickers, including children in sizeable numbers, who had been displaced due to urban demolitions. In the aftermath of a devastating fire in the area, Air Marshal (Retired) HL Kapur, who had directed me to accompany to inquire the cause of fire, in a strange turn of events offered space to initiate a project for the fire-affected homeless children in urgent need of care and protection, which marked the beginning of what would become Prayas and its six allied organizations today operating at the national level. Leveraging my role as Deputy Commissioner of Police overseeing the Missing Persons Squad and Juvenile Police Unit, the organization began to take shape. With its main office at New Kotwali Police Station, Central Delhi, the unit of the Juvenile Aid Centre (later named Prayas JAC) was established at Jahangirpuri, which grew through public–private partnerships and community policing initiatives with occasional guidance from senior police officials.

Prayas officially began operations on 14 November 1988, coinciding with Children's Day and the birth anniversary of Pandit Jawaharlal Nehru (the first Prime Minister of India). By that time, the organization had already been providing care to 25 fire-affected children. Drawing ideas from models such as the Juvenile Aid Police Unit in Bombay (now Mumbai) and some children and police related programmes in the UK and some other countries we had opportunities to visit, Prayas adopted innovative practices to support neglected and homeless children. Our visits to Bombay revealed the inadequacies of institutional homes and specialized treatment for such children in Delhi, underscoring the need for a more holistic approach. These insights, combined with collaborations with government and non-government agencies, laid the foundation for Prayas' distinctive model of child care, protection, development, rehabilitation through socio-economic reintegration, and empowerment.

A significant milestone in Prayas' journey came with the publication of the book *Neglected Child: Changing Perspectives* in 1993, which was the outcome of the National Consultation on Neglected Children organized with the support of the Ministry of Social Justice (later the Ministry of Women and Child Development was bifurcated), Government of India (GOI). Supported by UNICEF and the Ministry of Social Justice, the book highlighted various dimensions of neglected childhood and juvenile justice. Released by the then President of India, Honourable Shankar Dayal Sharma, it captured the proceedings of a national workshop held in 1992. This publication helped establish Prayas as a path-breaker in conceptualizing and addressing the needs of children in care and protection, promoting a holistic approach to child welfare. As a follow-up, Prayas pioneered numerous initiatives, including managing government custodial homes under the JJ Act. It emphasized the critical link between juvenile justice and children's rights, advocating for justice through the fulfilment of basic needs. Its programmes provided education, healthcare, shelter, and protection from abuse, aiming to restore childhood to vulnerable children. The organization also stressed the importance of family reintegration, advocating for children to return to their homes and schools whenever possible.

Advocacy became a cornerstone of Prayas' efforts, as the organization played a key role in shaping child protection policies and legislation. Its involvement in the amendment of the Child Labour Act and participation in the 11th Five-Year Plan showcased its influence on national frameworks. Through functional advocacy, Prayas connected grassroots action with policy changes, contributing to the elimination of child labour and trafficking. In partnership with the Norwegian Agency for Development Cooperation (Government of Norway), in 2000, it established the Prayas Institute of Juvenile Justice (PIJJ) in Tughlakabad Institutional Area in Delhi, which became a hub for research, training, and direct interventions. The institute aimed to serve as a working model for child welfare and juvenile justice in the region.

The growth of Prayas in terms of creating multiple projects for the children in need and in conflict with the law, alongside the evolution of the JJS in India, included the participation of the organization in the re-enactment of the Juvenile Justice (Care and Protection of Children) Act 2000. A landmark moment in Prayas' (PIJJ) history was the National Study on Child Abuse-including physical, emotional, sexual abuses, and neglect, conducted in collaboration with the Ministry of Women and Child Development, UNICEF, and Save the Children. The study revealed alarming statistics about child abuse in the country, with over 53% of children reporting sexual abuse, which ultimately led to the enactment of the POCSO Act in 2012. Through such efforts, Prayas solidified its role as a catalyst for change in the lives of neglected and vulnerable children across India.

The organization also collaborated with law enforcement to establish crisis intervention units and the first-ever Childline(s) 1098 (24X7 child helpline number), which handled issues like child labour, trafficking, and commercial sexual exploitation while becoming the lifeline for the neglected children in urgent need of care and protection within the framework of the JJ Act. Prayas' capacity for disaster response further expanded its scope. From the Gujarat earthquake in 2001, the tsunami in Andamans in 2004, the floods of Bihar in 2008, to the Nepal earthquake in 2016, Prayas took charge of the children in crisis situations, mobilizing resources to provide direct support through holistic projects in affected areas.

As Prayas entered its second decade, it reflected on its achievements, having supported nearly 10,000 children to date and nearly 2,98,000 CNCP (including 22000 CCL) on record, being holistically looked after through holistic projects for care, protection, development, rehabilitation, and social reintegration. The organization reaffirmed its philosophy that a child's struggles can be transformed into strengths. Prayas continues to uphold its commitment to addressing the fundamental needs and rights of children, offering hope and resilience to those facing the most challenging circumstances.

In 1997, Prayas' role in the JJS expanded significantly when it took over the management of the custodial (observation) home for boys at Delhi Gate, finding (corroborated by the National Crime Records Bureau analysis of the juvenile offenders) majority of these juveniles were neglected (CNCP) children as well. This decision followed incidents of maltreatment in government-run homes, culminating in the tragic death of a child. Acting on the recommendations of a High-Powered Committee, the Government of Delhi, decided to transfer the management of this home to an NGO. Prayas accepted the challenge despite having no prior experience in managing such homes. This decision marked a turning point in the history of institutional care in Delhi and provided Prayas with valuable learning opportunities. The experience became a testing ground for implementing changes that were later formalized in the JJ Act, 2000.

After taking over the home, Prayas transformed its environment. The physical infrastructure was renovated, meals were improved, and regular health check-ups were provided. The children were given access to non-formal education, recreation, counselling, and vocational training. Visitors were welcomed, ensuring transparency while maintaining the home's routines and discipline. Children were regularly taken on picnics, educational tours, and engaged in activities like painting and sports, earning prizes. Prayas turned the 'children's jail' into a nurturing home, offering opportunities for study, counselling, and recreation under constant supervision.

This transformation set the stage for the home to become a model for juvenile care, now classified as homes for juveniles/Children in conflict with the law and the children in need of care and protection. The success of this initiative led the government to transfer additional homes to NGOs like Prayas. This success also led to Prayas' involvement in the progressive implementation of the JJ Act of 1986. Through its operations, Prayas identified gaps in the Act and advocated for modifications, including changes in the composition of Juvenile Courts and Boards and the privatization of homes. These contributions influenced the JJ (Care and Protection) Act, 2000, which serves as a blueprint for child welfare in India.

Prayas rehabilitation services include the provision of non-formal/alternative education, followed by mainstreaming of children into the formal education system. Along with other support for the mid-day meals, weekly health check-ups, vocational/skilling training, recreation, community awareness, counselling, provision of special aids, child sponsorship, and aftercare are some of the salient features of the Prayas Rehabilitation Services. Further, Prayas has been providing major institutional care services to the CNCP through numerous Children Homes/Shelter, which are 24-hour facilities with holistic programmes for care, protection, development, rehabilitation, and social reintegration.

Today, Prayas operates across 316 community-based and targeted intervention centres/units for the CNCP, marginalized youth and women, including the homes/shelters as institutional care facilities, with 768 full-time co-workers directly benefiting nearly 50,000 beneficiaries on a day-to-day basis. The organization's unwavering commitment to child protection, safeguarding, and welfare, its innovative programmes, and its advocacy for systemic reform have cemented its role as a national leader in the fight for children's rights in India.

Launch of Yuva Connect Aftercare Programme

Launched in May 2011, the Yuva Connect programme aims to prevent juvenile delinquency (the majority of them being CNCP) by involving the community in rehabilitation efforts. This programme includes education, vocational training, family interventions, and counselling to ensure long-term positive outcomes for the juveniles.

Prayas' Role in Juvenile Justice Reforms

Prayas actively contributed to the drafting of the JJ Act, 2000, and subsequently raised concerns about reducing the age of culpability for serious crimes. They emphasized that the JJS should remain focused on rehabilitation rather than punitive measures, in line with international child rights standards.

Historic Judgements Related to Juvenile Justice

- *Salil Bali vs. Union of India* (2013): The Supreme Court rejected petitions to lower the juvenile age limit to 16 for serious crimes, reaffirming the principle that juveniles should be treated with rehabilitative measures.[33]
- *Dr. Subramanian Swamy vs. Raju* (2014): The Court upheld the JJ Act, rejecting attempts to treat juveniles as adults in cases of heinous crimes, reinforcing the goal of rehabilitation.[34]

  On the aforementioned matters which turned out to be historic judgements on the issues concerning JJS in India, Prayas JAC Society intervened alongside the Ministry of Women and Child Development and argued extensively through its representative (Mr. Amod Kanth, Founder, and General Secretary Prayas and former practitioner of the JJ Act as Chairperson of DCPCR highlighting the challenges of children in conflict with law and the significance of the JJ Act and its alignment with the International Conventions and the Constitution of India. We carried the Hon'ble Supreme Court in the aforementioned two matters, chaired by the successive Chief Justices, Justice Altamash Kabeer and Justice P. Sathashivam, through the journey of the JJS in India, arguing for the effective implementation of the law along with special focus on the rehabilitation and restoration of JCLs/CCLs. We requested the Hon'ble Court to avoid the regressive changes in the JJ Act related to reducing the age of children in conflict with law, and the Court fully accepted our contentions. We highlighted the need for a child-friendly approach in the adjudication and disposition of matters concerning children in conflict with law, and raised the points related to non-implementation of provisions under the JJ Act, 2000, in the true spirit, which hindered the rehabilitation and restoration of children in conflict with law.

Prayas' Advocacy and Role in Policy

Prayas continues to advocate for juvenile justice reforms in the larger context of child rights and the various types of CNCP, including the working, destitute, homeless, and street children, with a focus on restorative, rehabilitative, developmental, and educational methods, ensuring that the child protection system aligns with constitutional, legal provisions, and the ratified international principles. These efforts, including developing manuals for police officers and engaging with lawmakers and other stakeholders, are crucial in shaping the future of juvenile justice in India.

National Study on Child Abuse

Earlier in 2005–2007, the PIJJ had conducted a National Study on Child Abuse, including Physical, Emotional, Sexual, Neglected Child, and Girl Child, a large number among the 18,000 respondents being CNCP in 13 Indian states, focusing on the prevalence of child abuse and its impact on children aged 5–12. The study involved experts from various disciplines and a two-day Training of Trainers Programme. The study found that young children aged 5–12 are more prone to the risk of abuse and exploitation. Physical Abuse/Corporal Punishment was reported in two out of every three children, with 54.68% being boys. Sexual abuse was reported in 53.22% of children, with Andhra Pradesh, Assam, Bihar, and Delhi, reporting the highest percentage of sexual abuse among both boys and girls. This Study was carried out on behalf of the Ministry of Child & Women, GOI, being part of the UN's 'Global Study of Violence Against Children', and its recommendations resulted in the formulation of the POCSO Act 2012.[35]

Practical Experiences and Interventions

At the forefront of the rehabilitation efforts for CNCP, the Prayas JAC uses a multidisciplinary approach to meet the needs of these at-risk youth. Prayas JAC's solutions, which are based on the concepts of empathy, empowerment, and inclusion, go beyond traditional frameworks and include a range of comprehensive support mechanisms, from psychosocial counselling to education and skill development efforts.

The Rehabilitative Services

Non-Formal Education (Alternative and Innovative Education)

Thousands of CNCPs are brought within the educational programmes of Prayas, responding to their rights within the RTE Act and the developed programmes within the New Education Policy 2020. To raise the awareness level to a standard whereby a child is able to distinguish between good and bad in relation to his/her environment and through facilities for literacy, numeracy, life education, and initiating efforts for mainstreaming in the formal education system.

Empowerment Through Vocational Training

Imparting training in vocations has been made an integral part of all our educational programmes to make them meaningful. To enable the target group to ultimately move towards economic self-sufficiency as soon as they attain adulthood. Through the programme within the Prayas Institute of Economic Empowerment (PIEE)/NSDC (National Skill Development Corporation)/ JSS (Jan Shikshan Sansthan (translates to Mass Education Institute)), nearly 15,000 trainees undergo skilling cum livelihood programmes of Prayas, a large number of them being school dropouts and CNCP.

Production, Marketing, and Placement Services

These are aimed at job placements and entrepreneurship of the target group to earn a reasonable livelihood in due course of time. While learning skills, they also earn from the by-products of training. Prayas' allied organizations that include the Section 8 Company,[36] SPSS (Sanchay Prayas Swavalamban Sansthan (translates to 'Prayas Social Enterprise and Self-Reliance Institute') undertakes these activities towards livelihood and economic empowerment to children/youth 15 years and above at a reasonable scale.

Aftercare Programme

Aftercare services are needed to explore innovative, action-based programmes that help recently institution-released juveniles/young offenders and CNCP to re-enter the community in a healthy and respectful manner and, most importantly, to help their rehabilitation so that they live as responsible citizens. The aftercare programme plays an important role in the *rehabilitation and reintegration* of juveniles and young offenders and makes them self-reliant. Prayas JAC Society launched the YUVA CONNECT programme by Mr. B.K. Gupta, then Commissioner of Police, Delhi Police, on 21 May 2011, a joint initiative of Prayas, Delhi Police, and DCPCR aimed to empower the children in conflict with law and young offenders, stepping out from Prayas Observation Home. This was a unique public–private partnership of its kind in the country since July 1997. The initiative was strengthened under the aftercare programme of Prayas JAC Society to provide job-linked training to the young children/ offenders (CCL) or those from families in a dire state due to the incarceration of the bread earner of the family. More than 1000 juveniles/young offenders have successfully undergone deep counselling, socio-economic support, education, and training in skill development in various trades.

Recreational Services

These services are aimed at the restoration of the lost childhood and promotion of good mental health and well-being. Children in multiple forms of deprivation and crisis (CNCP) are provided with appropriate programmes, under both institutional and non-institutional settings.

The Protective Services

Amongst the broad category of UNCRC child rights, that is, survival, protection, participation, and development, the rights pertaining to protection are most essential and over-arching for children under difficult and adverse circumstances (CNCP), which organizations like Prayas are expected to fulfil. In consonance with the JJS, Prayas has developed a well-defined strategy of providing institutional care and protection through its integrated programmes. Prayas Children Home/Shelters, which apart from providing basic shelter and care, also provides routine services as listed here:

Health and Nutrition: To maintain the basic physical and mental well-being of these disadvantaged children who are otherwise deprived of their earnings and even two square meals. This also includes awareness generation towards the promotion of good health, hygiene, and the environment.

Social Awareness Programme: By its very character, the children (CNCP) who are being looked after by the organization, happen to be in myriad situations wherein the communities, government, and non-governmental agencies are to be made conscious about their respective duties towards them. To promote responsible citizenship and fellow feeling through group activities, self-help, and camaraderie.

Counselling and Referral Services: Apart from organizations own activities through its own professional, outreach services, and volunteers, support is elicited from the specialized agencies in respective areas of operation. To enable the target group to meet the challenges of the changing society and to upgrade the quality of life.

Some Stories of Prayas With CNCP and Challenges Faced

Case 1

Category: Orphaned
Age: 12 (At the time of induction in 2017)

Shruti (Name Changed) * was placed in Prayas in 2017 along with her sister. At the time of placement, the child was 12 years old. Shruti is an orphan. Her mother passed away before her placement in Prayas. Her father passed away shortly after her placement in Prayas.

Shruti and her sister were asked by their maternal uncle to stay with them; however, the uncle had sexually abused the child, due to which a case of

POCSO was registered against him, and the children do not wish to stay with them. She still has not received interim compensation in the case.

The child's maternal grandparents are incapable of taking care of the child and do not want to take the child. Shruti is intellectually disabled and has a low IQ. The child has also been diagnosed with attention-deficit hyperactivity disorder. The child has been prescribed psychiatric medicines.

Shruti is living with her younger sister in the institution. Shruti had to attend non-formal education classes for some time. She is currently enrolled in class 9 and attends regular school. She also attends tuitions as she requires individualized attention at times. Preeti struggles with studies, especially with subjects like English, Math, and science. Preeti has also been in fights and easily gets angry at other children. She has a close friend. She fights with her sister sometimes but is caring towards her. She thinks a lot and is worried about the time when she will turn 18 and will have to leave Prayas.

The child is provided regular counselling by the counsellors at Prayas, and she is also connected to the Institute of Human Behaviour and Allied Sciences for psychiatric and psychological treatment. The child also has medical issues and gets fits at times, which affect her physical and mental health. Prayas has provided her with appropriate and timely medical aid and support for dealing with physical and mental burdens.

Case 2

Category: Kidnapping
Age: 17 (at the time of induction in 2019)

Ritu (Name Changed) was placed at Prayas in 2019 when she was 17 years old. The family of the child consists of her parents, an elder brother who is married, an unmarried sister, and another elder sister who is married. Both parents are cooks, and the elder sister is also working. Ritu studied till class 8; after that, she dropped out.

Ritu was brought to Prayas after she was kidnapped and sexually harassed by an acquaintance. She went out with a friend to his place, where she was sexually and physically abused by him for a few days. She was forced to stay at his house. She then went back to her house, where she revealed the abuse. The parents of the child went to the police station to register a First Information Report (FIR), the next day of the incident (under Section 154 of the Code of Criminal Procedure (CrPC)). According to the statement recorded by the magistrate under Section 164 CrPC, the girl has accused four boys who had forcefully abducted her. After an FIR was filed (under Section 363 of the IPC for kidnapping), the CWC ordered the placement of the child in Prayas. After this, Section 376 IPC (for rape) and POCSO were added. One of the main accused was arrested, and the proceedings are in progress.

Ritu was enrolled in non-formal education again, and she appeared for her class 10 exams from an open secondary board examination. The child does not express a willingness to study any further. Ritu has turned 19 but continues to stay at Prayas by the order of CWC for aftercare, as the two accused have not been arrested, and the mother feels that restoration will not be safe for her. The Jhuggis (slum) in which Ritu was residing has also been demolished.

Ritu has been enrolled in vocational training in cutting, stitching, and tailoring. She earns a scholarship of Rs. 3000 in vocational studies. She goes through regular counselling sessions. Her confidence and self-esteem have gotten a boost since she started feeling independent.

Budgetary Allocation

The Union Budget 2023–24, with a decrease in the share to merely 2.30% of the budget, the stakeholders are facing major challenges in child protection-which primarily concerns the CNCP and the CCL, having the features of CNCP. The overall budget for children has increased by 11.92% compared to the previous year-alongside the decrease in child protection services. The Ministry of Minority Affairs saw a 37.81% loss in funding, while the Ministry of Labour and Employment saw a 33.33% reduction, which had allocations for such children.[37]

Resource mobilization strategies have also been challenged, with the Samagra Shiksha Abhiyan (translates to National Education Mission) (SMSA) receiving a meagre increase of 0.19% compared to last year's allocation.[38] The total allocation for SMSA stands at INR 37,453.47 crores, which must be examined in the context of the New Education Policy, 2020, which promises 6% GDP to be spent on education.[39]

Recommendations for Policy and Practice

The effective implementation of laws for CNCP is often impeded by barriers such as bureaucratic red tape, resource constraints, and inadequate training of personnel. Identifying gaps between policy and practice is essential to bridge the divide between legislative intent and on-ground realities. Additionally, the role of stakeholders and collaboration is paramount in addressing these challenges, requiring coordinated efforts from government agencies, NGOs, communities, and the judiciary. A holistic exploration of the rights and needs of CNCP, as outlined in the legal framework, is imperative for their well-being. Beyond mere legal provisions, addressing psychological, educational, and healthcare needs is crucial. Creating a child-friendly and supportive environment is essential to foster their rehabilitation and integration into society.

Innovative approaches for rehabilitation and support should be adopted, focusing on best practices from around the globe. Advocacy strategies play a pivotal role in enhancing awareness and implementation of laws pertaining to CNCP. Engaging with stakeholders and fostering collaboration is essential to drive systemic changes and ensure the rights of CNCP are upheld. Anticipating future challenges and changes in the landscape of juvenile justice is necessary to adapt and respond effectively. Organizations like Prayas must evolve their role in line with emerging realities, leveraging opportunities for research, advocacy, and policy interventions. Embracing technological advancements and evolving societal norms will be key in shaping the future of juvenile justice.

In conclusion, it appears that the resources available to serve millions of CNCP in India are extremely inadequate, considering their huge numbers, which are not enumerated in any form beyond the 2011 Census in India. Decidedly, India's CNCP partakes a sizeable chunk of the globally enumerated 160 million child labour, and the Socio-Economically Deprived Groups of 32.2 million out-of-school children (National Education Policy 2020). Prayas' journey embodies resilience, compassion, and unwavering commitment to the rights of CNCP. It calls for collective action to prioritize the rights of CNCP and cultivate a society where every child is valued, protected, and empowered. Through collective action, we can sow seeds of hope and cultivate a brighter tomorrow for generations to come.

Notes

1 Child Labour (Prohibition and Regulation) Act, No. 35 of 2016, India Code (2016).
2 Commissions for Protection of Child Rights Act, No. 4 of 2006, India Code (2006).
3 Right of Children to Free and Compulsory Education Act, No. 35 of 2009, India Code (2009).
4 Protection of Children from Sexual Offences Act, No. 32 of 2012, India Code (2012).
5 Ministry of Women and Child Development, Govt. of India, Status Report on CNCP in India (2023).
6 Prayas Juvenile Aid Centre (JAC) (Society), Annual Report 2023 (2023).
7 Delhi Commission for Protection of Child Rights (DCPCR), A Decade of Child Rights Protection in Delhi (2023).
8 United Nations Convention on the Rights of the Child, adopted Nov. 20, 1989, 1577 U.N.T.S. 3.
9 Juvenile Justice (Care and Protection of Children) Act, No. 2 of 2016, India Code (2016).
10 United Nations Convention on the Rights of the Child, adopted Nov. 20, 1989, 1577 U.N.T.S. 3.
11 Juvenile Justice (Care and Protection of Children) Act, No. 2 of 2016, India Code (2016).
12 Ministry of Women and Child Development, Govt. of India, Model Rules under the Juvenile Justice (Care and Protection of Children) Act, 2015 (2016).

13 United Nations Treaty Collection, Convention on the Rights of the Child, Status as at Dec. 2024.
14 The Standard Minimum Rules for the Administration of Juvenile Justice ('The Beijing Rules'), G.A. Res. 40/33, U.N. Doc. A/RES/40/33 (Nov. 29, 1985).
15 Committee on the Rights of the Child, Concluding Observations: India, U.N. Doc. CRC/C/IND/CO/4 (Jun. 13, 2014).
16 Children Act, No. 60 of 1960, India Code (1960).
17 Juvenile Justice Act, No. 53 of 1986, India Code (1986).
18 Juvenile Justice (Care and Protection of Children) Act, No. 56 of 2000, India Code (2000).
19 Juvenile Justice (Care and Protection of Children) Act, No. 2 of 2015, India Code (2016).
20 Juvenile Justice Act, No. 53 of 1986, India Code (1986).
21 D.K. Tiwari & S.K. Tripathi, Juvenile Justice in India: An Overview, 2 J. Legal Pol'y & Gov't 41 (2015).
22 United Nations Convention on the Rights of the Child, adopted Nov. 20, 1989, 1577 U.N.T.S. 3.
23 INDIA CONSTITUTION. Art. 15(3), Art. 39(f).
24 Children's Act 1960.
25 Vide G.S.R. 678(E) dated 1st September, 2022, w.e.f. 01.09.2022. The Juvenile Justice (Care and Protection of Children) Model Amendment Rules, 2022.
26 Vide G.S.R. 678(E) dated 1st September, 2022, w.e.f. 01.09.2022.
27 The Juvenile Justice (Care and Protection of Children) Model Amendment Rules, 2022.
28 Child Labour (Prohibition & Regulation) Amendment Act, No. 35 of 2016, India Code (2016).
29 MC Mehta v. State of Tamil Nadu, (1996) 6 SCC 756 (India).
30 The Protection of Children from Sexual Offences (POCSO) Act, 2012.
31 Juvenile Justice (Care and Protection of Children) Act, 2015.
32 Right to Education Act, 2009.
33 Juvenile Justice (Care and Protection of Children) Act, 2015.
34 Salil Bali vs. Union of India (2013): The Supreme Court rejected petitions to lower the juvenile age limit for serious crimes, reaffirming the principle that juveniles should be treated with rehabilitative measures.
35 Dr. Subramanian Swamy vs. Raju (2014): The Court upheld the Juvenile Justice Act, rejecting attempts to treat juveniles as adults in cases of heinous crimes, reinforcing the goal of rehabilitation.
36 Prayas Institute of Juvenile Justice, National Study on Child Abuse – Physical, Emotional, Sexual, Neglect, and Girl Child (2005–2007) (conducted under the aegis of the Ministry of Women and Child Development, Government of India).
37 A Section 8 company is a non-profit organization (NPO) in India that's registered under the Companies Act, 2013.
38 Ministry of Finance, Union Budget 2023–24, https://www.indiabudget.gov.in/.
39 United Nations Committee on the Rights of the Child, Joint Periodic Report Submission, https://www.ohchr.org/en/treaty-bodies/crc.

2

ROLE OF HIGHER JUDICIARY IN MONITORING JUVENILE CARE THROUGH JUVENILE JUSTICE COMMITTEES – AN INSIDER'S PERSPECTIVE

Justice Madan Bhimarao Lokur[1]

Introduction

Way back, in late 1991 or early 1992, I was initiated into the rights of children by an incident that shook the conscience of many, though not quite like the Nirbhaya gang rape and murder case of 2012. A 10-year-old girl, Ameena, was travelling in an Indian Airlines flight from Hyderabad to Delhi with a 60-year-old from the Middle East. It appears that throughout the journey, Ameena was sobbing, and this disconcerted one of the air hostesses, Amrita Ahluwalia. On enquiry by her, it appeared that Ameena had been married off to this man and was to be taken to the Middle East as a child bride.

After the flight landed in Delhi, Amrita Ahluwalia alerted the police, who arrested the 60-year-old foreign national. Initial investigations revealed that Ameena had been sold as a child bride by her parents. Pending further investigation, she was kept in a child care institution. Somehow, the entire episode came up for consideration before the Delhi High Court, and during the course of the hearing, I was directed by a bench of two judges of the High Court to visit the institution and report on Ameena's condition and the general upkeep in the child care institution. As directed, I visited the children's home for girls and submitted a report to the Court. Personally, I had come face to face with a stark reality of several young girls who were either trafficked or abandoned or rescued from a hellish existence. I was convinced that something needed to be done for them beyond submitting a report to the High Court.

Around that time, India ratified the Convention on the Rights of the Child on 11 December 1992. On learning of this momentous development, I believed that the rights of children, both boys and girls, would now be addressed by the state. It was not to be. It took several years for Parliament

DOI: 10.4324/9781003607076-4

to enact a law protecting the rights of children. Eventually, the Juvenile Justice (Care and Protection of Children) Act, 2000, was enacted, setting out a detailed framework for safeguarding the rights of children.

The Judiciary Takes Interest

It appears that despite our obligations under the convention and the law, we were not able to ensure that the rights of children were meaningfully made available to them or effectively recognized. Somehow or other, this came to the notice of the Chief Justice of India, who thought it appropriate to discuss it in the biennial Chief Justices' Conference held on 9–10 March 2006. After deliberations, the learned Chief Justices resolved as follows:

> That High Courts will impress upon the State Governments to set up Juvenile Justice Boards, wherever not set-up. The Chief Justices may nominate a High Court Judge to oversee the condition and functioning of the remand/observation homes established under the Juvenile Justice (Care and Protection of Children) Act, 2000.

This resolution became the real starting point for implementing the rights of children, at least by the judiciary. The resolution was in two parts – first pertaining to setting up JJBs and the second pertaining to nomination of a High Court Judge to oversee the condition and functioning of the remand/observation homes. The resolution was half-heartedly implemented on both counts. This was clear from the Agenda Notes for the next Chief Justices' Conference held on 14–15 August 2009, carrying a report on the establishment of JJBs in different state and union territories. The notes mentioned that the State Governments either did not establish a sufficient number of JJBs or failed to report on the progress made. The response for nominating a High Court Judge to oversee the condition and functioning of the remand/observation homes established under the Juvenile Justice (Care and Protection of Children) Act, 2000 (JJ Act), did not figure in the Agenda Notes. Such was the concern shown for the rights and dignity of children.

The Delhi High Court did take the resolution seriously and made a nomination, and I had the good fortune to be the nominated judge and designated as the Juvenile Justice Committee (JJC). While this revived my memories of the meeting with Ameena and gave me the opportunity to work on improving the conditions in homes for children, I had no precedent or guidance on how to move forward. At that time, several public interest litigations, somehow or other related to children, were pending in the Delhi High Court, and I decided to go through them to get an idea of the directions passed so that they could be implemented. After noting the directions passed in each public interest litigation, I prepared a list of 58 'things to do'. Each one was as important as the other, making it difficult to decide the priority for implementation. At this stage, a friend advised that I should close my eyes and put my finger anywhere on the sheet of paper and begin by implementing that direction. In one sense, it was sound advice, but, later, a visit to the Observation Home for Boys (OHB) was necessary to see whether implementation of any other direction should get equal priority, if not more. Therefore, my first visit to the OHB followed.

Visit to the OHB and the Prevailing Conditions

The conditions in which children were living in the OHB were deplorable. There were four dormitories, each for 25 children, but the resident children were 258. They were cramped in that space with little or no room to sleep at night. There were eight toilets for these children, but only four were functional. To add to my distress, I learnt from some children that their inquiry under the law was not progressing, and a few had spent more than the maximum sentence of three years (prescribed by the JJ Act) in the home; one child had been there for five years. Thus began my journey as the JJC of the Delhi High Court, with some of those scenes etched in my memory.

The first step I took after visiting the OHB was to make a request to the Principal Magistrate in the JJB to look into the case files and take a decision about the continued detention of some of the children. Fortunately, she and her social members took it upon themselves to open up each file and study it carefully. The exercise took them almost three weeks, but it resulted in the 'release' of 210 children. In other words, the JJB itself came to the conclusion that only 48 out of 258 children were required to be kept in detention in the OHB.

Having achieved something positive with the assistance of the JJB and there being no precedent for the duties and responsibilities of the JJC, there was clearly a necessity of co-opting the JJB, the Social Welfare Department of the Delhi Government, and some NGO friends for improving the living conditions of the children in the OHB. This was really the starting point for making systematic progress.

Getting the Stakeholders Together

To work out a strategy, I again met the Principal Magistrate. While extending her cooperation, she expressed the view that she had been given a 'punishment posting' – why should a judicial officer be made to conduct inquiries into offences allegedly committed by children, along with two social workers, particularly when the courts are overloaded with more important cases? I immediately realized that sensitizing the Principal Magistrate and social workers is an important and urgent task, since they make decisions impacting the life of an alleged juvenile offender. Their experience in going through the files and releasing the children from detention in the OHB made the task of sensitization that much easier and dispelled the idea of a 'punishment posting'. They were advised that their responsibility was not only to conduct an inquiry but also to ensure that children are not required to stay in a home longer than necessary, as detention is the last resort. They were also advised that their responsibility included taking steps for the rehabilitation and reintegration of a child by taking appropriate measures, including preparing a child care plan, which will, hopefully, take care of the immediate future of the child.

Unfortunately, and quite shockingly, my initial impression was that the Social Welfare Department of the Delhi Government did not seem to have the welfare of children on its radar. Fortunately, the secretary in charge did not remain in position for too long but long enough to get my goat. Her successors in office were far more empathetic and just the right people to discuss, chalk out, initiate, and implement plans to improve the living conditions of children. Infrastructure issues needed to be looked into, which were not confined only to maintenance of the building, but also the amenities, including wholesome food. Thus, some improvements began in the OHB in Delhi.

Over the next couple of years, I had occasion to visit OHBs in some other cities also. In one of them, the toilets did not have a door, water shortage was perennial, and electricity was non-existent. It was pathetic. I then realized that if improvements were necessary, and they were, visits to the homes for children, along with officials of the Social Welfare Department, are an absolute must. The officials need to actually see the ground reality through their eyes rather than through files put up to them for consideration.

In one sense, therefore, the task for the JJC is cut out. A lot needs to be done by way of improvements, and a lot can be achieved. The JJC must hold regular meetings with the JJB and the Social Welfare Department. In Delhi, meetings were initially held every fortnight, and after all stakeholders and duty holders appreciated that the JJC meant business, the living conditions of children improved, slowly but surely, and the frequency of meetings also staggered.

NGOs are, in a sense, the heart and soul of any positive activity concerning children. They have ground-level information about what exactly is or is not going on. They are in touch with both children and officials. Those NGOs that have their heart in the right place can greatly assist the JJC in bringing about necessary changes, including in policy. They are solid supporters of change, having seen the lives that children are leading. It is perhaps for this reason that government officials are reluctant to permit them access to the OHB and other Child Care Institutions (CCIs). The JJC must interact with NGOs and cannot afford to rely only on information provided by the government and statutory authorities, such as the child rights commissions.

Of course, there are some unscrupulous NGOs, and the JJC has to identify them and not deal with them. The horrendous activities of one such so-called NGO in Muzaffarpur (Bihar) were the subject matter of criminal prosecution when it came to be known that it was responsible for the trafficking of young girls for sexual purposes.

International organizations, particularly UNICEF, can play a crucial role in disseminating awareness of child rights. Although UNICEF did not get into the act, as it were, when I was the JJC in the Delhi High Court, they later played a crucial and significant role in fostering child rights and encouraging NGOs. In fact, as the chair of the JJC in the Supreme Court, UNICEF provided tremendous assistance and support. UNICEF agreed to hold four regional programs in a year for four years and a national program at the end of the year. The impact of these programs was quite remarkable.

These programs brought together JJCs of different High Courts, officers of the State Governments, police, and NGOs on one platform. The two-day programs held every quarter led to intensive and extensive discussions on problems children were facing and how to resolve them with the assistance and active cooperation of the administrators. The problems related not only to living conditions in OHBs and other CCIs (including Observation Homes for Girls) and functioning of State Governments in issues concerning child rights, but also issues of trafficking, child sexual abuse and child pornography, education and nutrition, among others. In other words, the entire range of issues concerning children was discussed and solutions were suggested, based on the experience of different stakeholders, including children. Such was the positive impact of these regional and national programs that UNICEF agreed to continue the national programs for a few more years.

UNICEF has also been instrumental in encouraging children to participate in events such as painting competitions. In one instance, the prize winner was rewarded by the JJC, and during the interaction, it transpired that he had not been produced before the JJB for almost eight months. The police report alleged that he was a thief, but the social investigation report under the JJ Act described him as a good and sincere student by his teachers and a friendly and helpful child by his neighbors. Not one of them believed that he could be a thief. Yet, due to a dereliction of duty by the JJB, the child spent several months in the OHB until the JJC ensured his release and rehabilitation.

What the JJC Can Achieve

JJCs in the High Courts can play a vital role in making us appreciate the meaning and content of child rights. JJCs are the glue that binds all stakeholders and duty holders to achieve one common objective – improving the lives of children and bringing all others on board as well. In a sense, the JJCs are a strong moral force. A signal from the JJC can set into motion changes required to be made not only at the official level but also at the level of citizenry. Experience has shown that individuals and relatively smaller civil society organizations (CSOs) have been forthcoming in rendering assistance when requested by the JJC and even otherwise. In the playground of one of the OHBs that I visited, the swings were broken. The authorities did little to repair the damage. A visit to the OHB by the JJC attracted attention, the reason being a so-called high-profile visit. One of those who came to the OHB premises, curious about the 'high-profile' visit, was a welder. During general discussions that the JJC had with the accompanying officials and people gathered there, the welder offered to repair the swings as his contribution to enjoyment in the life of children, perhaps much to the relief of the officials.

The JJC in Bengaluru intervened to ensure the return of a young girl to her parents in Arunachal Pradesh. She had been invited to Bengaluru to live with a 'friend' on social media. One day, she decided to travel from her village to Bengaluru via Delhi. The journey took her three days, and when she reached Bengaluru, her 'friend' was nowhere to be seen. The Railway Police produced her before the Child Welfare Committee, which placed her in a CCI. A visit by the JJC, followed by an interaction with the children, brought out her sorry story. Through the intervention of the JJC, she managed to contact her grandparents and return home.

A CSO took it upon itself to teach theatre and dance to the children in the OHB. A youthful threesome spent hours interacting with the children in the OHB in Delhi and virtually became an extended family for them. The reason for the expression 'extended family' is that the family of a child does not find it easy to visit an OHB for a variety of reasons, including belonging to a low-income group. Each visit is expensive. Moreover, the rules of some of the OHBs permit a limited number of visits per month. The threesome could meet the children almost every alternate day to give lessons to them, providing them solace and cheer which their family could not provide. This is what led to their being described by some of the children as their extended family.

A group of Indian Institute of Technology Delhi students took it upon themselves to impart computer education on Saturdays to children in a CCI for children in need of care and protection. Why were they doing it? They said they wanted to 'give back' to society through these children, and the time they spent with them was well worth it, as far as they were concerned. Similarly, a driving school gave free lessons to the children of the same CCI who were just short of 18 years of age so that they could get some employment after they came out. These children passed the driving test and were eligible to get a license. However, as luck would have it, the motor licensing authority desired to know the parentage of the applicants and their permanent address. The children were orphans or too young when they entered the CCI and did not know who their parents were and their permanent address was the CCI. This was not acceptable to the authority that rejected the application for a driving license. It was only later, with the intervention of the JJC that a driving license was issued to the children.

It is my belief that the role of the JJC is not and cannot be limited to concerning itself only with the functioning of JJBs and Observation Homes. It has a larger societal role to play and its concerns extend to involvement with the Child Welfare Committees (CWCs) for ensuring that they function in the best interest of the child. It must be appreciated that a child in conflict with law is also a child in need of care and protection. Therefore, on some occasions it may become necessary for the JJB to interact with members of the CWC. It is for this reason that whenever meetings are held by the JJC, members of all statutory authorities, that is, the JJB, CWC and members of the State Commission for the Protection of Child Rights are usually invited for discussions and brainstorming. In other words, the JJC has been given, by a resolution passed in the Chief Justice's Conference, the responsibility of overall supervision of ensuring that the dignity and rights of children are not only preserved and protected but are also fostered. To achieve this, the JJC has to reach out to all concerned and bring them on board for the best interest of the children. This can be easily achieved, and, frankly, I have been a witness to several such achievements in many States, if not all.

JJC in the Supreme Court

On my suggestion, the JJC was constituted in the Supreme Court in 2013 by Chief Justice Sathasivam. I had realized through my experience as the JJC in the Delhi High Court that importance must also be given to child rights at the national level and not only at the state level. After expressing my views and a brief discussion, the Chief Justice accepted my suggestion on the condition that I chair the JJC, to which I readily agreed. This decision had far-reaching consequences and enabled the Supreme Court JJC to bring together not only all JJCs across the High Courts but also officials at the Central Government level and NGOs from different parts of the country. Through the auspices of the JJC, judicial academies, including the National Judicial Academy at Bhopal, began to conduct awareness and sensitization programs for judges and judicial officers and even encouraged police academies to conduct such programs. Through the efforts of the Supreme Court JJC and support given by all concerned, particularly UNICEF, huge strides were taken in ensuring that the rights of children are protected and preserved. Judicial pronouncements given by the Supreme Court and almost every High Court added to the weight of efforts.

Some of these efforts yielded positive results such as the initiation of child-friendly courts,[2] one-stop centers for gender-related and child-related crimes and follow-up action, a responsive police force, and recognition through invitations to international conferences and the hosting of international conferences in India.

What More?

Oh yes, there's lots more that can be done and, in fact, should be done. When a child is accused of committing a heinous crime, the news is splashed all over, and the child is presumed to be guilty by the community. What happens when a child is the victim of a heinous crime? It hardly gets reported, usually on the grounds that it will adversely impact the child's future – a factor not considered when a child is accused of a crime. The National Crime Records Bureau, in its Crime in India 2022, has reported that as many as 162,449 cases of crime against children were registered. However, only 30,555 cases were registered against juveniles.[3] In other words, children who were victims of crime (such as kidnapping and sexual offences, including child rape) were more than five times the number of children in conflict with the law. Yet, we do not seem to pay serious attention to child victims of crime. Perhaps the JJCs can take up this problem.

Usually, when a victim of crime is identified, the first reaction of the state is to announce an ex gratia payment. It is time to realize that there is much more at stake as far as the child is concerned. This was chillingly brought home when the National Institute of Mental Health and Neuro-Sciences in Bengaluru studied the mental health impact on the victims of repeated sexual abuse in the Muzaffarpur[4] shelter home case that was unearthed in 2018, regarding the horrific incidences of sexual exploitation and also murder of female inmates of the home.[5] They had been traumatized not only physically but psychologically and emotionally drained and mentally disturbed beyond imagination. Would a few lakhs of rupees by way of ex gratia payment have brought normalcy to their lives? Issues of social acceptance arise when a child is sexually abused. Sometimes they are denied admission to a school for reasons that are impossible to accept. In the case of a child who has been kidnapped and later rescued, one can only imagine the mental trauma at the time of the incident, and recollections of which will perhaps be difficult to erase from memory for life.

To make matters worse, the ex gratia payment is dealt in a casual manner by the authorities. Child victims have little option but to wait for months to receive any compensation. I recall having considered the plight of a young girl (of just about 13 years) who was pregnant, carrying the child of her paternal uncle, who had raped her. It was too late and too dangerous for her to abort. After the birth of her child, she was abandoned by her family, and she had to be financially looked after. The CWC did not act with the necessary urgency, and, in addition, there was an unusual delay in giving her the necessary financial assistance. On inquiry, it transpired that she was number 33 in the queue and would have to wait for a couple of months before her case could be considered for financial assistance. How was she expected to survive for so long? How were those, higher up in the queue, surviving? These are troubling questions and deserve the consideration of the JJCs. The JJC must monitor all such cases, and there are many of them, through a secretariat of officers in the High Court dedicated to issues of child rights. High Court judges do not necessarily have the time to look into each and every issue that arises, and, therefore, there is a need for a secretariat.

Trafficking is perhaps the most heinous and unforgivable crime. A victim of sexual trafficking is more of a living corpse than anything else. Even when rescued, they have little hope of survival in the real world. While in the Delhi High Court, a case was brought to my notice that two young girls from Calcutta had been rescued from a brothel in Delhi. They were produced as accused persons before a Magistrate, in a case of immoral trafficking, rather than as victims of trafficking. Anyway, a person appeared before the Magistrate claiming to be the father of one of the girls and requested her custody. The Magistrate accordingly passed necessary orders giving him custody. A child rights activist happened to be present in court and asked the girl what had transpired. The activist learnt that the girl could not understand anything that had just transpired in the court, as she knew no language other than Bangla (her mother tongue), and the so-called father was actually the trafficker who had purchased her from her parents in Calcutta. Fortunately, the court staff could not complete the legal paperwork during the day, and so the girl was not handed over to the trafficker. Apprehending a similar fate to the other girl, the activist brought the events to my notice. As the JJC, I informed the Chief Justice of the events, and he, in turn, advised the Magistrate to exercise caution. The two girls were not handed over to the traffickers, but sensing trouble, the traffickers vanished. Did the girls return to their families? Were the traffickers ultimately apprehended? I do not really know.

In another incident of trafficking through child marriage, a young pregnant girl was not particularly fortunate. On directions of the Tripura High Court, arrangements were made to bring her from Jaipur to Agartala (capital of the north-eastern state, Tripura). However, her parents refused to accept her. Their reason was that she had been sold for child marriage (to traffickers) for Rs. 50,000, and the traffickers could come back to reclaim the girl, that is, their purchased commodity or demand return of the sale price, which the family did not have. So, the girl was left to her own fate and placed in a CCI.

There are several other unfortunate children who need the attention of the JJCs. Disabled children are one such category. Many of them are unable to attend school due to their disability, thereby depriving them of their rights and education under the Right of Children to Free and Compulsory Education Act, 2009. There are also children who are mentally challenged. The Chetna Institute for Mentally Handicapped in Lucknow is looking after many of them, but several more such homes are needed in different parts of the country. Wherever they are, they need to be well managed. Recently, in Asha Kiran in Delhi, described as a 'home for the mentally challenged', as many as 14 persons, including a minor and six women, died in a month.[6] Street children are another category that needs attention. There has been talk of rehabilitating them for several years, but no progress seems to have been made. Orphans are another category of children who deserve attention. Quite a few children became orphans during the COVID pandemic. Schemes were announced for their rehabilitation. Have such schemes been implemented? I could go on asking this and other questions.

Conclusion

The impact of the efforts made by the JJCs in the High Courts and the Supreme Court is difficult to assess, but there has definitely been a perceptible change for the better, in terms of attitudinal changes focusing more toward children. We need to empathize with them, not sympathize. It is only then that efforts will bear fruit. While a lot has otherwise been achieved through sustained efforts by JJCs and all those associated with them across the country, there is still a long way to go before we can confidently say that we have achieved the objectives of the Juvenile Justice (Care and Protection of Children) Act and allied laws including those relating to child sexual abuse, trafficking, child marriage, child labor, and so on. While these efforts are ongoing, the JJCs must widen their activities to include mental trauma that children suffer from, due to adverse circumstances and events, the rights of children with disabilities, meaningful education to children, and proper nutrition, which is one of the Directive Principles of State Policy mandated under the Constitution of India.

The JJCs in the High Courts and the Supreme Court may keep in mind the goal of Article 39 of our Constitution. This Article provides:

> The State shall, in particular, direct its policy towards securing – that children are given opportunities and facilities to develop in a healthy manner and in conditions of freedom and dignity and that childhood and youth are protected against exploitation and against moral and material abandonment.

With the above in focus and as their goal, the path for the JJCs is clearly laid out.

Notes

1 Former Judge, Supreme Court of India, Former Judge, Supreme Court of Fiji, and also Former Chief Justice of Gauhati High Court and Andhra Pradesh High Court and Former Judge of Delhi High Court.
2 Child friendly courts were established first in Delhi and have now been established in several other cities; one stop centers are now all over the country, and Bharosa, for example, in Hyderabad is doing excellent work.
3 NCRB, *Crime in India 2022*, 1 (2022), https://images.assettype.com/barandbench/2023-12/dc0ba053-a1f0-4e6a-a5f8-e7668ddd2249/NCRB_STATS.pdf.
4 In the state of Bihar, India.
5 Chronology of Events in Muzaffarpur Shelter Home Eexual Assault Case – India Today, https://www.indiatoday.in/india/story/chronology-events-muzaffarpur-shelter-home-sexual-assault-case-1645553-2020-02-11 (last visited 29 October 2024).
6 The deaths took place in July 2024. Overall, it is reported in the *Indian Express* newspaper that, between 2011 and 2017, as many as 123 male and 73 female inmates have died in Asha Kiran. The number of children who died, if any, is not known.

3

COMPARING THE ROLE OF CHILD CARE INSTITUTIONS IN REHABILITATION OF CHILDREN IN CONFLICT WITH LAW IN INDIA WITH GLOBAL BEST PRACTICES

Elisha Kanungo

Introduction

The modern world, including numerous developed countries like the United Kingdom and the United States, has witnessed the emergence of a movement calling for a unique approach to children alleged to have committed any offence, commonly referred to as juvenile offenders. The origin of this movement dates back to the 18th century. Juvenile offenders received similar treatment as adult criminals earlier than this. In the year 1989, the "General Assembly" of the UN enacted the "Convention on the Rights of the Child" (CRC), which sets guidelines that all member states must pursue for protecting the best interests of the child. International instruments and treaties have significantly improved the subjects of children's rights and the prevention of child abuse.[1] International organizations like UNICEF and the United Nations have historically paid more attention to children's growth and development. The focus on child well-being can be traced back to many early initiatives, like Pope Clement XI's proposal of the concept of "Instruction of Profligate Youth in Institutional Treatment" in the year 1704. Further, Elizabeth Fry then founded a different facility just for young criminals. "The Reformatory Schools Act" and "the Industrial Schools Act" were eventually enacted as statutory books in Britain.[2] Under the Juvenile Offenders Act, the first court for juveniles was founded in Chicago in 1899. The first court for juveniles was established in England in 1905. Additionally, the first probation laws were passed in England in 1887, as well as in the US state of Massachusetts in 1878. The issue of juvenile delinquency was covered in depth in the 2nd and 6th UN Congresses on the "Prevention of Crime and Treatment of Offenders" in 1960 and 1980. They concluded that the operation of juvenile justice

DOI: 10.4324/9781003607076-5

should follow the set of fundamental rules. It was later acknowledged that preventing juvenile delinquency required extra care.[3]

Juvenile justice–related matters are specifically covered in Articles 37 and 40 of the UNCRC. Article 37 states that a warrant is required for the arrest, custody, or confinement of minors. It is the task of governments to guarantee that minors who violate the law do not face cruel punishments or torture. It is not appropriate to place minors with adult prisoners. They are entitled to legal representation, the facility to plea their prison sentence, and the right to keep in touch with their relatives. Additionally, Article 40 guarantees children the right to a fair trial for those who have been accused of perpetrating an offence. This involves not having to testify against oneself or enter a plea of guilty, as well as the freedom to be presumed innocent until proven guilty and the right to legal representation and a trial. The minimum age at which minors can be prosecuted for crimes is set by their governments. Only in cases where a minor is found guilty of an exceptionally serious offence should imprisonment be handed down.[4] These articles build upon provisions articulated in the UN Standard Minimum Rules for the Administration of Juvenile Justice (1985 Beijing Rules), UN Guidelines for the Prevention of Juvenile Delinquency (1990 Riyadh Guidelines), and UN Rules for the Protection of Juveniles Deprived of Their Liberty (1990 Havana Rules). There are provisions in the 1989 CRC – adopted by the General Assembly through "Resolution 44/25 of 20" – that prohibit the exploitation, violence, and maltreatment of children. Every member-state must apply the Child Rights Convention's regulations in a manner consistent with its domestic legal systems. Additionally, it specifies the procedure for reintegrating the harmed child into the community. Articles 6, 7, and 8 of the 1989 CRC emphasize children's social and economic freedoms, as well as their right to a fair life and a basic education. Every country must guarantee that these children's rights are enshrined in its constitution and that an appropriate system for redress exists. For this reason, the National Council for the Protection of Child Rights was founded.[5] Afterwards, for safeguarding the rights of children, various international instruments and conventions have been signed by all the UN states. These are the UN Standard Minimum Rules for the Administration of Juvenile Justice (Beijing Rules). The Beijing Rules contain significant guidelines for treating juveniles in just and humane manners in the justice system. It believes that the normal trial procedure should not be followed for a juvenile, and every measure should be taken to reintegrate the juvenile into society. Counselling and community services should be ordered for the children to reintegrate into society and to divert them from anti-social activities. The rule further promotes institutionalization as the last option to treat the juveniles.[6] Further, "UN Guidelines for the Prevention of Juvenile Delinquency (Riyadh Guidelines)" prioritize education, which includes vocational education, so that the juveniles can be self-sufficient in the future for earning their livelihood, and this is in support of community-based rehabilitation rather than any institutional care for the juveniles.[7]

Another instrument, which was adopted in 1990 by the General Assembly, was the "UN Rules for the Protection of Juvenile Deprived of Their Liberty (Havana Conventions)". This guideline emphasized the rehabilitation detention policies. This made it a mandate that the detention facilities should provide a social reintegration programme. Another instrument adopted in 1997 by the Economic and Social Council was the "Guidelines for the Action on Children in Criminal Juvenile System (Vienna Guidelines)".[8] This guideline promotes community service and mediation as a mechanism for victim restoration between the offender and the victim, rather than any punitive measures. This guideline urged every member-state to bring juvenile laws that focus on the rehabilitation of juveniles. All the instruments mentioned earlier collectively focus on a child-centric approach, and children should receive adequate support for reintegration into society.

Children have received differential treatment since the Code of Hammurabi, which was established in 1790 BC and placed the family members in charge of their care and supervision. Rehabilitation of juvenile offenders through isolation has been prevalent in India. Lord Cornwallis founded the very first "Ragged School", an organization for such young children, in 1843, at the time of Indian colonialism. Between 1850 and 1919, there was significant economic and industrial chaos.[9] The initially enacted law, the Apprentices Act of 1850, mandated that children who were convicted between 10 and 18 years receive vocational education as an important component of their rehabilitation. Even the "Indian Penal Code (IPC)" of 1860 and the present Bhartiya Nyaya Samhita 2023 (BNS, which replaced the IPC) absolves minors below the age of seven of their criminal liability. Additionally, criminal liability does not apply to children within the age range of seven and 12, as they are still too young to comprehend the repercussions of their misconduct. Another important piece of statutes for regulating the treatment of young offenders was the "Reformatory School Act" of 1876 and 1897. According to the Act, offenders could be held by the court for two to seven years in a reformatory school; however, the court would not hold offenders in these facilities beyond the age of 18. Juvenile offenders were given particular care under the old Code of Criminal Procedure of 1898. Criminals up to the age of 21 were eligible for probation under the Code, depending on their good behaviour. The recommendations of the Indian Jail Committee (1919–1920) led to the Indian Children Act. Every province had the option to pass its own juvenile laws within its borders; the provincial governments of Madras, Bengal, and Bombay enacted their own separate acts relating to children in 1920, 1922, and 1924, respectively. These statutes included clauses pertaining to the creation of a unique system for treating minors.[10]

Following independence, India's juvenile justice system (JJS) is based on the mandates of the Constitution of India in Articles 15(3),[11] 21,[12] 241,[13] 39(e),[14] 39(f),[15] 45,[16] and 47.[17] It also draws from a number of internationally recognized agreements, including the UNCRC and the UN Standard Minimum Rules for Administration of Juvenile Justice (Beijing Rules). The Juvenile Justice Act 1986 superseded the Children Act 1960 and was initially introduced in the Lok Sabha on August 22, 1986, in accordance with the Beijing Rules.[18] All of the union territory governments were subject to the law when it came into operation, but states without juvenile laws were open to implement it in 1974 when India announced its National Policy for Children. Among other things, the policy covered the education and rehabilitation of impoverished, abused, neglected, and delinquent children. After India signed and ratified the CRC, the earlier Juvenile Justice Act of 1986 had to be replaced with the Juvenile Justice (Care and Protection of Children) Act, 2000, which brought compliance with the convention. Additional amendments to this Act were made in 2006, 2010, and 2015, respectively.[19] The Act offers a unique framework for children under the jurisdiction of the JJS in terms of their security, care, and rehabilitation. The Juvenile Justice Boards (JJB) was created to assist with "children in conflict with the law" (CCL), and the Child Welfare Committee (CWC) was formed to look into the issues of "Children in need of care and protection". Thus, it addresses both groups of children independently. Under this Act, juveniles who are detained or charged with committing crimes appear before the JJB rather than a standard criminal trial meant for adult offenders.[20]

Salient Features of the Juvenile Justice (Care and Protection of Children) Act, 2015

The Juvenile Justice (Care and Protection of Children) Act, 2015 (JJ Act) is a comprehensive statute that outlines the legal guidelines for dealing with children in India who are alleged to have committed an offence and/or who require care and protection.

A person who is below the age of 18 is considered a child or juvenile under the Act, although the JJ Act of 2015 no longer denotes a child even if he or she has committed an offence as a "juvenile". The Act mandates that JJBs be established in each district to deal with situations involving children who are in legal trouble. Determining if the child has breached any laws and what actions to take to assist them in getting back on track and reintegrating into society are the responsibilities of the JJB.[21] To address matters involving "children in need of care and protection" in every district, the Act also mandates the establishment of CWCs in charge of children who need care and protection, such as those who have been neglected or become orphans. Numerous initiatives for children's reintegration and rehabilitation are outlined in the Act, including learning, treatment, employment training, and community service. To provide children with care and protection, the Act promotes the use of non-institutional care alternatives like foster parenting, adoption, and sponsorship. To preserve the confidentiality of the children, the Act makes sure that the identity of the child who comes under the JJS is not divulged. The Act establishes a distinct process for handling cases involving any heinous and serious crimes perpetrated by minors between the ages of 16 to 18 years.

A child can be sent to a child care institution (CCI) under various circumstances as per the JJ Act, 2015. If a juvenile is not granted bail and while the enquiry is pending, they are first placed in an "observation home" (OH). In cases of serious offences, the child may be housed in a place of safety instead of an OH during the inquiry. Another CCI where the juvenile can be placed is the special home (SH). Upon final orders by the JJB, juveniles found guilty can be sent to an SH for a maximum period of three years, depending on the nature of the offence, with a possibility of early release based on their progress. If a juvenile above 16 commits any serious or heinous offence, the JJB may order their placement in a place of safety instead of an SH.[22] After completing their term, juveniles are entitled to rehabilitation and social reintegration through adoption, foster care, sponsorship, or aftercare programmes, which can extend for up to three years to help them transition to mainstream society. Each juvenile in a CCI must have an Individual Care Plan, which includes mental health care, education, skill development, and post-release support. These plans are regularly reviewed by management committees and overseen by probation officers, ensuring that juveniles receive proper rehabilitation and guidance.

Treatment of Juvenile Offenders in CCIs in India

The JJ Act 2015 under section 2(21) CCI means children's home, open shelter, OH, SH, place of safety, specialized adoption agency (SAA), and a fit facility recognized under this Act for providing care and protection to children who are in need of such services. To offer medical care, education, training, development, and rehabilitation for children in need of protection, the State Government may create or operate a children's home independently or through non-governmental organizations. For children with special needs, the government may assign certain homes that provide specialized assistance as needed. To ensure these homes follow established guidelines and give each child individualized care, the State Government may also establish guidelines for their management and supervision. Under Section 2(41), "open shelter" refers to a facility for children, created and operated by the State Government, either directly or via a voluntary or non-governmental organization, which must be registered in accordance with prescribed procedures. Section 2(40) defines OH as a home enrolled as such, for the purposes of temporary reception, care, and rehabilitation of any child alleged to be in conflict with law, either by itself, or through a voluntary or non-governmental organization, established and maintained in every district or group of districts by a State Government. The purpose of OH is to provide care and rehabilitation for the children who are alleged to have committed a crime and an enquiry is going on for the same. Section 2(56) defines SH as an organization established by a State Government or a voluntary or non-governmental organization for accommodation or offering rehabilitation assistance to children in conflict with law, who are found, through investigation, to have committed an offence and are taken to such establishment by an order of the Board. Under Section 2 (46), "place of safety" refers to any location or institution, excluding a police lockup or jail, that is either independently established or affiliated with an OH or an SH. The individual in charge must be prepared to accept and care for children who are alleged or determined to be in conflict with the law, as mandated by an order from the Board or the Children's Court, during both the inquiry and the rehabilitation phase following a guilty verdict, for a duration and purpose outlined in the order. A SAA is a place set up by the government or a registered non-governmental organization. It provides shelter for orphans, abandoned, or surrendered children, as directed by the authorities, with the goal of finding them adoptive families. (See Table no 3.1)

Various institutions are established to provide care, protection, and rehabilitation for children in different situations. An open shelter is a facility run by the State Government or registered NGOs to offer temporary support and protection to children who need a safe space. These shelters help children who may not have stable homes and provide necessary assistance for their well-being. An OH serves as a temporary residence for children alleged to have committed offences. These homes, established by the State Government or NGOs, provide care, protection, and rehabilitation while the legal inquiry is ongoing, ensuring children are not placed in police custody or jail. An SH is designed for children found guilty of an offence and is intended for long-term rehabilitation. Operated by the State Government or NGOs, these homes provide accommodation and reformation programmes based on the orders from the JJB. Similarly, a place of safety is a secure facility for CCL, used during the inquiry process or after conviction. Unlike jails or police lockups, these facilities ensure a child-friendly environment, focusing on care, protection, and rehabilitation. They may function independently or in connection with an OH or SH. A SAA is an institution set up by the government or registered NGOs to shelter orphans, abandoned, or surrendered children. These agencies work under the direction of the CWC to facilitate legal adoption, ensuring that children find permanent families and a safe, nurturing environment.

The children are kept in SH, where they are found to have committed a crime, and an order has been passed by the board. The place of safety is established for keeping the children between the ages of 16 and 18 who are accused of any serious or heinous crime or he/she has been convicted by the board. These institutions focus on rehabilitation, which helps the children to reintegrate into the mainstream of society, where their cognitive development can happen, and their behaviour will change by acquiring life skills.[23] However, the most difficult parts of institutional care are the rehabilitation and social integration of the children from the institutions into the family or society. From giving them food, clothing, shelter, and training to organizing and creating a personalized care plan for their recovery and social integration, it entails a number of tasks. It offers many services to help them get ready for the future and involves careful preparation regarding the best kind of rehabilitation and social integration. The tenderness, concern, sense of self, and social connections that families and communities can offer are not available in childcare facilities, which usually employ a small number of people. Due to a lack of engagement and attention, research shows that children in institutional care are more likely to experience growth problems. The CCIs play a predominant role in dealing with the rehabilitation of the children; however, their effectiveness also varies across countries while dealing with the rehabilitation of the juveniles.

CCLs are intended to receive care, security, and rehabilitation through the JJS in India. The JJ Act of 2015, which strives to establish a child-friendly legal system in accordance with the tenets of the United Nations CRC, serves as the framework for the system. Despite its good intentions, the JJ Act of 2015 has several operational issues. The absence of sufficient facilities for the care and rehabilitation of children in confrontation with the law or those in need of protection is a major problem, particularly in rural areas where many states lack them.[24] Furthermore, even with procedures for the prompt resolution of cases, courtroom delays continue to be a problem, resulting in extended imprisonment and delaying the rehabilitation and reintegration of impacted children. Even with this statutory structure in place, there has been much discussion about how effective India's JJS is. The system is frequently criticized for its lack of success in rehabilitating young offenders and keeping them from committing new crimes. Lack of facilities and funds, which also includes infrastructures for the JJS, has also been a source of worry. As a result, children's homes are overcrowded, and the rehabilitation services are subpar. In addition, there have been cases where the JJS has mistreated and abused young people. This calls into doubt the system's capacity to defend the rights of young CCLs. There are still certain difficulties and problems with the law's implementation, even though the JJ Act has enhanced the legal basis for handling children who are in legal peril, as well as those who need care and protection.[25] With an emphasis on their protection, dignity, and rehabilitation, India's JJ Act guarantees important rights for minors in jail. It ensures legal representation, upholds the presumption of innocence until proven guilty, and requires fair treatment devoid of handcuffs, unless absolutely necessary. CCLs have access to education and career at the CCIs. The Act permits such children to stay in touch with their families, unless doing so would be detrimental to their well-being. In accordance with international norms for children's rights, the Act's main objective is the juvenile's rehabilitation and social reintegration. According to the JJ Act, rehabilitation can start as quickly as the CCL is sent to a care facility or any correctional facility. Aftercare organizations can assist in the community reintegration of a child who conflict with the law. These are temporary residences where children are kept before being fully reintegrated into the community.

Aftercare organizations, as defined under Section 46 of the Juvenile Justice (Care and Protection of Children) Act, 2015, are facilities that support children who have turned 18 and are leaving CCIs. Their primary aim is to help these young adults transition to independent living by providing essential services. They offer housing and shelter, ensuring a safe place to stay. Additionally, they provide education and skill development programmes, helping individuals complete their studies or gain vocational training. Employment support, including job placements and career guidance, is also a key service. To address emotional well-being, these organizations offer counselling and mental health support. Financial assistance is provided for basic needs, along with training in financial literacy. They also offer legal aid and awareness, helping young adults understand their rights and access necessary legal documentation. By offering these services, aftercare organizations play a crucial role in ensuring that children transitioning out of institutional care can lead stable, self-sufficient lives.

The services provided at the aftercare organizations include the following:

1. Professional training which provides them economic ability to support themselves
2. Restorative training to develop emotional conduct
3. Conciliation about societal ethics
4. Exercises that promote both physical and mental well-being
5. Regular education[26]

After leaving the SHs and children's home, the CCLs are cared for in "aftercare organizations". Children in aftercare programmes are capable of leading moral and productive lives. Aftercare organizations aim to accomplish the main goal of helping minors and children cope with society. After living in institutional homes, the children and juveniles are encouraged to remain in the community. Children who are kept in aftercare organizations are encouraged to do trading, and they can play a part in assisting and maintaining the aftercare facility. Any volunteer-run facility or group that is recognized as an aftercare provider aims to endow young persons with the social and life skills they need to become fully integrated members of society. Children who join the aftercare programme also have access to legal, social, and health care, as well as suitable monetary support. The rehabilitative services offer children and juveniles standard vocational and academic opportunities to assist them in being self-sufficient and earning money for themselves. Following the child's reintegration into their community, the aftercare organization is responsible for ensuring they receive ongoing guidance and assistance. Members of different government agencies, such as CWC, JJB, the district child protection unit, and the social welfare department, collaborate to help the child reconnect with the world at large by giving them support following their integration with continuous monitoring, as well as emotional and financial support.

Juvenile Detention Centre in the United States

Numerous federal and state laws regulate the JJS in the United States. Although there isn't a single Juvenile Justice Bare Act in the United States, the framework usually consists of a number of important clauses or parts from both federal and state laws. The Illinois Juvenile Court Act of 1899 authorized the establishment of the nation's first juvenile court in Chicago in 1899. Under the statute, the court was granted authority over dependent, delinquent, and neglected children under the age of 16. The court's emphasis was on rehabilitation, not punishment (see Table 3.1). The statute further contains provisions which say judicial records relating to the offence of the minor are to be kept private to reduce the stigma of the juvenile. The law puts a restriction on minors' imprisonment. The minor who is under 12 cannot be confined in jail and should be kept apart from the adult offenders. Every court procedure should be carried out informally by the judges. This idea of introducing juvenile courts received traction very quickly. All the states in the United States had operational juvenile courts by 1925, except few states like Maine and Wyoming.[27]

In 1899, Cook County, Illinois, established the JJS in the United States with the goal of rehabilitation. The Act disbelieves that juveniles commit crimes because they are immature and impulsive. Therefore, rather than addressing offending children as offenders, the American juvenile system attempted to rehabilitate them.[28] The system recognized that these adolescents may be reformed into decent adults. In youth courts, the state took on the role of "parent of the nation", emphasizing the benefits the minor would have in the future. "The Illinois Juvenile Court Act 1899" framed specialized rules and procedures for deciding the matters of children below 16 years of age. The legal age of majority for US residents is also set by each state, and in

TABLE 3.1 Comparative analysis of the juvenile justice systems in Germany, the United States, the United Kingdom, and India

Aspect	*India*	*Germany*	*United States*	*United Kingdom*
Prevalent laws for juveniles	Juvenile Justice (Care and Protection of Children) Act, 2015 (JJ Act).	Youth Courts Act 1974.	Juvenile Justice and Delinquency Prevention Act, 1974 (JJDPA), state-specific laws.	Children Act 1989 and Crime and Disorder Act 1998.
Rehabilitation focus	Rehabilitation and reform through community-based care, foster care, and adoption.	Rehabilitation focused with a strong emphasis on reformation over punishment.	Focus on rehabilitation, with restorative justice programmes and diversion.	Focus on rehabilitation, community-based care, and reintegration into society.
Care approach	Children placed in CCIs receive basic care, education, and vocational training. Focus on trauma-informed care and psycho-social counselling.	Juvenile offenders are sent to educational institutions or placed in foster care, emphasizing education and psychological support.	Foster care, group homes, and juvenile detention centres with psychological support and educational programmes.	Secure Children's Homes (SCHs) or Young Offender Institutions (YOIs) offer education, psychological care, and vocational training.
Emphasis on education	Formal education, vocational training, and skill development programmes in CCIs.	Strong focus on educational programmes; most children receive vocational training in institutions.	Children in detention centres have access to education and vocational training programmes.	Children have access to formal education and may also participate in vocational training programmes.
Psychological and emotional support	Trauma-informed counselling, psychological services, and support for mental health issues.	Psychological services and psycho-social counselling are integral to rehabilitation.	Juveniles receive psychological counselling and therapy as part of rehabilitation.	Emphasis on mental health support, counselling, and therapeutic interventions in youth facilities.

(*Continued*)

TABLE 3.1 (Continued)

Aspect	*India*	*Germany*	*United States*	*United Kingdom*
Institutional environment	Government and NGO-run CCIs are often overcrowded and under-resourced, with varying quality of care. The Ministry of Women and Child Development sets standards.	Institutions are well-funded and maintained, ensuring children receive adequate care, education, and psychological support.	The juvenile detention system includes a mix of secure facilities and group homes, with varying standards across states.	Institutions like SCHs and YOIs are well-regulated, but overcrowding and understaffing can still be issues.
Legal and social support	Children have access to legal aid and legal representation and are represented by Child Welfare Committees (CWCs).	Children receive legal aid and are represented by juvenile courts in the legal process.	CIL has legal aid and representation in juvenile courts.	YOTs provide legal aid and social support during legal proceedings.
Successes	Focus on trauma-informed care and family reunification; growing emphasis on alternative care.	Strong system of juvenile rehabilitation and successful reintegration of many juveniles into society.	Effective restorative justice practices and diversion programmes have shown success in reducing recidivism.	Strong rehabilitation programmes in institutions focus on education, mental health, and reintegration.

most states, like New Jersey, New Mexico, and New York, anyone up to the age of 18 is considered a minor, barring some states like Mississippi, where people below 21 may be considered a minor. Anyone above 9 years but less than 21 years of age at the time of the commission of the offence is defined as a juvenile perpetrator according to the "Child and Youth Welfare Code", which was established by President Decree No. 603.

In *Re Gault, 387, US 1 (1967)* case for the very first time, it was decided that minors have identical privileges as adults, including being able to seek counsel, the right to be kept silent, and the right to be informed of the charges against them. This case continues to be an important component of the just procedural treatment that minors have been entitled to. In another case involving minors is *Roper v. Simmons, 543, US 551(2005)*, it has been decided that a sentence of death for violent crimes perpetrated by minors in the United States was deemed to be an unusually severe penalty. It was further noted that capital punishment was ever given only by the courts to those who committed extremely serious crimes. Justice Kennedy listed a few universal traits that distinguished juvenile offenders from adults and children who perpetrated terrible acts of violence. Firstly, minors are incapable of understanding the repercussions of the act they committed because they do not have the maturity and understanding of accountability. In addition, young people are susceptible to the influence of family or peers or any person in a fiduciary capacity. Lastly, a juvenile's personality differs from an adult as they are more impressionable, due to which the former has much greater potential for recovery and reformation.

Children in juvenile detention facilities in the United States are protected by a number of federal and state laws that are intended to protect their safety, welfare, and rehabilitation. Important rights involve the right to schooling, safeguarding from danger, legal representation, rehabilitative assistance, and separation from adults. In addition, minors are entitled to limited use of physical restrictions and health care, including mental health services. Regular evaluations of their detention status are carried out, and family communication is usually encouraged. State laws may offer additional protections and requirements for juvenile justice processes, even while federal guidelines such as the Juvenile Justice and Delinquency Prevention Act of 1974 (JJDPA) define fundamental criteria. The JJDPA, which was first enacted in 1974 and last renewed in 2002, offers vital support to state initiatives that help communities prevent juvenile crimes holistically and efficiently resolve the issues of juvenile offenders and their immediate families. Along with a juvenile planning and advisory system in every state, the JJDPA helps develop prevention strategies in both state and local JJS. Additionally, the Justice Department's Office of Juvenile Justice and Delinquency Prevention is responsible for training, developing technical aid and model programmes, conducting research and evaluation, and supporting state and local initiatives.

Juvenile Detention Centre in the United Kingdom

In the United Kingdom, the rights of children in juvenile detention centres are primarily outlined in the legal framework of the Children Act 1989 and the Crime and Disorder Act 1998. The Children Act 1989 contains some significant rights for juveniles by separating juvenile offenders from adult offenders. Further, it gives the right to access education and provides various rehabilitation programmes. The Act also emphasizes the value of family communication, legal representation, and routine assessments of jail placements. Local governments are in charge of ensuring children's safety and assisting in their reintegration into society.[29] These provisions aim to promote children's overall development and welfare while ensuring a fair and acceptable treatment strategy. One of the specialties of "the Crime and Disorder Act 1998" is that the rehabilitation of the juveniles is coordinated by a team, which is known as Youth Offending Teams. The team consists of various professionals such as psychologists, social workers, and probation officers whose primary function is to assess the needs of juveniles and set the appropriate rehabilitation methods suitable for the juveniles. The rehabilitation methods may include community services, counselling for the individuals, and providing education to the juveniles. A special category of home is established in the United Kingdom to deal with the juveniles known as "Secure Children's Home" for children who need a safe housing facility due to their heinous activity and severity of their actions. (See Table No 3.1)

Juvenile Detention Centre in Germany

To assist young offenders in becoming responsible adults, Germany's JJS, which is entirely modelled after the European Union's justice system, places more of a focus on educating than on punishing them. The "Jugendstrafrecht" legal system, which places a very special focus on assisting offenders between the ages of 14 and 20, creates specialized adolescent rooms in courts. In these chambers, judges, social workers, and psychologists collaborate to determine the best course of action for young offenders. Germany's strategy promotes alternatives like counselling and probation and prioritizes social assistance and education over punishment. (see Table 3.1) The late 19th and early 20th centuries saw the development of Germany's JJS. Only after World War II did the specific legislation achieve success, but a special court was created in 1908. But, in the year 1922, the Jugendwohlfahrtsgesetz (Junior Welfare Act) was enacted, which addressed the needs of children and adolescents.[30] The Juvenile Justice Act, which was created specifically for young offenders who had previously committed crimes as defined by general criminal law, was passed a year later, in 1923. Along with various procedural instructions for the juvenile courts and related processes, the Juvenile Justice Act specifies specific responses and consequences for minor offenders. The 1923 statute introduced three foundations for innovation. First, in contrast to the normal penal law, the 1923 legislation allowed for educational programmes instead of punishment. Second, the strictly enforced premise of mandatory prosecution could be waived. Last but not least, the criminal culpability age was raised from 12 to 14.

The Nazi era brought about several amendments to the Juvenile Justice Act of 1943. However, following World War II, the legislature once more raised the age of criminal culpability from 12 to 14. The 1953 revisions maintained "disciplinary measures" since other European countries adopted the same tactic. One of the main changes made in 1953 was the inclusion of young adults aged 18 to 21 in the juvenile court's jurisdiction. This court then determines whether to apply the JJ Act or the regular penal legislation. The 1922 Act included a clause known as "Parens Patriae", which specifies that the state will take the position of parents who were incapable or unwilling to carry out their responsibilities for their children's education. However, a more modern social support system known as Sozialstaat, or the social welfare state, replaced the Juvenile Welfare Act in 1990. Later, changes were made to the "German Juvenile Justice Act" to increase its effectiveness in rehabilitating young offenders. The background of this act, however, demonstrates that Germany is adopting a moderate policy towards its juvenile offenders, providing a reformation facility and only applying strict penalties under the most severe and violent conditions. The Youth Courts Act 1974, which deals with juvenile and young offenders, and the Child and Youth Services Act, which deals with children in need of care and protection, are the two laws that Germany has recently passed that deal with juveniles. Generally speaking, Germany's juvenile detention system places more emphasis on rehabilitation than punishment, highlighting the child's rights to education, psychological support, familial ties, and legal protection in consonance with the principle of restorative justice.

Comparative Analysis

It is seen from the previous study that restoration and integration are the universal goals of JJSs worldwide, with differential institutional settings, treatment philosophies, and legislative frameworks. The basis for dealing with young offenders is established by the JJ Act, 2015, in India, the Youth Courts Act 1974 in the United Kingdom, the JJDPA in the United States, and the Children Act 1989 and Crime and Disorder Act 1998 in the United Kingdom. Community-based care, foster care, and vocational education all play important roles in rehabilitation, which is still a primary priority. Some nations incorporate educational initiatives and restorative justice approaches into their systems, while others prioritize trauma-informed treatment, emotional counselling, and emotional wellness support. Another key difference is from institutional contexts; while the developed countries across the world have well-maintained infrastructures with adequate funding, others face resource limits and overpopulation like in India. There are special laws for children (or juveniles) in all countries, but the effectiveness mostly depends on the governmental support, legal representation, diversion programme ensuring betterment of the children, and most importantly focus towards the CCIs.

Conclusion

The global trend leans toward a more rehabilitative and child-focused approach in line with the international instruments, acknowledging that young offenders often require support, education, and intervention rather than strict punitive measures. Balancing the protection of society with the rights and well-being of juvenile offenders remains a complex challenge, requiring ongoing efforts to refine and improve JJSs worldwide.[31] India's Juvenile Justice Act emphasizes rehabilitation, protective rights, and a child-friendly approach. The focus on reintegration recognizes the potential for positive change in juvenile offenders. Implementation and consistent application of these principles, especially in diverse socioeconomic contexts, remain challenges. The United States has diverse JJSs with a focus on rehabilitation, legal representation, and educational rights. There's a growing awareness of the need to address disparities and avoid punitive measures for juveniles. Inconsistencies across states and concerns about the transfer of juveniles to the adult system highlight the need for greater uniformity and the protection of juvenile rights. The United Kingdom's welfare-based approach prioritizes the child's best interests and emphasizes rehabilitation. Involvement of families in the process and efforts to prevent re-offending are notable strengths. Balancing the welfare approach with public safety concerns and addressing issues of overcrowded youth detention centres are ongoing challenges. All three countries recognize the importance of rehabilitation, education, and protection of juvenile rights. Family involvement and community-based approaches are valued for successful reintegration. Challenges include the need for consistent implementation, addressing disparities, and balancing rehabilitative goals with public safety concerns. India may improve its JJS by adopting some of the best practices in the United States, the United Kingdom, and Germany. As observed in Germany and the United Kingdom, one of the main challenges is the infrastructure of CCIs, which is imperative to improve care and lessen overcrowding. India might potentially follow US restorative justice approaches, which emphasize rehabilitation over punishment. Children's psychological well-being would be enhanced by improving mental health and trauma-informed care, as is done in Germany and the United Kingdom. Additionally, reintegrating young people into society would be facilitated by offering more comprehensive educational and career training, as is the case in Germany and the United Kingdom. The system may be strengthened even further by ensuring long-term funding and improving social and legal support systems, as is the case in the United Kingdom. These changes would create a more effective and therapeutic environment for young offenders in India.

Notes

1 Prof Bernd-Dieter Meier et al., "*Juvenile Justice in Different Cultural Contexts: A Comparison of India and Germany*", Zeitschrift für Int. Strafrechtsdogmatik 491–501 (2010), https://zis-online.com/dat/artikel/2011_6_584.pdf.
2 M.W. Fox-Strangways, "*Reformatory and Industrial Schools*", 35 306–318, https://www.jstor.org/stable/43790284.
3 Fox-Strangways, "*Reformatory and Industrial Schools*", 306–318.
4 S.R. Chandolu, "*Child Rights Perspective of Juvenile Delinquency in India*", 1 The Rights 1–6 (2015), https://yior.org/wp-content/uploads/2019/01/Dr.-Sudharshan-Raju-Chandulu-1-min.pdf.
5 Nandini G Devarmani, "*Institutional Treatment for Juveniles in India – a Critical Analysis*", 3 Forensic Res. Criminol. Int. J. 256–260 (2016), https://medcraveonline.com/FRCIJ/institutional-treatment-for-juveniles-in-india-a-critical-analysis.html.
6 U.N. Standard Minimum Rules for the Admin. of Juv. Just., G.A. Res. 40/33, U.N. Doc. A/RES/40/33 (Nov. 29, 1985).
7 United Nations Guidelines for the Prevention of Juvenile Delinquency (The Riyadh Guidelines), G.A. Res. 45/112, U.N. Doc. A/RES/45/112, https://www.ohchr.org/en/instruments-mechanisms/instruments/united-nations-guidelines-prevention-juvenile-delinquency-riyadh.
8 United Nations Economic and Social Council. (1997). Guidelines for Action on Children in the Criminal Justice System (Vienna Guidelines). Resolution 1997/30, adopted 21 July 1997.
9 Meier et al., "*Juvenile Justice in Different Cultural Contexts*".
10 Dr. Ramesh Kumar Neeraj Bhardwaj, "*Juvenile Delinquency in India: A Study*", 9 Quest Journals 11 (1948), www.questjournals.org.
11 "*Nothing in this article shall prevent the state from making any law for women and children*".
12 *Right to life and personal liberty.*
13 *Prohibition of employment of children in factories.*
14 *"That the health and strength of workers, men and women and the tender age of children are not abused".*
15 *"That the children are given opportunities and facilities to develop in a healthy manner and in conditions of freedom and dignity and that childhood and youth are protected against exploitation and against moral and material abandonment".*
16 *"Provision for early childhood care and education to children below the age of six years".*
17 "*Duty of the state to raise the level of nutrition and the standard of living and to improve public health*".
18 Aayus Raj, "*Chapter 5 – JJS in India*", 3 Shimla Law Rev. (2020).
19 Teena Thomas, "*The Juvenile Justice System in India: A Brief Overview | Table of Contents*" (2020), https://sprf.in/the-juvenile-justice-system-in-india-a-brief-overview/.
20 Bhardwaj, "*Juvenile Delinquency in India*".
21 Rahul Sk & Dr. Raj Kumar Yadav, "*Challenges Faced by Children at Child Care Institutions under the Juvenile Justice (Care and Protection of Children) Act, 2015: A Legal Study*", 5 Int'l J.L. Mgmt. & Human. (2022).
22 Sec 2(19) JJ Act 2015.
23 Arlene Manoharan & Swagata Raha, "*The Juvenile Justice System in India and Children Who Commit Serious Offences – Reflections on the Way Forward*". Centre for Child and the Law (CCL), National Law School of India University, (2013), https://www.oijj.org/sites/default/files/documentos/the_juvenile_justice_system_in_india_and_children_who_commit_serious_offences.pdf

24 Suryansh Sharan, "*Juvenile Delinquency in India: Reasons, Justice and Solutions*" (2021), https://edubirdie.com/examples/juvenile-delinquency-in-india-reasons-justice-and-solutions/.
25 Aprajita Bharagava, "*Juvenile Justice in India*", 1 INT. J. INTERDISCIP. MULTIDISCIP. STUD. (IJIMS) 64–70 (2014), https://thelawbrigade.com/criminal-law/juvenile-justice-in-india.
26 "*New Guidelines on Treatment of Juvenile Convicts, Aftercare*", BUSINESS STANDARD, May 15, 2017, at 1–7, https://www.business-standard.com/article/pti-stories/new-guidelines-on-treatment-of-juvenile-convicts-aftercare-117051500989_1.html.
27 Gbolahan Osho, "*Is the United States Juvenile Justice System Working: An Empirical Investigation from the Life Course Approach*", 3 J. PUB. ADMIN. & GOVERNANCE 142 (2013).
28 Maram Deepika, "*Functioning of Juvenile Justice Systems in India, US*", ACADEMIKE 1–15 (2021), https://www.lawctopus.com/academike/juvenile-justice-systems/#:~:text=When a juvenile commits a,years should not be arrested'.
29 "*Her Majesty's Prison and Probation Service, GOV.UK. Guidance: Placing Young People in Custody: Guide for Youth Justice Practitioners*", Published 2014, updated 2020. https://www.gov.uk/guidance/placing-young-people-in-custody-guide-for-youth-justice-practitioners
30 Frieder Dünkel, "*Youth Justice in Germany*", in The Oxford Handbook of Juvenile Crime and Juvenile Justice (Barry C. Feld & Donna M. Bishop eds., 2016), https://doi.org/10.1093/oxfordhb/9780199935383.013.68O.
31 Aisvarya Chandran, "*Rehabilitation in the Juvenile Justice System*", 1 PLEADER 1–8 (2022), https://blog.ipleaders.in/rehabilitation-of-juveniles/#:~:text=After the Juvenile Justice Board, age%2C mental and physical makeup.

4

PROCEDURAL ASPECTS CONCERNING CHILD IN CONFLICT WITH LAW IN THE INDIAN LEGISLATIVE FRAMEWORK

Susmita Priyadarshini Mishra

Introduction

In all cultures younger children are considered vulnerable both physically and psychologically, therefore, less capable of self-sufficiency. Age restrictions formally represent society's assessment of the development of children's abilities and sense of responsibility. Age restrictions systematically govern children's activities: the permissible age for leaving school, marrying, voting, being treated as adults by the criminal justice system, enlisting in the military forces, and entering the workforce. However, age restrictions vary by activity and by country. The legal definition of a child has fluctuated in accordance with the intended goal. "Article 1 of the UNCRC, 1989" defines "a child as any human being under the age of 18 years, unless the applicable law designates an earlier age of majority".

The initial legislation concerning children in India was the "Apprentice Act of 1850". Nevertheless, this Act did not establish an independent juvenile justice system but rather operated within the framework of the adult criminal justice system. The separation of children from adults under "the criminal justice system in India" was initiated by the "Reformatories Schools Act of 1897".

The "Madras Children Act of 1920" was enacted in response to the suggestions put out by the "Indian Jails Committee between 1919 and 1920". This legislation marked a significant milestone as it became the first Children's Act implemented in India. The aforementioned legislation pertained to a specific province and encompassed the geographical region known as the Madras Province at that time. Subsequently, many legislations, like as the "Bengal Children's Act and the Bombay Children's Act", were enacted.

DOI: 10.4324/9781003607076-6

The Children's Act, which was applicable in Union Territories, was adopted by the Government of India in 1960. The abolition of all these legislations occurred with the passage of the Juvenile Justice Act (JJ Act) in 1986.[1]

A significant component of the children's acts is the establishment of a Children's Court, which is solely responsible for hearing matters that have been brought before it in accordance with the acts. A child who is of immature understanding and is at an impressionable age is the target of these laws, which establish differential arrangements for the treatment of such a child during inquiry and trial. When a child is in need of assistance, the aim of the juvenile court is not to punish them but to rehabilitate them. Social workers who have sufficient expertise and experience in child welfare are also involved with the operation of the juvenile court in order to provide assistance to the judicial authorities in the processing of cases from the perspective of welfare.[2]

Beyond India the first juvenile court was established in Chicago, Illinois, in 1899, starting the movement to build them. The Soviet Union passed a major child welfare law in January 1918. It was the Magna Carta for the poor Russian child.[3] It ordered the segregation of young criminals under 17 or 18 years old who could not be prosecuted. They could not be tried by the People's Court or imprisoned. "Commissions for juvenile affairs" handled matters related to children and were composed of judges, educators, and doctors. They addressed the juvenile's personality rather than his crime, focusing on the juvenile's "social neglect", physical status, and temperament determined his disposition. In spite of the severity of their offenses, the commission was not empowered to commit juveniles to prison. Using "medical-pedagogical" methods alone could help these adolescent criminals, as with time it was realized that punitive and retaliatory criminal legislation had not prevented youthful delinquency. In light of this, a new concept suggests that maladjusted youngsters should be treated individually through protective measures. Additionally, teens' unique needs must be considered as they mature.

The creation of Children's Courts created a new system. State intervention for children is the foundation of child guardianship, as a juvenile accused of a crime is considered a "ward in need of care and protection" rather than a criminal. The English departmental committee on the treatment of criminals rightly stressed that the child is more important than child protection authorities' vindication, which does not require proof of an offense. Since Children's Courts have no jury, prosecutor, attorney, or battles, the atmosphere is different and juvenile magistrates manage cases in ways that benefit the child and society.

In India, the JJ Act, implemented in 1986, was a significant milestone, being the first legislation pertaining to "juvenile justice in India" that possessed nationwide applicability. "This Act was revised and subsequently reenacted as the "Juvenile Justice (Care and Protection of Children) Act in 2000", to adhere to the requirements outlined in the United Nations Convention on the Rights of the Child (UNCRC). The legislation underwent subsequent amendments in 2006 with the enactment of the Juvenile Justice (Care and Protection of Children) Amendment Act[4], 2006, and in 2011. In June 2014, the Union Government proposed plans to modify the JJ Act, and the present Juvenile Justice (Care and Protection of Children) Amendment Act (JJ Act 2015) was promulgated.[5]

While the JJ Act provides the legal foundation, its effective implementation requires strong monitoring and enforcement mechanisms, which is where institutions like the National Commission for Protection of Child Rights (NCPCR) and State Commissions for Protection of Child Rights (SCPCR) play a crucial role. Established under the Commissions for Protection of Child Rights Act, 2005, these bodies ensure that child protection laws, including the JJ Act, are properly executed across the country. The NCPCR operates at the national level, overseeing policy implementation, investigating violations, and advising the government on child-related issues. Similarly, SCPCR functions at the state level, ensuring compliance with the JJ Act, monitoring juvenile homes, and handling complaints regarding child rights violations. These commissions have the authority to intervene in cases of child abuse, recommend policy changes, and work with law enforcement agencies to strengthen child protection measures. By bridging the gap between legislation and execution, they ensure that justice and rehabilitation reach every child in need, reinforcing the core principles of the Juvenile Justice framework. An Expert Committee, led by "Justice V R Krishna Iyer (Judge, Supreme Court (SC) of India), was constituted by the Government of India to design the National Commission for Children Bill 2000". Using this preliminary version as a basis, the government implemented the "Commissions for Protection of Child Rights Act, 2005".[6] The Act proposes the establishment of legal entities such as a "National Commission at the national level and State Commissions at the state level". The establishment of these commissions was intended to ensure the rigorous enforcement of children's rights and the efficient execution of legislation and initiatives pertaining to children. The guidelines for implementing the provisions of the Act on the "National Commission for Protection of Child Rights" were officially announced on July 31, 2006, and the NCPCR has been established. Additionally, some State Governments have established "State Commissions for the Protection of Child Rights". The commissions have the authority to take proactive measures to guarantee the protection of children and the promotion of their rights.

Initially, children were perceived as incapable of making autonomous decisions and hence had minimal agency in their own lives. Consequently, when children perpetrated infractions, they were labeled as "juvenile delinquents", a designation that emphasized their criminal conduct and bore significant stigma. The legal system attempted to reform rather than penalize juvenile criminals. The evolution of the term Child in Conflict with Law (CCL) in Indian juvenile legislation reflects the progressive shift from "punitive to rehabilitative approaches" to addressing juvenile delinquency. This transformation, evident in legislative terminology across legislations pertaining to juvenile justice, underscores India's commitment to aligning with international standards on child rights and adopting a rights-based framework. The Juvenile Justice System in India shifts from a primarily punitive framework to one focused on the care, protection, development, and social reintegration of children. The linguistic transition underscores this change in the conceptualization of children under the law. The term "juvenile delinquent" carries a substantial negative connotation and can irreversibly stigmatize a child. This stigma can hinder their reintegration into society and create barriers to their future success. CCL aims to de-stigmatize language, shifting focus from the child's inherent misconduct to their situational context. The new nomenclature advocates for a child-centered approach, prioritizing the "child's needs and best interests as fundamental". This transition is seen in the focus on child-centric protocols, the participation of social workers and experts in judicial processes, and the inclination toward restorative justice approaches rather than punitive actions.

Table 4.1 gives details about the comparative analysis between the three acts, the JJ Act of 1986, the JJ Act of 2000, and the JJ Act of 2015, under different criteria such as definitional ground, philosophical ground, and following of international standards.

TABLE 4.1 Comparative analysis between the Juvenile Justice Act of 1985, 2000, and 2015

Aspect	*Juvenile Justice Act, 1986*	*Juvenile Justice Act, 2000*	*Juvenile Justice Act, 2015*
Terminology	Delinquent juvenile	Juveniles in Conflict with Law	Children in Conflict with Law
Focus	Punitive	Rehabilitative	Rights-based, nuanced
Philosophy	Behavioral correction	Socio-economic and psychological reform	Child-centric rehabilitation and reintegration
Alignment with International Standards	Minimal	UNCRC, Beijing Rules 63	UNCRC, restorative justice
Age Differentiation for Heinous Crimes	No	No	Yes (16–18 years for heinous crimes)

Principles of Care and Protection and Relevance of Procedural Aspect

Under Section 3 of the JJ Act of 2015, there are certain principles that the Central Government, State Governments, the Juvenile Justice Boards (JJBs), and relevant agencies, while executing the provisions of this Act, should adhere to the following:

i. "Principle of the presumption of innocence" dictates that any child shall be regarded as innocent of any malicious or criminal intent until the age of 18 years. This principle is based on the notion that children's cognitive growth is continual, and they may lack a comprehensive knowledge of the repercussions of their actions. Like in the case of adults, this principle mandates that all legal processes concerning a child commence with a presumption of innocence.
ii. "Principle of dignity and worth" speaks that every individual will be accorded equal dignity and rights, which is also specified under Article 21 of the Constitution of India[7], [8]. This principle guarantees that CCLs are not exposed to harsh or degrading treatment throughout their interactions with the police, JJB, or other authorities. Rather than being perceived as offenders, they are viewed as individuals in need of direction, support, and rehabilitation. This protects their self-esteem and promotes a rehabilitation strategy that deters future criminal conduct.
iii. "Principle of participation" dictates that every child has "the right to be heard" and to engage in all processes and choices that impact their interests, with their perspectives considered in accordance with their age and maturity. The JJB is required to interact personally with the CCL prior to making determinations regarding their rehabilitation, restoration, or institutional transfer. By guaranteeing the child's participation, the system promotes accountability and personal development.
iv. "Principle of best interest" mandates that all actions concerning the child prioritize their welfare and facilitate the child's full developmental potential. The wellbeing and development of the child must be the paramount consideration in all choices regarding CCL. This principle inhibits the justice system from enforcing severe punishment measures that may jeopardize a child's future opportunities. Restorative and rehabilitative methods, including counseling, education, skill acquisition, and family reintegration, are advocated.
v. "Principle of family responsibility" asserts that the primary obligation for the care, nurturing, and protection of a child is with the biological family or the adoptive or foster parents, as applicable. The JJ Act dissuades institutionalization except where it is imperative. Efforts are directed at reintegrating the child with their family and community,

offering counseling and support to establish a stable environment. This notion underscores the family's essential function as a vital support system in a child's rehabilitation.

vi. "Principle of safety" states that all precautions must be taken to guarantee "the child's safety and to prevent any harm, abuse, or maltreatment" throughout their interaction with the juvenile justice system and subsequently. This principle mandates that strict measures be in place to ensure their physical and emotional safety at all stages – from apprehension to rehabilitation. Police officers, institutional staff, and JJB members must ensure that CCL are not subjected to coercion, ill treatment, or harsh interrogations. Safe housing in child care institutions, protection from violence in observation homes, and proper psychological support mechanisms are crucial components of this principle.

vii. "Principle of proactive measures" states that all resources, including those from family and community, shall be mobilized to enhance well-being, foster identity development, and create an inclusive and supportive environment, thereby mitigating children's vulnerabilities and the necessity for action under this Act.

viii. "Principle of non-stigmatizing semantics" dictates that adversarial or accusatory language should be avoided in matters concerning a child. Instead of terms like "accused", "convict", or "criminal", the law uses child-friendly language such as CCL. This prevents social stigma and psychological harm, which could otherwise lead to the child feeling permanently alienated from society. This is the reason for doing away with the term "juvenile" used in the 2000 Act and addressing such children as CCL under the present JJ Act 2015.

ix. "Principle of non-waiver of rights" stipulates that no waiver of any rights of the child is acceptable or legitimate, regardless of whether it is requested by the child, an individual acting on "the child's behalf, or a Board or Committee"; furthermore, the non-exercise of a fundamental right does not constitute a waiver. Children may not fully comprehend their legal rights. This concept guarantees that no child can be compelled, swayed, or deceived into relinquishing their rights, regardless of whether they – or an individual representing them – consent to do so. All legal protections, encompassing access to legal assistance, humane treatment, and equitable hearings, must be maintained consistently. This safeguards children from exploitation within the judicial system.

x. According to the "principle of equality and non-discrimination", discrimination against a child on any basis – including sex – will be forbidden. Regardless of their history or situation, every kid ought to be given fair treatment, legal defense, and rehabilitation chances.

Child in Conflict With Law

Under the Juvenile Justice (Care and Protection of Children) Act 2015 (JJ Act), the CCL is defined under Section 2 (13) as:

> Child in conflict with law means a child who is alleged or found to have committed an offense and who has not completed 18 years of age on the date of commission of such offense.

Procedural Laws Dealing With CCL

Those children who are found to be in violation of the law are dealt with by the JJB (Section 4. of JJ Act of 2015) preliminarily and after the assessment by JJB, by the Children's Court", while the Child Welfare Committee (CWC) (Section 27 of JJ Act) is responsible for dealing with children who have been neglected and are deemed to be uncontrolled. Therefore, the JJ Act separates the "child in need of care and protection (CNCP)" from those who have committed transgressions, that is, CCL, and offers counseling and education to the various groups of children in a distinct manner. The JJ Act also mentions the establishment of JJB (defined under Section 2(10)) and the Children's Court (defined under Section 2 (20)). Chapters III and IV of the JJ (Care and Protection of Children) Act, 2015 delineate the formation and duties of the JJB in adjudicating cases concerning CCL.

Juvenile Justice Boards

JJB is a legal entity constituted under the JJ (Care and Protection of Children) Act, 2015, in India. Its principal duty is to adjudicate issues involving children in legal disputes, facilitating their rehabilitation and reintegration into society. According to Section 4 of the JJ Act, 2015, the JJB is established by the State Government for each district or a consortium of districts. The Board consists of the following members:

i. Principal Magistrate: A Metropolitan Magistrate or a Judicial Magistrate of the first class, excluding the Chief Metropolitan Magistrate or Chief Judicial Magistrate, possessing a minimum of three years of service.
ii. Two Social Workers: Chosen according to the specified criteria, with a minimum of one being female. These members must have at least seven years of experience in health, education, or child welfare or hold degrees in law, sociology, psychology, or psychiatry.

The composition seeks to integrate legal competence with social welfare viewpoints, ensuring a comprehensive approach to juvenile justice. The

Board possesses exclusive jurisdiction over all matters pertaining to the JJ Act concerning children in dispute with the law within its domain.

i. Safeguarding Legal Rights: It guarantees the protection of the child's rights during the entire legal procedure, from apprehension to rehabilitation (Section 8 (3)(a)).
ii. Provision of Legal Aid: The Board enables access to legal aid for minors via legal services organizations (Section 8 (3)(c)).
iii. Investigation and Resolution of Cases: It performs investigations and issues suitable directives for the rehabilitation or reinstatement of children in legal conflict (Section 8 (3) (e)) (Section 14).
iv. Oversight Institutions: The JJB supervises the operations of observation homes and other facilities housing juveniles, assuring the maintenance of care and protection standards.
v. Collaboration with Other Agencies: It partners with CWCs, law enforcement, and non-governmental groups to guarantee holistic care and protection for juveniles (Section 8 (3) (h), (g) and Section 107 of JJ Act of 2015).
vi. The Board performs routine inspections of adult jails to guarantee that no minors are housed in these facilities and promptly facilitates their transfer to observation homes if discovered (under Section 8 (3) (j) and Section 8 3(m), JJ Act 2015). These functions emphasize the Board's responsibility in both adjudicating matters and safeguarding the welfare and rehabilitation of adolescents (Section 54).

A vital role of the JJB is to ascertain juvenility, which entails determining whether an individual charged with an offense was a CCL at the time of the purported crime. This determination is crucial as it dictates whether the individual will be adjudicated under the juvenile justice system or the standard criminal justice system. The procedure for ascertaining juvenility is delineated in "Section 94 of the JJ Act, 2015 read with Rule 10 and 10A of Juvenile Justice Model rules of 2016":

A. Age Authentication According to the documents:

- Matriculation or Equivalent Certificate: If accessible, this serves as the principal documentation for age verification.
- Birth Certificate from the Initial School Attended: This document is deemed acceptable in lieu of a matriculation certificate.
- Birth Certificate Issued by Municipal Authority or Panchayat: This document serves as legitimate evidence if the aforementioned two are unavailable.

B. Medical Examination: In the absence of the previously specified papers, the JJB may mandate a medical examination, which may include an ossification test or any other contemporary medical age assessment, to determine the individual's age.

The Board is required to render an age determination within 15 days of the evidence submission date. A claim of juvenility may be asserted at any point throughout a criminal proceeding, including post-disposal of the case, and also during appeals in the High Court and the SC. Procrastination in submitting such a claim cannot serve as a basis for its dismissal. Such a claim cannot be denied for delay. The accused receives the benefit of doubt when age determination tests reveal a range, in accordance with the presumption of innocence and child welfare. After determination of the age of the CCL, the Board has to determine whether the child will be tried as an adult, if the age is between 16 and 18 years. The basis of the determination is as per the mandate of Section 15 of the Act of 2015. The JJB's role in evaluating juvenility guarantees that juveniles are protected and rehabilitated rather than punished, reflecting the juvenile justice system's reformative attitude. The Indian juvenile justice system relies on the JJB to balance legal adjudication with the care and rehabilitation of lawbreakers. Restorative justice ideas guide its constitution, powers, and functions to treat adolescents with compassion and offer reform.

Children's Court

Children's Court is a Court established under the Commission for Protection of Child Rights Act, 2005, or a Special Court under the Protection of Children from Sexual Offences Act, 2012, wherever existing and where such courts have not been designated, the Court of Sessions having jurisdiction to try offenses under the Act. The Children's Court has the power to try the child either as an adult or a child (Under Section 19 of the JJ Act 2015[9]), after receiving the preliminary assessment from the JJB. It must ensure that the final order includes an individual care plan and follow-up details by the Probation Officer, District Child Protection Unit, or Social worker. The court also should ensure that CCL, till he/she attains the age of 21 years, should be placed in "place of safety" and after that he/she shall be transferred to jail. The court also must perform an annual periodic follow-up through a Probation Officer, DCPU, or Social worker. The JJB and Children's Court shall not hold any joint proceedings of CCL with an adult.

General Procedure for CCL Not Involved in Serious or Heinous Offenses

Upon apprehension, a CCL must be presented before the JJB within 24 hours, excluding travel time. Detention in police lockups or jails is explicitly forbidden. The JJB is authorized to issue bail, with or without surety, impose probation on the child, or assign the child to a suitable individual. Bail may be denied solely under particular conditions, and the JJB is required to document the rationale for the decision. The JJB initiates an investigation into the purported infraction. The investigation must be finalized within four months, with a potential extension of two months. The JJB must safeguard the child's rights during the entire procedure and offer legal assistance. The JJB also conducts a preliminary assessment where a CCL is alleged to have committed a heinous offense, and it may transfer him to the Children's Court for trial as an adult.

If the child is determined to have perpetrated a wrong, the JJB may issue a range of orders under Sections 17 and 18 of the JJ Act 2015, contingent upon the gravity of the conduct and the child's situation, including:

a. Counsel or admonition after guidance
b. Engagement in group therapy or community service activities
c. Levying a penalty on the child, parents, or guardian
d. Discharge on probation under the supervision of a parent, guardian, or suitable individual
e. Placement in a specialized facility for a duration not to exceed three years

Provisions for CCL Aged 16–18 Who Have Committed Serious or Heinous Offenses

The JJB conducts a preliminary evaluation for egregious offenses committed by individuals aged 16–18 years to analyze the child's mental and physical capability, comprehension of consequences, and the context of the offense. Professionals such as psychologists may aid the JJB in this evaluation.

a. If the preliminary evaluation suggests the necessity for an adult trial, the JJB may transfer the matter to the Children's Court.
b. "The Children's Court" thereafter decides whether the child should be prosecuted as an adult. Upon determining the child's guilt, the Children's Court mandates the issuance of a final order that encompasses a personalized rehabilitation care plan.
c. "The Children's Court" may mandate the placement of the CCL in a place of safety until the age of 21, following which transfer to an adult correctional facility is permissible. Nonetheless, the court must guarantee the availability of reformative assistance during the duration of the stay in the designated secure location.
d. The JJ Act specifically forbids condemning a CCL to death or life imprisonment without the possibility of parole, irrespective of the offense committed.

TABLE 4.2 Procedures depicting general provisions (not serious/heinous offenses) and special provisions (ccl aged 16–18 years, serious/heinous offenses)

Procedure	*General provisions (not serious/heinous offenses)*	*Special provisions (CCL aged 16–18 years, serious/heinous offenses)*
Apprehension	CCL produced before JJB within 24 hours (excluding travel). Police lockup/jail strictly prohibited.	Same as general provisions.
Bail	JJB may grant bail, place under probation, or entrust to fit person. Denial only under specific circumstances.	Same as general provisions.
Inquiry	JJB conducts an inquiry within four months (possible two-month extension). Ensures child rights protection and provides legal aid.	JJB does an initial evaluation to determine mental and physical capacity, comprehension of consequences, and the circumstances surrounding the offense.
Possible orders	Admonition after counseling. Group counseling. community service. Fine. Probation. Placement in a special home (maximum three years).	JJB may transfer the case to the Children's Court if preliminary assessment indicates the need for trial as an adult.
Trial	N/A	The Children's Court determines if a trial as an adult is necessary. Conducts trial if so, ensuring a child-friendly atmosphere.
Sentencing	Various orders, as mentioned earlier, based on offense severity and the child's circumstances.	Upon finding guilt, the Children's Court issues a final order with an individual care plan. May order placement in place of safety until age 21. **"Death penalty and life imprisonment without release are prohibited".**

Table 4.2 describes the procedures detailing the general procedures and special provisions followed in cases dealing with CCL, mentioned under the JJ Act of 2015.

Judicial Decisions Addressing CCLs

Procedural aspects of legislation with respect to CCLs have been discussed in this section through analysis of judicial precedents in terms of selected themes like age of juvenility and other procedural aspects of the JJ Act.

Age of Juvenility

In the *Umesh Chandra vs State of Rajasthan*[10] case where the SC stated that the date of occurrence of the crime is the correct date for the determination of the age of a juvenile and not the date on which the juvenile was produced before the court.

However, this apparently practical approach was challenged in the case of *Arnit Das vs State of Bihar*[11]. The key background fact is that the petitioner, Arnit Das, was arrested in connection with a murder (Crime No. 574/98 under Section 302, I.P.C.) that occurred on September 5, 1998. In this case, the SC determined that the criminal was below the age of 18 at the time the offense was committed. Therefore, the offender will be regarded as a minor under the provisions of the JJ Act of 1986. Hence, the determination age can be based on the following documents (under Section 94(2) of the JJ Act 2015);

a. Birth Certificate issued by a governmental organization or municipality
b. Matriculation certificate issued by a Board of Education
c. Birth Certificate issued by a school authority or any other competent authority

In the SC case *Pratap Singh v. State of Jharkhand & Anr,*[12] the appellant, Pratap Singh, was linked to a conspiracy resulting in a death by poisoning on December 31, 1998. He was arrested on November 22, 1999; after preliminary procedures, his age was determined to be around 18 years. Singh said, however, that he was a juvenile at the time of the act and presented school papers showing a December 18, 1983, birth date, therefore rendering him 15 years old on the day of the occurrence. The Court awarded him bail after considering this proof.

One of the issues was, irrespective of the date of occurrence, would be the reckoning date for determining the age of the alleged offender as a juvenile offender or the date when he is produced in the Court/competent authority?

The Court held that the date of the offense is the relevant date for determining whether an individual is considered a juvenile. This aligns with the earlier decision in *Umesh Chandra vs. State of Rajasthan* (1982), emphasizing that the intent of juvenile justice legislation is to protect young offenders based on their age at the time of the alleged crime. Following this judgment, the JJ Act was amended in 2006, which amended the definition of "juvenile in conflict" with law as one who has committed an offense and has not completed the age of 18 years as of the date of such commission.

The case of *Hari Ram vs State of Rajasthan and another*[13] centers on the determination of the appellant's age and the applicability of the JJ Act of 2000 in his case. On November 30, 1998, Hari Ram was arrested along with others for alleged offenses involving violence, assault, and murder. The alleged offenses took place on October 30, 1998. The Additional Sessions Judge determined that Hari Ram was below 16 years old at the time of the offense and declared him a juvenile. This decision was based on the date of birth provided by Hari Ram's father, which would have made Hari Ram 16 years and 13 days old on the date of the offense. The State of Rajasthan challenged the Sessions Judge's ruling. The High Court, relying on the same date of birth provided by the father, concluded that Hari Ram was over 16 years old at the time of the offense and, therefore, not subject to the JJ Act of 2000. A medical examination also placed his age between 16 and 17 years old. The case raised broader questions about the interpretation and implementation of the Act, particularly concerning:

i. The determination of a juvenile's age
ii. The Act's applicability to cases that were pending at the time it became effective on April 1, 2001
iii. The Act's "rehabilitative and restorative approach" as opposed to the adversarial nature of the general criminal justice system

The SC allowed Hari Ram's appeal and set aside the High Court's order. The Court ruled that Hari Ram was a juvenile at the time of the offense and, therefore, entitled to the protection and procedures afforded by the JJ Act, 2000. The case was remitted to the JJB for disposal in accordance with the law. The Court extensively analyzed the legislative history and amendments to the JJ Act. It highlighted the Act's "objective of rehabilitation and reintegration of juveniles", emphasizing its distinction from the punitive nature of the general criminal justice system. The Court emphasized the retrospective application of the JJ Act, 2000, as clarified by the amendments introduced in 2006. These amendments explicitly extended the Act's application to cases pending on April 1, 2001, "even if the offender was above 16 years old at the time of the offense but below 18 years old on the date the Act came into force". The Court pointed out that "Section 7A of the Act" allows for a claim of juvenility to be raised at any stage, even after the final disposal of a case. "Rule 12 of the Juvenile Justice Rules, 2007" outlines a clear procedure for "determining age, prioritizing documentary evidence over medical opinions". The Court highlighted the importance of following this procedure. In borderline cases where two views on age are possible, the Court stressed the principle of leaning in favor of holding the accused to be a juvenile. The Court underscored the need for a shift in the mindset of those entrusted with enforcing the Act. It advocated for a rehabilitative approach that prioritizes "the best interests of the child" and aims for their successful reintegration into society.

The case of *Salil Bali vs Union of India & Another*[14] challenges the constitutionality of the JJ Act, 2000, particularly concerning the age of juvenility and the treatment of juveniles involved in heinous crimes. The case was triggered by public outcry following the infamous Delhi gang rape case of December 16, 2012, where a juvenile was among the perpetrators (*Mukesh & Anr vs State for NCT of Delhi & Ors*[15]). Several writ petitions were filed challenging various aspects of "the JJ Act", including its "definition of a child and the leniency of punishments for serious offenses". The court had framed five issues in total.

i. Whether the JJ Act, 2000, or specific provisions within it, are ultra vires the Constitution of India?
ii. Whether the age of juvenility, defined as 18 years in the Act, should be reconsidered, particularly in cases of heinous offenses like "rape and murder"?
iii. Whether the JJB should have the discretion to impose punishments beyond the three-year limit prescribed in the Act for heinous offenses committed by juveniles?
iv. Whether the records of juvenile offenders should be maintained to identify repeat offenders and assess criminal propensities?
v. Whether the Act's focus on rehabilitation and reintegration is adequate in addressing the issue of juvenile crime, especially in cases of serious offenses?

The SC upheld the constitutionality of the JJ Act, 2000, and refused to strike down any of its provisions. The Court emphasized the Act's alignment with international standards and the Indian Constitution, highlighting the need for a restorative and rehabilitative approach toward juvenile offenders. The Court acknowledged the concerns regarding heinous crimes committed by juveniles but maintained that the current legal framework is sufficient, emphasizing the need for proper implementation and data collection before considering any changes. The Court clarified the misunderstanding surrounding the release of juveniles upon reaching the age of 18, emphasizing that the 2006 amendment to the Act ensures they serve the full term of their sentence, even if it extends beyond their 18th birthday. The Court ultimately dismissed all the writ petitions and transferred the case, upholding the existing provisions of the JJ Act, 2000.

The case of *Dr. Subramanian Swamy and Ors vs Raju Through Member Juvenile Justice*[16] challenges the interpretation of the JJ Act of 2000, specifically regarding the applicability of the Act to juveniles involved in heinous crimes. One of the perpetrators in the Delhi gang rape case, as mentioned earlier, was "below 18 years of age at the time of the crime". Public outcry and demands for justice for the victim led to several legal challenges to the JJ Act of 2000, aiming to hold the juvenile offender accountable under the adult criminal justice system. The court has framed the following issues:

i. Whether the "JJ Act, 2000" should be read down to exclude juveniles who have committed heinous offenses and possess a certain level of mental maturity from its purview?
ii. Whether the Act's uniform treatment of all offenders below 18 years, regardless of mental maturity or the gravity of the crime, violates Article 14 of the Constitution (the right to equality)?
iii. Whether the Act's provision barring criminal court jurisdiction over juvenile offenders infringes upon the core principles of the criminal justice system, thereby violating the basic structure of the Constitution?

The SC upheld the constitutionality of the JJ Act, 2000, and refused to read down its provisions. The Court held that the Act's language is clear and unambiguous in defining all persons below 18 years as juveniles, creating a distinct category for investigation, trial, and punishment, and acknowledged that while there might be differences within the under-18 category, the classification is reasonable and connected to the Act's objective of rehabilitation. The Court emphasized that Article 14 of the Constitution does not require absolute precision in classification. The Court rejected the argument that the Act replaces the criminal justice system, stating that it merely provides an alternative framework for dealing with juvenile offenders while still applying the same penal laws. The Court highlighted that the Act reflects India's international commitments and represents the legislature's considered judgment on the age of juvenility. The Court emphasized the principle of judicial restraint, recognizing the legislature's primary role in enacting and amending laws based on societal needs and data. Ultimately, the SC dismissed both the appeal and the writ petition, upholding the existing provisions of the JJ Act, 2000.

This case set the foundation for the societal public outrage and legislative introduction of the Bill of Juvenile Justice (Care and Protection of Children) Act of 2015, classifying the child into different categories depending upon their interaction with society and the gravity of the conflict committed. The Act retains the age of juvenility/childhood below the 18 years, but the objectionable area remained pertaining to relegating the child/juvenile between 16 and 18 years who alleged to have committed a heinous offense (offenses for which the maximum punishment prescribed is imprisonment for seven years or more) to the regular criminal system for adjudication by the Children's Court, which is only but a regular sessions court designated so. Sections 15 to 19 of the JJ Act have the pertinent clauses, respectively, treating the CCL as an adult after the careful preliminary assessment; this Act further classifies another category known as CNCP.

Procedural Aspect

The case of *Sanjay Singh, Babua @ Rajiv Singh and Rajendra Singh vs State of Madhya Pradesh, Through: Police Station Endori, Tehsil Gohad, District Bhind*[17] involves a criminal appeal challenging the conviction and sentencing of three individuals: Sanjay Singh, Babua @ Rajiv Singh, and Rajendra Singh. They were punished by the trial court in accordance with Section 302 of the Indian Penal Code (for murder) and pertinent provisions of the Arms Act. Appellant no. 2, Babua, was found to have been a minor at the time of the offense during the appeal. Using the JJ Act, 2000, the High Court overturned Babua's conviction, and his case was sent back to the JJB for further consideration. Babua's case was sent to the JJB for suitable adjudication within the juvenile justice system rather than being discharged, and the Board decided in favor of the High Court and overturned the punishment of the appellant no 2.

The case of *Sampurna Behura vs Union of India and Others*,[18] which was a Public Interest Litigation (PIL), addresses concerns about the implementation of the JJ Act of 2000, including the establishment of necessary institutions and the protection of children's rights. Sampurna Behura, concerned about the state of juvenile justice in India, filed a writ. The petition highlighted the failure of State Governments to implement provisions of the "JJ Act of 2000". These failures included:

a. The lack of establishment of CWCs, JJBs, and Special Juvenile Police Units.
b. The inadequate establishment of safe and secure homes for "children in need of care and protection".
c. Concerns about the living conditions of CCL.
d. Issues related to medical services for children in state custody.
e. The petition sought relief in these matters and urged the effective enforcement of the JJ Act of 2000.

The SC issued various directives to "the Ministry of Women and Child Development (MWCD) of the Government of India and the State Governments". The Court emphasized the state's duty under the Directive Principles of State Policy to ensure the care, protection, and fulfillment of the fundamental rights of children. The Court stressed the importance of fully staffing and operationalizing the NCPCR and SCPCRs. These commissions were seen as crucial for safeguarding children's rights and monitoring the implementation of the JJ Act. The Court urged the establishment of well-equipped and child-friendly JJBs in each district to ensure timely and fair trials for CCLs. It also highlighted the need for regular sittings to avoid delays and backlogs. The Court emphasized the importance of training legal aid lawyers, probation officers, Child Welfare Police Officers, and members of Special Juvenile Police Units to handle cases involving children effectively and sensitively. Recognizing the inadequate conditions in observation and shelter homes, the Court called for improvements in these facilities, ensuring education, healthcare, and proper nutrition for children. It also stressed the need for mandatory registration of all child care institutions to prevent trafficking and abuse. The Court ordered regular inspections and audits to monitor the implementation of the JJ Act nationwide.

The Sampurna Behura case is a landmark judgment that significantly impacted the landscape of juvenile justice in India. It led to crucial reforms and improvements in the implementation of the JJ Act, aiming to create a more "child-friendly and rehabilitative justice system". The judgment reasserted the importance of prioritizing the welfare and rights of CCLs and those in need of care and protection.

In the case of *Ajeet Gurjar vs The State of MP*[19], the appellant, Ajeet Gurjar, was accused in a criminal case involving severe charges, including murder and dacoit, under different provisions of the Indian Penal Code and the Arms Act. Upon ascertaining that the appellant was above 16 years of age at the time of the alleged violation, the JJB performed a preliminary assessment under Section 15 of the JJ Act. Subsequently, the Board forwarded the matter to the Children's Court as per Section 18(3) of the JJ Act. The appellant submitted an application to the Children's Court, requesting adherence to Section 19(1) of the JJ Act, which stipulates particular protocols for the transfer of juvenile cases for trial such as to conduct an inquiry to decide whether there is a need for trial of the child as an adult as per the provisions of the Code of Criminal Procedure, 1973 (now under BNSS of 2023). The Children's Court dismissed this application, causing the appellant to file a revision to the High Court under Section 482 of the Code of Criminal Procedure. The High Court rejected the petition, leading to the appeal before the SC. The issues framed are the following:

i. Whether the Children's Court is obligated to comply with the procedural requirements outlined in Section 19(1) of the JJ Act upon receiving a case transferred under Section 18(3)?
ii. Whether the failure of the Children's Court to adhere to these procedures vitiates the trial proceedings against the juvenile?

The SC underscored the statutory aspect of Section 19(1) of the JJ Act, which establishes the duty of the Children's Court upon receiving a case involving a juvenile. The Court stated that the Children's Court must guarantee that the juvenile is given a child-friendly setting, legal help, and other appropriate support. Furthermore, the Children's Court is obligated to perform an evaluation to decide whether the juvenile should be prosecuted as an adult or be referred back to the JJB for appropriate instructions. The SC determined that the Children's Court did not comply with the obligatory processes, therefore undermining the juvenile's rights under the JJ Act. The Court found that such non-compliance is not a minor procedural lapse but a major infringement that impairs the fairness of the trial. Consequently, the SC set aside the rulings of the Children's Court and the High Court, requiring that the matter be returned to the Children's Court for new consideration in strict conformity with the procedural protections established in Section 19(1) of the JJ Act.

In the case of *Child in Conflict with Law through His Mother vs. State of Karnataka and Anr*,[20] an FIR was registered against the appellant, a minor, for offenses of rape under Sections 376(i) and 342 of the Indian Penal Code, along with provisions of the Protection of Children from Sexual Offences Act, 2012. Here, this case remarkably presents the confusion regarding the treatment of CCL as an adult or a child; the JJB in this case simultaneously passed two orders through the same Board with different members, respectively, where in one case it passed the order to treat the child as an adult, and in another to treat the child as a child. The issue of procedural technicalities was raised in the Hon'ble SC, as the first order passed was not signed and was on hold for the same, and, in between, the second order was passed. The matter of prevailing one order initially was raised in the High Court of Karnataka, which after the examination concluded the child to be treated as an adult for the respective appeal. The mother of CCL was dissatisfied with the decision and appealed to the apex court to prevail over the second order passed by the JJB and to treat CCL as a child while setting aside the unfinished and unsigned order. The SC then struck down both the orders passed as the first one lacked the signature and the second one lacked the presence of the Principal Magistrate, both being essential requirements for the legitimate order of JJB. The Court also remanded the JJB for fresh consideration of this subject matter with proper care and attention to the technicalities, guaranteeing fair and reasonable process.

Conclusion

It is possible for the Juvenile Justice System in India to be improved by addressing legislative shortcomings, bolstering rehabilitation programs, providing specialized training, promoting restorative justice, and raising public awareness. The purpose of these measures is to achieve a balance between holding juvenile offenders accountable and the overall objective of rehabilitating and reintegrating them into society.

The JJ Act, 2015, represents a transition to a rights-oriented, rehabilitative model; nonetheless, its execution is plagued by discrepancies. The efficacy of juvenile justice reforms will rely on a collaborative strategy that incorporates legislative protections, child-centric processes, and community-oriented rehabilitation frameworks. Although India has made considerable progress in establishing legislative safeguards for children in confrontation with the law, the effective execution of these rules continues to pose difficulties. The procedural elements, as examined via judicial rulings, disclose variations in age assessment, initial evaluations, and trial procedures. Enhancing the functions of JJBs, Children's Courts, and child welfare institutions is essential for guaranteeing that juveniles obtain equitable, rehabilitative, and reintegrative justice instead of punitive actions that obstruct their future opportunities. Apart from the governmental agencies' involvement, there is a need for immediate involvement of NGOs and Children's Care Organizations from day zero, that is, from the start of Police Work. This way, the protection will be provided from the very beginning of the case, and the CCL will also feel protected, and the sense of reformation will grow as well.

Procedural deficiencies on the grounds, while implementing the provisions of JJ Act, 2015, in the execution of reformation of CCL, including delays in age verification, uneven enforcement of bail regulations, and insufficient psychiatric and social evaluations, underscore the necessity for more robust processes. Providing adequate training for judicial officials, law enforcement personnels, and probation officers in child psychology and trauma-informed methodologies would be essential in addressing these disparities, which is addressed in multiple cases by the SC of India as well. An enhanced monitoring mechanism by the National and State Commissions for the Protection of Child Rights might improve legal compliance.

The transition in legal perspective from perceiving CCL as delinquents to acknowledging them as children requiring care and protection signifies a progressive stance. Nonetheless, obstacles remain in facilitating their social reintegration. Increased focus on restorative justice techniques, skill development programs, and psychiatric therapy in juvenile facilities can provide enduring answers. Investing in post-release supervision and community involvement will prevent adolescents from entering the cycle of recidivism; whereas India has the provision of After Care Homes under the JJ Act of 2015, it can be analyzed that the benefit is seldom available to these children.

Future legislative modifications should focus on improving procedural efficiency, integrating restorative justice ideas, and reinforcing alternative sentencing options. Collaboration with child rights organizations, academic institutions, and adherence to worldwide best practices will be essential in developing policies that promote child welfare while ensuring social security.

> The JJ Act of 2015 aims to safeguard children's best interests. Therefore, in rendering their decision on the matter, JJB and/or the Children's Court should exercise additional care. One can see that the child is the ultimate victim as procedure relapses affect him. By implementing rigorous procedural safeguards and compulsory expert evaluation, courts may retain the rehabilitative goals of the JJ Act, 2015, therefore avoiding arbitrary transfers of young people into the adult criminal justice system.

From a legal standpoint, a child who has committed a crime requires a unique and subtle response within the system of justice for young offenders. The procedures concerning these children are governed by standards that put their rehabilitation and wellbeing over punitive actions. When conducting judicial procedures, it is crucial to thoroughly evaluate the child's age, level of maturity, and specific circumstances. The objective is to determine the course of action that is in the best interest of the child and will promote their growth and successful reintegration into society. The assessment of age is a crucial factor, frequently entailing the scrutiny of documents or a medical evaluation. The legal processes should provide an equitable and child-centric atmosphere, while considering the child's distinct requirements and susceptibilities. Incorporating rehabilitation initiatives, educational initiatives, and skill development opportunities should be fundamental aspects of the judicial process, with a primary focus on promoting constructive development and deterring future engagement in criminal behavior. Judicial rulings should demonstrate a fair consideration of both holding individuals responsible for their actions and acknowledging the opportunity for young offenders to change, encompassing the changing knowledge of how the legal system deals with CCL.

Notes

1 Sayanti Ganguly, A Short History of Juvenile Legislations in India: A Socio-Legal Perspective, 11 QUEST JOURNALS J. RES. HUMANIT. SOC. SCI. 2321 (2023), www.questjournals.org.
2 Sayanti Ganguly, A Short History of Juvenile Legislations in India: A Socio-Legal Perspective, 11 QUEST JOURNALS J. RES. HUMANIT. SOC. SC
3 Roscoe Pound, THE IDEAL ELEMENT IN LAW (2002).
4 THE JUVENILE JUSTICE (CARE AND PROTECTION OF CHILDREN) ACT, 2015, MINISTRY OF LAW AND JUSTICE, INDIA (2015).
5 Officially announced in the Gazette of India on January 20, 2006, as Act No. 4 of 2006.
6 Sayanti Ganguly, A Short History of Juvenile Legislations in India: A Socio-Legal Perspective, 11 QUEST JOURNALS J. RES. HUMANIT. SOC. SCI. 2321 (2023), www.questjournals.org.
7 B. R. Ambedkar et al., THE CONSTITUION OF INDIA, (1950), https://legislative.gov.in/sites/default/files/COI.pdf.

8 Malvika Singh, Claim of Juvenility: A Security for Ever, 2 HARYANA POLICE J. 1 (2019).
9 THE JUVENILE JUSTICE (CARE AND PROTECTION OF CHILDREN) ACT, 2015, MINISTRY OF LAW AND JUSTICE, INDIA (2015).
10 (1982) 2 SCC 202.
11 (2000) 5 SCC 488.
12 AIR 2005 SUPREME COURT 2731.
13 (2009) 13 SCC 211.
14 Writ Petition (C) NO. 10 OF 2013.
15 AIR 2017 SC 2161.
16 Criminal Appeal No. 695 of 2014 (Arising Out of SLP (Crl.) No.1953 of 2013).
17 Criminal Appeal No. 696 of 2011.
18 (2018) 4 SCC 433.
19 Criminal Appeal No. 3023 of 2023.
20 Criminal Appeal No. of 2024 (Arising out of Special Leave Petition (Crl.) No. 3033 of 2024)

PART 2

Addressing Specific Child Vulnerabilities

5

A SOCIO-LEGAL EXAMINATION OF CHILD MARRIAGE AND ITS SOCIETAL RAMIFICATIONS

Rajiv Ranjan and Dulung Sengupta

Introduction

In the Indian context, the institution of marriage has always been linked to the preservation of social order, rather than prioritizing individual autonomy and personal preferences. Traditionally, men in marriage have been bestowed with the duty to earn money and women have accepted household responsibilities. Though gradually this has changed in terms of women working outside the home, unfortunately, it has spread only to cities and not to rural regions. As per the 2011 census, about 21% of India's population is in the age group of 10–19, with 47% females. The same census shows that a considerable proportion of females within this demographic either are already married or will enter into matrimony prior to reaching the legally permissible age for marriage.1

Child marriage is a regressive and harmful practice that unfortunately still persists today, with women often taking the brunt. Marriage between children, defined as those below the age of 21 for males and 18 for females, is known as "child marriage."[1] No matter the gender of the child, child marriage is a social concern[2] and has dire life-long consequences.[3]

The world community is a victim of child marriage. Globally, 12 million women got married even before attaining 18 years of age, and in the least developed countries this situation is even worse, as the data collected by UNICEF shows nearly 40% of girls in under-developed countries get married before attaining majority.[4] Child marriages are highly prevalent in West and Central Africa, with more than 40% of young girls being married before they turn 18.[5]

Child marriage deprives children of their rightful childhood, and young girls are particularly vulnerable, since they are compelled to engage in household

DOI: 10.4324/9781003607076-8

responsibilities at an age that is detrimental to their well-being. For women, child marriage significantly influences maternal and infant health, inferior social status, and high fertility.[6] Similar to the practice of child brides, minor grooms are likewise compelled to assume adult duties which the child may not be prepared to shoulder. Early fatherhood is one example of that. The additional financial burden of managing the family forces the child to seek employment and contribute to the family's income, thereby preventing him from pursuing educational opportunities.

Child marriage has a significant impact not just on the individuals involved and their immediate families but also on the broader societal fabric. Females who enter into marriage before reaching the age of 18 have limited prospects for completing their education, economic self-sufficiency, and meaningful contributions to the national economy. There exists a significant likelihood that she may engage in sexual intercourse with her spouse and subsequently have a child, while lacking the necessary maturity to effectively nurture a child. Statistics have shown that a significant number of women experience mortality during childbirth.[7]

Data indicate that, within India, over 23 million girls have been married as minors, making child marriage a worrisome issue. The country's average growth rate is about seven,[8] yet the pace of decline in child marriage is just 1%.[9] This statistic is horrifying since its ramifications are not restricted only to the underage couple, but it also adversely impacts their families and society as a whole. When children are removed from school due to child marriage, they do not acquire the necessary qualifications for employment and fail to contribute significantly to the development of the nation.[10] As per the National Family Health Survey (NFHS5), 2019–2021, about 7% of the girls have been pulled out of school because of early marriage.[11]

The following chapters will elucidate the primary factors that contribute to child marriage in India, using analytical models. Additionally, they will endeavour to depict the current situation regarding India's efforts to eliminate child marriages, with a particular emphasis on select northern states of the nation. The chapter will attempt to delineate the primary rationales behind the practice, as well as the impact of early childbirth on young females.

Nature and Prevalence of Child Marriage in India

Child marriage is a societal issue with its roots well embedded in the historical context of this country. Although the government conducts awareness initiatives, this societal ailment persists in several regions of the nation. India represents 33% of all child brides globally, as reported by UNICEF in 2014.[12] This chapter will elucidate the factors contributing to the prevalence of child marriages in this nation.

In Indian culture, the selection of spouses is often done by the elders of the family, with the partners having little influence in the decision-making process. One explanation for this is that, if a girl gets married at an early age, her potential for childbearing would be maximized, and the husband would be provided with a chaste woman with whom he may engage in sexual intercourse.[13] This notion is further corroborated by several faiths, each expressing its support in distinct ways. In Islam, it is permissible for young women to marry after they reach the age of puberty. Furthermore, in rural areas, child marriage has been ingrained in the culture, having been practised since ancient times, and no one dares to challenge this religiously sanctioned custom. Household poverty is also one contributor to child marriages.[14] Families with unstable finances often want to have their daughters married to lessen their financial burden, and this also contributes to child marriages. For instance, the district of Jamui in Bihar had a prevalence rate of 85.3% for child marriages (percentage of girls married before turning 18 years old), with around 81% of these cases occurring among economically disadvantaged households in 2006–2007.[15] The child marriage prevalence rate in Jamui has reduced to 51.9% in 2019–2021, but it records one of the highest numbers of child marriages in Bihar.[16] The district of Sawai Madhopur in Rajasthan exemplifies a scenario where 73.3% of child marriages have occurred, with roughly 53.1% of poor families.[17] Similarly, in the district of Murshidabad, West Bengal, the prevalence rate of child marriage is very high at 71%, with 57.5% of that figure being from low-income households.[18] Marriage enables families to shift the financial responsibilities of daughters to the husband's family, relieving them of some of the financial strain that comes with living in poverty.

The presence of entrenched patriarchy is also a contributing factor to the occurrence of child marriages. Women are often confined to domestic duties, and their ability to generate income is restricted. Many families believe that marrying their daughters at an early age would ensure their future stability. Additionally, illiteracy contributes to this social problem. Families lacking in education fail to recognize the significance of women's empowerment and education. Furthermore, they are not informed that coercing a minor into matrimony is a legally punishable offence under the law. Supported by UNICEF India in West Bengal, a case study on child marriage during the lockdown revealed that parents appear to be torn between adhering to socio-legal justifications against child marriage and common fears that their adolescent daughters will be trafficked, run away, be married, or be abused or their "familial honour" will be tarnished due to late marriage.[19]

Implications and Impacts of Child Marriage

Child marriages set in motion an entire cycle of disadvantages and vulnerabilities. The prevalence of child marriages has seen a reduction from

47% in 2006 to 23.3% in 2019–21.[20] However, it has been observed that child marriages are still prevalent among certain sections of the country in the name of customs, practices, and religious beliefs.[21] Qualitative studies also cite that some parents prefer to get their children married after they attain 18 but are compelled to resort to child marriage due to financial limitations and lack of educational opportunities.[22] Child marriages and adolescent childbearing are significantly high in the poorest 20% of the population.[23] Although the legal age of marriage is 18 for girls and 21 for men, as per the NHFS-5, 2019–21, 25% of women in the age bracket of 18–29 years and 15% of men in the age bracket of 21–29 years get married before they attain the legal minimum age;[24] 38% of women who are currently in the age bracket of 20–49 years have been child brides.[25] Child marriages among women are the highest in the states of West Bengal, Bihar, Tripura, Jharkhand, and Andhra Pradesh. Among men, it is highly prevalent in the states of Bihar, Gujarat, Rajasthan, Madhya Pradesh, Jharkhand, Arunachal Pradesh, and West Bengal.[26] As per a report published by UNICEF in 2023, one-third of the world's child brides reside in India.[27] More than half of these girls live in five states in India – Uttar Pradesh, Bihar, West Bengal, Maharashtra, and Madhya Pradesh.[28] It is also noted that the likelihood of child marriages among girls is six times greater than among boys.[29] A UNFPA report projects that more than 40% of women were married below 18 in West Bengal, Bihar, and Tripura.[30] Although there are certain disparities in the data presented by different organizations, which are to some extent caused due to the differences in their methodologies and objectives, there is a general consensus that child marriages are affected by other factors such as poverty, the educational status of children and parents, work status, customs, traditions, community pressures, and awareness. The National Crime Records Bureau (NCRB) has recorded a steady increase in the number of cases registered under the Prohibition of Child Marriage Act (PCMA), 2006, from 2017 to 2021.[31] In 2021, 1050 cases were registered under the Act,[32] which is a positive indication of increased awareness and higher reporting among the citizens, but, still, the numbers are far less than the number of actual child marriages solemnized in the country. There has been a decrease in the general national rate of child marriages in India, yet there are still particular locations in which the number of child marriages is comparable to the rate that existed in India 15 years ago.[33] Child marriages have a never-fading impact on the lives of children and proximately impact their social, economic, and sexual autonomy. It violates their rights to education, health, and protection, which are basic inalienable rights for living a life with dignity. It makes them socially vulnerable and pushes them into further despair and poverty. Not just that, in several instances, they are more vulnerable to being victims of violence and trauma.

Teenage Pregnancies and Higher Fertility Rates

Age at first marriage is a proxy indicator of the age of first sexual intercourse.[34] Exposure to sexual activity at a young age increases the threat of teenage pregnancy. Teenage pregnancies are associated with higher risks of complications during pregnancy and childbirth.[35] As per the WHO, maternal mortality is the second-ranked cause of death among adolescent girls. Girls who bear children before adulthood are generally anaemic and underweight, which puts both the child's and the mother's life at risk.[36] Teenage pregnancies also increase the chances of neonatal mortality.[37] Surprisingly, the brides and grooms of child marriages, as well as their parents, are aware of the ramifications of teenage pregnancies and higher fertility.[38] As per the NHFS-5, 7% of women in India bear children when they are in the age bracket of 15–19 and more than half of the currently married women in the same age group either are pregnant or have delivered their first child.[39] Tripura, West Bengal, Andhra Pradesh, Assam, Bihar, and Jharkhand record the highest number of teenage pregnancies in India.[40] The number of children a woman bears depends on the age she begins childbearing and her sexual autonomy. The occurrence of teenage pregnancies and higher fertility is relatively higher among rural women, who have less or no schooling.[41] Women belonging to lower economic strata and scheduled tribes are more vulnerable to teenage pregnancies and have more children.[42] This is directly attributable to the fact that these women get married earlier than their counterparts. Although there has been a significant decline in fertility among teenage girls, the numbers remain worrisome.

Violence and Trauma

Child marriages expose children to a higher risk of violence, exploitation, and abuse.[43] Child marriages are characterized by spousal age gaps, which lead to power imbalances between the spouses and a lack of female autonomy. A higher degree of marital control by husbands is observed in marriages where the wife is aged between 15 and 19 years.[44] Child brides are more likely to face intimate partner violence (IPV).[45] It can be in the form of physical, emotional, and sexual violence,[46] which is a source of trauma for many girls and women.[47] As per NFHS-4, 2015–16, women aged 15–19 face either emotional, physical, or sexual violence or a combination of more than one of these.[48] Sexual IPV is highly prevalent among child brides in India and is closely associated with the expectation of sexual intercourse and childbearing soon after marriage in Indian society. Many child brides have reported that they were not familiar with sexual acts and their partners before marriage.[49] The lack of familiarity with sex, compounded with the lack of familiarity of their partners, produces a severely traumatizing experience.[50] As a result, the child brides suffer from poor concentration, flashbacks, intense sadness, hyperarousal, irritability, and hopelessness.[51] Apart from sexual IPV, child brides are more susceptible to domestic violence. Lack of education, economic independence, and less autonomy in the household make child brides socially vulnerable. Their physical mobility is restricted to the extent that some of them are not even permitted to visit their parents or socialize outside the four walls of the house.[52] This isolates them socially from their friends, families, and other support systems after marriage.[53] They are often beaten and threatened and are made to believe that their husbands are justified in beating their wives.[54] Almost 40% of women married before the age of 18 believe that wife beating is justified.[55] The child brides are often tortured mentally by their in-laws and are forced to do all the household work.[56] India has the highest rate of domestic violence among women who were child brides.[57] More than half of the women who were married before they turned 18 have reported being victims of domestic violence.[58] Girls belonging to lower wealth quintiles and having less or no education are at an elevated risk of facing domestic and spousal violence in India. Instances of spousal violence in any of the forms are prevalent in all the Indian States.[59]

Adverse Effects on Education and Empowerment of Women

Child marriage, deep-rooted gender roles, and adolescent pregnancies have been major factors impacting school dropouts among girls belonging to rural and poor households. Although India has made significant progress over the years in minimizing child marriages and enhancing access to education, a lot more needs to be done. More education generally leads to later marriages and childbearing; on the other hand, child marriages and early pregnancies are major roadblocks to education, especially among girls. It has been seen that child marriages adversely affect secondary school attendance among girls in most of the South-Asian countries, including India. The marital status of children has a significant impact on their school attendance rates. A recent study reveals that 78.32% of single children in Gujarat attended school compared to 48.28% of married children.[60] The same study also shows that only 57% of married girls were attending schools as compared to 80% of married boys.[61] A child bride has a lower probability of completing primary and secondary school in India.[62] As per data collected by UNICEF, among women aged 20–24, there were higher levels of school dropouts after the primary level, where the girls were married before they turned 18.[63] Almost eight out of ten married girls drop out of school;[64] 57% of women in this age bracket completed only primary schooling, and, sadly, only 10% completed secondary school;[65] 16% of women in the same age bracket belonging to the poorest wealth quintile are further affected by adolescent pregnancies and childbirths, which makes their condition more deplorable.[66] In the case of child grooms, the primary reason for school dropouts is due to increased financial and family responsibilities that compel them to start working at an early age.[67] Non-completion of schooling also affects the future employment opportunities of the children, as they have fewer skills and knowledge, which makes them financially insecure.[68] Child marriages can lead to an inter-generational cycle of poverty.[69] A study by the World Bank assesses that child marriages affect the ability of children to participate in the labour force, especially women, and also adversely impact the type of work they are engaged in.[70] In a study carried out by Child Rights and You (CRY), the majority of the respondents who were child brides were either engaged in doing paid or unpaid household chores or were working as agricultural labourers. Child brides have lesser autonomy in making decisions for entering the labour force due to their social vulnerability.[71] Even higher fertility rates at a young age that result in quick and multiple pregnancies influence the role of women in the labour market and act as an impediment by causing a reduction in the hours they are able to work.[72] They can also cause frequent interruptions in their employment.[73]

Legislative Framework on Child Marriages in India

India took its first steps for preventing child marriages by enacting the Sharda Act of 1929, which was later renamed as the Child Marriage Restraint Act of 1929 (CMRA). It prohibited marriages of girls below the age of 15 and of boys who were below 18. In 1978, the Act was amended, which increased the minimum age of marriage of girls to 18 and of boys to 21. The objective of the Act was to eradicate child marriages, taking into account the horrific and irreversible impacts it had on the psychological and physical well-being of children, especially girls. The penal provisions of the legislation did not apply to children as they were considered mere passive actors. However, the penalty was imposed on adult males who were contracting parties to the marriage with a child bride. The Act placed greater liability on adult males who were above the age of 21, keeping in mind that they would have greater awareness and foreseeability to be deterred from child marriage. The legislators had also taken into consideration the active role played by parents, guardians, and all other persons who performed, conducted, or directed the solemnization of any child marriage. However, the maximum imprisonment under the Act was only up to 3 months, which failed to create the necessary deterrence for preventing the contracting parties or their relatives from solemnizing child marriages.

The CMRA was replaced by the PCMA. The new Act was armed with provisions for providing relief to victims and stricter penalties for eliminating the menace of child marriage from Indian society. However, like the CMRA, the PCMA also does not render the child marriage void but only makes it voidable at the option of the parties to the marriage, which can invalidate their matrimonial relationship only after obtaining a decree of nullity from the court.[74] The application for the annulment of marriage can be filed within two years after attaining a majority.[75] It can also be filed by a minor through their guardians or next of kin, along with the Child Marriage Prohibition Officer.[76] Besides annulling the marriage, the court shall direct the parties and their parents to return all the money, gifts, jewellery, and other valuables that were exchanged at the time of the marriage.[77] Child marriage is expressly declared as null and void in certain cases where the child is taken out of the custody of the lawful guardian through enticement, is compelled by force, or is induced to go from any place through deceitful means, or is sold either for marriage or after the marriage for being used for immoral purposes.[78]

Under the PCMA, legislators have taken into account the need to provide financial and social security to the female contracting parties post the annulment of marriage by incorporating maintenance provisions for them. The court may pass interim or final orders directing the male contracting parties or their parents, in case the male contracting party is a minor, to pay maintenance to the woman till her remarriage.[79] While deciding the amount of maintenance, relevant factors such as the needs of the child and her lifestyle are to be taken into consideration.[80] The court is also equipped with the power to issue orders for the residence of the female party until she remarries.[81]

The PCMA provides for enhanced penalties for adult males who marry a child and persons who perform, promote, conduct, direct, abet, permit, or in any manner facilitate a child marriage.[82] The offences are punishable with rigorous imprisonment extendable up to two years and a fine which up to one lakh rupees. It is perceived that when the child is under the custody of their parents, guardians, or any member of any organization or association, who is duty-bound to act in the best interest of the child, should not promote or permit child marriages to be solemnized. They should not be negligent, and even the act of attending or participating in the marriage makes them liable for a penalty under the Act.

Furthermore, the government introduced the Prohibition of Child Marriage (Amendment) Bill in 2021 to raise the minimum age of marriage of women to 21 and bring it in line with that of men. The proposed bill also seeks amendments to various personal laws to bring uniformity in the minimum legal age for the marriage of women. Although the primary objective of the amendment is to reduce the infant and maternal mortality rates in the country, it will also be a boon for girls who are victims of child marriages owing to the disparities in the personal laws.

Reporting and Rates of Disposal of Child Marriages

The PCMA, 2006, was enacted to prevent child marriages and take punitive actions against those who are associated with such marriages.

Under the Act, the Child Marriage Prohibition Officers (CMPOs) are entrusted with the responsibilities of preventing the solemnization of child marriages, creating awareness, and advising the people of the concerned localities not to indulge, promote, or allow the solemnization of child marriages. The Act also provides for the setting up of District Child Protection Units (DCPUs) that are responsible for coordinating and implementing the activities for child rights and protection at the district level. The machinery at the district or block levels must function efficiently for the proper implementation of the Act and the fulfilment of its objectives. The Eleventh and Twelfth Five-Year Plans emphasized that the panchayats also play a central role in the empowerment of women and girls and the eradication of social menaces like child marriage.[83] However, a study conducted by CRY mentions that in certain districts of UP and Maharashtra, there is no separate CMPO, and a member of the DCPU team is working as the CMPO as well.[84]

Although there is a rise in the number of reported cases of child marriages in India, underreporting remains a pressing concern, which is evident in the wide disparity between the number of cases recorded by NCRB and the NFHS data. There are certain clusters where child marriages are rampant prevalent but no cases are filed.[85] The same report also states that there is no uniform mechanism followed by the police for investigating and handling the cases registered under the PCMA.[86] In the same districts, the DCPUs did not maintain any records of the number of households visited or the parents counselled by them.[87] They were maintaining only the list of child marriages that were prevented by them in their jurisdiction.[88] After the cases are registered, the Child Welfare Committees constituted under the Juvenile Justice (Care and Protection of Children) Act, 2015, play a pivotal role in the rehabilitation and protection of the children who are rescued from child marriages. Unfortunately, in some blocks like Chandauli of UP, where there is a very high incidence of child marriage, such a mechanism is nonexistent.[89]

In 2021, only 1050 cases of child marriages were recorded in India, while 561 cases were yet to be investigated from the previous year.[90] The highest number of cases was recorded in Karnataka, followed by Tamil Nadu, West Bengal, Assam, Maharashtra, and Odisha. Disposal of cases by the police is impaired by insufficient evidence. In 2021, there were 44 such cases where the police observed that, despite the cases being true, they could not find sufficient evidence.[91] The pendency percentage of the police disposal under the PCMA is 41.6%.[92] The conviction rate of cases under the PCMA is very low (9.7%), while the rate of pendency is 96.4%.[93] This clearly showcases the lack of proper implementation of the Act by the police as well as the Judiciary, which is highly dismal. Proper sensitization coupled with legal and institutional machinery is indispensable for curbing child marriages.

Role of the Indian Judiciary Addressing Child Marriages

Child Marriages have been regarded as a gross human rights violation by the Indian Judiciary.[94] The Courts have criticized child marriages, stating that they reflect the chauvinistic attributes of the Indian society that have existed historically and sadly continue to exist even after the enactment of the Prohibition of Child Marriage Act, 2006.[95] The Judiciary has been confronting several cases over the years, which makes them revisit the objectives of the legislation and analyse the gaps to ensure better protection of minors from the menace of child marriage and ensure effective implementation of the legislation. The High Court of Delhi reiterated the rationale behind the enactment of the PCMA in *Association for Social Justice & Research v Union of India*.[96] It held that the children lack physical and psychological fitness for marriage, which has severe ramifications on their physical, mental, and social well-being. The court associated child marriages with early pregnancies, health risks, lack of education, poverty, maternal and child mortality, and domestic violence. Through different judicial decisions, they have pressured the "state" to make sure that the enacted laws are enforced and implemented effectively. The apex court decision in *Independent Thought vs. Union of India*[97] has been a very transformative decision, which criminalized intercourse with a minor wife (under 18 years of age). This case needs to be credited for recognizing minors as individuals with rights. Additionally, this changed the outlook of the society by prioritizing well-being over marital status. The court adopted a protectionist approach towards the victims of child marriages and recognized the need to provide them with adequate care and protection. The court in another case also directed the government to register the marriages so that accountability could be fixed in case of child marriages.[98] Additionally, the Judiciary has emphasized that child marriages cannot be conducted in the guise of personal laws.[99] The PCMA is a secular legislation, and its benefits should reach all children irrespective of their religious or social background. Personal laws or customary practices cannot override the Rights guaranteed under Article 21 of the Constitution. In *Society for Enlightenment & Voluntary Action v. Union of India*,[100] the apex court had the opportunity to look into the issue of child marriage along with the steps taken by the state to curb the problem. The court also analysed the policies of the government to effectuate the purpose. The court held that child marriages violate the right to self-determination[101] and personal autonomy.[102] In relation to the state, the court stated:

> *States also have an obligation to monitor and enforce compliance with these laws and to work closely with civil society organizations to implement effective interventions. The State's role is not limited to merely punishing offenders but extends to creating an enabling environment where*

children can exercise their rights freely. This includes the responsibility to not only to legislate against child marriage but also to address the underlying socio-economic factors – poverty, lack of education, and gender discrimination – that perpetuate this practice.

The apex court reminded the state that a child is a "national asset" as per national policy and thus the state has a responsibility to nurture the child by ensuring their full development. This judgement is of paramount significance as it lays down critical guidelines aimed at the prevention and eradication of child marriage. The court has directed the state governments to appoint CMPOs at the district level, ensuring that they are exclusively tasked with addressing child marriage without being assigned any other responsibilities so that they can focus exclusively on preventing child marriages. Additionally, the Ministries of Women and Child Development and Home Affairs in each state and union territory are required to conduct regular performance reviews to assess the effectiveness of implemented measures. The judgement also emphasized setting up specialized police units and providing the magistrates with the authority to take suo moto actions and issue injunctions for preventing child marriages. Considering the gaps in the implementation of the legislation, the guidelines prescribe strict disciplinary actions against negligent public servants. The court has also considered the barriers in the delivery of speedy justice and has suggested exploring the possibilities of establishing special fast-track courts for cases involving child marriages. Child marriage, being a social issue, requires community participation and preventive measures from the grassroots level. The guidelines emphasize the adoption of the Child Marriage Free Village Initiative and call for the active measures taken by CMPOs for conducting awareness campaigns in schools, religious institutions, and panchayats. Sensitization at the right age is of utmost importance, and the court has rightly focused on the inclusion of comprehensive sexuality and rights education in the school curriculum to educate the children about their legal rights, the benefits of delaying marriage, and provide them with an understanding of their sexual and reproductive health. The judgement addresses another very important aspect, that is, the capability building of children, especially girls who are at risk of getting married before 18. The court has directed the Ministry of Women and Child Development to provide scholarships, stipends, and financial support to the girls or their families so that they can choose education over early marriages. Furthermore, the judgement discusses how access to vocational training and skill development programmes can improve the economic status of the families of girls who are at risk of getting married and help in preventing child marriages. The Indian Judiciary has conveyed its strong opposition to child marriages through various pronouncements and has time reaffirmed the objectives of the PCMA. It has always given recognition to the rights of children and considered child marriages to be a gross violation of their basic rights, which not just takes away their childhood but also creates several hardships and impediments that stall their development. The courts have stressed enhancing the accountability of the public servants assigned the duty to prevent and eradicate child marriage. With recent pronouncements such as in the case of *Society for Enlightenment and Voluntary Action & Anr v. Union of India*,[103] the courts have analysed the loopholes in the implementation of the PCMA. The courts have not limited themselves to the role of being custodian of the rights of the children who have been victims of child marriage but have also tried to fill up the grey areas by issuing appropriate directives and guidelines through their progressive pronouncements.

Conclusion

At the global level, India is a signatory to several international instruments that aim to protect children from all forms of abuse and exploitation and uphold their basic human rights. These include the Universal Declaration of Human Rights, the UN Convention on the Rights of the Child, the International Covenant on Economic Social Cultural Rights, and the Convention on the Elimination of Discrimination against Women. These instruments reiterate the importance of the protection of human rights for the holistic development of children and building capabilities to ensure that they live a dignified life. They place responsibilities on the member nations to protect children from human rights violations and provide protection and safe rehabilitation wherever necessary. Child marriage has been recognized as a major concern and violation of the human rights of children, which affects their present and future in innumerable ways. It has horrific effects on the physical and mental well-being of children and blocks their road to a dignified social life. It impedes their access to education, which has far-reaching effects on their skill and knowledge development and hampers their chances of good employment opportunities. Therefore, India, being a member of the international instruments, has a greater responsibility to prevent human rights violations like child marriages.

Article 39(f) of the Constitution of India enshrines that children are provided with opportunities and facilities that are required for their healthy development in a free and dignified manner. The government is bestowed with the responsibility to protect the childhood of children and keep them safe from exploitation, abuse, and moral and material abandonment. The government is incessantly trying to curb child marriages through adopting policies such as the National Policy for Children,[104] the National Plan of Action to Prevent Child Marriage in India in 2013, and the National Action Plan for Children of 2016. These policies and plans work on the effective enforcement and implementation of the PCMA by developing effective measures such as enhancing access to education, conducting programmes for changing social norms and attitudes, and providing training to boys and girls for capacity building. These policies focus on a child's right to nutrition, education and development, protection, and participation. These policies are positive changes that can address the root causes of child marriages and help bring about the desired changes in societal attitudes and practices. Complementing the laws and policies, schemes such as Beti Bachao Beti Padhao[105] (translates to Save the Daughter Educate the Daughter), Rashtriya Kishor Swasthya Karyakram[106] (translates to National Youth Health Programme), Scheme for Adolescent Girls (SAG) at the national level,[107] and Kanyashree (translates to Daughter's Prosperity) programme in West Bengal,[108] Girl Child Protection Schemes Ladli Lakshmi Yojana (translates to beloved daughter as Goddess of Prosperity Scheme) in Madhya Pradesh,[109] Ladli Social Security Allowance Scheme in Haryana[110] (translates to beloved daughter social security allowance scheme), Chief Minister's Girl Child Protection Scheme in Tamil Nadu[111], and so on, at the state level are instrumental for protecting rights of children and prevent child marriages.

India has made significant progress in reducing child marriages nationwide, but totally eliminating it remains a daunting task. The elements contributing to this malpractice include poverty, patriarchy, cultural customs, and illiteracy. Internationally, programmes such as the Sustainable Development Goals have also inspired governments to address this societal problem that hinders young people from fully experiencing and celebrating their youth. States such as Bihar, West Bengal, and Maharashtra must make significant progress in addressing the issue of child marriages. Government programmes like as Beti Bachao, Beti Padhao, and others have made great strides in highlighting the importance of women's empowerment and in neutralizing the stereotyping of girls as a financial burden on their families and communities. Community participation and non-governmental organizations working at the grassroots level can play a major role in the eradication and reporting of child marriages. In addition, the law enforcement authorities, like the Police, Child Marriage Prohibition Officer, District Magistrate, and District Women and Child Development Office, need to be more active, particularly in rural areas, to bring to light instances of child marriage and prevent the same. The Police, Child Marriage Prohibition Officer, and District Magistrate should take all necessary measures to prevent the solemnization of child marriages under their jurisdictions, especially the organization of mass marriages. The police and the Child Marriage Prohibition Officer should collect adequate evidence to facilitate the prosecution of the wrongdoers. Timely action and effective measures on the part of the law enforcement agencies can have a positive impact on lowering the instances of child marriages. Appropriate enforcement of the provisions of the PCMA and imposition of the punishments on the wrongdoers would instil a sense of deterrence throughout the population, which would help to reduce the instances of child marriage. However, child marriages have been historically practised in India, and they continue to be practised due to social perceptions and economic hardships. Therefore, deterrence alone is not adequate to eradicate child marriage. It has to be supplemented with measures to spread awareness, educating children and families about its long-term repercussions and providing financial support and vocational training to combat the causes of child marriages. It is important to recognize that the ramifications of child marriage go beyond the individuals involved in the marriage and impact society as a whole, which denigrates the nation. If young people are not burdened with marital responsibilities early on, their energy and potential may be tapped effectively, leading to significant accomplishments for the country. The impediments faced by these young couples in pursuing education are a matter of concern not just for the individuals themselves but also for society as a whole. Getting married at a young age not only robs individuals of their youth but also hinders their ability to contribute positively to society.

Notes

1 The Prohibition of Child Marriage Act, 2006, § 2, Act No.6 of 2007.
2 B. Pramila, "Child Marriage: Scenario in India." Proceedings of the Indian History Congress 74 (2013): 998–1008, http://www.jstor.org/stable/44158905.
3 Nisha Varia "Ending Child Marriage: Meeting the Global Development Goals' Promise to Girls." In World Report 2016: Events of 2015, 1st ed., 33–40. Bristol University Press, 2016, https://doi.org/10.2307/j.ctvndv9bj.6.
4 Child Marriage Is a Violation of Human Rights, But Is All Too Common, UNICEF Data: Monitoring the Situation of Women and Children, https://data.unicef.org/topic/child-protection/child-marriage (last visited December 2, 2023).
5 UNICEF: For Every Child, Child Marriage in West and Central Africa at a Glance, 4, 2018, https://www.unicef.org/chad/media/246/file/Child-Marriage-in-WCA-At-a-Glance.pdf.
6 Jennifer Parsons, Jeffrey Edmeades, Aslihan Kes, Suzanne Petroni, Maggie Sexton & Quentin Wodon, "Economic Impacts of Child Marriage: A Review of the Literature," The Review of Faith & International Affairs 13:3 (2015): 12–22, https://doi.org/10.1080/15570274.2015.1075757.
7 UNICEF Global Databases, 2022, https://data.unicef.org/topic/child-protection/child-marriage/ (last visited Dec. 5, 2023).
8 World Bank National Accounts Data, and OECD National Accounts Data Files, https://data.worldbank.org/indicator/NY.GDP.MKTP.KD.ZG (last visited December 4, 2023).
9 This analysis is based on the data collected till 2012.
10 UNICEF: For Every Child, Ending Child Marriage and Adolescent Empowerment, https://www.unicef.org/india/what-we-do/end-child-marriage (last visited December 2, 2023).
11 Table 2.28, National Family and Health Survey (NFHS-5), 2019–21, https://dhsprogram.com/pubs/pdf/FR375/FR375.pdf. (last visited November 3, 2023).
12 Child Rights and You, Causes of Child Marriage Can Have Long-Term Effects on Young Girls, https://www.cry.org/blog/child-marriage-can-have-long-term-effects-on-young-girls/ (last visited December 2, 2023).

13 https://globaljustice.regent.edu/2022/02/child-marriage-in-india/ (last visited November 3, 2023).
14 S.J. Jejeebhoy, Ending Child Marriage in India, Drivers and Strategies, New Delhi: UNICEF, 2019.
15 Jyotsna Jha et al., Reducing Child Marriages in India a Model to Scale Up Results, Centre for Budget and Policy Studies and United Nations Children's Fund, 2016.
16 National Family Health Survey-5, 2019–21, District Fact Sheet Jamui, Bihar, Ministry of Health and Family Welfare, https://dhsprogram.com/pubs/pdf/OF43/BR_Jamui.pdf.
17 Reproduced from "District-Level Study on Child Marriages in India: What Do We Know about the Prevalence, Trends and Patterns?" ICRW and UNICEF, 2015.
18 Reproduced from "District-Level Study on Child Marriages in India: What Do We Know about the Prevalence, Trends and Patterns?" ICRW and UNICEF, 2015.
19 UNFPA-UNICEF Global Programme to End Child Marriage, 2020 Country Profiles, https://www.unicef.org/media/111381/file/Child-marriage-country-profile-India–2021.pdf (last visited November 25, 2023).
20 Ministry of Women and Child Development, https://pib.gov.in/PressReleaseIframePage.aspx?PRID=1947773 (last visited November 25, 2023).
21 Ministry of Women and Child Development, https://pib.gov.in/PressReleaseIframePage.aspx?PRID=1947773 (last visited November 25, 2023).
22 Child Rights and You (CRY), "Child Marriage in India: A Research Study," December 2021, New Delhi.
23 A. Bajracharya, S. R. Psaki & M. Sadiq, Child Marriage, Adolescent Pregnancy and School Dropout in South Asia, Report by the Population Council for the United Nations Children's Fund Regional Office for South Asia, Kathmandu, Nepal, 2019.
24 International Institute for Population Sciences (IIPS) and ICF. 2021, 209, National Family Health Survey (NFHS-5), 2019–21, India: Volume I. Mumbai: IIPS.
25 International Institute for Population Sciences (IIPS) and ICF. 2021, 209, National Family Health Survey (NFHS-5), 2019–21, India: Volume I. Mumbai: IIPS.
26 International Institute for Population Sciences (IIPS) and ICF. 2021, 209, National Family Health Survey (NFHS-5), 2019–21, India: Volume I. Mumbai: IIPS.
27 Ending Child Marriage: A Profile of Progress in India, UNICEF, 2023.
28 Ending Child Marriage: A Profile of Progress in India, UNICEF, 2023.
29 Ministry of Women and Child Development, https://pib.gov.in/PressReleaseIframePage.aspx?PRID=1947773 (last visited November 25, 2023).
30 Child Marriage in India: Key Insights from the NFHS-5, 2019–21, https://india.unfpa.org/sites/default/files/pub-pdf/analytical_series_1_-_child_marriage_in_india__insights_from_nfhs-5_final_0.pdf (last visited November 25, 2023).
31 Reproduced from "District-Level Study on Child Marriages in India: What Do We Know about the Prevalence, Trends and Patterns?," ICRW and UNICEF, 2015.
32 Reproduced from "District-Level Study on Child Marriages in India: What Do We Know about the Prevalence, Trends and Patterns?," ICRW and UNICEF, 2015.
33 https://www.cry.org/downloads/safety-and-protection/Child-Marriage-in-India-A-Research-Study.pdf.
34 Child Rights and You (CRY), "Child Marriage in India: A Research Study," December 2021, 210, New Delhi.
35 International Institute for Population Sciences (IIPS) and ICF. 2021, 210, National Family Health Survey (NFHS-5), 2019–21, India: Volume I. Mumbai: IIPS.
36 Child Rights and You (CRY), "Child Marriage in India: A Research Study," December 2021, New Delhi, https://www.cry.org/downloads/safety-and-protection/Child-Marriage-in-India-A-Research-Study.pdf (last visited Nov. 27, 2023).

37 International Institute for Population Sciences (IIPS) and ICF. 2021, 210, National Family Health Survey (NFHS-5), 2019–21, 111, India: Volume I. Mumbai: IIPS, https://rchiips.org/nfhs/NFHS-5Reports/NFHS-5_INDIA_REPORT.pdf (last visited November 27, 2023).
38 Child Rights and You (CRY), "Child Marriage in India: A Research Study," December 2021, 210, New Delhi.
39 Child Rights and You (CRY), "Child Marriage in India: A Research Study," December 2021, 210, New Delhi at 116.
40 Child Rights and You (CRY), "Child Marriage in India: A Research Study," December 2021, 210, New Delhi at 117.
41 Child Rights and You (CRY), "Child Marriage in India: A Research Study," December 2021, 210, New Delhi.
42 Child Rights and You (CRY), "Child Marriage in India: A Research Study," December 2021, 210, New Delhi at 117.
43 International Institute for Population Sciences (IIPS) and ICF. 2021, 209, National Family Health Survey (NFHS-5), 2019–21, India: Volume I. Mumbai: IIPS.
44 Child Rights and You (CRY), "Child Marriage in India: A Research Study," December 2021, 210, New Delhi at 583.
45 Shankey Verma & Rashmi Choudhury, "Child Marriage and Intimate Partner Violence in India: A National Study," Journal of Loss and Trauma (2023), https://doi.org/10.1080/15325024.2023.2259292 https://tandfonline.com/doi/full/10.1080/15325024.2023.2259292 (last visited November 30, 2023).
46 Verma & Choudhury, "Child Marriage and Intimate Partner Violence in India."
47 Anjali Menon, "Intimate Partner Violence in Indian Brides: Mechanisms of Trauma, Applied Psychology Opus," 2023, https://wp.nyu.edu/steinhardt-appsych_opus/intimate-partner-violence-in-indian-child-brides-mechanisms-of-trauma/ (last visited November 29, 2023).
48 International Institute for Population Sciences (IIPS) and ICF. 2017. National Family Health Survey (NFHS-4), 586, 2015–16: India, Mumbai: IIPS.
49 Ending Child Marriage: A Profile of progress in India, UNICEF, 2023.
50 Ending Child Marriage: A Profile of progress in India, UNICEF, 2023.
51 Ending Child Marriage: A Profile of progress in India, UNICEF, 2023.
52 Reproduced from "District-Level Study on Child Marriages in India: What Do We Know about the Prevalence, Trends and Patterns?," ICRW and UNICEF, 2015.
53 https://india.unfpa.org/sites/default/files/pub-pdf/analytical_series_1_-_child_marriage_in_india_-_insights_from_nfhs-5_final_0.pdf.
54 United Nations Children's Fund, Early Marriage: A Harmful Traditional Practice. A Statistical Exploration, New York, NY: UNICEF, 2005.
55 Ending Child Marriage: A Profile of progress in India, UNICEF, 2023.
56 https://www.cry.org/downloads/safety-and-protection/Child-Marriage-in-India-A-Research-Study.pdf.
57 United Nations Children's Fund, Early Marriage.
58 United Nations Children's Fund, Early Marriage.
59 NFHS-5, 2019–21.
60 Jacqueline Bhabha & Orla Kelly, Child Marriage and the Right to Education: Evidence from India, FXB Centre for Health and Human Rights, Harvard University, 2013, https://www.ohchr.org/sites/default/files/Documents/Issues/Women/WRGS/ForcedMarriage/NGO/HavardUniversityFXB3.pdf (last visited November 29, 2023).
61 Bhabha & Kelly, Child Marriage and the Right to Education.
62 A. Bajracharya, S. R. Psaki, & M. Sadiq, "Child Marriage, Adolescent Pregnancy and School Dropout in South Asia," Report by the Population Council for the United Nations Children's Fund Regional Office for South Asia, Kathmandu, Nepal, 2019.

63 Bajracharya, Psaki, & Sadiq, "Child Marriage, Adolescent Pregnancy and School Dropout in South Asia."
64 "Ending Child Marriage: A Profile of Progress in India, UNICEF," 2023, UNICEF India, https://data.unicef.org/resources/ending-child-marriage-a-profile-of-progress-in-india 2023/#:~:text=The%20practice%20of%20child%20marriage,additional%20efforts%20will%20be%20required (last visited November 30, 2023).
65 Q. Wodon, A. Savadogo, & A. Kes, Economic Impacts of Child Marriage: Work. Earnings, and Household Welfare, Washington, DC: The World Bank and International Center for Research on Women, 2017. https://documents1.worldbank.org/curated/en/312761498512784050/pdf/116835-BRI-P151842-PUBLIC-EICM-Brief-WorkEarningsHousehold-PrintReady.pdf (last visited December 3, 2023).
66 Wodon, Savadogo, & Kes, Economic Impacts of Child Marriage.
67 Child Rights and You (CRY), "Child Marriage in India: A Research Study," December 2021, 210, New Delhi.
68 "Ending Child Marriage: A Profile of Progress in India, UNICEF," 2023.
69 Note 72.
70 Wodon, Savadogo, & Kes, Economic Impacts of Child Marriage.
71 Boender, Carol, The Relationship between Child Labour and Child Marriage: A Discourse Analysis, UNICEF Kathmandu, 2021.
72 Id.
73 Id.
74 The Prohibition of Child Marriage Act, 2006, § 3, Act No.6 of 2007.
75 The Prohibition of Child Marriage Act, 2006, § 3, Act No.6 of 2007 at §3 (3).
76 The Prohibition of Child Marriage Act, 2006, § 3, Act No.6 of 2007 at §3 (3).
77 The Prohibition of Child Marriage Act, 2006, § 3, Act No.6 of 2007 at § 3(4).
78 The Prohibition of Child Marriage Act, 2006, § 3, Act No.6 of 2007 at § 12.
79 The Prohibition of Child Marriage Act, 2006, § 3, Act No.6 of 2007 at § 4.
80 The Prohibition of Child Marriage Act, 2006, § 3, Act No.6 of 2007 at § 4.
81 The Prohibition of Child Marriage Act, 2006, § 3, Act No.6 of 2007 at § 4.
82 The Prohibition of Child Marriage Act, 2006, § 3, Act No.6 of 2007 at § 9, 10 and 11.
83 "Working Group on Development of Children for the Eleventh Five Year Plan (2007–2012)-A Report," https://www.aicte-india.org/downloads/girl_child_XI_five_year_plan.pdf (last visited December 4, 2023).
84 Child Rights and You (CRY), "Child Marriage in India: A Research Study," December 2021, 210, New Delhi.
85 Child Rights and You (CRY), "Child Marriage in India: A Research Study," December 2021, 210, New Delhi.
86 Child Rights and You (CRY), "Child Marriage in India: A Research Study," December 2021, 210, New Delhi.
87 Child Rights and You (CRY), "Child Marriage in India: A Research Study," December 2021, 210, New Delhi.
88 Child Rights and You (CRY), "Child Marriage in India: A Research Study," December 2021, 210, New Delhi.
89 Child Rights and You (CRY), "Child Marriage in India: A Research Study," December 2021, 210, New Delhi.
90 Child Rights and You (CRY), "Child Marriage in India: A Research Study," December 2021, 210, New Delhi at 342.
91 Child Rights and You (CRY), "Child Marriage in India: A Research Study," December 2021, 210, New Delhi at 344.
92 Child Rights and You (CRY), "Child Marriage in India: A Research Study," December 2021, 210, New Delhi at 345.
93 Child Rights and You (CRY), "Child Marriage in India: A Research Study," December 2021, 210, New Delhi at 357.

94 *T. Sivakumar v Inspector of Police*, Thiruvallur Town Police Station, Thiruvallur District, 2011 SCC OnLine Mad 1722.
95 *Yunusbhai Usmanbhai Shaikh v. State of Gujarat*, 2015 G.L.R. 2512.
96 2010 SCC OnLine Del 1964.
97 W.P. Civil 382 of 2013.
98 *Seema v. Ashwini Kumar*, AIR 2006 SC 1158.
99 2024 SCC Online SC 2922.
100 2024 SCC Online SC 2922.
101 *National Legal Services Authority v. Union of India*, AIR 2014 SC 186.
102 *KS Puttaswamy v. Union of India*, AIR 2017 SC 416.
103 *KS Puttaswamy v. Union of India*, AIR 2017 SC 416.
104 The National Policy for Children 2013.
105 Beti Bachao Beti Padhao, Ministry of Women and Child Development, Government of India, https://www.myscheme.gov.in/schemes/bbbp (last visited Nov. 3, 2023).
106 Rashtriya Kishore Swasthya Karyakram, Ministry of Health and Family Welfare, Government of India, https://rksk.in/home (last visited November 3, 2023).
107 Scheme for Adolescent Girls (SAG), https://www.india.gov.in/scheme-adolescent-girls-sag?page=2#:~:text=SABLA%20aims%20at%20empowering%20Adolescent,guidance%20on%20existing%20public%20services (last visited November 3, 2023).
108 Kanyashree Prakalpa, Department of Women Development and Social Welfare, Government of West Bengal (DWD&SW), https://www.wbkanyashree.gov.in/kp_scheme.php (last visited November 3, 2023).
109 Chief Minister Ladli Lakshmi Yojana, Department of Women and Child Development, https://www.cmhelpline.mp.gov.in/Schmedetail.aspx?Schemeid=246 (last visited November 3, 2023).
110 Ladli Social Security Allowance Scheme, Directorate of Social Justice and Empowerment, Haryana Government, https://socialjusticehry.gov.in/ladli-social security-allowance-scheme/ (last visited November 3, 2023).
111 Chief Minister's Girl Child Protection Scheme, Social Welfare and Women Empowerment Department, Government of Tamil Nadu, https://www.tnsocialwelfare.tn.gov.in/en/specilisationschild-welfare/chief-ministers-girl-child-protection-scheme (last visited November 3, 2023).

6

LEGAL RIGHTS OF THE CHILDREN BORN OUT OF LIVE-IN RELATIONSHIPS

Ayushi Srivastava

Introduction

Live-in relationships, also known as cohabitation in many Western countries, involve two unmarried individuals living together in a relationship that resembles marriage.[1] Live-in relationships, or cohabitation, have seen a significant rise in prevalence over the years, transforming from a relatively uncommon practice to a more visible and accepted reality in many parts of the world, though not uniformly. This shift is marked by both an increase in the number of couples choosing to live together outside of marriage and a growing, although not universal, legal and social recognition of these relationships.[2]

In India, this concept is relatively new and is often perceived as a Western cultural import. While live-in relationships are becoming more common, particularly in urban areas, they still face significant social and legal challenges due to the country's deeply rooted cultural and traditional norms.[3] Similarly, in the United States, cohabitation was once seen as rare and deviant behavior.[4] Data from the U.S. Census Bureau shows a dramatic increase in cohabiting couples, from about 450,000 in 1960 to nearly 3 million in 1990.[5] In India, the trend has also been upward, particularly since around 2000.[6]

A live-in relationship is generally defined as two unmarried individuals cohabiting with the intention of sharing their lives, responsibilities, and emotional bonds, similar to a married couple but without undergoing a formal legal or religious marriage ceremony. Despite the increasing prevalence of such relationships, Indian society largely views them with skepticism. Traditional values still dominate public perception, and older generations,

DOI: 10.4324/9781003607076-9

especially in rural areas, often see live-in relationships as immoral or socially unacceptable.[7] However, younger generations, influenced by globalization and changing societal norms, are more open to this arrangement, particularly in metropolitan cities.

The debate surrounding live-in relationships in India often hinges on the tension between societal morality and legal recognition. While these relationships remain highly stigmatized and are widely perceived as immoral, the Supreme Court has consistently maintained that morality and criminality are distinct concepts.[8] This distinction aligns with the broader principle of constitutional morality, which ensures that individual freedoms are upheld regardless of prevailing social prejudices.[9]

Despite some legal acknowledgment, there is no specific law comprehensively regulating live-in relationships in India. This lack of a clear legal framework creates uncertainty regarding the rights and obligations of partners, particularly concerning property, inheritance, and financial support. Unlike marriage, which imposes well-defined legal and social responsibilities, live-in relationships remain largely unregulated, making them more flexible but also legally ambiguous.[10]

Another significant concern is the perception that live-in relationships are "walk-in and walk-out" arrangements, meaning that either partner can leave without legal repercussions. While this flexibility may be appealing to some, it also raises concerns about stability, particularly in cases where one partner (often the woman) is financially or emotionally dependent on the other.[11] However, it is worth noting that modern marriages, too, are increasingly subject to dissolution, with rising divorce rates in India, thereby challenging the notion that live-in relationships are inherently less stable than formal marriages.

Live-in relationships have also been compared to adultery, especially in conservative circles. However, the two concepts are legally and morally distinct. While adultery involves extramarital affairs and was previously criminalized under Indian law,[12] live-in relationships involve two consenting unmarried individuals and are not inherently illicit. The judiciary has clarified that granting legal recognition to live-in relationships does not equate to validating adultery.[13]

Live-in relationships in India represent a shifting social landscape where traditional norms are being challenged and re-evaluated. While the judiciary has taken steps to provide legal protection to individuals in such relationships, societal acceptance remains inconsistent. The increasing recognition of live-in relationships highlights the need for a more explicit legal framework to safeguard the rights of partners, particularly women and children. As Indian society continues to evolve, the legal system will likely need to adapt to these changing dynamics, balancing personal freedoms with social stability.[14]

International Scenario

The international scenario regarding live-in relationships, also known as cohabitation, reveals a diverse landscape with varying degrees of social acceptance and legal recognition across different countries. While some nations, particularly in the West, have made significant strides in acknowledging and regulating these relationships, others still face legal ambiguities and societal resistance, resulting in inconsistent recognition and protection.

In many Western countries, cohabitation, often termed "de facto" relationships, has achieved substantial legal recognition, with laws designed to protect the rights and responsibilities of cohabiting partners.[15] These laws frequently address property division, inheritance, and financial support upon separation. For instance, in the United Kingdom, legal protections are in place concerning the economic rights of women within these relationships, which are similar to concerns in the United States.[16] The existence of these various laws and policies can be considered as one step toward access to justice for women.

In the United States, cohabitation has transitioned from being a rare and atypical behavior to a more common experience, especially among younger adults, though legal recognition can vary considerably between states. There are specific laws that address the rights of cohabitants but no uniform approach. The legal system in the United States may use the concept of "palimony"[17] when addressing the rights of cohabitants, but some courts may require cohabitation to maintain a claim, while others do not. Courts in the United States might recognize property rights based on unjust enrichment or an express contract.[18]

Several countries also have family maintenance schemes that allow courts to override a deceased's estate plans to provide for dependents, which sometimes include cohabiting partners. These schemes exist in the United Kingdom, New Zealand, Australia, and Canada.[19] In England and other Commonwealth jurisdictions, the Testator's Family Maintenance scheme allows judges to revise a will to support dependents and relatives.[20]

Sweden has enacted laws concerning cohabitants' mutual homes, which have also been extended to same-sex relationships. The Swedish Law on Cohabitants' Mutual Home makes a five-or-more-year period of cohabitation strong evidence of a fully matured relationship.[21]

In Queensland, Australia, there is a proposed intestacy statute that includes de facto partners and requires that the couple live together on a genuine domestic basis, while also balancing factors similar to those listed in Professor Waggoner's proposed statute. This proposal, along with that of New Hampshire, also includes a requirement that the cohabitants must have been living together for a fixed time before the death of one partner.[22]

China's inheritance system incorporates the value of reciprocity, which can result in courts considering a potential heir's behavior toward the decedent when making decisions about inheritance rights. This means that Chinese courts might adjust the share of an estate, rewarding someone who cared for the decedent or punishing someone who did not.[23]

Across these various countries, a common theme is the determination of whether a live-in relationship is "marriage-like," with courts considering the duration, commitment, and public presentation of the relationship. Many jurisdictions also face the problem of how to address the lack of a comprehensive legal framework, which often results in ambiguities and uncertainties in the rights of cohabiting partners. Legal systems also struggle to balance the need to recognize evolving relationship models with long-standing social and legal traditions. While some countries have adopted comprehensive measures, others are still trying to navigate this complex issue.

Children Born Out of Live-In Relationships

In India, there are conflicting views in terms of the status of a live-in relationship. The choice concerning a partner is an individualistic decision, one which cannot be forced upon by the state. So, whereas, on the one hand, the social perception is that such relationships are immoral and should not be practiced, there is another set of petitions in the court seeking protection orders.[24]

In cases like *S. Khushboo v. Kanniammal*[25] and *Indra Sarma v. V.K.V. Sarma*,[26] the Supreme Court clarified that while live-in relationships may not conform to traditional societal expectations, they are neither illegal nor criminal. This stance reflects the principle established in *Manoj Narula v. Union of India*,[27] where the court emphasized that constitutional morality, rather than fluctuating public morality, should guide legal interpretations. The judiciary has repeatedly invoked this doctrine in landmark cases such as *Navtej Singh Johar v. Union of India*[28] and *Joseph Shine v. Union of India*,[29] reinforcing that legal protection cannot be denied merely because a practice is deemed unacceptable by a section of society.

The recognition of live-in relationships under laws like the Protection of Women from Domestic Violence Act (PWDVA), 2005, demonstrates this shift toward constitutional morality. The Supreme Court of India has affirmed that living together falls under the right to life and personal liberty as enshrined in Article 21 of the Indian Constitution.[30] PWDVA includes live-in relationships under the definition of "domestic relationships,"[31] thereby providing legal protection to women in such partnerships.[32] This development acknowledges the vulnerability of women in live-in relationships and ensures that they have some legal recourse in cases of abuse or abandonment.[33]

A key legal phrase associated with live-in relationships in India is "relationship in the nature of marriage," as outlined in the PWDVA. This term has been the subject of judicial debate, as courts have had to determine whether live-in partners qualify for legal protections similar to those granted to married couples. The judiciary has emphasized that not all live-in relationships can be considered equivalent to marriage – only those that exhibit characteristics similar to a marital union, such as exclusivity, shared responsibilities, and long-term commitment, may be recognized under this category.[34]

Legal Status

In India, the legal status of children born within live-in relationships has been progressively defined. The issue of the legitimacy of children born out of live-in relationships comes into the picture as the legal status of such relationships is questionable, and the difficulty of the same percolates to such children. Section 16 of the Hindu Marriage Act, 1955, and Section 26 of the Special Marriage Act, 1954 confer legitimacy upon children born out of marriages that are either void or voidable. These provisions state that "children born from a marriage that is null and void or where a decree of nullity is granted in the case of a voidable marriage shall be considered legitimate or deemed to be legitimate, respectively."

It is firmly established in the legal framework of the country that no child should be deprived of their rights merely because they are born out of a void or voidable marriage. This legal stance is grounded in the principle that children should not be denied fundamental rights simply because their parents were not legally married, ensuring that they are treated as legitimate by construction.[35] The aim is to shield children born to such relationships from systemic discrimination.

In the case of *Tulsa v. Durghatiya*,[36] the Supreme Court held that a child born from such a relationship should not be considered illegitimate. Along with this, it was also held that the cohabitation between the parents should be for a substantial period of time, demonstrating genuine commitment to the relationship. Now the understanding gained through this interpretation forms part of a workable system, but it is not clear on the point of a "substantial period of time" to determine the consequent rights of the child in such relationships. The Supreme Court held in *S.P.S. Balasubramanyam v. Suruttayan*[37] that

> if a man and woman are living under the same roof and cohabiting for some years, there will be a presumption under Section 114 of the Evidence Act that they live as husband and wife and the children born to them will not be illegitimate.[38]

Legal Implications on Children

In India, the legal and social rights of individuals in live-in relationships, and particularly the rights of their children, can be categorized into property rights, custody, maintenance, and social implications. While the legal system has made some strides toward recognizing these rights, social acceptance remains a challenge.

Property Rights

Section 16,[39] through the jurisprudential interpretation, may confer legitimacy upon a child born from a live-in relationship. When read strictly, it can be made out that Section 16(3) imposes restrictions on the inheritance rights of such children, limiting them solely to the property of their parents. This means that children born from live-in relationships have a legal right to inherit any property a parent has acquired independently, rather than through inheritance, which can be passed on to their children, irrespective of the parent's marital status.[40] This recognition ensures that such children are not left without financial security solely due to the nature of their parents' relationship.

However, a significant limitation exists concerning ancestral or coparcenary property.[41] The Supreme Court has ruled that children born to live-in relationships do not have an automatic claim to such property. Ancestral property refers to assets inherited across generations, typically within a Hindu Undivided Family. Unlike children born within marriage, those from live-in relationships do not enjoy the same legal presumption of inheritance rights in this regard, restricting their entitlement to family wealth.[42]

Despite this limitation, there have been judicial observations suggesting a potential shift in inheritance laws. Some interpretations of Section 16(3) of the Hindu Marriage Act indicate that children of live-in relationships could, in the future, be granted rights over ancestral property. In the landmark case of *Vidyadhari v. Sukhrana Bai*,[43] the Supreme Court set a precedent by recognizing the inheritance rights of children born from a live-in partnership and granting them the status of "active heirs." In the case of *Revansidapa v. Malikarjun*,[44] the court highlighted that the term "property" in this context does not differentiate between ancestral and self-acquired property. Therefore, children from live-in relationships may inherit both types of property. The Supreme Court, in the case, recognized the inheritance rights of four children born from a live-in relationship, designating them as "legal heirs."

Custody

Custody of children is determined primarily by the principle of the best interests of the child, irrespective of the parent's marital status or sexual orientation. The courts are expected to consider the child's physical, emotional, and financial well-being when making custody decisions. While there are established legal frameworks for married couples,[45] the legal landscape is less clear for unmarried couples, especially those in live-in relationships or non-heterosexual unions. Children from non-traditional families may face discrimination or lack adequate support, highlighting a need to ensure that legal protections are extended to all children, regardless of their parents' relationship. This includes not only children born to unmarried couples but also those adopted by single parents or unmarried couples, especially in the event of relationship breakdown, and the legal mechanisms for enforcing this are not fully developed. In addition, if a single person adopts a child and enters a relationship, the law is not clear about the custody of the child should the relationship break down.

Maintenance

The responsibility to provide for the well-being of another person is also legally defined as maintenance. This becomes exceptionally crucial for a child born out of a live-in relationship. Section 21 of the Hindu Adoptions and Maintenance Act, 1956, outlines that a legitimate son or a minor son of a predeceased son, or a legitimate unmarried daughter, or an unmarried daughter of a son, or the unmarried daughter of a predeceased son shall be considered dependents entitled to maintenance from their father or the estate of their deceased father. However, this section of the Act does not directly cover an infant born from a live-in partnership, resulting in the denial of the right to claim maintenance under this law but states that a son, whether born within or outside of a legal marriage, has the right to maintenance from his father or his deceased father's estate if he is a minor. In the landmark case of *Dimple Gupta vs. Rajiv Gupta*,[46] the judiciary utilized its authority to promote the goals of social justice by declaring that an illegitimate child from an illicit relationship is eligible for maintenance under Section 125 of the Code of Criminal Procedure, 1973, which provides support to minor children, regardless of their legitimacy, and extends even after they reach adulthood if they are unable to support themselves.

Courts generally treat children from legal and illegitimate unions equally regarding maintenance rights, prompting calls for equitable treatment of property rights. Denying maintenance to a child born to a live-in couple may be challenged under Article 32 of the Indian Constitution, asserting a violation of constitutional rights of life and personal liberty. The Kerala High Court, in *PV Susheela vs. Komalavally*,[47] emphasized that such denial could deprive a person of their right to lead a dignified life. Despite court declarations emphasizing fair treatment of children born from various relationships, disparities persist. Notably, children born outside of live-in situations are treated fairly after assertions that differential treatment would breach Article 14.

Section 13[48] of the Hindu Minority and Guardianship Act, 1956, underscores that the child's welfare is paramount and should be interpreted broadly, prioritizing the child's development over other considerations. The state has the duty to act as parens patriae in such cases.[49]

Conclusion

The evolving landscape of live-in relationships in India represents a significant departure from traditional societal norms. Judicial pronouncements have progressively recognized the legitimacy of such unions, affirming the right to choose one's partner and acknowledging the legal status of children born from these relationships. However, despite these advancements, a critical gap remains due to the absence of a comprehensive legal framework explicitly addressing the rights and responsibilities of live-in partners and their children. The judiciary has played a crucial role in dismantling legal barriers and also consequently social barriers in some ways. The issues of inheritance, financial security, parental rights, and protection from exploitation need more function-based approaches. A function-based approach focuses on the purpose or role something serves rather than its inherent nature or status.[50] It comes from a more flexible and dynamic understanding of the relationships. For example, instead of only providing protection from abuse to spouses and a limited class of cohabitants, a function-based approach would provide protection to anyone who has an interdict against abuse, based on the need to prevent harm, regardless of their relationship status. Similarly, a functional view of the family would consider how the relationship operates rather than its precise legal status and may include same-sex couples, step-parents, and other individuals who fulfill a parental role.[51]

The Model Code on Indian Family Law 2024[52] offers a forward-looking approach to family law reform, advocating for the recognition of stable unions beyond traditional marriage. This includes revising inheritance laws, ensuring gender justice, and recognizing diverse family structures based on care, dependency, and mutual responsibility. The proposed framework acknowledges the changing realities of relationships and seeks to provide equitable rights to partners and children in non-marital relationships.[53]

To ensure legal clarity and protection for live-in relationships in India, a distinct legislative framework should differentiate them from marriage while providing safeguards through registration or declaration mechanisms. Succession laws must recognize inheritance rights for children and long-term partners based on financial dependency. Safeguards should prevent exploitation, ensuring vulnerable partners have legal recourse. A functional parenthood model should uphold caregiving roles, joint custody, and child welfare. Family law must be modernized to eliminate gender bias, simplify succession, and clarify maintenance rules. Judiciary and executive bodies should adapt to evolving family structures, and public awareness campaigns should reduce stigma.

Notes

1 Surbhi Yadav, *Live-In Relationship Is the Vanishing Point of Marriage*, 5 Indian Journal of Law and Legal Research 2 (2023).
2 Larry L. Bumpass & James A. Sweet, *National Estimates of Cohabitation*, 26 Demography 615, 624 (1989), https://doi.org/10.2307/2061261 (last visited Aug 31, 2024).
3 Yadav, *Live-In Relationship Is the Vanishing Point of Marriage* at 54.
4 Larry L. Bumpass, R. Kelly Raley & James A. Sweet, *The Changing Character of Stepfamilies: Implications of Cohabitation and Nonmarital Childbearing*, 32 Demography 425, 426 (1995), https://read.dukeupress.edu/demography/article/32/3/425/170979/The-Changing-Character-of-Stepfamilies (last visited Feb 2, 2025).
5 Lawrence W. Waggoner, *Marital Property Rights in Transition*, 59 Missouri Law Review 63 (1994).
6 Deepshree Chauhan & Anshul Agrawal, *Security of Live-in Relationship*, 4 International Journal of Law Management & Humanities 123 (2021).
7 Indra Sarma vs VKV Sarma, (2013) 15 SCC 755, 52.
8 *S. Khushboo vs Kanniammal and Ors.*, 2010(2) AC R2082(SC), 30.
9 *Reena vs State of Rajasthan*, S.B. Criminal Writ Petition No. 2183/2024, 10.
10 Anand Singh Prakash, *Legal Conundrum of Live-In Relationship in India: A Judicial Approach*, 9 Law and World 47 (2023), https://lawandworld.ge/index.php/law (last visited Feb 3, 2025).
11 Pronema Bagchi, Anuradha Parasar & Pournima Inamdar, *Changing Dynamics of Marriage as an Institution: An Examination of Normativity into Translation*, 18 Palarch's Journal of Archaeology of Egypt/Egyptology 2452 (2021).
12 Before being struck down in Joseph Shine vs Union of India, AIR 2018 SC 4898.
13 The Times of India, *Live-In Acceptable, Why Not Adultery*, 28 January 2011, http://articles.timesofindia.indiatimes.com/2o11-o1-28/mumbai/28356o771adultery-live-in-relationshipscriminal-offence (last visited Jan 31, 2025).
14 Yadav, *Live-In Relationship Is the Vanishing Point of Marriage* at 54.
15 Amartya Bag, *Succession Rights in Case of Live-in Relationships: An Analysis in the Indian Context*, SSRN Journal (2011), http://www.ssrn.com/abstract=2011751 (last visited Aug 29, 2024).
16 Yadav, *Live-In Relationship Is the Vanishing Point of Marriage* at 60.
17 Marvin vs Marvin (1976) 18 C3d660.
18 D. Velusamy vs D. Patchaiammal, AIR 2011 SUPREME COURT 479, 24.
19 E. Gary Spitko, *An Accrual/Multi-Factor Approach to Intestate Inheritance Rights for Unmarried Committed Partners*, 81 Oregon Law Review (2002) 281.
20 Waggoner, *Marital Property Rights in Transition* at 41.
21 Waggoner, *Marital Property Rights in Transition* at 79.
22 Waggoner, *Marital Property Rights in Transition* at 84.
23 Spitko, *An Accrual/Multi-Factor Approach to Intestate Inheritance Rights for Unmarried Committed Partners* at 282.
24 Suman Meena and Anr. vs State of Rajasthan, S.B. Criminal Writ Petition No. 792/2024 vide order dated 02.08.2024.
25 2010(2) AC R2082(SC).
26 (2013) 15 SCC 755.
27 2014 INSC 568.
28 AIR 2018 SC 4321.
29 AIR 2018 SC 4898.
30 Shafin Jahan vs Ashokan K.M. & Ors., 2018 INSC 222, 16F.
31 Protection of Women from Domestic Violence Act, 2005, § 2(f).
32 Indra Sarma vs VKV Sarma, (2013) 15 SCC 755, 52 at 24.

33 Indra Sarma vs VKV Sarma, (2013) 15 SCC 755, 52 at 10.
34 D. Velusamy vs D. Patchaiammal, AIR 2011 SUPREME COURT 479, 24 at 33.
35 Revansidapa vs Malikarjun, (2011) 11 SCC 1.
36 Appeal (civil) 648 of 2002.
37 AIR 1992 SC 756.
38 AIR 1992 SC 756 at paragraph 6.
39 Section 16, Hindu Marriage Act 1955. [16. Legitimacy of children of void and voidable marriages. (1) Notwithstanding that a marriage is null and void under Section 11, any child of such marriage who would have been legitimate if the marriage had been valid, shall be legitimate, whether such child is born before or after the commencement of the Marriage Laws (Amendment) Act, 1976 (68 of 1976), and whether or not a decree of nullity is granted in respect of that marriage under this Act and whether or not the marriage is held to be void otherwise than on a petition under this Act. (2) Where a decree of nullity is granted in respect of a voidable marriage under Section 12, any child begotten or conceived before the decree is made, who would have been the legitimate child of the parties to the marriage if at the date of the decree it had been dissolved instead of being annulled, shall be deemed to be their legitimate child notwithstanding the decree of nullity. (3) Nothing contained in sub-section (1) or sub-section (2) shall be construed as conferring upon any child of a marriage which is null and void or which is annulled by a decree of nullity under Section 12, any rights in or to the property of any person, other than the parents, in any case where, but for the passing of this Act, such child would have been incapable of possessing or acquiring any such rights by reason of his not being the legitimate child of his parents.]
40 *Bharatha Matha vs R. Vijaya Renganathan*, AIR 2010 SC 2685.
41 Section 16(3), Hindu Marriage Act 1955.
42 *Bharatha Matha vs R. Vijaya Renganathan*, AIR 2010 SC 2685.
43 CIVIL APPEAL NO. 7108 of 2003.
44 (2011) 11 SCC 1.
45 The father is considered to be the natural guardian of his legitimate minor children, according to Article 6 of the 1956 Hindu Minority and Guardianship Act. However, Section 6(b) gives mothers custody rights to children born in illegal relationships. Even if there is a case where the court grants custody of the child to a married male partner, such an interpretation should be only in the child's best interest.
46 Appeal (crl.) 1139 of 2002.
47 I (2000) DMC 376.
48 Section 13. Welfare of minor to be paramount consideration. (1) In the appointment of declaration of any person as guardian of a Hindu minor by a court, the welfare of the minor shall be the paramount consideration. (2) No person shall be entitled to the guardianship by virtue of the provisions of this Act or of any law relating to guardianship in marriage among Hindus, if the court is of opinion that his or her guardianship will not be for the welfare of the minor.
49 Supriyo @ Supriya Chakraborty & Anr. vs Union of India W.P.(C) No. 1011/2022, 134.
50 Alison Cleland, Claire Mcdiarmid & Elaine Sutherland, *Family Dynamics: Contemporary Issues in Family Law* (Jane Scoular ed., Butterworths Tolley 2001) 132.
51 Alison Cleland, Claire Mcdiarmid & Elaine Sutherland, *Family Dynamics: Contemporary Issues in Family Law*, 132.
52 The Model Code on Indian Family Law, https://vidhilegalpolicy.in/research/the-model-code-on-indian-family-law/ (last visited Feb 3, 2025).
53 The Model Code on Indian Family Law, https://vidhilegalpolicy.in/research/the-model-code-on-indian-family-law/ (last visited Feb 3, 2025) at 48.

7

MYRIADS OF VULNERABILITIES OF DISTRESSED CHILD MIGRANTS

A Case Study From Odisha

Sohini Mahapatra, Nikita Pattajoshi, and Rishika Khare

Introduction

With the increasing pace of globalisation and the development of the economy, earning a livelihood amidst growing unemployment has led the working class to go beyond their home states. Migrating for work, whether across international borders, within the country to other states, or within the state to other districts, is not a new trend, and such migration induced by socio-economic factors is often identified as 'distress migration'. While there are no yardsticks to differentiate distressed migration from other types of migrations, according to the Food and Agriculture Organisation, 'all migratory movements made in conditions where the individual and/or the household perceive that the only viable livelihood option for moving out of poverty is to migrate' amount to distressed migration.[1] The distress might be owing to a range of factors like drought or crop failure, resulting in food insecurity or a lack of livelihood options.

Understanding Child Migration

While the migrant labour force or the 'invisible workforce' is one of the most exploited sections in the labour force market, one section that reels under additional layers of vulnerability is the migrant children. The impact that migration has on the rights of children and child welfare could be varied. Children affected by migration can fall into one of the following three categories: firstly, children of migrant workers who are left behind in the home states; secondly, children who migrate with their families looking for better opportunities or means of livelihood; and thirdly, children who migrate

DOI: 10.4324/9781003607076-10

in search of opportunities for themselves, independent of their parents. The Government of India's Protocol on Prevention, Rescue, Repatriation and Rehabilitation of Trafficked and Migrant Child Labour, 2008 (hereinafter referred to as the Child Migrant Rescue Protocol), defines a 'migrant child labour' as 'a child who has moved with or without the family across State borders or even within the same State and is engaged in hazardous work as specified under the Child Labour (Prohibition & Regulation) Act'.[2] It goes on to identify the role of various stakeholders in the rescue and repatriation of migrant children, among others.

The number of children who can be identified as migrants in India is immense. As per the National Sample Survey Office (NSSO), a governmental organisation that conducts large-scale sample surveys, in the year 2007–2008, 62.7 percent of migrant households have child/children in the age group 0–14 years.[3] According to the census in 2011, India has a population of 92.95 million migrant children.[45] As per a study by UNICEF, in 2011, one out of every five migrant workers was a child.[6] It is also worth noting that there has been a steady increase in the number of migrant children since 1991.[7] While these figures by themselves are not alarming, what is worrisome is that the migrant children are as vulnerable as, or sometimes even more vulnerable than, their adult counterparts.

Theoretically, migration amongst children has the potential to open new horizons and make a host of social and economic opportunities available to a child. However, there is no dearth of literature to show that the reality is quite the contrary.[8] Even the National Plan of Action for Children, 2016, identifies 'migrant children' as a category of 'vulnerable children', which is the focal area of the action plan.[9] Migrant children are not only at a high risk of exploitation but also more susceptible to becoming child labourers or victims of trafficking. Even among child labourers as a class, migrant children have longer working hours, are paid less, and have a higher mortality rate.[10]

Further, child migration as a phenomenon is very complex and has varied dimensions interacting with each other, like age, gender, caste, and educational qualification level. Migrant children in themselves cannot be studied as a class, since, within the larger group, they can be further re-grouped into smaller categories based on the parameters mentioned earlier, each facing a different level of vulnerability. For instance, the level of vulnerability of a girl child who migrates with her parents is not the same as that of her male counterpart. Likewise, the plight of a child in a rural-to-rural migration might not be as concerning as that of a child in a rural-to-urban migration. It has been seen that rural-to-urban migration has been one of the causes for increased violence against children.[11] To add to this, some migrant children go on to face caste-based discrimination in the workplace.[12] These migrant children are at a higher risk of being pushed into child marriage. As per the Census,

2011, 33 percent of migrant children were married, in contrast to only 4.5 percent of non-migrant children who were married. These figures represent only the reported cases of child marriage, while many go unreported.

Therefore, migrant children constitute a very heterogeneous group in themselves, and hence any attempt to understand the nature of their vulnerabilities must be done in light of these specific parameters and categorisations.

Background of the Study

Although existing literature and scholarship on child rights and child welfare have justifiably identified child migrant workers as a vulnerable class and studied the nature of their vulnerabilities, there has been little evidence-based research in the context of Odisha to study the ground-level realities.[13] An UNICEF report on migrant children in India has recognised the need for macro- and micro-level studies to aid better planning to address the needs of such children.[14] Even the National Plan of Action for Children, 2013, has identified a lack of adequate data on children and a lack of comprehensive research and data on child migration as key challenges from a policy planning perspective.[15]

This chapter is one such micro-survey across 200 Gram Panchayats in the state of Odisha that fills the gap to a certain extent by providing evidence-based research from the state of Odisha to corroborate the proposition that child migrant workers have multiple layers of vulnerabilities and hence need special attention. Only internal migration, that is, migration to various places within the Indian territory, has been considered for this study. The operational definition used for a 'child migrant' in this context is children who migrated with their families for better livelihood opportunities, for the family and children who migrated for better livelihood opportunities, for themselves, independent of their parents.

Distressed migration from the State of Odisha has been a cause of concern for the Government of Odisha. Historically, western Odisha has seen a huge outflow of migrants owing to various socio-economic reasons, specific to regions in western Odisha like depletion of forest resources and recurring droughts. The 'Dadan' system of labour (i.e. a non-institutionalised method of recruiting workers through contractors and agents for mostly the unorganised sector) and migration has fraught the Odisha labour market for ages. A study by Civil Society Organisations shows that child labour constitutes an important part of such migration, as children from western Odisha accompany parents to work in brick kilns in other states, particularly in southern Indian states like Andhra Pradesh and Tamil Nadu, and are often referred to as *pathurias*.[16] In view of the gravity of the phenomenon, the Government of Odisha has instituted a State Action Plan for Safety and Welfare of Inter-State Migrant Workmen from Odisha and has been undertaking various social mapping exercises to identify key drivers of distress migration and propose policy solutions accordingly.

Methodology

The primary data used in this chapter is an outcome of one such social mapping exercise based on a survey conducted in 200 Gram Panchayats in four districts in the western part of Odisha – Kalahandi, Nuapada, Bargarh, and Balangir. The survey was conducted in the year 2021–22, and the data was collected from September 2021 to January 2022. The research tool used was an interview using a structured questionnaire of all households in migration-prone Gram Panchayats in the four identified migration-prone districts of Odisha. The questionnaire aimed at capturing both quantitative and qualitative information on socio-economic conditions, livelihood patterns, causes and consequences of distress migration, and the perception of the migrant workers.

This study is based on data pertaining to migration, which happened voluntarily, through either a contractor or otherwise. It does not include cases of forced migration, that is, migration owing to being trafficked into another state. This chapter relies on data collected in the previous study to capture varied aspects of child migration.

Limitations

The master dataset used for this chapter captures data on migrations that have happened during the period of three years only preceding 2021. Since the study was focussed on identifying migrating households in particular districts, some of the responses collected indicate the response of the household in general and need not necessarily apply to that of a child in the household.

Law and Policy Framework

Terms like 'child labour' or 'child migrant workers' should be more fictitious rather than real, considering that the Indian legal landscape provides bolstering legislation to prevent the same. 'Child migrant workers' stand at the point of convergence of, primarily, three legislations – the Child Labour (Prohibition and Regulation) Act, 1986 (hereinafter referred as the Child Labour Act), the Inter-State Migrant Workmen (Regulation of Employment and Conditions of Service) Act, 1979 (hereinafter referred as the ISMW Act), and the Right to Free and Compulsory Education Act, 2009 (hereinafter referred as the RTE Act). Each of these legislations was passed with the intention of protecting children and securing their rights, in one form or the other. However, the data collected through the household survey clearly reveals that somewhere the implementation of these legislations has been frustrated.

The Constitution under Article 24 expressly prohibits the employment of children below the age of 14 years, in any factory, mine, or hazardous employment. The primary legislation prohibiting child labour is the Child Labour (Prohibition and Regulation) Act, 1986, which clearly mandates that no child, that is, a person who has not completed 14 years of age, shall be employed or permitted to work in any occupation or process.[17] The only exceptions to this are children working in the audio-visual entertainment industry and in family enterprises, though they should be non-hazardous and not during school hours. To understand whether an industry is hazardous or not, reference to the schedule of the statute is pertinent, wherein mines and factories using inflammable substances or explosives and hazardous processes as defined under Section 2(cb) of the Factories Act, 1948, have been listed as hazardous industries. Furthermore, the Factories Act, 1948, in its First Schedule provides an elaborate list of industries which involve hazardous processes. The Odisha Child and Adolescent Labour (Prohibition and Regulation) Rules, 1994, further bifurcate in its schedule into 'occupations' and 'processes' wherein employment of children is completely prohibited.

In addition to this list, Section 87 of the Factories Act prohibits employment of children in any manufacturing process or industry, which, in the opinion of the State government, is a 'dangerous operation'. Rule 96 of the Odisha Factories Rules, 1950, provides an extensive list of 'dangerous operations'. Thus, it may be inferred that the employment of children in any occupation whatsoever, especially in hazardous industries or dangerous operations, is violative of the fundamental right of children as well as of the Child Labour Act and Factories Act.

The Child Labour Act cannot be viewed in isolation but rather must be contextualised conjointly with the RTE Act. The objective of the RTE Act is to fulfil the goal of Article 21A of the Constitution, which makes free and compulsory education for children between the ages of 6 and 14 a fundamental right. Both the statutes, the Child Labour Act and the RTE Act, emphasise children going to school. The proviso to Section 3 of the Child Labour Act clearly states that even when children are helping in family enterprises it should be beyond school hours or during vacations. The corresponding 1994 Odisha Rules further elucidate this, expressly mentioning that a child shall not be engaged in any task or helping, which interfaces with or hinders the right to education of a child.[18] Thus, the education of children is non-contestable. Furthermore, as per the RTE Act, providing 'compulsory education' creates an obligation on the appropriate government as well as the local authorities to ensure free elementary education, as well as ensuring that 'children belonging to the disadvantaged group'[19] and 'children belonging to the weaker section'[20] are not prevented from pursuing and completing elementary education on any grounds.[21] As per the 2017 notification of the School and Mass Education Department, Government of Odisha,[22] a child belonging to disadvantaged group means

> the child belonging to SC, ST and SEBC categories and child without any home and settled place, ostensible means of subsistence, found begging, child labour, street child, child with special needs, child in a foster care, rescued child, child of manual scavenger, migrants, construction/building worker, road worker, child of landless agricultural labour, child of single/ widow parent, child of war martyr/war widow and child living with or affected by HIV

and child belonging to weaker section means 'child belonging to below poverty line (BPL) family or beneficiary or card-holders of different poverty elimination programmes of Government'. Therefore, any child migrant worker pursuing employment or the child of any migrant worker belongs to the disadvantaged group and weaker section. Thus, such children forgoing their education due to any compulsion, whether they are working due to financial needs or working because they are accompanying their migrant parents, are being deprived of their fundamental right to education.

The Constitution, coupled with the Child Labour Act and the RTE Act, makes it quite unambiguous that the employment of children or merely a child working in any occupation or process compromising on their education is not permissible under the law. The law states penalties for the acts and specifies that such children shall be rescued and rehabilitated. Migration of children often forces them to drop out of school and become part of the workforce, either reluctantly or voluntarily, to contribute towards the financial status at home. However, migration must not necessarily lead to dropping out of school. Section 5 of the RTE Act provides for the transfer of the child from one school to another, either within or outside the State, where the head teacher or teacher-in-charge is supposed to facilitate the process by issuing a transfer certificate. Not just the State, local authorities, or school staff but even the parents and guardians of a child have the duty to ensure that their child or ward receives elementary education. An understanding of all the legislation, together with the State rules, clearly indicates that, *first*, every child is entitled to compulsory elementary education and, *second*, a child must not be thrown into the shadows of child labour. The onus in both cases lies upon the State, local authorities, school authorities, parents, as well as guardians, except the child themself. A child who is a victim of the circumstances is dependent on others to secure their fundamental right to education and the prohibition of child labour is duly protected.

Article 39(e) of the Constitution entails that 'the State shall direct its policy towards ensuring that the tender age of children are not abused and that citizens are not forced by economic necessity to enter avocations unsuited to their age or strength'. Children migrating for purposes of work fall under both categories: firstly, they are abused due to the inherent vulnerabilities associated with their tender age. This kind of abuse could range from being exploited by the employer, physically and/or verbally or just being compelled to work when they should be focusing on education. Secondly, they are often forced into avocations not suitable for their age or strength, driven by economic necessity. Many child migrant workers accompanying their migrant parents end up doing the same kind of work that their parents as adults are employed to do. This may sometimes require lifting heavy loads to working in extreme inhuman conditions or working for long duration of hours at abysmal or almost no pay. Further, Article 39(f) directs the State to ensure 'that children are given opportunities and facilities to develop in a healthy manner and in conditions of freedom and dignity and that childhood and youth are protected against exploitation and against moral and material abandonment'. Thus, even a single child migrant worker is a testament to the State's failure to implement these directives.

The idea is not to take away from the initiatives that the States take to tackle these issues, especially the State of Odisha, but rather to bring forth the gap between the initiatives and beneficiaries. As part of the Sarva Siksha Abhiyaan Odisha initiative, the Government of Odisha has established 'Seasonal hostels' – a scheme dedicated specially for children of migrant families in the districts of Balangir, Kalahandi, Nuapada, Bargarh, and Mayurbhanj. The scheme is directed towards targeting child labourers, dropout children, and out-of-school children. The objective of the scheme is twofold:

1. Setting up seasonal hostels (residential) at the source points to prevent migration in the first place
2. In case of migration, to provide elementary education at the destination points, that is, Cuttack and Khordha, through non-residential Special Training during school hours

The idea of seasonal hostels is to prevent discontinuity of education propelled through migration. However, the scheme is applicable only to destination points within the State. The premise that children will not migrate out of state with their parents or on their own, no matter what, may not always be correct. While residential seasonal hostels for children of migrant workers in the migration-prone districts are a good starting point, the possibility of even a few children accompanying their parents or going on their own to find work, thereby forfeiting their education cannot entirely be negated. There needs to be a system wherein inter-state migrant children also get access to elementary education at the destination points beyond their home State. Thus, the percolation of this idea to the actual intended beneficiaries needs to be tested through the findings of the survey.

The third legislation which hovers over child migrant workers is the ISMW Act. This legislation is the primary act governing all inter-state migrant workers, in establishments where five or more such workers are employed and to contractors who employ five or more inter-state migrant workers.[23] Additionally, the Act defines inter-state migrant workers as 'migrant workers who are recruited by or through a contractor in one State under an agreement or other arrangement for employment in an establishment in another State, whether with or without the knowledge of the principal employer'.[24] Thus, at the very onset, the statute confines the meaning and understanding of an inter-state migrant worker, as in cases of less than five migrant workers either working in an establishment or working for a contractor, the Act would have no relevance. Also a person who, without an intermediary or a contractor, on his/her own, goes to another State in search of employment will also be outside the purview of the statute. This could essentially leave out a significant number of people outside the ambit of the ISMW Act. Presuming that the Act is applicable to an establishment or to a contractor, the legislation still does not, whether directly or indirectly, address children who are inter-state migrant workers. This does not imply that children do not migrate; it means only that the wage rates, conditions of service, issuing a passbook, displacement allowance, journey allowance, and other facilities that are applicable to adult migrant workers will not be extended to children because the Act does not impose such obligations. The statute also directs that every establishment and contractor employing inter-state migrant workers must maintain a register with the particulars of each worker, such as name, age, sex, nature of employment, and other pertinent details as prescribed in the State rules. However, since children fall outside the purview of the Act, and combined with the fact that child labour is prohibited, it is highly probable that child migrant workers do not find an entry in any of these registers, thereby making them entirely invisible in the workforce yet prone to exploitation.

While analysing the vulnerabilities of child migrant workers, it is also pertinent to look at it through the lens of marriage. The definition of a child in the context of child labour and right to education is starkly different from that given under the Prohibition of Child Marriage Act 2006 (hereinafter referred to as the 'Child Marriage Act'). Under Section 2(a), a male below 21 years of age and a female below 18 years of age are a 'child'. Therefore, hypothetically, if a girl is somewhere between the ages of 14 and 18 years and is migrating for employment, she may not be child labour as per the law, and her right to education may not be getting violated even if she is not pursuing education. Nonetheless, she is a child as per the Child Marriage Act and, if married, is a punishable offence under the said Act. Though there has been a move to increase the minimum age of marriage of females to 21 years, the law is still pending with the Indian parliament. Marriage is one of the chief reasons for migration across age groups, and even if children migrating are not employed but are migrating because they are married and have to accompany their spouses, they are equal victims at the hands of the non-implementation of the law.

Findings and Analysis

The findings in this chapter are a result of surveying a total of 82,620 households. Out of the 1,23,481 respondents, 62,053 were found to be migrants. Within these 1,23,481 respondents, 8607 were children aged between 1 and 14 years who migrated with their parents and hence fall within the operational definition of 'child migrants' laid down in earlier parts of this chapter. While there are many ways to assess the vulnerability of migrant children, this chapter starts with assessing their vulnerability based on three parameters: education status, marital status, and migration status.

Level and Status of Education of Migrant Children

As mentioned earlier, the right to free and compulsory education, that is, elementary education, is guaranteed under the Constitution as well as the RTE Act, for children between the ages of 6 and 14 years. Out of the total children who were surveyed, 18,319 were found to be in the said age group.

Figure 7.1 shows that in the age group of 6 to 14 years, 8 percent (1237) of children are still illiterate and not part of the education system at all, while only a mere 1691 have completed elementary level of education. The

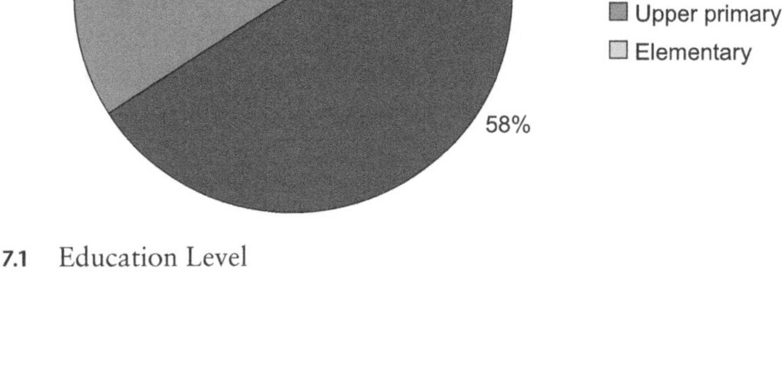

FIGURE 7.1 Education Level

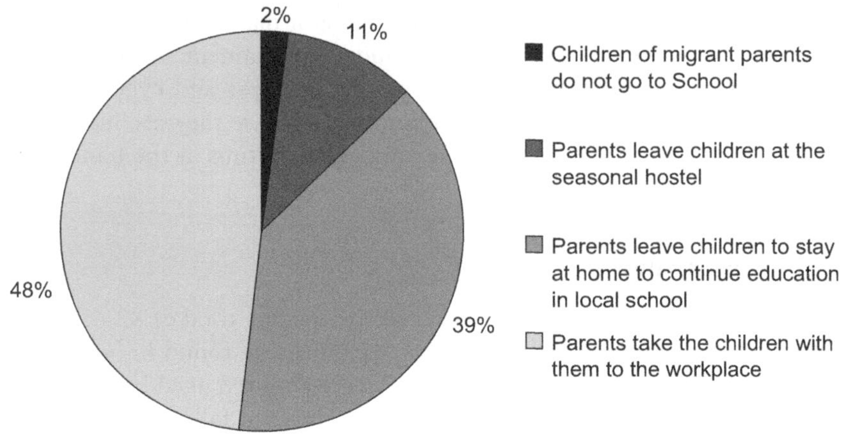

FIGURE 7.2 Status of Education When Parents Migrate

majority of the children, that is, 58 percent (8978), have completed only primary education, whereas 23 percent (3593) have completed upper primary. Thus, the findings clearly reflect the poor implementation of the RTE Act as well as the guarantee Article 21A.

To further understand the status of the education of children, it is noteworthy to look at the response of parents who are migrating. Figure 7.2 represents situations where both parents are migrating to other States. The majority of the parents who migrate (6908) take their children with them to the workplace. This results in children either becoming part of the workforce themselves or assisting their parents in domestic duties. In either situation, these children have to sever ties with the education system. An ancillary problem with children accompanying parents to other States is also language. Most public schools offer education in the regional language, and pursuing education becomes a challenge for a child migrating from Odisha to another State, with a language that he/she is not accustomed to. It is assuring to see that 39 percent of parents (5603) leave their children behind at home and 11 percent (1518) leave them at government seasonal hostels to continue with their education in the local schools. Thus, it may be deduced that seasonal hostels as a welfare measure to tackle migration of children and ensure continuity in education are somewhat working; 309 parents have responded that their children do not go to school. This could imply two things – either their children are not of the school-going age or they are out of school by dropping out or not being enrolled in the first place.

Marital Status

To assess whether there is a prevalence of child marriage among females aged 18 years and males up to 21 years (the legal cut-off age) has been considered,

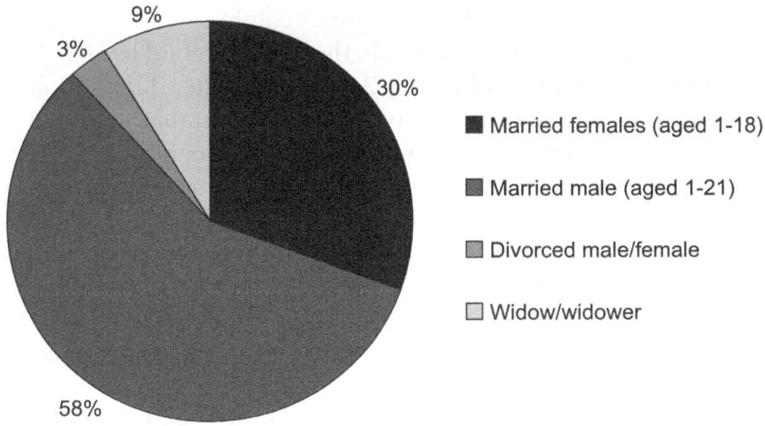

FIGURE 7.3 Marital Status

unlike for education and migration, where the age group considered is only up to 14 years.

While child marriage is entirely prohibited and is a punishable offence, Figure 7.3 shows extensive violation of the statute. Out of the total number of children in the age bracket, 394 females have married before the completion of 18 years of age. The trend of child marriage among males is comparatively higher, with 742 males being married below the age of 21 years. Not only were children found to be married, but they have also been either married and divorced or married and lost their spouse, even before attaining the legal age of marriage. While 3 percent (40) of children were divorced, 9 percent (111) were widowed.

Migration Status

Out of the total number of children in the age group of 1 to 14 years, almost 33 percent were found to have migrated to other States due to one reason or another. Migrating children are broadly of two categories: firstly, those who have their own purpose of migration and the second category is those who accompany their parents. In either case, they are a vulnerable group deprived of their fundamental rights, and the numbers reflected are rather worrisome. A significant number of children, that is, 2078 of them, migrated in search of employment. Thus, irrespective of their educational status, marital status, and the kind of work that they do in the destination State, these children fall under the category of child labour. It also implies that these children going to other States looking for livelihood opportunities clearly are out of school and have forgone their education. About 1721 children migrated to take up employment, which could mean that they are either certain of the place of work that they are going to or have been offered employment in the destination State. Thus, both these categories combined indicate that 52 percent of the migrating children fall within the ambit of child labour. This demonstrates the clear violation of Article 24 as well as the Child Labour Act.

One percent (81) of the children have responded that they migrated primarily to cook for other migrants in the family, and 11 percent (777) migrated to take care of siblings. Both of these categories indicate that children are compelled to fulfil family obligations or provide caregiving duties at the cost of their education and wellbeing. A child migrating to take care of another sibling also indicates that, apart from the respondent child, there are other younger children involved in the situation, who would perhaps have the same fate as the caregiver. It is pertinent to note that when asked about the purpose of migration 2600 children have responded that their purpose of migration is beyond the four specifically indicated in the questionnaire (provided in Figure 7.4). It may be safe to presume that these children could be simply accompanying their parents or family. Irrespective of the purpose of migration, it is clear that in all the situations mentioned these children are certainly not pursuing education. Children are permitted to work or help only in family enterprises, subject to that not affecting their education. However, the data clearly indicates otherwise.

Nature of Employment

Since the primary reason for migration amongst children is employment, it is pertinent to delve into the nature of employment as well. The law prohibits engaging children in any occupation or hazardous processes whatsoever. However, the survey findings reveal that children are employed in hazardous

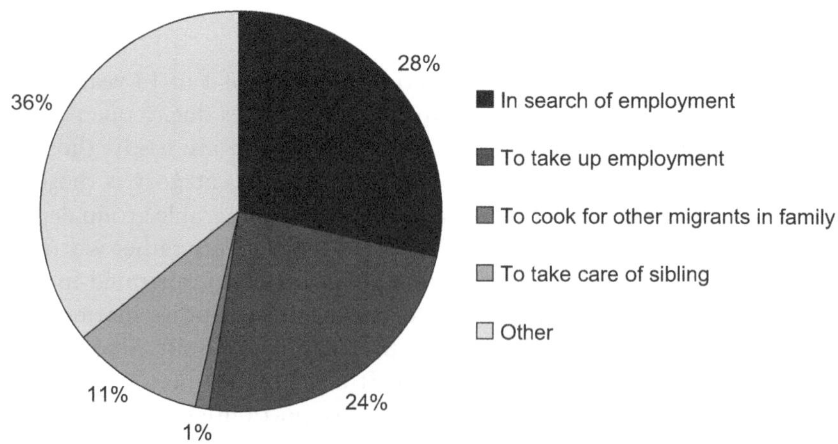

FIGURE 7.4 Purpose of Migration

or dangerous operations as well. The majority of children (2909 of them) were said to have been working in brick kilns. This may possibly be because the majority of the adult respondents in this survey were also found to be employed in brick kilns. Thus, it may be presumed that these children working in brick kilns are either accompanying their parents, who are employed in brick kilns and therefore end up working there, or it could be that brick kilns are the most sought-after option for migrant workers from Odisha. 'Manufacture of refractory bricks' is listed as a dangerous operation under the Odisha Factories Rules; however, the survey does not clarify the kind of brick-making process that the children are involved in.

Children have also been found to be working as daily labourers (159), in textile and cotton industries (1), as well as working at building and construction sites (13), as domestic servants (10) and bakery (1), amongst others. Only 63 children are employed in skilled work. While to the naked eye the graph distribution might seem to be very marginal for these occupations, however, the numbers in themselves are quite concerning: 159 children employed as daily wagers or 13 employed at construction sites may be prone to exploitation due to long duration of work, unpaid or lesser wages, and other such labour right violations.

It is also pertinent to note that a sizeable number of children (592) have migrated to be mere unpaid family workers fulfilling domestic duties, such as cooking and child care. This may also be overlapping with the purpose of migration mentioned earlier; nonetheless, it is clearly perceived as 'unpaid work' by the respondents. A large and substantial number of children (1729) have responded 'any other' as their nature of employment, acknowledging that they are certainly engaged in employment, but the kind of industry/occupation/process or nature of work is not listed herein.

Twenty-six of them have responded that they are self-employed at the destination point. These children, perhaps, pose a perturbing issue – do they qualify as child labour? As per Section 3 of the Child Labour Act, a child is prohibited from being 'employed' or 'permitted to work' in any occupation or process. A self-employed child is not 'employed' by anyone and may not necessarily require 'permission to work', and the kind of work may not be an 'occupation or processes'. Is such a child then covered under the ambit of the Child Labour Act? These children, however, are well within the scope of the RTE Act, and not pursuing education is a clear violation of the legislation and their fundamental right to education.

Socio-Economic Dynamics of the Families of Migrating Children

A simple answer to 'why does distress migration happen?' could perhaps be – to seek better employment opportunities and wages. However, the answer is affected by the social and economic dynamics of the family, society, and the interested persons in the process of migration. Often, factors like social exclusion, limited access to public resources, and infertility of land may propel a family or its members to migrate.[25] These considerations become relevant when the distress migration amongst children is studied so that any remedial state measure attempting to redress the challenge of distress migration could better target the propelling factors. This section of the chapter explores the socio-economic dynamics of the families of the children who have migrated and assesses the contributing role of these dynamics in furthering the distress migration amongst the surveyed population. The section also explores whether migration has helped families to be in a better socio-economic position, considering the challenges faced by the migrants at their destination.

The survey data indicate that major triggering factors for the migration of families include poverty, landlessness, lack of local employment (including lack of employment for skill-based work), and poor wages in the local employment. These factors together contribute to be responsible for migration of more than 87 of the households. Other reasons include lack of work during the non-agricultural seasons and displacement from the original place of residence.

While the majority are migrating due to financial distress, such challenges appear to be consequent to the social placements of these families through caste and education. In terms of education, the relationship between migration with educational level shows a negative trend. The lower the educational level, the higher the ratio of migration. A very limited migration is reported in persons with degrees of graduation or above. In conjunction with this, the data on the relationship between migration and marital status show that married persons are more likely to migrate than persons who are still single. Arguably, financial responsibilities in a family structure after marriage increase, particularly after having children, nudging the need to migrate for better wages and employment. A combined observation of the education level and marital status indicates that a married person with a better education is less likely to migrate, compared to a married person with lesser education. This potentially gives rise to the possibility that the education of children with educated parents is less likely to be adversely affected due to distress migration. Further, the education of children with parents who migrate with a lesser level of education continues to be hindered. Therefore, the education level and migration patterns can affect the educational outcome of children through generations; as this vicious cycle repeats, the children who become adults with low educational levels get pushed into migration, which in turn affects their children's education too.

The Indian Constitution recognises and categorises certain historically marginalised communities into three broad categories: scheduled castes (SCs), scheduled tribes (STs), and other backward classes (OBCs) for purposes of affirmative action measures and other special safeguards. In line with the constitutional provisions, the caste/social categories recognised for the survey were SCs, STs, OBCs, and the general castes. The survey data also display a strong caste – migration nexus. Migrations among the three constitutionally recognised backward categories are starkly high compared to general category persons – a total of 36 percent migrants from the four districts belong to the ST category, followed by 32.7 percent of SC migrants and 28.6 percent of OBC category persons, whereas only 2.4 percent of persons migrating from the four districts belong to the general category. This indicates the limited opportunities or accessibility that the backward categories have towards employment and the skills needed to undertake employment. The caste factor or social backwardness cannot be looked at in isolation. It must be understood in the context of the resultant economic disadvantages that it can create, by limiting opportunities, accessibility of resources and generational deprivation of social security. Social backwardness, therefore, has a relation to economic backwardness because the migration pattern in the four districts indicates that most of the migrant families are also BPL card holders. All the persons or families holding the BPL cards admitted that they travelled for better wages. Trends of migration also suggest that families that have taken loans are migrating to explore opportunities to pay off their debts with better wages. Traditionally, one of the economic factors that is considered to provide financial stability is the ownership of land. However, land ownership of the families has not necessarily prevented the migration. This is possibly due to the factor of improper irrigation facilities, which is a challenge,[26] as reported by many migrants. Additional challenges may include limited access to credit for agriculture or fertilisers.

The high figures concerning migration raise questions about the effectiveness of the multiple social and financial security measures being offered by the Government of India and the Government of the State of Odisha. In line with the trend of migration among families of BPL cardholders, the data from Balangir, Bargarh, Kalahandi, and Nuapada also indicate that migration is high even when the families hold job cards under the National Rural Employment Guarantee Act, 2005, which ensures a compulsory minimum of 100 days of wage employment to the cardholders per year. Similarly, migration is also persistent in families that get financial benefits through pension schemes of the government, like disability pension or old-age pension. Despite the schemes of the government existing when the data collection was conducted, like the *Kalia Yojana*,[27] *Biju Krusak Kalyan Yojana*,[28] *Ujjwala Scheme*,[29] and affordable housing schemes[30] by the Centre and the State Government, migration continues to be a challenge.

It is evident that the social and economic distressing factors conjunctively contribute to the reasons for families or their members to undertake distress migration. While the purposes of migration are to take up employment with better wages or to search for better employment opportunities, their fulfilment is laden with multiple challenges as well. Major challenges faced by the migrant families (including child migrants as workers and companions) are lack of housing facilities; unsafe work conditions; delay in wage payment; lack of health safety; no wages for overtime work; lesser wages to females; sexual, physical, and verbal abuse; language problem; long working hours; restriction to use mobile phones; fear of local goons; absence of opportunities for recreation; and so on. The survey data also suggest that the wages paid to the workers do not comply with the legal requirement of minimum wages against the hours of work put in by the migrant workers. The challenges faced at the destinations highlight the deplorable work conditions that the migrants have to face. Children migrating as workers see a clear violation of their basic rights as employees, due to the absence of proper and safe working conditions. Further, sexual abuse, overtime working hours, lesser wages, and delayed wages not only violate the basic right against exploitation of child labour[31] but also violate the right against bodily and labour exploitation as a human being.[32] In cases where the child is not migrating as a worker himself but is accompanying parents as they migrate, the challenges like lack of proper housing facility, fear of local goons, and delayed wages (affecting the family's survival) hamper the stable living conditions of the children and violate the sheer dignity of life as a human being which is protected under the right to life[33] guaranteed by the Indian Constitution.

In terms of public services, more than 2000 families with migrants have reported that they did not have access to basic amenities like public distribution services, Anganwadi centres, schools, and primary health care centres at the destination. Some of the reported reasons for the lack of facilities are the long distance between the facility and the workplace, lack of an Aadhaar Card (provides proof of identity and address for Indian citizens) or its copy with the migrant to avail the public service,[34] lack of proper communication due to language problems, and so on. These facilities are a mandate as per the current legal framework; their absence indicates a lack of implementation by the administration. The lack of these basic public services, as reported by the respondents, hampers the children's rehabilitation in the destination, limits their development, and again violates the right to life of children.

The overall assessment of the impact of migration on these families indicates that the financial improvement amongst these families is very limited. Forty-five percent of the migrants have reported that the migration has just helped them to survive without any major upliftment, and 16 percent have reported that there was no change in their economic condition and 'admitted that their life was no less miserable in destination centres than in their home villages'.[35] Only 27 percent of the migrants report that they have been able to save some money. Therefore, while we see an influx of inter- and intrastate migrants from these four districts in Odisha, the purposes for which migration takes place do not seem to be getting fulfilled, yet the families' living conditions get distorted with just the hope of a better future through migration.

The Government of India and the State of Odisha have rolled out multiple social security measures to ensure that distress migration is prevented. The trend in Odisha shows gaps in the complete dissemination of the benefits of the schemes. The concerns are heightened, particularly when the absence of benefit percolation in society creates an opportunity for exploitation of the vulnerable. The vulnerability of these families proves beneficial for the contractors, middlemen, and employers at the destinations to exploit them and avoid upholding the basic rights of the workers and their families. In this default system, children become the ultimate sufferers whose future is stuck in a vicious cycle of vulnerabilities due to the lack of protection and resources in the present.

Conclusion

The National Policy for Children, 2013, identifies four key priority areas for safeguarding the rights of children's education and development; health and nutrition; protection; and participation.[36] The results and findings in this chapter indicate how, in two of the four priority areas (education and development, and health and nutrition), child rights protection is jeopardised.

The results and findings on the level of educational qualification of the migrant children (Figure 7.1) reflect a very sad state of affairs about the child's right to education and development. Even for children who have migrated with their parents, continuing their education has sometimes become a challenge, as inferred from Figure 7.2.

Further, as discussed under socio-economic dynamics, many migrant households with children do not have access to public services like the Public Distribution System (PDS) system (an affordable food grain distribution system managed by the Government of India). Lack of access to such basic amenities can have adverse impacts on the level of impoverishment and health of the children associated with the migrant households. While attempts have been made to ensure greater accessibility to the PDS system by allowing portability of various benefits from one state to another, the Supreme Court's direction to the Centre to implement the 'One Nation One Ration card' scheme,[37] enabling inter-state migrants to obtain food provisions even in their destination States, the scheme has not been given full effect. Further, there are findings that raise doubts about the availability of stable living arrangements for the migrant households. This, in turn, can impact the level of development and protection available to a child.

Therefore, the results and findings in this chapter indicate a clear violation of various aspects of the rights of the child as envisaged by the National Policy of 2013.

Violation of Other Laws

The results and findings not just throw light on the violation of the rights of children, as discussed earlier but also highlight the under-enforcement of various other welfare legislations like the Right to Education Act. The findings and analysis on the educational aspect have shown how the children of migrant workers have either stopped going to school or have never enrolled in a formal education system. The data also speak volumes about the under-enforcement of the child marriage prohibition laws, as 1136 instances of child marriages have been seen amongst these migrant children.

Figure 7.5 indicates that at least ten of the migrant children under study worked as domestic help in the destination state. This is also in gross violation of legal provisions on child labour in light of the Government of India notification in October 2006[38] to list employment of children as domestic workers as one of the hazardous occupations under the Child Labour (Prohibition and Regulation) Act 1986.

Further, as indicated in Figure 7.5, some of the migrant children work in the unorganised sector or in workplaces which may be called a 'regulatory

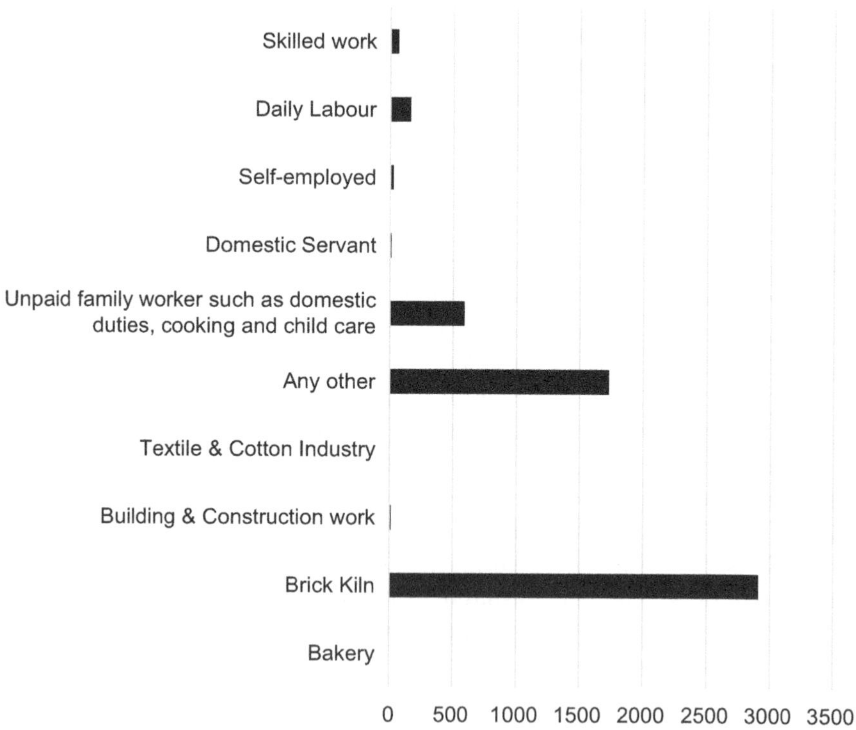

FIGURE 7.5 Nature of Employment

blind spot'. Some of these workplaces engaging migrant children, like a *dhaba* (roadside eatery) or a brick kiln, remain unregulated under any law, and, therefore, such cases of child migration and child labour usually go unnoticed and unreported.

Suggestions for Policy Framework

Framing legal and policy responses to curb distress migration among children is way more complex than legal and policy responses to curb distress migration among adults. Since the key push factor for distress migration of adults is a lack of employment opportunities or adequate means of livelihood in the origin state, this can be remedied by providing employment opportunities to such adults. However, the problem of children migrating in search of work cannot be remedied by providing work/employment at the origin, in view of the ban on child labour. Therefore, curbing child migration needs the development of a multi-pronged strategy.

At the outset, attempts to curb distressed migration among children must start with attempts to stop child labour and child marriage in India. It is worrisome when 'marriage' becomes a reason for child migration, exemplifying how one social evil becomes the cause for another, and this deserves policy attention. Though the dataset analysed in this chapter does not indicate marriage as a cause for migration among children, a study by NSSO has found that, for 43.1 percent ST and 35.6 percent SC migrant population, marriage is a significant driver for migration. Also, as per a UNICEF study, one out of three girls has cited marriage as a reason for migration, as per the 2011 census.[39] This indicates that child marriage is a causative factor for child migration. Likewise, child labour as a prevalent practice in many parts of the country has prompted children to migrate in search of such opportunities. Also, a gradual increase in the number of migrations has been contributing to the problem of child labour.[40] Thus, effective implementation of the Child Labour (Prohibition and Regulation) Act, 2016, as well as the Child Marriage Prohibition Act, is the need of the hour.

Secondly, as discussed under socio-economic dynamics, it has been observed that often the levels of education and migration are two parameters that turn into a vicious cycle. There is often an early transition of the children (with minimal education) to the labour market. One way of breaking this cycle is to provide more skill-based education or a vocational curriculum[41] to children so that they enter the workforce with a certain skill set. While this may not solve the problem of child migration altogether, it will ensure that the migrant children are less vulnerable or exploited at the hands of the employers.

The Indian Government's Child Migrant Rescue Protocol has many solutions to offer, none of which are legally binding. Further, though the Protocol has identified specific roles for various stakeholders like the Labour Department and the District Administration, it is fraught with ambiguities regarding the procedure and the stage of intervention.[42]

Any policy intervention by the Government must be wary of the fact that migrant children as a community are not homogeneous, and hence targeted policies may be made for each vulnerable group among migrant children. Therefore, a holistic approach must be taken while framing policies to arrest migration among children. Such policy making must not only focus on improving access to education as a strategy to arrest child migration but must take note of all causative factors. Studies of this nature help to flag various causative factors and socio-economic dynamics in which child migration as a phenomenon operates and thus ensure more informed policy making.

Notes

1 Laura Deotti and Elisenda Estruch, Social Policies and Rural Institutions Division, *Addressing Rural Youth Migration at Its Root Causes: A Conceptual Framework*, United Nations Food and Agriculture Department (Rome) 2016 (Dec. 10, 2023, 10:23 AM) https://www.fao.org/3/i5718e/i5718e.pdf.

2 Ministry of Labour and Employment, Government of India, *Protocol on Prevention, Rescue, Repatriation and Rehabilitation of Trafficked & Migrant Child Labour*, 2008, p. 18 (Nov. 11, 2023, 05:45 PM) https://megpolice.gov.in/sites/default/files/protocol_trafficked_migrant_child_labour.pdf.

3 National Sample Survey Office, M/o Statistics and Programme Implementation, Government of India, *Employment and Unemployment and Migration Particulars in India*, Report No. 531, 64th Round (Jun. 2007–2008).

4 *Census considers any migrant in the age group 0–19 years as a child migrant.*

5 Young Lives Research to Policy Centre, *Understanding Child Migration in India (Research and Policy Brief)* UNICEF (Mar. 2020) https://www.unicef.org/india/media/3416/file/Child-migration-India2020-policy-brief.pdf.

6 Young Lives Research to Policy Centre, *Understanding Child Migration in India (Research and Policy Brief)* UNICEF (Mar. 2020) https://www.unicef.org/india/media/3416/file/Child-migration-India2020-policy-brief.pdf.

7 Ministry of Women and Child Development, Government of India, *National Plan of Action for Children, 2016* (Dec. 2016) https://wcd.nic.in/sites/default/files/National%20Plan%20of%20Action%202016.pdf.

8 S. N. Tripathy, *Distress Migration among Ultra-Poor Households in Western Odisha*, 9(2) Journal of Land & Rural Studies 241 (2021); Ankit Anand, *Understanding Socio-Economic Vulnerabilities in Child Malnutrition between Migrants and Non-Migrants in India*, 15 Child Indicators Research Journal 1871 (2022); Anindita Sengupta, *Migration, Poverty and Vulnerability in the Informal Labour Market in India*, 36(4) The Bangladesh Development Studies 99 (2013).

9 Ministry of Women and Child Development, Government of India, *National Plan of Action for Children, 2016* at 5.

10 International Labour Organization, *Child Labour and Migration* (Dec. 4, 2023, 07:32 PM) https://www.ilo.org/ipec/areas/Migration_and_CL/lang-en/index.htm.

11 Enakshi Ganguli Thukral & Parul Thukral, India Child Rights Index (HAQ Centre for Child Rights, New Delhi 2011).

12 *See* Kavita Chowdhury, *Intersection of Caste and Child Labour in Bihar* 54(4) Economic & Political Weekly (2020).
13 *See* Migration Information and Resource Centre, *Incidence of Child Migration in Western Odisha* (2009), https://lawsdocbox.com/Immigration/103273774-Incidence-of-child-migration-in-western-odisha.html; S.N., *Distress Migration among Ultra-Poor Households in Western Odisha*; Centre for Policy Research, *Improving Social Protection for Migrant Affected Children: Spotlight on Odisha*, UNICEF (2021) https://cprindia.org/wp-content/uploads/2022/02/Odisha-unicef.pdf.
14 Young Lives Research to Policy Centre, *Understanding Child Migration in India (Research and Policy Brief)* at 5.
15 Ministry of Women and Child Development, Government of India, *National Plan of Action for Children, 2016*, at 3 & 32.
16 Migration Information and Resource Centre, *Incidence of Child Migration in Western Odisha*.
17 Child Labour (Prohibition and Regulation) Act 1986, § 3, No. 61, Acts of Parliament, 1986 (India).
18 Odisha Child Labour (Prohibition and Regulation) Rules 1994, Rule 7.
19 Right to Free and Compulsory Education Act 2009, § 2(d), No. 35, Acts of Parliament, 2009 (India).
20 Right to Free and Compulsory Education Act 2009, at § 2(e)
21 Right to Free and Compulsory Education Act 2009, at § 8 & 9.
22 Notification no. SME-EL2-EL2-0035-2017-11360 (Jun. 27, 2017).
23 Inter-State Migrant Workmen (Regulation of Employment and Conditions of Service) Act 1979, § 1(4), No. 30, Acts of Parliament, 1979 (India).
24 Inter-State Migrant Workmen (Regulation of Employment and Conditions of Service) Act 1979, at § 2(e).
25 Labour and ESI Department, Government of Odisha, *Social Mapping of Migrant Workers in Odisha: Phase II*, 2023, p. 162.
26 For the purpose of the study, irrigation facility available to the families owning or having access to land, were divides into three parameters – land is wholly irrigated, partially irrigated or there is no irrigation facility. 86 percent respondents from Balangir district and 81 percent of respondents from Bargarh district have no irrigation facility.
27 *Odisha Kalia Yojana* (Krushak Assistance for Livelihood and Income Augmentation) was started in 2019 to 'increase farmer's livelihood and income'. The scheme aims to 'provide freedom of choice of financial support to the farmers of the state and to motivate them for their empowerment as well as growth and development of agriculture in the state'.
28 *Biju Krushak Kalyan Yojana:* The scheme provides financial support to the farmers by providing health and accident insurance
29 *Pradhan Mantri Ujjwala Yojana:* The scheme was launched in 2016 by the Government of India with an objective to phase out use of traditional fuels for cooking and instead increase rural households' accessibility and affordability of cleaner fuels like LPG.
30 Schemes applicable in the State of Odisha for affordable housing include *Indira Awas Yojana, Pradhan Mantri Awas Yojana, Biju Pucca Ghar Yojana*.
31 India Const. art. 24.
32 India Const. at art. 23, cl. 2.
33 India Const. at art. 21.
34 Yogima Seth Sharma, *Aadhaar Mandatory for All Workers to Avail Social Security Benefits*, Economic Times (May 5, 2021, 04:14 PM) https://economictimes.indiatimes.com/news/economy/policy/aadhaar-mandatory-for-all-workers-to-avail-social-security-benefits/articleshow/82401711.cms.

35 Labour and ESI Department, Government of Odisha, *Social Mapping of Migrant Workers in Odisha* at 163.
36 Ministry of Women and Child Development, *National Policy for Children, 2013*, Resolution No. 16–1/2012/CW-I (Apr. 26, 2013) https://wcd.nic.in/sites/default/files/npcenglish08072013.pdf.
37 In Re: Problems and Miseries of Migrant Labourers with Bandhua Mukti Morcha v. Union of India & Others, 2021 SCC Online SC 441 (India).
38 Notification No. S.O. 1742 (E) (Oct. 10 2006) (Gazette of India, Extraordinary).
39 Young Lives Research to Policy Centre, *Understanding Child Migration in India (Research and Policy Brief)*.
40 HAQ: Centre for Child Rights, *Still Out of Focus: Status of India's Children: Summary Report*, HAQCRC New Delhi (2008) https://haqcrc.org/wp-content/uploads/2016/07/still-out-of-focus-status-of-indias-children-2008-summary-report.pdf.
41 Young Lives Research to Policy Centre, *Understanding Child Migration in India (Research and Policy Brief)*.
42 Ministry of Labour and Employment, Government of India, *Protocol on Prevention, Rescue, Repatriation and Rehabilitation of Trafficked & Migrant Child Labour* at 40–43.

8

ARE THE CHILDREN LACKING AN EXCLUSIVE GREEN SAFEGUARD IN INDIA?

Tanaya Raha

Introduction

Worldwide environmental contamination is the issue which shatters the core existence of human civilization. It seems like the self-ruin of the most intellectually advanced and sophisticated species of the ecosystem to enjoy the optimum material growth. As the whole scenario is absolutely a global issue, collective effort is the only way. Eco-centrism is the elementary philosophy that can only resist the civilization from such natural annihilation through artificial ammunitions in the form of socio-economic proliferation. Though the human race is quite optimistic about its self-assured, scientific and extraordinary existence, eco-centrism actually de-emphasizes the importance of human supremacy for the promotion of the significance of other living creatures like animals, plants, and other living and non-living organisms. In the 19th century the notion of environmental jurisprudence came into prominence to co-relate a balance between human-centric and eco-centric issues.

This balance actually navigates the universal journey of sustainability, which is the most cherished goal to be achieved by the nations. The elemental theme of sustainability is based on the most important notion of inter-generational equity. It values the interest of our descendants, leaving aside any consideration. The present generation should explore nature and natural resources for socio-economic upsurge with appreciable preservation and maintenance for the generations to come. The theory of sustainability is the nucleus of the present global environmental protection expedition, and it has judiciously put emphasis on environmental ethics to maintain inter-generational equity. What environmental jurisprudence lacks is the emphatic focus on both present and future generations. We cannot deny the truth that

DOI: 10.4324/9781003607076-11

the multidimensional nature of child rights neglects their environmental rights the most. If the future of the global citizens is uncared for with regard to their environmental rights, Mother Earth must be heading towards ruinous truth. In the vast area of legal regime, children possess a good number of legal protections in so many international instruments, constitutions, civil and criminal laws, and rules and regulations only except in environmental laws. The rights of those budding prospects are somehow neglected and suppressed in the wide area of environmental jurisprudence. Their tenderness and most fragile social status definitely need some more specific legal safeguards than a normal adult citizen. Environmental harm is a type of silent killer. So, it is just impossible for a minor victim of ecological debasement and climate disorder to combat the threat independently. Actually, they do not receive sufficient recognition as the environmental right-holder.

Rights Connected to the Environmental Rights of a Child

Initially, as a human being and a citizen of India, a child is entitled to exercise the right to life and livelihood in a pollution-free environment under Article 21 of the Constitution of India.[1] Though Article 21 has a wide ambit to embrace all other rights to grow up freely for a young soul, specifically, other rights are the right to survive, right to good health and hygiene, right to play, right to growth and development, right to food, right to sanitation, and right to rest, leisure, and amusement – all substantive rights are susceptible to be hampered. Children should be free from all kinds of respiratory threats. Therefore, it is imperative that children have adequate pollution-free space to play; each and every child of the nation should have the right to inhale purity and to drink clean and pure water. As they are incapable of claiming their environmental rights, so special initiative is certainly required. Enjoyment of a pollution-free environment is definitely a prerequisite for the benefit of other fundamental rights, as well as human rights, especially the physical and mental growth of a child.

International Instruments Relating to Environmental Rights of the Children

UN Convention on Child Rights (CRC), 1989

The most prominent and leading UN Convention on the Rights of the Child[2] (CRC), 1989, seems apt to steer the child rights initiatives globally. CRC is meant for guiding the nations to prioritized children's interests, and it is a real breakthrough to give an impetus to the highest interests of the children. For the appropriate growth and advancement of a child, the word 'environment' denotes a two-fold meaning, that is, physical environment and the emotional environment that predominantly has an impact on mental health.

The physical environment involving the ecological, geological and climatic comfort that are part of the elementary human rights assuring a healthy development for a child is our core area of concern in this chapter.

The Preamble to the CRC echoes the cardinal theme of the universal charter that recognizes the egalitarian shield of inherent rights and dignity of the human family, irrespective of everything. A parallel recognition of the most tender phase of human life, along with the necessity of its special care, attention, and assistance, has also been assured decisively. It affirms a comprehensive safeguard for all groups of children irrespective of their socio-economic status, whether having satisfactory supports for mental and physical development or struggling with helplessness, unfortunate harm and miseries. As the future backbone of society, they have every right to be protected and nourished both physically and mentally.[3]

Article 3 of the CRC articulates that the best interests of all children should be an ultimate matter of concern. Well-being of a minor is the responsibility of several institutions, like parents, family, school, and society at large, on the one hand, and the administrative institutions, law-making institutions, judicial bodies, welfare institutions, and non-governmental organizations, on the other. Moreover, the state has the overall responsibility to monitor and control all those organizations.[4] Article 6 of the Convention is another key assurance to ensure the right to life[5] of a child with all its maximum extent possible including the right to survive and to be developed properly.[6] Both the concepts of best interest and right to survive and develop assure the right to healthy living and upbringing. Article 12 is the other ventilation for a child that assures respect for the child's view. If the child has adequate maturity to express their discomfort, the nation should ensure the right to be heard for the child.

Though an exclusive and substantive right of the environment to the children is yet to be prescribed, the CRC is the sole foremost document to prove it a precondition for the fruitful enjoyment of other innate rights of this vulnerable group. From several provisions, it is clear that, though not having an exclusive status, the ecology-based rights of the future stakeholders are not negligible at all, and it seems an essential ingredient to the accomplishment of a dignified and peaceful human life.

UN Convention on the Rights of the Child (CRC) – Amplification of the Scope of the Issue

The UN CRC, for the first time, widens the scope of environmental rights of children from different aspects. Blending of different general principles broadens the jurisprudential ambit of the matter. Those principles are

i. Survival and Development Principle: As children are blooming buds, healthy survival and comprehensive growth are inalienable to their lifeline. The right to survive and to avail all available developmental measures is the cardinal right which absorbs all related basic human rights. A clean and healthy environment is one of the leading supports to enjoy a dignified and healthy life. As a child is a future flower, its growth and development involve immense importance as its survival.[7]

ii. Non-Discrimination Principle: Discrimination amongst children on the basis of any adverse and unjustifiable distinction like colour, language, sex, religion, political opinion, ethnicity, social origin, race, birth status, any disability, nationality, and financial status of the child or his/her parents. The state obligation should not discriminate against the child in any way while providing any measure to prevent them from environmental harm.[8]

iii. Best Interest Principle: The Best Interest Principle is the principle which simply involves the welfare measures. This provision is applicable in all actions concerning child rights. The environmental rights of a child are one of the most delicate rights due to its vitality. Without fresh air to breathe, without a glass of pure water, a child will never be able to achieve the other rights and accomplishments of life in a healthy manner.[9]

3.1 (b)(iv). The Participation Principle: The best interest of a human being can never be achieved without participation and involvement in different relevant events. Participation acknowledges the right of a person to express their own views and exchange of views and definitely nourishes the mental ability to take part in the nation's growth. Children are somehow neglected due to their age to express their views in state initiatives. In the matter of environmental pollution, they need to express their grievances, explaining their own suffering. General Comment No. 26 is the best example where children from different countries echoed their environmental plight.[10]

Declaration of the Environment Leaders of G8 Countries on Children's Environmental Health (1997)

A good environment is an integral part of perfect health and hygiene. The first major international development with regard to child health-oriented environmental issues is the initiative taken by the developed and industrialized nations, Group of Eight, countries, that is, G8 countries[11] (United States, Canada, France, Germany, Italy, Japan, Russia, and the United Kingdom). It is also popularly known as the Miami Declaration, as issued in Miami in 1997. Those nations clearly express their commitments to remove lead from petrol, to improve air quality and also the quality of drinking water. Another vital part of this declaration is those nations' realization to improve the scientific risk assessments, to align the regulatory measures for direct incorporation of children and to set forth further research on endocrine-disrupting chemicals, causing endocrine dysfunction, autism, low-level lead toxicity, and so on.[12]

World Summit on Sustainable Development, 2002

In the World Summit 2002 held in Johannesburg, South Africa, the World Health Organization (WHO) declared the initiative to improve the environmental protection of children. Actually, the WHO prioritized the risk of children and youth as vulnerable to environmental hazards.[13]

In the next year, the WHO published the report of its 56th World Health Assembly on 5 March 2003. In the report of the WHO, the outcomes of the Global Summit on Sustainable Development were focused on. Moreover, the WHO report is emphatic on the execution of the inference and the implementation plan included new agreements and reaffirmation of previous commitments. Along with other matters, the Summit chalked out its plan for controlling disease and health care issues, including environmental health and lifestyle matters. In its 12th point, it focuses on the improvement of human health to decrease infant and child mortality. Furthermore, special attention is paid to clean water supply, improvement of sanitation and poverty reduction strategies. Poverty reduction strategy is such an issue that has a notable impact on child rights development. Moreover, during the World Summit, WHO plays a notable role as the organizer of a series of health-related events like a panel discussion on the 21st century's health and environment, focusing on the strategies to secure the future of children jointly with UNICEF, UNEP (United Nations Environmental Programme), and physicians contributing to Social Responsibility, and so on. The result of this discussion outlined the key policy actions in the areas of health, environment, and Sustainable Development. In another one-day parallel event, in collaboration with the Health Department of South Africa, there was a ministerial round table on health, which included discussions on child health and investment in the health sector.[14]

Another initiative by the WHO, named Healthy Environment for Children introduced by the Director General of the WHO, a global alliance aimed to raise worldwide action to prioritize the environmental risks and health dangers in such places where children live, play, and study. World Health Day 2003 was celebrated with the theme 'Healthy Environment for Children' as a follow-up action of the World Summit. Following the global summit, a type 2 initiative was also introduced on Children's Environmental Health indicators by the United States, where the governments, non-governmental organizations, and international and inter-governmental organizations were included to proceed hand in hand, and the focus was on the test indicators of the environmental health of children to combat problems in a better way.[15]

A World Fit for Children Declaration (2002)

Another noteworthy declaration allied to the Optional Protocols on the Rights of the Child is 'A World Fit for Children Declaration', 2002, which involves the Millennium Development Goals[16] to be pledged by the United Nations Member States by 2015. With other aims, the seventh goal is to ensure environmental sustainability. These goals are followed by a declaration specifically related to the children. 'A world fit for children' is an exclusive oath note to save, protect and develop the green rights of the children. It seems a kind of plea from the children's forum to the world community, *praying for the shields*, essential for their proper growth and development. Eradication of poverty, protection of the environment, and active participation of children were significantly highlighted there. 'We are the World's children' was the heart-touching starting note of the prayer of this declaration. Respecting their plea, the world leaders committed to providing a better future to every child across the world. A global call to join the movement by upholding the commitments fixed different objectives, including the 'Protection of Earth for the Children'. The oath demonstrates the basic theme of the sustainability goal, ensuring a safeguard to the natural environment with all its varieties, beauty, and resources. It seems a great effort to protect and preserve the rejuvenating natural resources to ensure a quality life for all generations, present and future. Every kind of support for the protection of the little souls and to minimize the effects of environmental degradation and natural disasters is assured firmly. Consequently, a series of plans of action has been framed to materialize those noble oaths.[17]

Declaration on the Rights of Indigenous Peoples (2007)

The UN Declaration on the Rights of the Indigenous Peoples[18] is another instrument where several articles interlinked to the children's right to the environment are mentioned clearly. Indigenous people belonged to a vulnerable group of society, and an indigenous child should be paid more attention, care, and protection by the State agency to make them aware of their own rights, including environmental rights. It is noteworthy that, specifically, Articles 2, 14, 21, 22, 24, 28, 29, 32, and 40 acknowledge those rights in the absence of which the right to environment for a child seems meaningless.[19]

Article 2 ensures the state's obligation of non-discrimination, as indigenous people are more susceptible to discrimination in society. They should get every kind of opportunity to be treated alike. Article 14 speaks of the rights of the indigenous people to set up and control their own educational system, using their native languages and comprehensible teaching and learning methods, and this provision also includes their right to have environmental education. Article 21 guarantees their rights to live as human beings with all amenities and dignity available to the rest of the society. The comprehensive ambit of the adequate scope of livelihood invariably includes the environmental standards. The dignified standard of living, with other comforts and security, includes proper housing with sanitation, health, and social security. This article, as well as Article 22, also secured special attention for indigenous youth and children. Article 24 is truly significant as it requires preservation of natural plants and habitats for the conservation of the practice of herbal treatment, which is very common and popular in their social structure. Article 24(2) specifies the equal right to reach and enjoy the optimum level of physical and mental health. This right signifies the entitlement of Life, Health, and Environment indeed. Article 28 of the Convention represents the state obligations to provide remedies to the indigenous people, and these remedies include their right to get sufficient compensation, along with the rehabilitation and resettlement process in case of land grabbing by the states. This acquisition process should not harm the natural resources at all, and to avoid destruction, an environment impact assessment is essential. Article 29 is that provision which reflects the ardent necessity of all three elements – life, health, and environment for the indigenous community. It directly ensures that, like others, the indigenous community has their right to the preservation of not only the nature and ecology of the lands they inhabit but also the arability of their lands and the capacity of their natural resources. The State should always help them to maintain their natural resources, and Article 29(2) ensures the responsibility of the State to initiate effective measures to affirm that all lands and territories of the indigenous people remain free from any kind of storage or disposal of hazardous materials. Such a kind of storage and disposal can only be done with their prior consent. The next para, Article 29(3), implies the State's obligations to take care of their health issues by constant monitoring and restoration. When Articles 21 and 22 are read with Article 29, a clear view of the right to the environment of indigenous children is distinctly visible. Articles 32 and 40 again provide the protection for the indigenous population by assuring the State's responsibility to aid them to access their financial and other technical rights through international cooperation and to access their right to decide freely in case of conflict with the State through a just and fair process without any kind of compulsion or manipulation. All aforementioned provisions are equally applicable to all types of rights of the indigenous communities, as well as their youth section, including their rights to the environment and health.[20]

The Functions of the Human Rights Commission on Child Rights and Environment: Human Rights Perspective

A movement to prove the significance of environmental resources for children could never be eventuated without the inalienable connection of human rights, as all basic child rights are based on the innate rights of human beings. The formal address of the Human Rights Commission took place in the same year of adopting CRC, that is, 1989, to articulate the environmental issues along with a resolution on the movement.[21] It signified some more moves to dump dangerous, toxic products and wastes. Article 24 is the most crucial and thought-provoking declaration of the UN officials as it directly addresses the necessity of environmental rights of children in an unconditional manner. Actually, frequent resolutions on environment and sustainable growth by the Commission on Human Rights are very common every year, like 1994 to 1996 and again in 2002, 2003, and 2005. Subsequently, as the successor of the Human Rights Commission, the Human Rights Council adopted the resolutions each year during 2011–2015. In the years 2012 and 2014, the resolutions granted the necessity to be linked with the rights of the children to environmental protection. It is an acknowledgement indeed, despite any direct and specific address regarding the human rights of every child and their right to the environment. The Human Rights Council in 2016 issued a statement regarding the deleterious effects of climate disorder, specifically on children's health. Following this, in 2017, the resolution of the Council seems unique to involve the children in environmental decision making, which was not materialized, and the 2018 resolution mentioned children as belonging to a vulnerable group only.[22]

Report of the Special Rapporteur on the Human Right to a Healthy Environment (2018)

Out of the basic realization that children as the worst sufferers of climate disasters and ecological degradation can be a part of environmental decision making, the Council moved by directing the Special Rapporteur to continue to research those environmental obligations with special care to the ecological rights of every child in coordination with human rights mechanisms, governments, civil society organizations, and others. The Special Rapporteur submitted the report on the 37th session of the Council and flagged children as the most fragile group in society exposed to all kinds of pollution and contamination in a true unhealthy manner and probably the most helpless group of society, incapable of accessing effective remedies. Moreover, they are most of the time incapable of exercising their basic rights, including their right to be informed, right to participation, and so on. The report cited the data of the unfortunate yearly death of 1.5 million children below the age of 5 due to different pollutions and exposure to toxic substances. It has a prolonged effect on their health and mind. Biodiversity and climate change contribute to different diseases and disabilities in their lives. The report suggested joint initiatives by other Special Rapporteurs; the Committee on the Rights of the Child; organizations like UNICEF, OHCHR, and WHO; and other individuals who submitted their valuable views during the preparation of the report.[23] The Report recommended specific responsibilities for the States by organizing

i. educational programmes to raise the understanding ability of every child to point out environmental issues and to build up their capabilities to react to environmental and climatic challenges;
ii. testing of probable after effects of proposed measures and elimination of any negative impact detected before their approval and implementation;
iii. collection of data regarding the sources of environmental attacks on children and the appropriate utilization of information and data collected for public awareness;
iv. policies to involve children in the environmental policy-making processes and their participation with expressed views on environmental issues.[24] The report put parallel emphasis on the International Environmental Soft Law Principle based on the notion of Sustainable Development, inter-generational equity, environmental impact assessment (EIA), Information and Consultation, precaution, and prevention.[25]
v. The basic rights interconnected to the human rights, as well as environmental rights, of the children are those inalienable rights strengthening their wholesome growth and well-being. These rights are

    Right to life, health and environment[26]
    Right to adequate standard of living[27]
    Right to play and recreation[28]
    State obligations of environmental education[29]
    State obligations of information[30]
    State obligations of assessment
    State obligations to consider the views of children[31]
    State obligations to provide remedies[32]
    State obligations of non-discrimination
    State obligations as a regulatory authority to control private actors.[33]

The report thus recommended a handful of obligations of the States to ensure and protect the supreme interests of each and every child across the world. Their best interests are always to be prioritized as the preliminary consideration of the State powers in all kinds of decision making, which may have the propensity to yield to environmental attack on the youngsters specifically.[34]

The Global Children's Environmental Rights Initiative (CERI), 2019

CERI was another initiative (in 2019) by the UN Human Rights Commission to strengthen and collaborate on the issue of environmental rights of a child and the sustainability goal. This initiative emphatically prioritized the sustainable development goal that could elevate the recognition of children's sustainable environmental rights. It chalked out certain steps to be taken to boost the involvement, as well as awareness and protection of the youth.[35]

Firstly, the empowerment of children and youth to take part in the movement with regard to their environmental rights,

Secondly, raising awareness and building capacity among the global decision makers at different levels, like regional, national, and global, and also to increase State obligations with regard to the relationship between children's rights and the environment.[36]

Thirdly, the coordination facilitating stronger cooperation among the key stakeholders,

Lastly, the framing and safeguarding of the worldwide recognition of the set of principles controlling the negative effects of environmental pollution on the youth.

As an outcome of those guidelines, the Special Rapporteur organized a series of regional consultations to coordinate with the children, youth and expert minds to discuss different relevant issues. In addition, it organized some additional digital consultations, capacity building tools and technical guidance for the awareness and promotion of the issue.[37]

UNHRC General Comment No. 26 (2023): A Special Focus on the Adverse Impact of Climate Change on the Children

Key Theme and Objective

A General Comment or recommendation is the interpretation cited by the Treaty Body of any UN Committee to explain the treaty provisions, methods of work, and other relevant clarifications. The Committee on the Rights of the Child has very recently expressed its concern for the environmental rights of the child jeopardized by the threat of alarming biodiversity and climate change. UNHRC General Comment No. 26 is the General Comment of the Committee on the Rights of the Child and environmental degradation, with a special focus on climate change.[38]

The Draft General Comment No. 26 welcomes the response from the joint submission of the Child Rights Connect Working Group[39] by the UN Committee on the Child Rights. Several social service networks working on child rights representing different countries are the parties here to reflect their valuable thoughts and suggestions for this specific alarming issue of the impact of climate change on the global youth. Those members of the working group are Alana Institute, Child Rights International Network (CRIN), CRC Asia, DKA-Austria (a Catholic faith based funding agency in Austria), Global Action Plan, Heirs to Our Oceans, Environment Africa, Franciscans International, One Ocean Hub, Save the Children International, Make Mothers

Matter, Plan International, World Council of Churches, Soka Gakkai International, and World Vision International.[40]

Children are suffering from worldwide contamination of air, water, land, ocean acidification, toxic pollution affecting natural resources, shattered ecosystem, and the most threatened climate disaster. The term 'children' has that magical essence of tenderness and delicacy that it can always be used as prioritized for any positive move and reformation. A plea on their part to save the world for them is definitely a mystic force behind the Draft General Comment No.26. The most remarkable feature of this comment is that it has gained remarkable strength from the contribution of youth in the Committee's 2016 day of general discussion on their own rights affected by environmental lapse.[41] The uniqueness of this procedure lies in the working of a diverse and committed Child Advisory Team that arranged a global process of consultation with 7,416 children from a total of 103 nations, consisting of 13 child experts, between 10 and 17 years of age and belonging to different regions, backgrounds, and experiences. The team conducted through online survey along with in-person consultations, both regional and national. Thus, the advisory team played a pivotal role in collecting experiences and ideas from the youth through a global children's questionnaire. The reports of the advisory team were based on the findings of the questionnaire. The questionnaires were distributed globally in two phases: 31 March to 20 June 2022, and November 2022 to February 2023.[42] Most of the young minds reflect the negative impact of environmental degradation on their lives, and they blame the choking, dirty, and polluted environment for their unhappy lives; they actually blame the adults for this degradation, of which they are the worst victims. They are scared of their endangered existence in future. Thus, the prayer of the little souls is the true motivation to proceed further. Though General Comment 26 aimed to focus on climate change, its attention covers a wide spectrum of environmental harm, having adverse effects on children both direct and indirect. The key objectives of the Committee are:

(i) To put stress on the urgency to highlight the dreadful impact of environmental degradation and change of climate change on children,
(ii) To encourage a comprehensive understanding of the rights of a child as applicable in the case of environmental protection,
(iii) To explain the obligation of the State parties ratifying the Convention and to guide the other agencies like legislature and administration, in an authoritative manner with regard to environmental issues, emphasizing on climatic catastrophe.[43]

Thus, the basic objectives resemble a rights-based approach to the environment, which reflects a keen understanding or realization of the necessity of child rights. This understanding can only hammer the core concern of the

State. Every child should be recognized and honoured as a respectable citizen having the immediate right to be protected from all environmental harm, including climate change.

Different forms of pollutants affecting child health:

Various forms of pollution affecting the children are air and water pollution, climate disorder, toxic and chemical substances and non-biodegradable waste, lack of biodiversity, and loss of ingress to nature. The report of the Special Rapporteur marks ambient air pollution from transport, factories, the use of wood for household functions, and the use of coal, coal products, and other solid fuels. Children are susceptible to being affected by this common type of pollutant, mainly the household pollutants.

According to the WHO most serious diseases affecting children are skin cancer and other ailments due to overexposure to ultraviolet radiation (UV). Ozone depletion by the substances emitted from different human activities is another alarming issue affecting children's health badly. Smoke haze, as an obvious result of land and forest fires, is another pollutant that often disturbs the human respiratory system. To control transboundary haze pollution, ASEAN, which means the Association of South East Asian Nations, adopts an agreement at the regional level, not specifically for the children but to protect general human health.

Air pollution and water pollution all are basically controlled by the national law and related rules and regulations. Like air pollution, water contamination is another problem that has a transboundary effect. Apart of the national laws of each nation, two global agreements to which countries belonged to UNICEF are the parties to control the rivers flowing across national borders. A Treaty on International Watercourses, the UN Watercourses Convention (UNWC), is appropriate to monitor the States to prevent, control, and reduce water pollution. The only member nation is Vietnam.[44]

Regarding the Mekong River Basin issue, an Agreement on the Cooperation for the Sustainable Development of the Basin, such as UNWC, is signed on 5 April 1995, where four nations, namely, the Kingdom of Cambodia, the Leo People's Democratic Republic, the Kingdom of Thailand, and the Socialist Republic of Vietnam mutually joined to reorganize, protect, and cooperate the Mekong River Basin and conservation, utilization, and management of resources. Article 3 of the treaty distinctly mentions the protection of Ecological and Environmental balance, and Article 7 states the concept of prohibition and cessation of harmful effects. Both articles are helpful in achieving the Sustainable Development Goal by reducing and preventing water pollution in the particular region. Though the Mekong River Commission is a good step for the present and the future generation, it has no specification for the suffering of the child community there.[45] The utility of this sustainable treaty will somehow be suspected of

> threatening the Sambor Dam project of China, while China is not a party to this treaty. This type of transboundary step to save the world, especially the children, from contamination of water bodies, is much needed.[46] Polluted air may cause slow poisoning, but a glass of contaminated water can cause it instantly. So, soft law should be more specific and stricter with regard to the best environmental interests of the child.

Climate change is another environmental nuisance that has a disproportionate ill effect on children. It is a threat to the children's health worldwide. The United Nations Framework Convention on Climate Change and the parent treaty Paris Agreement (2015) have fixed the aim of maintaining the worldwide average temperature rise within 1.5 degrees Celsius above pre-industrial levels and to reduce the emission of greenhouse gases. As kids are the most vulnerable group, their health tends to be affected more, with the disastrous effects of ozone layer depletion and greenhouse gases. An EPA Report of 2023 shows that the impact of climate change is more fatal on child health than on adults. Two to four degrees of global warming have a deleterious effect on child health.[47] Different respiratory diseases have increased, like:

- Childhood asthma cases have increased between 4% and 11% due to increasing air pollution.
- Childhood asthma-related emergency hospital visits have increased from 17% to 30% owing to an increase in pollen levels.
- Lyme disease cases of children cite an increase from 79% to 241% or an additional new case from 2,600 to 23,400 per year.[48]
- A decrease in school performance due to a heat wave leads to 4% to 7% reduction in academic achievements, and this affects their future career.
- Displacement due to natural calamities like floods, earthquakes, and cyclones has a deleterious effect on their livelihood, growth, and development.
- Global warming has increased diseases like dengue, malaria, Zika, Lyme disease, and new types of viruses.
- Due to the burning of fossil fuel, every year, 1000 children below 5 die every year.[49]
- Two reports published by the WHO in the year 2017 reveal that 1.7 million children below five years of age die due to indoor and outdoor air pollution, contaminated water, poor sanitation, and insufficient hygiene.[50]

Recommendations on the draft:

The Child Rights Connect Working Group recommends[51] certain points that

- Certain terminology like 'environmental citizens' and 'child rights defender' should be replaced with 'child environmental human rights defenders', while mentioning the young souls defending environmental lapses for obstructing their basic human rights.

- The term 'children in vulnerable situation' suggested to replace 'susceptibility of children'.
- Suggested replacement of the term 'environmental harm' with 'environmental degradation and climate change'.
- The introduction to the General Comment should recognize the children's right to a clean, healthy, and Sustainable Development.[52]
- Children's participation process should be encouraged, and the views and suggestions cited by the children should be heard by the stakeholders. The present generation of youth is more mature to understand the depth of the issue. The views, ideas, and suggestions from the youth can be collected from different area-based campaigns or school-oriented awareness camps, creative/essay writing competitions, and debates on environmental issues and through their participation in different national and international platforms and in meetings arranged by regulatory authorities with the support of local authorities and non-governmental organizations. Movies and documentaries on environmental degradation and climate change and its devastating effect on child health can be shown area-wise. It will enable them to meet the gravity of the problem. Their voice can be the echo of their own suffering. Moreover, an online poll for adolescents can be another way to feel the pulse of the youth.
- Amongst many other child rights as specified in CRC, those rights violated due to the direct effect of environmental degradation and climate change should be separated like

i. Right to food (during any natural calamity due to climate disorder, the State should ensure the distribution of healthy, fresh, and raw food instead of frozen or processed one)
ii. Rights of the displaced children (rights of the migrant and displaced children should be secured at the earliest possible opportunity)
iii. The rights of children with disabilities (this specific category of children should occupy a considerable part of the State obligation)
iv. Rights of the indigenous children (the State should be more careful in dealing with them, as they live closer to nature and are more susceptible to environmental harm)
v. Link between environmental degradation, climate change, and violence against children (the children affected by climate disasters tend to be tortured by several types of exploitation, abuse, violence, and especially the foundling girl children should be protected from an optimum level of physical exploitation and mental trauma)
vi. Right to education (introduction of environmental science at the elementary stage of school education)

vii. A systematic access to information and best available science by the children, their parents, and caregivers (that will protect the child from misinformation and misguidance)

Environmental Rights of the Children in India: A Critical Analysis

In India, though children are treated as normal citizens with regard to their environmental rights, their environmental safety and security are not ignored at all. Rather, they are fortified with lots of connected rights like the right to health and hygiene, right to food, right to education, right against different abuses like child labour, and so on. Parts III and IV of the Indian Constitution are still silent about any direct constitutional safeguard of this vulnerable group and ensure provisions that have resemblance with the mission of the United Nations Conventions on the Rights of the Child (UNCRC) guidelines.

Constitutional Safeguards

As the mother law it does not ensure any classified provision in the form of a fundamental right for an exclusive ecological right of the children in India. In compliance with the UNCRC mandates regarding the right to life, health and survival (Article 6), Article 21[53] assures the right to life and livelihood for every Indian citizen. This provision has a very extended range of application, which includes all rights to enjoy a dignified life. The right to live a life in a pollution-free nature is one of the most important rights that can be availed by exercising Article 21. Judicial activism in India provides enormous support to the citizens to access their environmental rights as a basic human right assured in the form of fundamental rights. Any child irrespective of their age has the right to access the wide ambit of Article 21 as a citizen of India.[54]

Article 24 is more specific in controlling the unfortunate phenomenon very prominent in India, that is, child labour. Prohibition of employment of children in the factories can save them from toxic and hazardous substances, which keeps them away from respiratory ailments.[55] In the matter of *M.C. Mehta v. State of Tamil Nadu*,[56] the Apex Court decided that the employment of children in the matchstick manufacturing unit is a devastating and preposterous activity. Through a series of remarkable judgements, the honourable Apex Court has repeatedly warned different industrial units to stop their production causing harm to the vicinity or to continue their process after having infrastructural modification and advancement necessary to decrease the pollution. In this regard, the Court utilized the concepts of Precautionary Principle, Polluter Pays Principle, Doctrine of Inter-Generational Equity, Public Trust Doctrine, and so on, considering the concept of sustainability. Even the honourable Court never hesitate to remind different local authorities and administrative bodies to exercise their power and authority for regulating the industrial, crushing, and mining units.

In *M.C. Mehta v. U.O.I. (2004) 6 SCC 588* the Court authenticates that to live in an atmosphere congenial to human existence is a part of the right to life, and the State is duty-bound to exercise its sovereign power to maintain ecological balance and a hygienic environment. Furthermore, the honourable Court instructs not to delimit the process within the residential area of illegal colonization, but the whole town.[57]

Article 39 is the next provision that belongs to Part IV, that is, the Directive Principles of the State Policy that ensures the State's obligations towards the citizens. Article 39(e) confirms that a child should not be abused in any way due to their tender age. This kind of abusive activity may even violate the rights of a child to get pollution-free air, pure water, and a green land to play. Article 39(f) gives mandates to the State to give the children the opportunities as well as facilities to be developed in a healthy, dignified, and free manner. Moreover, both childhood and youth are to be safeguarded against any kind of exploitation and moral or material abandonment.[58]

Article 47 is another directive to the State, which is most relevant with regard to the issue of the environment and the rights of children. It imposes the duty on the State to raise the level of standard of living and nutrition and to improve public health. Both issues here are directly connected to the environmental risks.[59]

A considerable number of effective judicial decisions can be cited here regarding the protection and maintenance of public parks and open space for recreation that is out an out connected to the purpose of right to health and right to environment of the children. Physical activities in a pollution-free and environment-friendly open space are an inevitable support to their physical and mental health growth and development. Specially, in the urban areas, they lack to enjoy it. So, any kind of infrastructural development, construction, encroachment, and conversion of a park for any other purpose on the part of any private entity or the State is instantly directed to be stopped by the Apex Court.

The consequence of this vital issue had persistently been amplified in several cases by the Indian judiciary. In *Calcutta Youth Front v. State of West Bengal*[60] the Supreme Court allowed the grant of sub-soil rights of a public park to construct a basement air-conditioned market by explaining it would not hamper or disturb the ecological balance of the park. In *Bangalore Medical Trust v. Muddappa, (1991) 4SCC 54*, the Court baffled the conversion of a public park to a nursing home under the development scheme for the extension of the city of Bangalore that was initiated by the City Improvement Board of Bangalore. The Court preferred the importance of the public park, clarifying it as 'a necessity not a mere amenity'. Even it focused on the absence of open space due to rampant urbanization, causing health hazards, and suggested the City Improvement board take a preventive measure to get rid of the alarming ecological disturbance.[61] *Virender Gaur v. State of Haryana, (1995) 2SCC 577* is another notable decision where the honourable Court cited the United Nations Conference on the Human Environment and the Stockholm Declaration to emphasize the importance of the right to life and enjoyment of basic human rights. The case evolved around the same issue, that is, construction on the land reserved for better sanitation, ventilation, and recreational purposes.[62]

In the issue of *Dr. G.N. Khajuria v. Delhi Development Authority*,[63] the Delhi Development Authority wrongfully allotted a land reserved for a park in a residential colony to the respondent for the construction of a nursery school. It was a clear violation of the provisions of the Delhi Development Act, 1957.[64] In *C. Uma Devi. Govt. of Andhra Pradesh*[65] the Andhra Pradesh High Court restricted the local authority to not to converting a park into a garbage dumping yard.[66]

Article 48A and Article 51A(g) are the constitutional provisions directly dealing with environmental protection issued to all citizens. The former is the shield of the Directive Principles of State Policy, and the latter is the fundamental duty imposed upon the citizens. In both spheres, access by the children is directly denied, though environmental rights fulfil the theory of best interest from all aspects. Most interestingly, such a vital issue is not listed in the Seventh Schedule of the Constitution of India, enumerating the list of subject matter for law-making, which could have paved the way for a specific statute.

Statutes Relating to Child Rights and Environment

India was a signatory to the UNCRC; the child rights movement in India is actually very lively and working with the help of a good number of laws enacted by the Indian Parliament, with the aid of different child rights-related policies and the active role of the non-governmental agencies to secure the socio-economic rights of a child. Children in the poverty-stricken areas of India are still suffering from different issues like malnutrition, illiteracy, sexual abuse, and socio-economic sufferance like child marriage, child trafficking, and abortion. There are specific statutes for all aforementioned issues that include procedural safeguards for children. Again, on the other hand, a considerable number of environmental legislations are there, but not a single one is specifically focusing on the environmental rights of the Indian children. Only the laws relating to the prohibition of child labour in India, formerly the Child Labour (Prohibition and Regulation) Act, 1986,[67] and now the Child Labour (Prohibition and Regulation) Amendment Act, 2016,[68] provide protection to children from engaging in any occupation and prohibit the engagement of adolescents in hazardous occupations and processes. Section 3A of the statute strictly prohibits any hazardous occupation as mentioned in the schedule, like mines, inflammable substances or explosives, and occupations involving hazardous processes. Another labour law statute, the Factories Act, 1948, in its Chapter VII (Employment of Young Persons) provides a comprehensive safeguard to child labours.[69]

Relevant Child Rights Policies and Action Plans

- The National Policy on Children (1974)[70] is a policy to consider children as an asset, so they must be protected before and after their birth, and they should be assured with full physical, mental, and social development and balanced growth. A comprehensive health programme, along with other measures, was suggested.
- The National Policy on Child Labour (1987) instructs a strict implication of the child labour–related statutes to confirm that the working conditions of the children are non-hazardous. It further identified some additional occupations and processes harmful to the child's health.
- The National Nutrition Policy (1993) aims to eradicate undernutrition, which disturbs physical growth and health. Both physical growth and health depend not only on adequate food but on an appropriate environment and an undisturbed ecology.
- The National Health Policy (2002) has its target to reduce the infant mortality rate to 30 per 1000 live births and maternal mortality rate to 100 per lakh live births by 2010.[71]
- The National Charter for Children (2003) includes a plan to secure the inherent rights of the child, to secure a happy and healthy childhood for them. It ensures the life and liberty of all children, health and nutrition, and the right to play and leisure. All those rights are extremely relevant in the context of the guideline initiated by UNCRC.
- The National Plan of Action (2005) is the most effective policy in this context as it suggests:

  i. Consider the child as an asset and as a human being having basic human rights,
  ii. Assure equality amongst the children
  iii. Recognize different stages of childhood, identifying the requirements of each stage.
  iv. Prioritize the poorest and disadvantaged children who are least served.
  v. Improve water and sanitation in both rural and urban areas.

The aforementioned points of the national plan of action comply with the theories of participation, non-discrimination, best interest, and right-based approach as recognized in the global journey against environmental pollution and climate change. Out of innumerable governmental schemes, a few are directly dealing with the environmental rights of the child. However, they are to some extent a step ahead of the goal, subject to their appropriate implementation.[72]

Commendable Role of Non-Governmental Organizations

In India, the non-governmental organizations (NGOs) are truly active to uphold and ensure a healthy and promising growth of children. They are to provide constant support to government agencies, as well as work on their own initiatives. They are trying to uphold the aim of Comment No. 26.

CRY (Child Rights and You):

CRY is a leading one, to give constant support to this vulnerable group, combining the goal of the internationally accepted mandates, the constitutional rights of the children, and other governmental aims and policies. CRY has recently chalked out the synchronization of the internationally ensured fundamental rights of the children and their effective contribution to the young minds. The right to survival proclaims a good start to nurture some basic supports like adequate nutrition, healthcare, and a safe environment during childhood. Secondly, the educational right is a cornerstone of youth development, and it helps the young minds to explore their rights and interests. This right empowers a child to be a conscious citizen in the future and to be a conscious environmental citizen also especially to combat the threat of climate disaster. Next is the right to participation, which empowers a child to raise their voice in the decision-making process. The right to development is a comprehensive factor ensuring all kinds of well-being, both physical and emotional. It is designed to go through holistic growth and development. The most specific and vital one, as mentioned by CRY, is the right to safe environment to protect and preserve the future world. Youth power can be utilized in the best possible manner to regenerate the vitality of the green planet.[73]

Joint venture of Save the Children and the Pricewaterhousecoopers India Foundation:

Two prominent organizations are working hand in hand to challenge the impact of climate change on children globally and the disturbance caused by it in the timely accomplishment of Sustainable Development Goals. Save the Children India is one of the world's largest NGOs supporting the child rights movement. Both organizations have tried to specify the challenges faced by the children due to climate change, and they worked together to raise awareness in the disaster-prone areas like Jammu and Kashmir, flood-prone Kerala, drought-prone Maharashtra and Madhya Pradesh, and cyclone-prone Odisha. They are of the opinion that the extent of the impact of the climate disaster is somehow unprecedented. Children, as a disadvantaged, vulnerable group, are at higher risk of adverse consequences due to climate change.[74] This collaboration aimed to identify the key problems, like

a. Identification of the principal effects of the climate crisis on children,
b. To appraise the inherent socio-economic conditions that make the children vulnerable to climate hazards,
c. To identify the risk mitigation and most importantly the adaptation measures to reduce the impact of climate disasters on the children, in short, medium, and long terms,
d. To provide a proposed roadmap for the appropriate implementation of the adaptation strategies.[75]

A clear methodology of their research work on the issue has put emphasis on the sensitivity and adaptive capacity of the children, which actually turns them vulnerable.
Nine is Mine Campaign:

Nine is Mine Campaign, a magnificent move in the form of a participatory children's advocacy initiative, is the brainchild of Nelson Mandela. In India, several NGOs supported the campaign specially initiated for and by the children across India to ensure their educational and health rights, which are aligned to their ecological rights also.[76] Actually, the root of this campaign is embedded in the intention and true spirit of the UNCRC, and it believes that children having the capability of forming their own views should have the right to frame and express their opinions freely. It allows children all over the country to belong to different schools and NGOs to have access to the system, ensuring their rights.[77] This campaign has been launched with the participation of more than 4500 children in Delhi on 16 October 2006. It is a children's advocacy move to demand 9% of the gross domestic product (GDP) for the purpose of their education and health, 6% for their education purpose, and 3% for their health purpose means. A total of 9% of the GDP should be secured for basic two fundamental rights essential for their growth and development.[78]

PRATYEK (translates to 'Each and Every'), a registered organization on child rights working with UNESCO, is popular for its child-led advocacy initiative. This organization is set up to ensure a free and happier childhood to all children. This organization has been started by Steve Rocha, who is influenced with the teachings and vision of Edmund Rice. Rocha is the convener of Nine is Mine national campaign, which arranged an online event named 'No Cop Out' (means not to avoid or escape from doing something) on 4 and 5 November 2022, along with some other organizations like World Vision India, Wada Na Todo Abhiyan (translates to 'Do not break the trust Mission'), Vanshakti (translates to 'Forest-Strength'), Kids 4 Tiger, Brian Rhyme, Save the Children, Child Rights Connect Geneva, Terres des Homes Switzerland, and Edmund Rice International, Geneva. This was a unique initiative to involve the children in policy-making process. Steve Rocha, the National Convener of NINEISMINE from PRATYEK, expressed that each generation should get an opportunity to change the course of history and the children should be given opportunity at the forefront of this historic moment to reverse climate change that demands their own ecological rights and the rights of the Mother Earth too. The number of children registered for this event was more than 600. Over a year, 3500 young voices expressed their demands for a global-ecological-rights for children. Kartik Verma, a 16-year-old representative from the Uttar Pradesh, is the young delegate to present the Ad Vocal report at the event with other international diplomats.[79] The No Cop Out event is an online platform for the youth (almost 900 participants) to discuss and address their proposals and plea to the world leaders to respect their ecological rights. For a fruitful incorporation of their 'earth rights' the little brains also have suggested an amendment in the Indian Constitution as well as the Constitution of other countries.[80] The youth further demands that had they been given the right to cast vote, their voices definitely echoed the plea of the mother earth, the voice of the endangered (species), and the voice of the excluded (children). They recommend for innumerous relevant issues, which may really bring a revolutionary wave in the motion of environmental pollution movement. Issues proposed by them are

- Right to green child-specific risk and impact assessment,
- Right to adequate green information,
- Right to holistic green education,
- Right to recover and complain,
- Right to protection when vulnerable,
- Right to genuine expression and participation,
- Right to corporate earth responsibility,
- Right to best green laws and standards,
- Right to green budgets and green policies
- Right to expect good green governance.[81]

Riddhima Pandey Case: a notable example of child participation in India:

Participation of youth to claim their demands and necessary clarification from the regulating authorities regarding their failure to fulfil the climate change targets has a reflection in the matter of Riddhima Pandey v. Union of India,[82] where a nine-year-old girl belonged to Uttarakhand, sued the

Government of India through a case filed in the National Green Tribunal (NGT) Delhi. Her petition pointed out the lacunas in mitigating the implication of the Public Trust Doctrine, the commitments of the nation under the Paris Agreement and the shortcomings of India's present environmental laws and climate change-related policies. This case involved a substantial question pertinent to environmental degradation. The petition cited the noteworthy concepts of Indian Environmental laws like the concept of Sustainable Development, Inter-Generational Equity, and Precautionary Principles, as well as included several foreign decisions on similar legal concepts. The foreign cases mentioned in the petition are Urgenda Foundation v. Kingdom of the Netherlands (a case of Netherland), Juliana v. United States (a case of United States), and Leghari v. Pakistan (a case of Pakistan).[83] Her main plea was that she, along with all children in India and the generations to come, had their right to pollution-free healthy environment on the basis of the concept of the inter-generational equity. The petition also mentioned the increasing vulnerability of the children to the alarming impacts like heat waves, diseases, malnutrition, and displacement. The petition also suggested preparation of 'Carbon Budget' needed to be implemented by the government. The case was dismissed by the NGT on the basis of the explanation that it would become irrational to presume that the mission and vision of the Paris Agreement and other international protocols were not reflected in the policies of Indian government. The NGT stated that it was sufficiently considered during the EIA.[84] This case is now under appeal before the honourable Supreme Court of India.[85] This matter also focused on the definition of 'environment' under the Environment Protection Act, 1986. The main focus was whether the wide ambit of the definition is inclusive of the term climate or not.[86]

Conclusion and Recommendations

To evaluate the environmental rights of the children in India, it can be said that India still lacks protection of the ecological interest of the children of the present time and the upcoming generations. India ratified the sustainable goal, so the concept of inter-generational equity is not unknown to Indian policy framers. There must be more emphasis on the child rights-based approach. Unless the absence and requirement of the core right is realized, the policy framers lack to give it a proper legal shape. Participation of Indian children in several global and national movements raised and led by the young minds has gained a motion with the active support of notable NGOs, ceaselessly working with different child rights including their environmental rights. It goes without saying that leading NGOs in India are full of enthusiasm to save the environmental rights of the children focusing on the climate change issues. Their ardent activities may get a vigour with the support of direct legislative aid with regard to the specific issue. Specific legislation is the need of the moment. The legislation must prioritize the environmental rights of children on the basis of the theories of best interest, participation, and so on. The key goals of the General Comment No. 26 should be considered earnestly. To lead a wholesome and effective global movement, eradication of poverty, spread of education, proper sanitization system, and related issues should be dealt with utmost care. Environmental education must be introduced from the primary level instead of higher level. Children need to familiarize with nature and should realize the consequence of destruction of priceless natural resources. From the early childhood they should come to know the environmental threats and their fundamental duties as per Article 51A(g) of the Constitution through their syllabus oriented studies. Every child should be entrusted with the responsibility to save the earth and to pave a smooth future for them as well as for the next generations to come. The voices of the green heroes like Kartik Sharma and Riddhima Pandey should reach all Indian children through the inclusion of their stories in the school syllabus and through awareness camps in school and showing of documentaries on their lives initiated by the governments and local authorities. Innocent minds should be endowed with duties as the protector of mother earth. Their right to participation should be highlighted by organizing effective awareness camps, sapling distribution, audio-visual show, and street play, which can be effective modes to motivate the innocent minds more and more to spread the Green Movement. Company Social Responsibility should be more focused not only on general environmental issues but on the specific crisis involving children. Thus, the environmental protection of future stakeholders should be secured by realizing its disastrous effect. Unless children are environmentally secured, an apocalypse is not too far.

Notes

1 Protection of Life and Personal Liberty: No person shall be deprived of his life and personal liberty except according to procedure established by law, *The Constitution of India*, 18 (Eastern Book Company, 2011).
2 Ian Brownlie, *Basic Documents on Human Rights*, 243 (Oxford University Press, 2002).
3 Brownlie, *Basic Documents on Human Rights*.
4 Brownlie, *Basic Documents on Human Rights*.
5 *The Constitution of India* (2011).
6 *The Constitution of India* (2011).
7 Thoko Kaime, Children's Right and the Environment, in *International Human Rights of Children*, 1 (2018), 4–19, https://www.researchgate.net/publication/325104353_Children's_Rights_and_the_Environment?shem.
8 Kaime, Children's Right and the Environment, 4–19.
9 Kaime, Children's Right and the Environment, 4–19.
10 Kaime, Children's Right and the Environment, 4–19.
11 G7 Information Centre, https://www.g8.utoronto.ca (last visited Dec. 22, 2024).

12 Philip J. Landrigan & Giorgio Tamburlini, *Editorial: Children's Health and the Environment: A Transatlantic Dialogue*, Environmental Health Perspective: National Library of Medicine (Oct. 2005), https://pmc.ncbi.nlm.nih.gov/articles/PMC1281297 (last visited Nov. 29, 2023).
13 Kaime, Children's Right and the Environment.
14 Kaime, Children's Right and the Environment.
15 *Report by the Secretariat of the World Health Organization on World Summit on Sustainable Development, Fifty-Sixth World Health Assembly*, World Health Organization, https://apps.who.int/gb/ebwha/pdf_files/WHA56/ea5613.pdf?shem (last visited Dec. 2, 2023).
16 *A World Fit for Children-Text-4X6, UNICEF Humanitarian Aid Organization*, https://www.unicef.org/serbia/media/7321/file/A%20world%20fit%20for%20children (last visited Dec. 22, 2024).
17 *A World Fit for Children-Text-4X6, UNICEF Humanitarian Aid Organization.*
18 *www.un.org*, https://www.un.org/development/desa/indigenouspeoples/wp-content/uploads/sites/19/2018/11/UNDRIP_E_web.pdf (last visited Nov. 30, 2023).
19 *www.un.org.*
20 *www.un.org.*
21 Patricia Moore, *Background Paper on: Environment and Children's Rights in International Law and National Jurisprudence*, Report of UNICEF (EAPRO), i, iv (2020), http://unicef.org/eap/media/5911/file/Environment%20and%20Children's%20Rights.pdf.
22 Moore, *Background Paper on.*
23 *Children's Right and the Environment: Special Rapporteur on the Human Right to a Healthy Environment*, http://www.ohchr.org/en/special-procedures/sr-environment/childrens-rights-and-environment (last visited Nov. 27, 2023).
24 *Children's Right and the Environment.*
25 Moore, *Background Paper on*, at 4.
26 Moore, *Background Paper on*, at 4.
27 Moore, *Background Paper on*, at 4.
28 Moore, *Background Paper on*, at 4.
29 Moore, *Background Paper on*, at 4.
30 Moore, *Background Paper on*, at 4–5.
31 Moore, *Background Paper on*, at 4–5.
32 Moore, *Background Paper on*, at 4–5.
33 Moore, *Background Paper on*, at 4–5.
34 Moore, *Background Paper on*, at 4–5.
35 Children's Environmental Rights, https://ceri-coalition.org (last visited Nov. 30, 2023).
36 Children's Environmental Rights.
37 Children's Environmental Rights.
38 *Child Rights Connect*, https://childrightsconnect.org/general-comments (last visited Nov. 30, 2023).
39 *Child Rights Connect.*
40 *Child Rights Connect.*
41 Committee on the Rights of the Child, Draft General Comment No. 26 (202x), *Children's Rights and the Environment with a Special Focus on Climate Change*, https://childrightsenvironment.org/wp-content/uploads/2022/11/First-Draft_General-Comment-No_26_November-2022.pdf (last visited Nov. 30, 2023).
42 *Report of the First Children and Young People's Consultation*, https://childrightsenvironment.org/wp-content/uploads2022/09/Report-of-the-first-Children-and-Young-Peoples-Consultation.pdf (last visited Dec. 1, 2023).
43 *Report of the First Children and Young People's Consultation.*

44 Moore, *Background Paper on*, at 9.
45 *Mekong River Commission for Sustainable Development*, https://www.mrcmekong.org (last visited Dec. 2, 2023).
46 *Georgetown Law*, https://www.law.georgetown.edu/environmental-law-review/inprint/volume-32-issue-1-fall-2019/the-sambor-dam-how-chinas-breach-of-customary-international-law-will-affect-the-future-of-the-mekong-river-basin/ (last visited Dec. 2, 2023).
47 *Children's Health*, Harvard T.H. Chan School of Public Health, https://www.hsph.harvard.edu/c-change/subtopics/climate-change-and-childrens-health/ (last visited Dec. 2, 2023).
48 *Children's Health.*
49 *Children's Health.*
50 *Child Rights Connect*, 38, at 1.
51 *Child Rights Connect*, 38 at 3.
52 *Child Rights Connect*, 38 at 3.
53 *The Constitution of India* (2011).
54 INDIA CONST. art. 21.
55 INDIA CONST. art. 24.
56 M.C. Mehta v. U.O.I. A.I.R. (1997) SC 699 (India).
57 Dr. Paramjit Jaswal, Dr. Nistha Jaswal & Vibhuti Jaswal, *Environmental Law*, 60 (4th ed. reprint 2018).
58 INDIA CONST. art. 39. cl (e), (f).
59 INDIA CONST. art. 47.
60 A.I.R. (1988) S.C. 43 (India).
61 Jaswal, Jaswal & Jaswal, *Environmental Law*, at 197–198.
62 *Asian Development Bank*, http://lpr.adb.org/resource/virender-gaur-and-orsvs-stateharyanaand-ors199-2scc-577-india (last visited Dec. 18, 2024).
63 (1995) 5 SCC 762 (India).
64 Jaswal, Jaswal & Jaswal, *Environmental Law*, at 198.
65 (2001) A.I.R. A.P. 460 (India).
66 Jaswal, Jaswal & Jaswal, *Environmental Law*, at 199.
67 The Child Labour (Prohibition and Regulation) Act, 1986, Ss. 3,13,14, Part A, Part B of the Schedule, No.61, Acts of Parliament, 1986 (India).
68 The Child Labour (Prohibition and Regulation) Amendment Act, 2016, S.5, No.35, Acts of Parliament, 2016 (India).
69 The Factories Act, 1948, Ss.67–77, No.63, Acts of Parliament, 1948 (India).
70 *Policies and Programme for Children in India*, eGyankosh, https://egyankosh.ac.in/bitstream/123456789/1/Unit2.pdf?shem (last visited Dec. 4, 2023).
71 *Policies and Programme for Children in India.*
72 *Policies and Programme for Children in India.*
73 *10 Fundamental Rights of a Child in India-Ensuring a Bright Future*, www.cry.org, https://www.cry.org/blog/rights-of-child-in-india/ (last visited Dec. 4, 2023).
74 *Protect a Generation: Climate Security for India's Children*, https://resourcecentre.savethechildren.net/document/protect-generation-climate-security-indias-children / (last visited Dec. 4, 2023).
75 *Protect a Generation.*
76 *Nineismine Campaign*, https://www.hamraahfoundation.org/nineismine-campaign/ (last visited Dec. 15, 2024).
77 *Nineismine Campaign.*
78 *Nine Is Mine Campaign*, https://www.comminit.com/content/nine-mine-campaign (last visited Dec. 1, 2024).
79 Editor's Desk, *Children Demand Ecological Rights at the No COP Out*, Tattva News-https://en.tattvanews.com/national/children-demand-ecological-rights-at-the-no-cop-out/ (Nov. 4, 2022), (last visited Dec. 1, 2024).

80 Anwesha Majumdar, *At COP27, over 900 Children Formulate Draft Seeking Ecological Rights, Republic World*, (Nov. 13, 2022), https://www.republicworld.com/world-news/at-cop-27-over-900-children-formulate-draft-seeking-ecological-rights-articleshow (last visited Dec. 15, 2024).

81 *Children Demand Ecological Rights Ahead of COP-27*, https://www.indiawaterportal.org/articles/children-demand-ecological-rights-ahead-cop-27 (last visited Dec. 3, 2023).

82 (2017) SCC Online NGT 30.

83 *Climate case chart*, https://climatecasechart.com/non-us-case/pandey-v-india/ (last visited Dec. 19, 2024).

84 *Climate case chart*.

85 Riddhima Pandey v. Union of India, (2019) SCC online NGT 843 (India).

86 M.P. Ram Mohan, Els Reynaers Kini & Sriram Prasad, *India's Progressive Environmental Case Law: A Worthy Roadmap for Global Climate Change Litigation*, 54, Georgetown Journal of International Law, 489, 527–528, (2023) https://www.law.georgetown.edu/international-law-journal/wp-content/uploads/sites/21/2024/03/GT-GJIL240010.pdf.

PART 3

Protection of Children in the Online Platforms

9

BALANCING PROTECTION AND PARTICIPATION

Children's Data, Online Privacy, and Age of Digital Consent

Ananya Singh

Introduction

Despite significant social and legal progress, childhood remains a domain where many stakeholders continue to rely on outdated assumptions and rigid frameworks – most notably, chronological age as a proxy for capacity. The prevailing belief is that children should be kept under parental watch and societal control till they come of age. Age becomes a substantial distinguishing factor between who is a child and who is an adult. Consequently, regardless of a child's level of understanding or competence in a particular domain, they are often limited by the constraints of their age.

While age remains a practical benchmark for designing protections, an uncritical reliance on it risks underestimating children's evolving competence across diverse contexts. The fixation on age as the primary criterion of maturity has two underlying fallacies. First, the universalization of children's growth and competence acquisition trajectories is misleading. To assume that all children constitute a homogeneous group and that the development of their capacities is equally influenced by the same set of factors is far from the truth. In fact, a wide range of factors impacts how children's capacities develop and how such capacities may be interpreted by the world around them. For example, in conflict contexts like mass migration and/or refugee situations, children often take on roles as translators, cultural brokers, and caregivers. They learn new languages faster and navigate bureaucratic systems, helping parents with forms, transport, and appointments. Despite this clear display of social and practical competence, they are still seen as "dependents". Further, what may be considered an adult's responsibility in some cultures may, in fact, be a chore regularly performed by children in other cultures. While

DOI: 10.4324/9781003607076-13

protective frameworks in Western contexts play a critical role in preventing exploitation, they may also overlook the forms of agency and skill development embedded in other culturally specific forms of child participation.

Second, it is unfair to measure children's abilities and capacities based on adult benchmarks. As seen in figures like Greta Thunberg and echoed in numerous local youth movements, children's civic engagement is often disregarded not because of a lack of competence but because critics focus on "age" rather than the content of the message. This illustrates how adult standards of legitimacy silence even highly competent young voices. This blocks adults from seeing or valuing what children do, can do, or wish to do. Similarly, in standardized school systems, a child who is cognitively advanced in, say, mathematics, but "young" by birthdate, is often held back from skipping grades due to rigid age norms. Conversely, a child struggling emotionally or socially is still pushed forward with their age group. This undermines the recognition of developmental asynchrony – emotional, cognitive, and physical maturity do not progress uniformly. As a result, the broader tendency to vest parents with substantial authority over children's rights and decision-making has resulted in the invisibilization and negation of children's capacities.

Against this backdrop, the appearance of the phrase "evolving capacities of the child" in the text of the UN Convention on the Rights of the Child (UNCRC) represented a radical departure. A child was no longer viewed as just a passive recipient of protection but rather s/he was now being seen as an active participant in her/his life.

Now, more than 30 years later, thanks to technology, we stand at the brink of a watershed moment. In the third decade of the 21st century, with increasing access to digital devices from early childhood, questions arise not only about screen time but about how children's identities, learning patterns, and data footprints are being shaped in ways beyond their control. Although massive amounts of data are increasingly being collected about everyone, children's data needs our special attention. Children need to be afforded the agency to define who they are for themselves, without having their future pathways predetermined or their learning styles unduly narrowed down by algorithms.

Hence, over the years, laws have been passed to "protect" children in the online space by handing over the decisions related to their "participation" in the digital arena to their parents. This is based on a two-fold reasoning: (a) children have limited understanding of the risks and rights regarding the processing of personal data, and (b) adults (such as a child's parents) are better equipped to provide meaningful consent for the collection and use of children's data. While it is true that parents act with their child's best interests in mind, the growing complexity of digital contexts introduces new risks that may exceed parents' technical or ethical foresight.

This chapter digs deeper into the concept of "evolving capacities of the child", situating it in the context of the digital era. By contrasting the existing legal frameworks around children's data protection, privacy, and consent, it examines whether it is time to critically re-evaluate the longstanding reliance on chronological age as the primary measure of competence and capacity in children's legal and digital lives.

Age-Gating and Evolving Capacities of the Child

Age-based consent is a pivotal concept in legal frameworks, determining the minimum age at which individuals can legally engage in specific activities, including sexual relations, legal contracts, and voting. In many socio-legal systems, the age of consent is defined based on assumptions about an individual's maturity and capacity to understand the consequences of their actions. Universally, this age is fixed at 18, though it may vary in some national/cultural contexts.

The designation of 18 as the age of adulthood has evolved through a confluence of factors: biologically, most individuals have completed puberty by this age; educationally, it aligns with the typical end of secondary schooling; and, from a civic perspective, it coincides with the age at which individuals become eligible for voting, military service, and jury duty. Historically and politically, the 20th century witnessed a significant shift, particularly during and after the World Wars, when 18-year-olds were widely conscripted into military service. This gave rise to the argument that those old enough to fight for their country should also be granted full civic rights. In 1969, Britain became the first major democratic nation to lower the voting age from 21 to 18. In the United States, the voting age was lowered from 21 to 18 through the 26th Amendment in 1971. India amended its Constitution in 1988 through the 61st Amendment, reducing the voting age from 21 to 18. The United Nations Convention on the Rights of the Child (1989)[1] further reinforced this standard by defining a child as anyone under the age of 18, unless majority is reached earlier under national law.

Common examples of areas where age determines important socio-legal-political functions in India include:

TABLE 9.1 Examples of areas where age of consent is required

Matter	*Age of consent*	*Relevant law*
Voting	18	Representation of the People Act, 1950
Executing legal contracts	18	Indian Contract Act, 1872 (minors cannot enter into binding contracts)
Driving license	18	Motor Vehicles Act, 1988
Marriage	18 (female), 21 (male)	The Prohibition of Child Marriage Act, 2006
Sexual consent	18	Protection of Children from Sexual Offences Act, 2012
Digital consent (data processing)	18	Digital Personal Data Protection Act, 2023

Examples of areas where the age of consent is required.

However, adulthood is ultimately a social construct rather than a purely scientific one. Science can indicate when an average person completes physical growth, but development continues throughout life, and it varies widely among individuals. The digital domain, in fact, further complicates this gradual evolution of responsibility. Unlike driving or voting, where physical and cognitive maturity can be more clearly measured, the digital domain requires an ongoing process of access, learning, and adaptation. The digital age blurs the conventional line between childhood and adulthood, raising important questions about when children are ready to assume responsibility for their actions online. The digital world demands a nuanced understanding of maturity and autonomy, one that more readily embraces the evolving capacities of a child.

The concept of a child's "evolving capacities" emerged during the UNCRC Working Group's discussions on freedom of thought, conscience, and religion.[2] While some expressed concern that children were not being recognized sufficiently as individuals with rights, critics argued that granting too much recognition of a child's capacities could conflict with the established scope of parental rights under international, national, or religious laws. To address these issues, the Canadian Delegation proposed a draft that included the phrase "evolving capacities of the child". Following this, the draft text was altered to read:

> The States Parties shall respect the rights and duties of the parents and, where applicable, legal guardians, to provide direction to the child in the exercise of his right in a manner consistent with the evolving capacities of the child.

Later, the delegations from Norway, Canada, Sweden, and Argentina agreed that there was indeed "need for a general provision dealing with the evolving capacities of the child". In the 1987 Working Group session, a preliminary document was presented by the United States and Australia, which highlighted the significant role of parents as the main holders of rights.2 The Canadian Delegation asserted that the main focus should be on safeguarding the child's rights, rather than simply restating the rights of parents. Later, Australia, Austria, the Netherlands, and the United States submitted the following new draft text:

> The States Parties to the present Convention shall respect the rights and duties of the parents and, where applicable, legal guardians, to provide direction to the child in the exercise of his or her rights enumerated in the present Convention in a manner consistent with the evolving capacities of the child, having due regard for the importance of promoting the

> development of the skills and knowledge required for an independent adulthood.

While certain delegates continued to express concerns about the perceived lack of protection for parental rights, the members of the Working Group emphasized that the Convention had already recognized and emphasized the important roles parents have in the upbringing of children. They argued that it was now crucial to shift the focus toward the child's evolving capacities. The final version of Article 5 of the UNCRC now reads:

> States Parties shall respect the responsibilities, rights, and duties of parents, or, where applicable, the members of the extended family or community as provided for by local custom, legal guardians or other persons legally responsible for the child, to provide, in a manner consistent with the evolving capacities of the child, appropriate direction and guidance in the exercise by the child of the rights recognized in the present Convention.

The UNCRC, thus, recognizes that, as children grow, their capacities evolve and that parents should adjust their approach to help children take more responsibility for their decisions. "Evolving capacities" as a policy principle breaks away from the traditional notion that children lack capacity until they cross a specific age threshold or achieve adulthood.[3] Children's capacities develop progressively as they grow, gaining skills in reasoning, communication, and decision-making. While they may initially require significant support, over time, they become more capable of engaging with and responding to their environment. Recognizing this progression means allowing children increasing opportunities to express their views, assume responsibilities, and participate in decisions that affect their well-being.

However, while this recognition made children visible as rights-holders under international law, it did not – and still does not – grant children the right to independently exercise these rights based solely on their evolving capacities. Instead, it ensures that children are entitled to receive appropriate direction and guidance from their parents or guardians to fully enjoy these rights. This cautious, "guarded" approach likely arose from the drafters' concerns that acknowledging a child's evolving capacities could conflict with established parental rights and the sanctity of the family, potentially undermining the child's best interests. This concern is based on the assumption that children lack full capacity, meaning they must reach a certain age threshold before they can be entrusted with decision-making rights.

Article 12 of the UNCRC asserts that:

> States parties 'shall assure to the child who is capable of forming his or her own views the right to express those views freely in all matters affecting

the child, the views of the child being given due weight in accordance with the age and maturity of the child'.

While this chapter recognizes children as active agents entitled to participate in decisions that affect their lives, the words "age", "capable", and "maturity" are subjective. While a five-month-old and a five-year-old are entitled to the same rights, their capacities are significantly distinct. But age may not always correlate with enhanced capacities or higher maturity. For instance, a 10-year-old child may demonstrate a higher level of maturity than a 12-year-old child, who may still need guidance in making responsible choices. Therefore, standardizing consent requirements across age groups may prove to be counterproductive to children's preparation for and participation in society and the economy.

It has also been pointed out that children's development can be very different based on their socio-economic circumstances. A 14-year-old belonging to a low socio-economic status might have similar knowledge and digital literacy as a 10-year-old from a high socio-economic status. Therefore, solely relying on age as a determining factor may overlook the diverse range of abilities and knowledge that different children possess, based on their personal circumstances. This lopsided approach may significantly disadvantage the children growing up in the Global South.

The "deficit model" of childhood, which views children primarily as passive recipients of protection, contrasts with the UNCRC's vision of recognizing children as active participants with rights and agency. The idea that a number is the ultimate parameter to judge a child's capacity fails to acknowledge the immense variability and complexity of human development. It overlooks the fact that children, even at a young age, possess unique talents, insights, and capabilities that can surpass the limitations imposed by their chronological age. Maturity is, in fact, a function of a multiplicity of factors such as a child's "evolving" individual experiences, personal potentials, cognitive abilities, emotional intelligence, social competence, and moral reasoning. Therefore, this over-reliance on age as the ultimate criterion to decide who is capable and who is not leads to the oversimplification, homogenization, and standardization of children's evolving capacities and varying childhood experiences. Hence, the question remains: *should chronological age remain the sole determinant of a child's capacity to have and/or exercise rights?*

While age-gating may provide clarity and consistency in determining children's autonomy, such rigid criteria may erroneously universalize and oversimplify the diverse capacities and needs of individual children. Findings indicate that children's competencies are developed through experiences, cultural factors, and parental involvement, not just by the passage of time.[4] This highlights the need for policymakers to consider children's right to participate in and take responsibility for decisions they are capable of, while also ensuring adequate protection. On the other hand, operating in a sans-age floor manner might risk exposing some children to greater harm online. Therefore, it is in fact a Herculean task to specify the different age thresholds at which children should be afforded varying degrees of autonomy and agency to take responsibility (such as providing consent). Lansdown (2005) outlines several potential models for determining children's rights, each with its own advantages and disadvantages. One approach is the current convention of establishing fixed, prescribed age limits in the law. Alternatively, age restrictions could be eliminated and replaced with a system of individual assessments to evaluate a child's ability to exercise a specific right. Under this approach, the law would presume competence, placing the responsibility on adults to prove a child's incapacity if they wish to limit the child's rights. Another possibility would be to maintain age limits but permit children who show sufficient competence to access certain rights at an earlier age. Lastly, a more differentiated approach could be adopted, where age limits are applied only to those rights most vulnerable to abuse or neglect by adults, while other rights would operate under a presumption of competence, enabling children to exercise them more freely.

Digital Natives and Age of Digital Consent

The internet transcends time and space, offering unprecedented opportunities for connection, creativity, and self-expression. As a result, children, today, are exposed to a wealth of information, resources, and tools online. They are actively engaging in and with online communities to express their opinions and participate in discussions that shape their understanding of the world. They are displaying a new level of sensibility and independence in the digital realm.

Today, even very young children commonly use digital devices, almost all of which operate by monetizing data collection, processing, and usage. While children are the original creators and owners of the resulting data traces, in most cultural and legal contexts, it is their adult guardians who have the final say over who can collect, process, and store their data. Simply put, while they are afforded the freedom to participate in potentially risky activities online, their status as children leaves them without the autonomy and agency required to navigate digital experiences and/or negotiate any control over their data footprints. This has paved the way for the discourse on the age of digital consent. The age of digital consent refers to the minimum age at which children can provide consent to companies/organizations to collect, process, use, and store their data.

In the United States, under the Children's Online Privacy Protection Act (COPPA) of 2000,[4] digital service providers must acquire verifiable parental consent for users under the age of 13. "Verifiable parental consent" refers to any reasonable process by which a parent is informed that their child's personal data is being collected and processed and then gives their consent. This can be done through methods such as video or phone calls, parental payment systems, electronic scans, or the use of government-issued IDs, among others. Further, multiple bills pertaining to securing a safe online space for children have been tendered in the US over the years. One such bill is the Protecting Kids on Social Media Act,[5] which proposes mandating social media companies to obtain parental or guardian consent to allow those between the ages of 12 and 17 years to use social media. The Kids Online Safety Act[6] seeks to require companies to obtain parent's/guardian's consent before allowing children under the age of 17 to use their platforms. COPPA 2.0[7] proposes to tighten the age-gating mechanisms by potentially raising the age of protection from under 13 to 16 years of age. All of these acts and bills, while being in conflict with one another over minimum age, meet at the "over-reliance on parental consent" square.

The European Union's General Data Protection Regulation[8] requires children between the ages of 13 and 16 to provide verifiable parental consent for the processing of their data. But EU member states remain free to set a different age of digital consent. For example, the Netherlands[9] and Germany[10] have set the age of digital consent at 16, France[11] at 15, Italy[12] and Spain[13] at 14, and Denmark[14] and Sweden[15] at 13. China's[16] Personal Information Protection Law states that parental consent is an absolute must for processing the data of anyone younger than 14 years of age. China and the EU lower the minimum age of consent compared to others, but both tend to standardize "minorhood" and children's capacities, which may overlook individual differences.

Although Australia's Privacy Act of 1988[17] does not define an age upon reaching which an individual can make his/her own privacy-related decision, it states that consent is deemed to be valid only when it is given by an individual who has the capacity to provide such consent. According to the act, platforms are tasked with assessing the capacity of users under the age of 18 to provide consent on a case-by-case basis. By empowering platforms to evaluate capacity on a case-by-case basis, Australia sets the precedent for taking a more nuanced, non-standard, and sensitive approach to diverse children, their varying childhoods, and their different evolving capacities to make privacy decisions. However, the Act's ambiguous language places significant responsibility on platforms, which could result in inconsistent protection for children.

India's Digital Personal Data Protection Act of 2023[18] mandates that, prior to processing the data of any individual below the age of 18, entities must obtain parental consent. Results from the National Statistical Office's 78th Round Survey in 2020–21[19] indicate that ICT skills are higher among younger age groups. Hence, by overly relying on parental consent, it ignores empirical and anecdotal evidence wherein parents in fact seek advice from their children about navigating digital devices and the internet. Moreover, this "one-size-fits-all" approach pegs the minimum age of digital consent at a much higher level than the aforementioned contemporary global legal frameworks.

Except for Australia, most frameworks apply uniform age thresholds that fail to account for children's individual developmental differences. Children are mostly lumped into overly broad categories such as under-13s and under-18s. Instead of recognizing the unique developmental journey of each child, these frameworks rely on arbitrary age thresholds to determine a child's capacity to provide digital consent. This approach risks underestimating or overestimating children's capacities and may not adequately protect their rights and well-being. Moreover, though the rapid pace of technological advancements often outpaces parents' understanding and knowledge of digital platforms and data privacy, the frameworks continue to rely on parental consent for the processing of children's digital personal data. This lack of awareness or complete information on the part of the parents may inadvertently expose their children to privacy risks. Additionally, overlooking the valuable insights and perspectives that children themselves can offer when it comes to their own digital privacy is a mistake that will cost dearly.

Recommendations

While the current reliance on uniform age thresholds for digital consent faces valid criticism for oversimplifying children's diverse capacities, it is important to recognize the practical reasons behind this approach. A differential age of consent recognizes that children's ability to understand and make informed decisions about digital interactions is not uniform but influenced by various factors, including social, economic, political, and demographic conditions; it is also inherently subjective, which risks inconsistency in applying the law, leaving room for exploitation or misunderstanding. Because platforms and regulators often lack the tools to assess each child's consent capacity, fixed age limits provide a practical legal benchmark. Policymakers often favor clear, fixed ages because they facilitate consistent legal enforcement and provide straightforward guidance for parents, educators, and technology companies. Uniform ages reduce ambiguity and help ensure that protections are applied broadly and efficiently, especially in complex digital environments where assessing individual capacity on a case-by-case basis can be challenging and resource-intensive. However, balancing these practical considerations with more flexible, context-sensitive approaches could better respect children's evolving abilities while still ensuring clear protection and legal clarity.

On the other hand, while the involvement of parents in their children's digital lives is typically seen as beneficial, this arrangement has significant drawbacks. Many parents lack the digital literacy necessary to fully assess the complexities of digital environments and/or understand the implications of online agreements. For example, in rural areas where digital literacy is often lower and access to technology is limited, parents may struggle to understand the implications of consenting to data collection, leading to uninformed or hesitant decisions. In contrast, urban parents might have better digital skills but face challenges navigating complex privacy policies often presented only in dominant languages, which excludes non-native speakers. Additionally, socio-economic disparities further complicate digital literacy efforts, as families with fewer resources may lack access to education or the tools necessary to fully grasp the risks and rights involved in digital consent. The use of complex, jargon-ridden language by technology companies is another hindrance. A parent may unknowingly authorize an app that collects excessive personal data or that includes harmful content, simply because they do not understand the app's terms of service or privacy policies. Additionally, there exists a generational gap in digital fluency, with many parents struggling to keep up with rapidly evolving technologies and platforms. As a result, they may be unable to anticipate the full range of risks their children may face online. Moreover, there is a concern that some parents, out of an abundance of caution, may impose overly restrictive measures on their children's digital access. This parental overreach may hinder children's ability to develop critical digital literacy skills and autonomy, potentially straining the parent-child relationship and fostering a lack of trust. Thus, placing the responsibility of evaluating the appropriateness of a platform or application's data protection and privacy policies on parents is an exorbitant miscalculation. Rather, children, who often have firsthand experience with evolving risks (compared to adults), may be better placed to exercise caution and make informed decisions regarding their data, privacy, and safety online.

Given these complexities, a balanced approach is necessary. First, as children have firsthand experience of what it means to grow up in the digital age, their perception of the digital world should be integrated into any policy or framework concerning safeguarding children's privacy online. This could be done by creating a system that allows for the evaluation of a child's capacity to give informed consent based not solely on age but on demonstrated digital literacy and cognitive maturity. Such a framework would avoid the rigid application of age-based laws and instead recognize the "evolving capacities of children". An all-encompassing, nuanced, and context-specific rubric to determine the level of a child's capacities and his/her ability to participate in the digital world should be developed. This rubric must factor in a child's gender, age, family background, social standing, financial health, educational level, cultural context, and national environment to determine the quality of capacities the said child evolves/may evolve. This holistic approach will recognize the multifaceted nature of a child's development and ensure that their digital experiences & opportunities are appropriately tailored to their unique circumstances.

Second, it is imperative to enhance digital literacy education for both children and parents. Schools, communities, and digital platforms should collaborate to provide accessible educational programs that equip parents with the knowledge needed to make informed decisions about digital consent and help children develop critical thinking skills regarding online risks. Children and parents should also be provided with resources and support networks, such as helplines or online forums, where they can seek advice and guidance regarding their digital privacy. Technology companies should also be legally mandated to provide their terms and conditions in child-friendly, jargon-free, and (wherever possible) local languages.

The road to granting children the agency to exercise their rights in a manner that is consistent with their evolving capacities begins with a multi-national, multi-stakeholder consultation to revisit and review what "evolving capacities" mean in the 21st century in general and in the digital age in particular.

Matters of child protection and child participation in the digital era are not mutually exclusive events. The conceptualization of a reasonable non-zero-sum game between child participation and child protection necessitates ensuring that protection does not diminish the room for respectful recognition of children's agency and that participation does not prematurely burden children with responsibilities typically associated with adulthood. There is an urgent need to recognize children as rights-holders, agents, and equal stakeholders in any conversation concerning their digital personal data. Therefore, affording intergenerational justice mandates moving beyond "age" as the sole determinant in the recognition of children's capacities and exercise of rights. Respecting children's evolving capacities in the digital age is like nurturing a creeper plant. One must do everything that one would normally do for an upright tree. But when the creeper starts charting its own path (however twisty), choosing its own direction, and embracing its independence, all one should do is to provide it a safe environment to flourish in.

Notes

1 *Convention on the Rights of the Child*, art. 5 & 14, G.A. Res. 44/25, U.N. GAOR, 44th Sess., U.N. Doc. A/44/49 (1989). UNICEF.

2 U.N. Comm. on the Rts. of the Child, Report of the Working Group on a Draft Convention on the Rights of the Child, paras. 15–16, U.N. Doc. E/CN.4/1984/71 (1984); *Compilation of General Comments and General Recommendations Adopted by Human Rights Treaty Bodies*, U.N. Doc. HRI/GEN/1/Rev.9 (Vol. I), at 455 (2007), as cited in S. Varadan, The Principle of Evolving Capacities under the UN Convention on the Rights of the Child, 27 *The International Journal of Children's Rights* 306, 308 (2019).

3 Sheila Varadan, The Principle of Evolving Capacities under the UN Convention on the Rights of the Child, 27 *The International Journal of Children's Rights* 306 (2019), https://doi.org/10.1163/15718182-02702006.
4 Children's Online Privacy Protection Act of 1998, 15 U.S.C. §§ 6501–6506 (2000).
5 Protecting Kids on Social Media Act, S. 1291, 118th Cong. (2023).
6 Kids Online Safety Act, S. 1409, 118th Cong. (2023).
7 Children and Teens' Online Privacy Protection Act, S. 1418, 118th Cong. (2023).
8 Regulation (EU) 2016/679 of the European Parliament and of the Council of 27 April 2016 on the protection of natural persons with regard to the processing of personal data and on the free movement of such data (General Data Protection Regulation), 2016 O.J. (L 119) 1.
9 *Implementing Act for the General Data Protection Regulation*, art. 5 (2018) (Netherlands).
10 *Bundesdatenschutzgesetz* (BDSG), the German Federal Data Protection Act.
11 *Loi n° 78–17 du 6 janvier 1978 relative à l'informatique, aux fichiers et aux libertés* [Law No. 78–17 of 6 January 1978 on Information Technology, Files, and Freedoms], art. 8, (as amended by *Loi n° 2018–493 du 20 juin 2018*), art. 45 (2018).
12 *Codice in materia di protezione dei dati personali* [Personal Data Protection Code], art. 2-quinquies (2018).
13 *Ley Orgánica 3/2018, de 5 de diciembre, de Protección de Datos Personales y garantía de los derechos digitales* [Organic Law 3/2018 of 5 December 2018 on Personal Data Protection and Guarantee of Digital Rights], art. 7 (2018) (Spain).
14 *Lov om behandling af personoplysninger* [Act on Processing of Personal Data], § 106 (2018) (Denmark).
15 Swedish Code of Statutes, Act containing supplementary provisions to the EU General Data Protection Regulation, ch. 2, § 4 (2018).
16 *Personal Information Protection Law of the People's Republic of China*, art. 31, 2021.
17 Privacy Act 1988 (Cth) (Austl.).
18 *Digital Personal Data Protection Act, 2023 (India).*
19 *(National Statistical Office, 78th Round Survey Report 35, Appendix A (Table 14) (2020–21)).*

10

SAFEGUARDING THE VULNERABILITIES OF CHILDREN RELATING TO CYBERBULLYING FROM THE SOCIO-LEGAL-TECHNICAL DIMENSIONS IN INDIA

Parimita Dash and Soumya Mohapatra

Introduction

The ongoing evolution of social media and digital technologies is changing the way we live, making it easier to connect with more people and build relationships with the simple click of a keyboard. These advancements have a profound impact on how we socialize, do our work, and interact with one another, and also how we perceive and think of ourselves, as these communications have become a part of our identity. A significant amount of our interactions today is virtual and relies heavily on the internet for accessing information and engaging in collaborative endeavors using tools like email, instant messengers, and video conferencing. Be it the middle-aged, the elderly, the youth, or children, everyone's life has been touched by these technologies. But as far as children are concerned, cyberspace poses specific risks.

As technology continues to reshape the world across all age groups, this chapter focuses on children due to their distinctive characteristics in the digital landscape. Children stand out as the demographic with the highest level of access to computers and the internet, a trend emphasized by Watkins.[1] Moreover, they represent the generation with extensive access to mobile phones, tablets, laptops, and other gadgets from a young age, enabling them to stay connected with social media and friends through internet at all times, without the need for any physical proximity. Recognized as enthusiastic early adopters of technology, children and youth effortlessly integrate various forms of technology into their daily lives.

During adolescence, children undergo a crucial phase of identity development, which is formed along with socialization. This process involves learning societal norms, values, and morals; the socially approved ways of

DOI: 10.4324/9781003607076-14

thinking and behaving; and, in the process, becoming functional members of society. This contributes to the formation of a unique identity or personality. As society introduces new modes of interaction like social networking and instant messaging, the dynamics of communication are undergoing significant changes. The advent of the internet, with its array of both positive and negative aspects, lacks the conventional monitoring mechanisms found in traditional forms of socialization, which operate to control and regulate behavior through a system of rewards and punishments. This absence of social control significantly increases the likelihood of adolescents engaging in risky behavior, making them susceptible to various forms of cyberbullying, which prominently marks the biggest vulnerability that children and young adolescents are exposed to in cyberspace. This issue of cyberbullying, along with other risks associated with social media and the internet, has emerged as a prominent challenge in the 21st century. While it spans across the lifespan, the bulk of research and attention has concentrated on children and young individuals, where the prevalence of cyberbullying appears to be most pronounced. This chapter aims at exploring the various sociological dimensions of the issue of cyberbullying, of which the children often become victims in today's digital world, along with analyzing to what extent the various legal and technological measures that have been adopted in India to deal with the issue of cyberbullying have been effective.

Cyberbullying and Its Implications: The Sociological Perspective

Cyberbullying is defined as 'an aggressive and intentional act carried out by either an individual or a group through electronic means, repeated over time against a victim who is unable to easily defend themselves'[2] by a peer of the same age, exerting power. According to this definition, cyberbullying is an act that is repeated and refers to intentional aggressive behavior perpetrated by an individual within the same age group who exercises dominance over a victim who is unable to readily shield themselves through electronic media.

The internet and personal gadgets grant children continuous access to their personal face-to-face networks, operating 24 hours a day. While this accessibility can be advantageous for adolescents navigating social challenges or who are 'socially awkward', providing extended supportive peer networks, it also carries negative implications, notably in the form of cyberbullying, where unflattering content such as photographs, rumors, and communications can be rapidly and widely disseminated.

Distinction Between Traditional Bullying and Cyberbullying

The digital space serves as a liberating arena for young individuals,[3] offering a lot of opportunities for self-expression. Similar to offline or physical interactions, the digital world is governed by certain emerging norms that dictate acceptable technology use, which are distinct from the norms related to interactions in physical settings.[4] These norms are altered compared to the 'real world', where rules of 'impression management'[5] are very different. Additionally, when one compares the physical setting that a school offers to the digital environment, one can decipher the unique characteristics that it possesses. In a school, bullying is mostly direct as there is physical proximity between the perpetrator and the victim. Digital technology use is private and unlimited and allows for the rapid, secretive spread of cyberbullying incidents.[6]

Another notable distinction that can be observed in the digital space, in contrast to direct and personal interactions, is the absence of spatial or physical boundaries. Digital technology enables cyberbullies to victimize a substantial number of individuals almost effortlessly and without being limited by physical confines.[7] In other words, cyberbullying can take place easily even when the perpetrator and the victim are not present within the same geographical space. Consequently, in comparison to physical bullying and targeting, there is the potential for limitless perpetrators and targets in the digital space.[8]

Moreover, the digital space is not limited by any social norms or rules, with less restrictive standards governing social interactions as compared to the direct physical ones. As a result, the youth in the digital space have a lot more opportunities to present different shades of their personalities and identities as well as opinions, both positive and negative. This is something that they might not be too comfortable with in the 'real' world. Young individuals perceive cyberspace as an impersonal environment, providing them with the perceived freedom to express themselves without constraints. This perception is associated with the essence of disinhibition in the digital or virtual world, where scholars have contended that there is a high probability of transformation of an individual's online behavior due to the absence of social censorship seen in face-to-face interactions.[9] Unlike direct, physical bullying, cyberbullying lacks the immediate interpretation of non-verbal cues and responses of witnesses, leading to an absence or minimization of social checks.

Bussey et al. argue that when it comes to the digital space, factors which more personal in nature, for example, morality, become significant. Morals, acting as guiding principles for appropriate behavior in social interactions, can be selectively disengaged as the perpetrator cannot see the reaction of the victim. This enables individuals engaging in cyberbullying to suspend their moral beliefs during specific episodes, avoiding internal conflict or psychological distress. When there is a perception among individuals that there would not be any negative consequences of their behavior, then the chances become highly likely that they will indulge in behavior which they would normally avoid. Thus, this perception modifies the boundaries of acceptable virtual/online behavior.[10]

Espinosa and Clemente[11] have theorized online behavior in terms of what they call the 'time displacement hypothesis', suggesting that the time spent online by young people may detract from face-to-face socialization opportunities, impacting their cognitive and social skill development. Increased digital engagement, as supported by empirical evidence, is associated with a higher likelihood of an individual being both a victim and an offender of cyberbullying.[12] The multitude of technology forms used by young people contributes to a unique aspect of cyberbullying, where they can feel bombarded due to various channels, which is different from direct bullying.[13] Darden adds that the digital realm also allows for documenting and recording cyberbullying incidents, a capability often lacking in physical situations.

Furthermore, the power relationship in cyberbullying is different from direct, physical bullying. An implication of this is that disparity between the victim and the perpetrator is not always based on might or toughness but on knowledge of the digital world and technology, as well as facelessness.[14] In cyberbullying, this discrepancy of power dynamics reflects the target's perceived lack of power rather than the dominance of the offender.[15] Since the perpetrators are able to conceal and generate suspicion about their identities, this gives them more power[16], [17]

This difference in the power relationship significantly increases because the victims are not able to properly and efficiently react to these incidents of cyberbullying. Butler and Campbell[18] posit that there is a global reach of cyberbullying's potential audience, which renders its targets powerless. As mentioned earlier, young individuals often lack the capability to remove publicly available information resulting from cyberbullying episodes. To address this, they must request website owners or intermediaries to intervene, a process that is not always straightforward. Unlike incidents of direct bullying and harassment in school settings, which are generally subject to direct administration by teachers and other staff with specific, formally codified rules, the nature of digital technology dilutes the level of surveillance. Consequently, this diminished control by authority figures has a tendency to encourage perpetrators who indulge in cyberbullying to resort to behavior which would, under normal circumstances, be curtailed by both formal and informal norms.[19]

Moreover, in the usual cases of direct bullying, the victims can usually identify the perpetrator directly, whereas in cases of cyberbullying, accurately determining the real identity of the offender may prove more challenging. Digital technology provides individuals with the ability to feel anonymous and, as a result, invincible by either concealing or manipulating their real identity. According to some scholars, this perception of facelessness granted by the internet, along with a lack of restrictions, gives the offenders greater liberty to act.[20]

Children's Vulnerabilities in Cyberbullying

The advent of the internet and its easy access today has expanded the avenues for communication, offering various platforms like message boards, blogs, emails, and instant messaging. These tools have made an important contribution in helping individuals to express their thoughts on diverse topics, share multimedia content, and engage in conversations. Social networking sites, such as Facebook, consolidate these communication channels, enabling users to create profiles, exchange messages, chat in real-time, and update statuses.

While these technologies bridge physical distances among friends after school, they also harbor the potential for negative consequences. Unfortunately, they can become spaces where rumors are spread, and peers are socially sabotaged, causing a sense of panic, shame, and vulnerability[21], [22] So, it is important to comprehend the essence, attributes, and magnitude of the issue of cyberbullying and cyber victimization within the shared school environment.

In social network environments and instant messaging programs, connections are labeled as being 'friends' with a particular person or persons. However, it's essential to acknowledge that these virtual connections may not always correspond to genuine friendships, as a lot of these 'friends' could be individuals whom one might not have met or ever is likely to meet. Similar to the complexities of categorizing relationships in the physical world, online connections may involve acquaintances or individuals only partially known. Actions taken on social network sites occur in front of a virtual audience of 'friends', with limited visibility and potential unfamiliarity, and no knowledge of what information is revealed and what is concealed. Despite the virtual nature, it's vital to recognize the overlap between face-to-face and virtual worlds through interconnected peer networks.[23]

Cyberbullying in the Indian Context

According to the National Crime Records Bureau of India, the number of cyberbullying cases in the country reported a 63.48% surge from the year 2018 to 2019. Even though comprehensive data about cyberbullying in India is not available, different studies point to two facts. Firstly, the cases of cyberbullying in India are rising, and the cases of cyberbullying have regional variations across India.[24]

In India a study conducted in 2020 reported that 9.2% of adolescents in the National Capital Region experienced cyberbullying.[25] One such case states about the ordeals a now college-going woman in New Delhi had to face as a pre-teenager when one of her classmates collected her photographs and personal information and used those to impersonate her on Facebook, leading to a lot of mental agony for the woman. In another case in New Delhi, a woman had to face abusive trolling for almost half a decade for a post on Facebook which was critical of the government. These cases are the tip of the iceberg, which points to a larger problem that plagues society.

Victims of cyberbullying encounter different kinds of aggressive behavior, such as harassing messages or emails, abusive and denigrating comments, cyber-stalking, and public shaming. In India, the modus operandi of cyberbullying among adolescents includes online threats, identity theft, trolling, body shaming, and spreading rumors. Adolescents, being particularly vulnerable, experience cyberbullying through text messages, phone calls, social media, and other digital platforms. Social networking sites such as Instagram, Facebook, Twitter, and WhatsApp are frequently used for these activities. Many victims experience multiple forms of cyberbullying, which underlines the widespread nature of this issue.

A 2022 survey conducted by global computer security firm McAfee came up with a report, 'Cyberbullying in Plain Sight',[26] which uncovered disturbing trends. For example, it discovered that almost 85% of Indian children have reported experiencing cyberbullying, which is the highest proportion globally. The study aimed to uncover significant trends related to cyberbullying across ten countries. The survey, conducted from June 15 to July 5, involved a little over 11,000 parents and their children from ten different nations, including India, among others. It was carried out through online questionnaires.

In addition to being the most targeted as victims, Indian children were reported to engage in cyberbullying at a rate twice the international average. According to the aforementioned McAfee report, about 45% of Indian children admitted to cyberbullying strangers, as contrasted with 17% globally. Moreover, 48% of Indian children acknowledged cyberbullying someone they were familiar with, in contrast to 21% in other countries. The predominant ways in which cyberbullying took place in India included circulating gossip (39%), shunning out from groups or discussions (35%), and slandering or name-calling (34%).

The study highlighted that children in India faced the maximum occurrences of 'extreme forms of cyberbullying' worldwide, encompassing instances of racial discrimination, sexual harassment, and intimidating threats of bodily harm. Approximately 42% of Indian children experienced racist cyberbullying, a figure 14% higher than the global average of 28%. Other extreme forms included intentionally making inflammatory statements or trolling (36%), personal attacks (29%), sexual harassment (30%), intimidating by threatening personal harm (28%), and publishing private and personal information with the intention of harming (23%), all of which were described as twice the international average.[27]

This report shows that in India the instances of cyberbullying were quite high, where more than one in three children, sometimes at an extremely young age (around 10 years), faced issues like digital racism, sexual harassment, and intimidation by threatening physical injury. These statistics make India the leading country with the maximum reported cases of cyberbullying. The study also revealed that the group most vulnerable to online bullying was girls in the age group of 10 to 16 years. This age group, according to the McAfee Corp report, reported facing sexual harassment, intimidation by threatening personal injury in the range of 32–34%, which is much more than the world figures.[28] Surveying 14 social media platforms, including Snapchat, Facebook, and Instagram, the study found that the reported instances of cyberbullying among Indian children are approximately one and a half times more than their counterparts from other nations on these digital spaces. Additionally, this report shows that in India 45% of the children concealed the fact from their family that they were being cyberbullied, a rate lower than the global average of 64%, potentially due to a lack of understanding of the issue. The report also showed that Indian parents displayed significant knowledge gaps about cyberbullying, and children often did not perceive behaviors like bullying and slandering as malicious online behavior. As there is a lack of meaningful communication, assistance from any support group, Indian children were reported to address cyberbullying by themselves, with the most common response being deletion of the account (58%) to avoid further problems, and a significant number of them confided in their friends about their experiences (87%).[29]

Professor Halder, who is the founder of the Centre for Cyber Victim Counseling, is of the opinion that among adolescents in India cyberbullying is not only verbal but also takes various sexually explicit non-verbal forms, such as the use of pictures, memes, and graphics interchange format. He also notes that a lot of the parents of the victimized children, instead of supporting and motivating their wards, end up normalizing this violence by saying that it is a part of growing up, and one should be strong enough to deal with it, or that they should have been more careful and avoided the whole situation. All this ends up pushing the child into a shell. Moreover, school management also evades or brushes off these issues, as it would dent their image.[30]

Technology and Cyberbullying

Cyberbullying, an outcome of interactions in the digital world, requires technological interventions to combat its menace. Technology can be a facilitator of cyberbullying and also can be instrumental in combating cyberbullying, depending on the intention with which it is being used. Hence, technological measures to prevent cyberbullying are an important issue that needs special focus, and hence constant debates and deliberations are needed to come up with new-age technology that will restrict interaction in the digital world with age-appropriate standards, which will definitely restrict children from getting exposed to such online interactions which may lead to their bullying.

Parental control software is one of those technology-driven measures which can restrict children's access to some online platforms that might appear as unsafe for their consumption. Such apps, once downloaded on the phone/laptops/PCs which the children use, do not allow them to access content on certain online platforms which are not age appropriate for them. In this way they are barred from being exposed to such platforms, which may make them vulnerable by compromising their privacy or the privacy of the data shared by them online in good faith, which may have exposed them to blackmail at a later instance as victims of cyberbullying. Hence, it is essentially necessary that, when it comes to the children's online activities, parents must take more care and be more cautious toward such vulnerabilities to which their children may be exposed. And one of the effective ways of showing caution in this regard is to allow parental control software to do its job, while the child interacts in the digital world.[31] This is more effective for the parents of children below 10 years of age, where the online activity of the children is regulated by their parents in a true sense, as such children are dependent on their parents when it comes to their interactions in the digital world.

Another such technology-driven measure to deal with the issues of cyberbullying that children face in cyberspace is 'keyword-spotting' blockers.[32] These blockers help in identifying such keywords, which might not be conducive enough for children and block all such content associated with such keywords from popping up on the screen while the child is using the device to connect to the digital space. These are the kind of apps/software which work on the keyword algorithm, in which some keywords may be identified by the user as restrictive, and once the user enables the restrictive settings on the device, any content on the internet corresponding with those keywords would automatically get filtered and access to such content will be completely prohibited. Most of these apps suggest many such keywords on their own which are already embedded in them, and the user just has to enable the restrictive access based on those keyword settings on the device. A few of these apps/software also allow the user to choose his/her own keywords based on which the user wants to restrict the content. This feature may be in addition to the availability of the suggestive keywords already embedded in those apps. The keywords may be with regard to hate speech, toxic or abusive content, violence, and nudity. Once such content is restricted from a child's consumption, half of the battle is already won in not exposing the child to volatile interfaces and hence eliminating any possibility of the privacy of the children or their personal data being compromised, leading to cases of cyberbullying and hence creating a safe ambience for the child to grow and learn using the digital platforms.

Machine learning is another way of ensuring cyber-security and often regarded as an effective measure to find out any malware targeted at one's device, which can be potent enough to compromise on privacy of the individual.[33] Kids, while interacting in an online space, often are careless or do not appreciate the dangers of clicking unknown prompted links and sometimes end up clicking on such links, which in turn are found to be malware which automatically gets downloaded in their devices, compromising the security of such devices, making all data and information residing in the device vulnerable. Such malware allows the devices to be operated remotely once they are downloaded, giving a third-party sitting at a far-off place all the power to operate the device and control it from the other end. This risks the privacy of the young children to an extent that they often become victims of blackmail and bullying, affecting their mental peace hugely, forcing them often to take drastic steps in their lives. Machine learning comes as a savior in such situations. Machine learning is one of the finest technological innovations that studies the patterns of the data and logs of a device and tries to find out malware which cause the cyber-attack. It then tries to fix them by running counter-cyber-attack software, thereby ensuring minimum damage to the data residing in the device and also ensuring that the privacy of such data is not further compromised.[34]

One of the greatest technological innovations of late has been the advent of artificial intelligence (AI). These days AI is being often used to regulate bullying or offensive or abusive content online. Many of the social media companies are heavily relying on AI to create such algorithms that will find out any kind of hate speech or abusive language in the digital space which may trigger cyberbullying.[35] AI not only filters the expression of abusive language or hate speech but also can analyze subtle sarcastic comments leading to bullying, and on this count it stands out from various other software created earlier with the same objective of identifying bullying content in the online space. AI has better analyzing capabilities and hence better serves the purpose of identifying such content, which can be bullying not only expressly but also can be implied bullying. Meta, formerly known as Facebook, has of late heavily used AI to take down any such abusive, toxic, and bullying content found by the AI on its platform before inviting any legal troubles for itself, invoking liability on its part in this context. AI has its own pros and cons and is definitely not free from flaws, but it has definitely come up as the next big thing in the technology domain, penetrating into almost all fields of invention and innovation, making the human race dependent on it more and more for varying purposes. AI has proved itself to be effective enough in maintaining cyber-security, because of which giant online service providers have started resorting to AI for maintaining their cyber-security.

In light of the discussions made previously, technological measures are definitely an effective measure to curb cyberbullying by protecting children from becoming victims of such cyberbullying in the first place. However, these measures do not provide any sanction for the wrong-doers who propagate cyberbullying in cyberspace, thereby leaving room for discussions on the effectiveness of legal measures in combating these issues of cyberbullying.

Cyberbullying and Its Implications: The Legal Perspective

The gravity of cyberbullying cannot be underscored by highlighting the fact that this act of bullying someone in the digital space, often operating on anonymity, makes it difficult to trace the wrong-doer, but it can affect the person so bullied to such an extent that he/she might even take the drastic step of committing suicide. If this act of cyberbullying can have such a grave cascading effect, it is pertinent to deliberate on addressing this issue with stringent laws across the countries in the world. In a country like India with a huge population and even a sizeable internet population, effective laws against cyberbullying are the need of the hour.

However, India to date doesn't have a comprehensive law on cyberbullying. Other laws regulating cyberspace and its interactions do provide provisions relating to cyberbullying in an implied manner. Also, the Indian Penal Code provides for cyberbullying in an implied manner. The Government of India has also come up with policies, schemes, guidelines, and initiatives from time to time to combat various issues pertaining to cyberspace and its interactions, including the issue of cyberbullying. This segment of the chapter will involve an analysis of the various relevant provisions of the existing laws on cyberbullying making an attempt at evaluating whether such existing legal provisions are effective to ensure cyber-security and prevent online bullying or whether India needs a sui generis law on cyberbullying considering the growing dependence of people on the digital space, thereby causing a substantial rise in the number of cyberbullying cases over a decade.

As mentioned earlier, India lacks specifically dedicated provisions to cyberbullying in any of its existing laws. And in the absence of any specific legal provisions, what is referred to most when it comes to any issues pertaining to cyberspace is the provisions of the Information Technology Act, 2000 (IT Act), which regulates the interactions in cyberspace.

A. *Cyberbullying under the IT Act, 2000:*
   No specific provision is dedicated to cyberbullying under the IT Act, 2000, but references may be drawn to the issue of cyberbullying in the light of more than one provision of the Act, which are analyzed as under:

   - IT Act, 2000, provided for the provision, which made the act of sending messages and emails, which are abusive in nature and have the potential to cause injury or harm to the person to whom such message or email is targeted, a punishable offence drawing out a liability on the part of the sender of such message/email. However, this provision of the IT Act was struck down when the Apex Court of the Country declared it to be unconstitutional.[36]

- Another provision of the IT Act, 2000, which can be interpreted to be invoked against an act of cyberbullying where the Act, provided for a liability in terms of an imprisonment, which may extend to five years and a fine, which may extend up to ten lakh rupees, upon a person who publishes or transmits obscene material in electronic form with an intention to defame the other person and blackmail, thereby leading to cyberbullying of the person to whom such online material is transferred.[37]
- The IT Act also provides for liability in terms of imprisonment up to three years and a fine of three lakh rupees for a person who intentionally violates the privacy by transmitting, capturing, or publishing the personal pictures of another person, thereby facilitating cyberbullying.[38]
- The most appropriate provision under the IT Act, 2000, is the provision which makes the act of creating, recording, or advertising anything which depicts children in a vulgar and obscene manner in sexually explicit conduct. This is the closest provision which can be invoked in case of cyberbullying of children as this becomes a major reason for cyberbullying of children.[39]

B. *Cyberbullying under the Bhartiya Nyaya Sanhita, 2023*

Bhartiya Nyaya Sanhita, 2023 (BNS), which came into effect on July 1, 2023, replacing India's old penal law, that is, the Indian Penal Code, has not expressly incorporated 'cyberbullying' as an offence within its ambit, unlike many other countries like the United States, where cyberbullying per se is considered an offence under their legal system. However, some of the provisions of BNS can be interpreted to address the issue of cyberbullying in an implied manner. A pertinent point that needs to be highlighted here in this context is that many of the provisions of the BNS, which can be interpreted in the light of cyberbullying being gendered in nature, are only applicable to women as victims, and men are kept beyond the purview of such provisions. Hence, these provisions of BNS seem to lose relevance when it comes to cyberbullying of children, as gender cannot be a consideration, as boys equally fall prey to cyberbullying. Some of these provisions of BNS are discussed in the following text for better clarity in terms of interpreting them in the light of the essence of cyberbullying impliedly, along with the corresponding provisions of the old law, that is, IPC.

- Anyone who intends to insult the modesty of any woman by any words of gestures in any form (including electronic form), which is targeted to be heard or seen by her, respectively, or intrudes upon the privacy of a woman, shall be punishable under BNS[40] with a simple imprisonment, which may extend to a term of three years and also with fine. The same provision was also provided under the IPC.[41] The provision, though clearly, has a scope to get interpreted to incorporate bullying/cyberbullying; however, this provision has a limited scope in case of invoking it for cyberbullying of young boys, as the provision is not a gender-neutral provision.
- Another penal provision which addresses criminal intimidation through the use of anonymous communication using a fake id or an unknown telephonic source, which provides for an imprisonment up to two years or a fine or with both, can be interpreted in the light of cyberbullying, where the bullying is done using any fake id or under the veil of an unknown source. This provision is well stipulated under both the new criminal law[42] and the old criminal law.[43]
- Provision relating to defamation as laid down under both the old law[44] (IPC) and the new law[45] (BNS), which states that any harm caused to the reputation of a person by another by making or publishing words, signs, and visible representations in any manner including such publication made online will be considered as defamation/cyber defamation, which shall be punishable with a simple imprisonment which can extend up to two years or with fine or with both. Cyberbullying can be interpreted as a form of cyber defamation, and hence BNS's provision of defamation can very well be invoked in a case of cyberbullying.
- Stalking is another important provision of the BNS,[46] which can be discussed in the context of cyberbullying, as cyber-stalking under BNS also includes monitoring the activity of a woman online through various online communication methods or following her on various online platforms even after a clear indication of disinterest on her part. However, this provision of BNS again is a gender specific law and can be invoked only in case of women being stalked online, leading to cyberbullying of only the female population or young female children or adolescents' population. This provision relating to stalking was also a part of the old criminal manual, that is, the Indian Penal Code.[47]

C. *Cyberbullying under the Digital Personal Data Protection (DPDP) Act, 2023:*

The recent law relating to protection in the form of digital data, also shortly known as the DPDP Act, 2023, provides several provisions for ensuring the protection of data against unauthorized use or misuse in the digital space. A few of these provisions, which appear relevant considering the cyberbullying of children, are discussed here:

- One of the provisions of this law, which has been constantly under scrutiny, is the definition of a child under this law.[48] As per this law, anybody who has not attained 18 years of age will be brought under the ambit of a child. But this appears to many as a flawed interpretation of a child, as there cannot be such a wide spectrum starting from 3 years to 17 years being considered as under the single category of children for thc purpose of this law. Many critics are of the opinion that the law must make age-appropriate provisions within the spectrum of 3 to 17 years; otherwise, this law will remain lip service in tackling the issues faced by children of different age groups in the digital space will not be effective.[49]
- As per this law, the various online platforms need to take 'verifiable parental consent' before processing any data of the child interacting in the digital space. This mandate would require everyone below the age of 18 to first verify their age before accessing some sensitive data. Though it is a welcome step toward regulating the behavior of a child in cyberspace, this will increase the surveillance by the government, which will be a real challenge on the part of the government, considering the huge internet population in India.
- As per this law, the online platforms are mandated not to process any data relating to children if such processing will have a detrimental effect on the child, where the scope of detrimental effect has not been defined, leaving room for discussion on the same from case-by-case basis. This mandate, if followed by the online platforms diligently, will be effective against cyberbullying involving children, as in most cases of cyberbullying, the basis of bullying remains the misuse of the personal information/data of such children.[50]
- The law also prohibits online platforms from tracking or monitoring children based on the information/data shared by them on their platforms and sending them suggestions based on such monitoring. This provision promotes ethical practices by the online platforms, making them extend more care and caution toward children whose data, at any cost, should not be compromised to prevent chances of cyberbullying targeted at them because of this data breach at the end of the online platforms that collected such data pertaining to the child in the very first place.[51]
- However, the law also comes up with certain exceptions to the provisions mentioned earlier, whereby it enables the Central Government to exempt certain websites from collecting this 'parental verified consent' or exempt them from mandating the compliance of 'no tracking'

policy when it comes to data given by a child. This exemption can only be possible when the Central Government is convinced that the online platform is handling the data of the child in a 'verifiably safe manner'.

Best Practices to Curb Cyberbullying

Various countries have implemented different legal frameworks to counter the growing menace of cyberbullying. In the United States, the Children's Internet Protection Act requires schools to have such policies which address cyberbullying, especially access to harmful and/or inappropriate content over the internet, ensuring children's security while using emails, chat room conversations, and so on.[52] Realizing the importance of education in addressing cyberbullying, Australia has introduced integrated digital citizenship programs as a part of the school curriculum, which teach students about being responsible when online, how to secure one's privacy, and the impact of cyberbullying.[53] Programs like this aim to make children more empathetic, respectful, and accountable toward themselves as well as others. In Japan, with 21,900[54] recognized cases of cyberbullying among students, the government has established hotlines and counseling services specifically for cyberbullying victims, providing them with immediate assistance and guidance. Moreover, in a few schools, a practice has started where children are shown animated videos of the harms of cyberbullying and internet addiction, with experts talking to them about these issues.[55] Malaysia, which has also seen a sharp rise in cases of cyberbullying from 42,904 cases in 2023 to around 51,000[56] cases from January to March 2024, has urged social media companies to intensify efforts against cybercrimes, calling for greater cooperation from platforms like Facebook, Instagram, and TikTok to remove harmful content.

Conclusion

All these provisions under three different laws, that is, the IT Act, 2000, the Bhartiya Nyaya Sanhita, 2023, and the DPDP Act, 2023, in India, though do not expressly provide for cyberbullying in general and in the case of children, in particular, but to a fair extent, address the issue of cyberbullying in children and its implications. Hence, even in the absence of a sui generis law on cyberbullying, the Indian legal regime has proved itself to be fairly effective in terms of dealing with cases of cyberbullying, with three main laws providing for different provisions of cyberbullying in an implied manner. So, in the current scenario, there may not be a requirement for a sui generis law to address the singular issue of cyberbullying. But the analysis of different provisions of

BNS, 2023, IT Act, 2000, and DPDP Act, 2023, which can be interpreted to bring cyberbullying within their ambit, clearly states that there is a lack of express incorporation of cyberbullying as an offence to date in any law in force in India. Also, it can be stressed that no law in India, including the three laws mentioned earlier, has expressly defined the word 'cyberbullying' in any of its provisions. Hence, there may not be a need for a standalone law on cyberbullying in India currently, but a serious need is being felt to at least have a specific statutory provision expressly dedicated to cyberbullying, considering the growing cases of cyberbullying in India. Such provision must clearly define 'cyberbullying' and set out the various forms/types of cyberbullying committed using different modus operandi. Similarly specific provision must be dedicated to address the concerns posed by the growing cases of children being victims of cyberbullying. When it comes to the incorporation of penal provisions against the act of various types of cyberbullying, punishments need to be determined proportionate to the gravity of the type of cyberbullying, and aggravated sanctions need to be incorporated against an act of cyberbullying targeted against children.

Apart from the legal provisions, as discussed earlier, a strong technological regime with new-age technological measures to ensure cyber-security will go a long way in combating cyberbullying, especially involving children, as it will help to ensure the privacy of the data pertaining to the children. Hence, it's high time the Indian government must deploy enough funds toward creating a strong infrastructure for innovating new technological measures to ensure data privacy in the digital world. Data science engineers need to be motivated and duly compensated to help them bring these much-needed innovations in encryption technology for ensuring online data privacy. In the same way, looking at the issue of cyberbullying from a sociological viewpoint, the role of parents and teachers in schools and colleges is very crucial, as they are the stakeholders who would instill a sense of responsibility in the children when they interact in cyberspace. Awareness among these stakeholders regarding their responsibility toward building responsibility and accountability for children and young adults in the digital world should be the major focus in this context, which must be reflected in various schemes of the government. Strategies for awareness campaigns in schools and colleges, highlighting the importance of ensuring the privacy of personal data in cyberspace to protect our young children from any form of cyberbullying, should be a priority. The success of combating cyberbullying rests on the fair balance of the sociological, technological, and legal intent toward the issue. It is therefore the need of the hour that in a country like India with a huge digital population, the government must strive to effectively deal with the concerns of cyberbullying involving children, which has become the biggest vulnerability which children are exposed to in cyberspace in the present digital world.

Notes

1 S. Craig Watkins, *Young and the Digital: What Migration to Social Network Sites, Games and Anytime, Anywhere Media Means for our Future* 1–19 (Beacon Press 1st ed. 2009).
2 Peter Smith et al., Cyberbullying: Its Nature and Impact in Secondary School Pupils, 49 *Child Psychology & Psychiatry* 376–385 (2008).
3 Ozen Erdur-Baker, Cyberbullying and Its Correlation to Traditional Bullying, Gender and Frequent and Risky Usage on Internet-Mediated Communication Tools, 12 *New Media & Society* 110 (2010).
4 K. Runions et al., Cyber-Aggression and Victimization and Social Information Processing: Integrating the Medium and the Message, 3 *Psychology of Violence* 12 (2013).
5 Erving Goffman, *Presentation of Self in Everyday Life* 208–237 (Doubleday 1959).
6 Qing Li, Cyberbullying in Schools: A Research of Gender Differences, 27 *School Psychology International* 157–170 (2006).
7 David B. Sugarman and Teena Willoughby, Technology and Violence: Conceptual Issues Raised by the Rapidly Changing Social Environment, 3 *Psychology of Violence* 1–8 (2013).
8 David B. Sugarman and Teena Willoughby, Technology and Violence: Conceptual Issues Raised by the Rapidly Changing Social Environment, 3 *Psychology of Violence* 1–8 (2013).
9 Kay Bussey et al., The Role of Moral Disengagement and Self-Efficacy in Cyberbullying, 14 *Journal of School Violence* 30–31 (2015).
10 Ruth Festl and Thorsten Quandt, Social Relations and Cyberbullying: The Influence of Individual and Structural Attributes on Victimization and Perpetration via the Internet, 39 *Human Communication Research* 103–104 (2013).
11 Pilar Espinosa and Miguel Clemente, Self-Transcendence and Self-Oriented Perspective as Mediators between Video Game Playing and Aggressive Behaviour in Teenagers, 23 *Journal of Community & Applied Social Psychology* 68–80 (2013).
12 Robert Didden et al., Cyberbullying among Students with Intellectual and Developmental Disability in Special Education Settings, 12 *Developmental Neurorehabilitation* 146–151 (2009).
13 Edwin C. Darden, The Cyber Jungle, 196 *American School Board Journal* 54–56 (2009).
14 Roberto Slonje and Peter K Smith, Cyberbullying: Another Main Type of Bullying?, 49 *Scandinavian Journal of Psychology* 147–154 (2008).
15 Julian J. Dooley et al., Cyberbullying Versus Face-to-Face Bullying: A Theoretical and Conceptual Review, 217 *Zeitschrift für Psychologie/Journal of Psychology* 183–184 (2009).
16 Kathryn Davies et al., 'I Was Bullied Too': Stories of Bullying and Coping in an Online Community, 18 *Information, Communication & Society* 359 (2014).
17 Sameer Hinduja and Justin W. Patchin, Bullies Move beyond the Schoolyard: A Preliminary Look at Cyberbullying, 4 *Youth Violence and Juvenile Justice* 148–169 (2006).
18 Deborah Butler et al., Cyber Bullying in Schools and the Law: Is There an Effective Means of Addressing the Power Imbalance?, 16 *Murdoch University Electronic Journal of Law* 85–86 (2009).
19 Sameer Hinduja and Justin W Patchin, Bullies Move beyond the Schoolyard: A Preliminary Look at Cyberbullying, 4 *Youth Violence and Juvenile Justice* 148–169 (2006).
20 Sameer Hinduja and Justin W. Patchin, Personal Information of Adolescents on the Internet: A Quantitative Content Analysis of MySpace, 31 *Journal of Adolescence* 125, 138–139 (2008).

21 Sameer Hinduja and Justin W. Patchin, *Bullying beyond the Schoolyard: Preventing and Responding to Cyberbullying* 19–42 (Corwin Press 1st ed. 2008).
22 Kimberly Mason, Cyberbullying: A Preliminary Assessment for School Personnel, 45 *Psychology in Schools* 323–348 (2008).
23 Nicole L. Weber and William V. Pelfrey Jr., *Cyberbullying: Causes, Consequences, and Coping Strategies* 85–97 (LFB Scholarly Publishing LLC 1st ed. 2014).
24 M. Vijayarani et al., Silent Screams: A Narrative Review of Cyberbullying among Indian Adolescents, 16 *Cureus* (2024).
25 Rhea Maheshwari, In One Year Alone, Cyberbullying of Indian Women and Teenagers Rose by 36%, *The Scroll*, 2024, Available at: https://scroll.in/article/956085/in-one-year-alone-cyberbullying-of-indian-women-and-teenagers-rose-by-36; (Last accessed on 13. 1. 2025, at 10.05 am).
26 Vats, Sukriti, 85% Indian Kids Have Experienced Cyberbullying, Highest in the World, Finds New Survey, *The Print*, 2022, Available at: https://theprint.in/india/85-indian-kids-have-experienced-cyberbullying-highest-in-the-world-finds-new-survey/1074175/; (Last accessed on 11. 1. 2025, at 10.15 am).
27 Chengyan Zhu et. al., *Cyberbullying among Adolescents and Children: A Comprehensive Review of the Global Situation, Risk Factors, and Preventive Measures*, Available at: https://www.frontiersin.org/journals/public-health/articles/10.3389/fpubh.2021.634909/full; (Last accessed on 14. 1. 2025, at 11.20 am).
28 Sukriti Vats, 85% Indian Kids Have Experienced Cyberbullying, Highest in the World, Finds New Survey, *The Print*, 2022, Available at: https://theprint.in/india/85-indian-kids-have-experienced cyberbullying-highest-in-the-world-finds-new-survey/1074175/; (Last accessed on 11. 1. 2025, at 11.05 am).
29 Emily A. Vogels, *Teens and Cyberbullying*, 2022, Available at: https://www.pewresearch.org/internet/2022/12/15/teens-and-cyberbullying-2022/; (last accessed on 19. 1. 2025, at 8.30 pm).
30 Pooja B. Jaiswal, Why Prevalence of Bullying in India Is Very High, *The Week*, Aug. 31, 2024, Available at: https://www.theweek.in/health/cover/2024/08/31/bullying-in-india-cases-statistics-tips-to-deal-with.html; (last accessed on 11. 1. 2025, at 11.35 am).
31 Shivangi Gautam and Sapna Sharma, *Cyberbullying: Repercussions and Strategies for it Prevention*, July-December 2023, Available at: https://www.mastersindatascience.org/resources/prevent-cyberbullying-with-technology/; (Last accessed on 30. 11. 2023, at 3.15 p.m.).
32 Shivangi Gautam and Sapna Sharma, *Cyberbullying: Repercussions and Strategies for it Prevention*, July-December 2023, Available at: https://www.mastersindatascience.org/resources/prevent-cyberbullying-with-technology/; (Last accessed on 30. 11. 2023, at 3.15 p.m.).
33 Gordon Gottsegen, *Machine Learning in Cybersecurity: How It Works and Companies to Know*, Available at: https://builtin.com/artificial-intelligence/machine-learning-cybersecurity (Last accessed on 30. 11. 2023, at 7.20 p.m.).
34 Akhilesh Deshmukh and Eleanor Barlow, *Debunking the Myths: How Machine Learning (ML) Benefits Cyber Security*, Dec. 2020, Available at: https://www.securityhq.com/blog/debunking-the-myths-how-machine-learning-ml-benefits-cyber-security/; (Last accessed on 30. 11. 2023, at 7.20 p.m.).
35 Wasyihun Sema Admas, Yirga Yayeh Munaye and Abebe Abeshu Diroc, *Cyber Security: State of the Art, Challenges and Future Directions*, 2024, Available at: https://www.sciencedirect.com/science/article/pii/S2772918423000188; (Last accessed on 18. 1. 2, at 11.15 a.m.).
36 Sec 66 A of the IT Act, was struck down when the Apex Court declared the provision to be unconstitutional stating it to be curtailing the Freedom of Speech and Expression granted by the Indian Constitution under Article 19 (1) (a) in *Shreya Singhal V Union of India*.

37 Sec.67, Information Technology Act, 2000.
38 Sec. 66 E, Information Technology Act, 2000, added in the Information Technology (Amendment) Act, 2008.
39 Sec. 67B, Information Technology Act, 2000.
40 Sec 79, Bhartiya Nyaya Sanhita, 2023.
41 Sec 509, Indian Penal Code, 1860.
42 Sec 351, Bhartiya Nyaya Sanhita, 2023.
43 Sec 507, Indian Penal Code, 1860.
44 Sec 499, Indian Penal Code, 1860
45 Sec 356, Bhartiya Nyaya Sanhita, 2023.
46 Sec 78, Bhartiya Nyaya Sanhita, 2023.
47 Sec 354 (D), Indian Penal Code, 1860
48 Tim Maurer and Arthur Nelson, *The Global Cyber Threat*, 2021, Available at: https://www.imf.org/external/pubs/ft/fandd/2021/03/global-cyber-threat-to-financial-systems-maurer.htm; (Last accessed on 2. 12. 2023, at 1.30 p.m.).
49 Tim Maurer and Arthur Nelson, *The Global Cyber Threat*, 2021, Available at: https://www.imf.org/external/pubs/ft/fandd/2021/03/global-cyber-threat-to-financial-systems-maurer.htm; (Last accessed on 2. 12. 2023, at 1.30 p.m.).
50 Anirudh Berman, *Understanding India's New Data Protection Law*, Aug. 2023, Available at: https://carnegieendowment.org/research/2023/10/understanding-indias-new-data-protection-law?lang=en; (Last accessed on 2. 12. 2023, at 11.45 a.m.).
51 Anirudh Berman, *Understanding India's New Data Protection Law*, Aug. 2023, Available at: https://carnegieendowment.org/research/2023/10/understanding-indias-new-data-protection-law?lang=en; (Last accessed on 2. 12. 2023, at 11.45 a.m.).
52 Federal Communications Commission Consumer and Governmental Affairs Bureau, Consumer Guide, Children's Internet Protection Act (CIPA), Available at: https://www.fcc.gov/sites/default/files/childrens_internet_protection_act_cipa.pdf; (Last accessed on 23. 1. 2025, at 1.30 p.m.)
53 Chan Nee Nee et.al., *The Digital Defence against Cyberbullying: A Systematic Review of Tech-Based Approaches*, Dec. 2023, Available at: https://www.tandfonline.com/doi/full/10.1080/2331186X.2023.2288492; (Last accessed on 24. 1. 2025, at 3.30 p.m.).
54 Manichi Japan, *Cyberbullying among Kids on Rise in Japan: What Can Schools Do to Address It?*, Jan. 2023, Available at: https://mainichi.jp/english/articles/20230127/p2a/00m/0na/028000c; (Last accessed on 28. 1. 2025, at 3.40 p.m.).
55 Manichi Japan, *Cyberbullying among Kids on Rise in Japan: What Can Schools Do to Address It?*, Jan. 2023, Available at: https://mainichi.jp/english/articles/20230127/p2a/00m/0na/028000c; (Last accessed on 28. 1. 2025, at 3.40 p.m.).
56 Ulum Islamiyyah, *Risk and Protecting Factors of Cyberbullying in Malaysia: A Comparative Analysis*, Dec. 2021, Available at: https://www.researchgate.net/publication/358193699_Risk_and_Protecting_Factors_of_Cyberbullying_in_Malaysia_A_Comparative_Analysis; (last accessed on 30. 1. 2025, at 10.15 a.m.).

11

PROTECTION OF MENTAL HEALTH OF CHILDREN IN DIGITAL ECOSYSTEM

A Socio-Legal Study

Shrilekha Banerjee

Introduction

Social distancing mandates during the post-COVID-19 period have activated the propensity among most of the children, from kindergarten to teenagers, to adopt the *new normal* as an available coping mechanism for daily avocation of life, even beyond studies. The significant impact of advanced media technologies, being the gateway of innovative information and communication, e-governance, and so on has made today's young generation children *digital natives to a great extent*. The on-screen habits thus affected not only the learning process, social relationships, amusement, in a word, overall development, rather laid out the exemplary addition to online habits among the children. Such exposure of the children to the range of information available on the internet adversely affects their cognitive, behavioral, and emotional development, particularly in the transition group, that is, those who are from childhood to adulthood. The enormous impact of such on-screen activities is having its concentration upon the physical, physiological, psychological, and social domains of such young generations. The mental health of such children and the young generation, thus, is not only averse to the extant socio-cultural values, social norms, attitudes, personal and interpersonal relationships at home-fronts and beyond but rather perpetuates a range of systemic challenges to the biomedical or psycho-social approaches in providing comprehensive remedies to the mental health problems of such children and young generations. Such a rapid shift toward on-screen activities has influenced users to voluntarily put themselves in solitary confinement at home, espoused with sedentary behaviors, staying away from peer groups and/or outdoor recreations, and any healthy interpersonal as well as pro-social relationships.

DOI: 10.4324/9781003607076-15

Among the school-goers, the most reflected behaviors are negative attitudes toward people, increasing absenteeism, non-participation in institutional programs, and aversion to taking challenges and risks. And the young generation that has either completed or is undergoing the transitional shift-over from childhood to adulthood is exposed to anxiety, stress, depression, panic, irritation, impulsivity, delinquency, somatization, sleep disorder, emotional liability, and in worst situations suicidal behavior.[1] It has been observed that once internalization of such sedentary behaviors starts to reflect in childhood, the mental health problems evolve, thereby mostly persist in adulthood and manifest in external behavioral problems and life outcomes.[2] One more factor that isolates the parents from their children and indirectly contributes to such a crisis is the case of working parents. In the age of consumerism, the increased financial insecurity has put competing time demands to look after the children. What warrants the consideration on the part of the State is to take into account the practical implications pertaining to the protection of the mental health of the children, appropriate and periodic legislative, administrative, and other schematic measures necessary and contributory to implement the Child's Rights. The economic, social, and cultural rights of the children cannot be enforced through policy tools due to some unresolved divisions and internal limitations. However, opportunities through schematic approaches may be accommodated in the policy responses. According to the latest report of the World Health Organization (WHO), almost 14% adolescents out of a billion people were accounted in 2019 to have been suffering from mental disorders and concluded that mental disorders are pre-eminent and influential grounds of disability and early mortality.[3] What is more significant is that the concentration of such mental disorders is reported to be higher in high-income countries.[4] The inextricable link of on-screen activities is more practiced than adequacy levels in well-to-do families.

Youngsters' Lifestyle During the COVID-19 Pandemic

The suspension of a physically active lifestyle during COVID-19 is but a coincidence that triggered the impetus to explore and experience the correlations between the physical activities and their associated psychological traits afresh and the traumatic effects thereof. It is COVID-19 that underscores how, in the rat-race of the new normal platform, the incremental on-screen activities gradually suspended the movement behaviors and appreciated the sedentary behavior among the children and young generations. Some of the remarkable negative physical health effects on the children are sleeplessness, obesity, vision problems, and longer periods of on-screen activities. The contents of the digital platform insinuate and involve the minds of most of the children to interact with the contents due to attractive rewards or virtual stickers/coins to the users, particularly the online games, and thereby cause the sensory stimuli that can cause the secretion of the release of dopamine in the brain. These enmesh the children to indulge their sedentary behaviors and encourage the ailments both physically and psychologically in the near future.[5]

Connection Between Physical and Mental Well-Being

The positive correlations between physical activities and wellness and the development of mental health are not the subject of recent studies. It has long been medically established that the beneficial impact of regular physical activities among children aged five years and below contributes to developing healthy weight, fundamental motor skills, cardio-metabolic health, enhanced muscular and skeletal health, cognitive and learning social skills, and so on.[6] The WHO has addressed that body movements may be as part of recreational purposes or walking, cycling, or even household chores, enabling the skeletal muscles to promote energy expenditure, resulting in healthy consequences and reducing the tendency of a sedentary lifestyle. Sedentary behavior is considered where the physical activities require energy expenditure < 1.5 Metabolic equivalents (MET). Insufficient physical activity is associated with a higher risk factor to experiencing cardiovascular diseases. Further, an experimental study has revealed that, on measuring the disability-adjusted life years and years of life lost, it is concluded that the symptoms of mental disorders appear at a very early stage of life and may often lead to premature mortality.[7] The fact that mental health services are not independent and isolated treatment but rather they confine, besides the physical body, the psyche, brain, mind, and soul, and variances of physical afflictions makes variances in the diagnosis and treatment. What is more significant is that such issues are to be viewed from socio-cultural factors as well. However, the mental well-being of children is predominantly related to their physical activity. It is found that children who are physically active face less stress, depression, and anxiety than children who are fixated on screens, video games, and social media. Going outside doing some form of moderate activity lowers levels of depression and anxiety symptoms and promotes a better lifestyle. Moderate to vigorous exercise, for at least an hour every day, is the recommendation of the WHO for adolescents, which includes sweating and breathing hard.[8] Sedentary behaviors among children and adolescents, often among emerging adults, become a public health concern across the globe as depression, anxiety, and distress influence to adopt mostly substance use among emerging adults. Thus, piecemeal attention to the mental status during the formative stages of children would adversely affect their future cognitive and social-emotional health.[9]

Sedentary Life and Screen Time

Prolonged use of screen time fosters ADHD, that is, attention deficit hyperactivity disorder, which results in poor academic results in addition to various mental health outcomes and leads to evolving higher depressive symptoms and psychological distress.[10] The positive correlation between physical activities and well-being of mental health has been endorsed in various studies,[11] for example, improvement in cognitive function, enhanced self-esteem, decreased depression and anxiety, and academic achievement. The perceptual control; psychoanalytic, behavioral, humanistic, and other psychodynamic counseling and psychotherapy; and so on have been theorized to sort out the root causes and to treat people suffering from mental health issues.[12]

In rural areas consistent and reliable services and/or community care is a challenge as there is a lack of compound and complex categorized requirements for effective mental healthcare services; hence, much focus is made on the physical aspects of the treatment. Thus, consistent association of physical activities has positive health benefits, for example, metabolic, cardiovascular, immunologic, endocrine, and neurotransmitter, on the physical aspects, while reinforcing self-esteem, social relationships and interactions, sense of mastery and control, and so on, on the mental health aspects.[13] The outcomes of sedentary behaviors have been primarily categorized into two divisions: (a) intermediate outcomes, like blood lipids, blood pressure, and fitness; and (b) clinical outcomes, like cognition, mood, quality of life, and cardiovascular events,[14] which have long-term effects. It has further been observed that engaging in on-screen activities manifests poor cardio-metabolic health, lower fitness, and sleep disorders, and, based on typologies of sedentary behaviors, various credible interventions like school-based activities (structured physical-education, sports, recreations, etc.), and device-measure activities, for example, multiple composite scenarios-based game that appreciates therapeutic value,[15] have incremental benefits on mental health. Specific symptoms require intervention of special services for management and provide adequate curative services, like pharmacological, non-pharmacological, and psychodynamic approach; psychotherapy approach; cognitive behavior therapy; and dialectical behavior therapy. Some prescribed physical activities having mental health benefits are like cardio-respiratory fitness, muscular fitness, aerobic exercise, and walking and cycling, which reduce depressive symptoms and improve positive cognitive functions.[16]

Indian Perspective on Mental Health of Children

In India there is a negative mindset to treat the mental health of children, particularly among socially and economically disadvantaged strata of the society. The National Education Policy (NEP) 2020, though, has made ample provisions for the e-learning mechanism to fulfill the basic requirement for expanding education for all; however, the digital divide has come in the way of inclusive accessibility and participation and mass involvement of students in the e-learning process. Sufficient expansion of internet infrastructure facilities coupled with adequate training of the teaching staff to equip the teachers with required pedagogical development, adequate digital devices, and distribution of accessory resources for the rural students are yet to be completed in a full-fledged manner. Like the healthcare sector, the budgetary allocation for education is also marginal in India, as education is also the subject that comes within the purview of the State List under the Indian Constitution. In pursuance of the NEP 2020, the Massive Open Online Courses are being promoted by the regulatory bodies of the government to inculcate a learning environment within the digital maps of the country. The Educational Institution Regulatory Bodies have issued the mandate to the higher educational institutions to effectuate the e-learning process on elementary subjects to enrich the learning depositories with more resources of e-learning; however, the financial constraints have kept major educational bodies from accentuating the mandate of the Educational Regulatory Bodies. In the context of a changing demographic socio-cultural ecosystem, the significance of e-learning is considered to be the inclusive approach to promote the fundamental right of education under Article 21A of the Constitution of India.[17] Post-liberalized transformation has created major opportunities for economic advancement that led the traditional family relationships into a number of dual-earning nuclear families to mitigate the need of the time, in turn, reducing the parental involvement in the development of children's lives. In addition, the competitive social contexts induced by liberalization have influenced the social milieu toward more materialistic lifestyles, hence replacing the traditional lifestyles with present technology-driven modern lifestyles that appreciate more dependency on electronic appliances and on-screen activities. Thus, the psycho-social correlations have gradually changed pro-social behaviors, reduced support, and contact with the extended families. As a result, prolonged engagement with on-screen activities caused an incremental increase of sedentary behaviors and the consequent anxiety, conduct disorder, depression, intellectual disability, and mental disorders. Those outcomes are incalculable and deemed to have adverse effects upon health, education, life outcomes, earnings, and so on. In an estimation made by WHO 2020, it has been observed that "between 2012–2030 India may have to suffer the economic loss due to such mental health conditions up to the tune of USD 1.03 trillion."[18] According to a recent study,[19] the need for mental healthcare services is for around 150 million Indians, while only one-fifth are availing of the same.[20] It has also been suggested that a safe ecosystem for the children in the schools, positive peer relationships, loving caregivers, and so on may reduce such risks. It has also been observed that social stigma and lack of budgetary allocation are two notable barriers in dealing with such challenges.[21] No comprehensive assessment on sedentary behaviors of children, adolescents, and emerging adults has been made; as such, the Mental Health Care Act, 2017, particularly in the post-COVID period, has lesser relevance relating to the changing paradigm of mental health issues in Indian social contexts.

Mental Healthcare Services in India

Mental healthcare service in India has been integrated within the fold of the primary healthcare system. The functional apparatus has been set at the district level, and its performance is far from the actual treatment necessary to address and deliver the mental healthcare services. Governmental scheme,[22] though, has surfaced to extend the mental healthcare services to the priority area; however, the extant remedial mechanism and administrative framework in reference to the increased variances of mental disorders since the COVID-19 pandemic have hardly been considered to mitigate. To deal with the issues of mental health for the school-going children, effective tools for providing information related to mental health and care services to adolescents are essential, and these can be done via digital intervention, mental health (m-health), and tele-health platforms. These platforms can provide the preliminary care and also safeguard those who are on the verge of having mental health problems.[23] PRIDE – the Pilot Trial of an Online Digital Problem-solving Intervention for School-Going Adolescents in Goa, a trust-funded program (2016–22) in India, addressed a significant part of the mental health issues of adolescents. It was designed primarily for lower-class urban adolescents, belonging to New Delhi and Goa,[24] in view of the parameters envisioned by the WHO[25] to make improvements in health and well-being, which corresponds to physical activity. The productive result of such physical activity on mental health and severe mental disorders has been medically established. For a country as diverse as India, popular sports may vary from place to place, and the "Fit India" provides a list of sports that are popular in our country. FIT India Movement is the initiative undertaken by the Ministry of Higher Education in the year 2018 to address the increasing lifestyle diseases, like diabetes and hypertension, among the young generations in India. To engage the students in physical activities while undergoing the educational career is the main purpose of such program. Though under this initiative, monthly sharing of data to the extent of fitness plan undertaken by the higher educational bodies is to be uploaded in the web portal of the FIT India, but no allocation of funds has been provided from the ends of the government for this. Thus, in addition to the financial constraint to effectuate such program and that the main challenges are "lack of time" and "lack of motivation", which have an effect on Indian's lack of physical activity. Lack of financial resources, coupled with increasing dropouts, and the inadequate institutions compared to the increasing students, children are reluctant to participate in such program as their physical activity mainly happens in schools (including transportation). The National Health Portal of India sorts out a handful of safe public places with access; however, there is an apprehension of strong-arm tactics in public areas that render such places unsafe for children, and this may also dissuade children from opting for physical activity in public areas.[26]

Post-Independence Journey Toward Mental Health

Post-1947 independent India has adopted and appreciated the biomedical model of healthcare delivery in its legal framework of mental health and relevant programs. The primary focus during post-independence for mental health was mainly on infrastructure development in healthcare facilities, an increase in the number of accommodations of the patients in the hospitals, to construction of distinct child psychiatry units, and overcoming the deficiency of human resources to mitigate the mental health sector. The community psychiatry concept gained its momentum under the influence of international developments in the second half of the 1970s in India. Global progress relating to community psychiatry induced India to adopt the concept of community psychiatry during the post-1970s. With international developments and supported by WHO, for the developing and under-developing countries state-led mental health program was introduced, that is, National Mental Health Program (NMHP) whose initial objectives were (i) to ensure the accessibility and affordability of plinth level uniform mental healthcare for each one, especially for the marginalized and persecuted ones; (ii) to upgrade the primary healthcare, homogenizing the mental healthcare as well, and (iii) to foster participation of communities in expanding mental health services. Consequently, in the year 1997, the NMHP had been enlarged, cutting across the district level in four districts, which, in turn, spread over 704 districts across the country. Reformative measures related to mental health legislation were put up since the 1950s and ultimately surfaced as legislation in the year 1987, in the name and style of the Mental Health Act (MHA) was enacted. Surprisingly, the policy frameworks on mental healthcare have undergone its transition from an institutional model to a community engagement model, ultimately ending as of now in the MHA as a custodial law.[27]

The core objectives of the MHA are to harbor, foster, and make progress for the well-being of the mental health of the people at large and to provide protection to the mentally ill people without discrimination. The basic principles, which have been introduced by WHO for the mental healthcare purpose that should be taken into consideration before amending laws on mental health by any country, are as follows:

i. To promote mental healthcare (including restrictive type, self-determination, and/or assistive right of self-determination, and prevent mental disorders)

ii. To give access to basic mental healthcare facilities
iii. To follow international principles on mental health

To recognize the due validation of the rule of law (including accessibility of review procedure, periodic auto-review mechanism, etc.), the central government, on ratification of the international instrument of 2006,[28] has introduced the principles of the said convention imperative in its policies and laws. As the narrative of the expression "health," as explained by WHO, is more holistic and broader, the new legislation on mental health has confirmed the preservation, safeguarding, fostering, mitigating, and rehabilitating the mental disorders for attaining the global standards of health. As a consequence of a new legislation on mental healthcare has substituted the earlier MHA, 1987. However, a paradigm shift was found in recent times from charity-based custodial care to a rights-based community care approach. Keeping pace with progressive trends in medical technology and diagnostic patterns in treating mental disorders, the present legislation, that is, the Mental Health Care Act, 2017, is more proactive in nature. The rights-based approach led to the evolution of the human-rights group. The difference between the primary mental health policy, 2014, with that of the Act of 2017 is that whereas the earlier policy compiled the inclusive approach and provision for the recovery from mental illness but as collective rights, the genre of the present legislation, that is, the MHA, 2017,[29] is more prone toward protecting the individual's right focusing on the provisions of accessibility, affordability, quality health, and social care. The policy, to foster the mental healthcare services, has extended its purview, supplemented by enhancing the availability of medical resources (including professionals' support) and, for its due enforcement, enhances monitoring, keeping accountability, uniformity, and universal access to mental health services. Moreover, for the furtherance of care services, the community participation, research, monitoring, and evaluation have also been duly endorsed.

Very few states have their own mental health policy, and Kerala is one of them. With respect to budgetary allocations relating to mental health, Kerala is at the top of the list out of the total allocated budget in the health category, which is 1.16%, in comparison to other states of the Union of India. The model scheme, namely, UNARV – the district model of telemedicine services for the adolescents suffering from mental illness or emotional distress in Kerala state, is operationalized at the schools at the district level by the state to take care of the mental health of the adolescents. The adolescents (between the age group of secondary and senior-secondary) who require behavioral therapy were being consulted, advised, and counseled by their school teachers, besides solving their (students) problems in academic pursuit. They were specially educated and trained in the area of adolescent developmental psychology and mental health disorders. For the purpose of recovery, those rural students who have been suffering from mental illness or emotional distress are prepared with various kinds of therapies such as cognitive behavioral therapy, problem-solving skill therapy, and anger management skills. Such integrated conscientiousness process regarding mental healthcare, espoused with primary healthcare services by the medical professionals through systematic assistance of the state government, was initiated in the year 2011 in coordination with the DMHP team. With the passage of time, it has been expanded to 98 centers across the state and monthly 28 clinics across each district. These clinics are the nodal points for the preliminary mental healthcare services. All such socio-beneficial measures have been undertaken besides the Accredited Social Health Activist scheme, that is, to identify mental health problems, figure out such cases on completion of the prescribed training, and conduct a survey in various gram panchayats.[30]

Much progress has been made by the government in bridging the delays and developmental disorders as part of the School Health Program under the "Ayushman Bharat" scheme. The Boards of Secondary Education, like the Central Board of Secondary Examination, have suggested engaging counselors for the psychological exercises for the secondary and senior-secondary students to inculcate among them a few notions like self-concept and self-image, and the ability to stand up for themselves in adverse circumstances of life. For instance, in Goa, an NGO called *Sangath* (translates to "companionship") has designed a program for students of 5th to 12th grade named School Health Promotion and Empowerment. On putting it into practice, positive results have come to light relating to children's health behaviors. Training provided by the lay counselors regarding the conduct of the Society of Metabolic Health Practitioners has also been implemented. Like Social Empowerment Through Health Education And Research, the multicomponent school-based intervention for promoting adolescent health program in government-run secondary schools that enables intervention through a school-, evidence-based approach to identify and promote adolescent health program in Bihar through its Adolescence Education Program. This is a low-cost approach method utilizing the services of trained teachers and lay counselors. Also, the Indian Psychiatric Society, Kerala, introduced training in 2021 *Sneha Kavacham* (translates to "affectionate shield"). The objective of the program is to address digital addiction, with a special target audience, that is, students, teachers, and parents.[31]

Paucity in Healthcare Sector

Long-accustomed sedentary behaviors, based on sensitivity analysis, lead to major psychiatric disorders. In the vocabulary of medical science, the different types that are often recognized under different categories of disorders are neurotic and mood disorders (bipolar and personality disorders), psychotic disorders, neuro-developmental disorders, addictions, conduct disorders, intellectual disabilities, and other psychiatric disorders. The higher cost of treatments for such disorders is chiefly due to:

a. Lack of required specialized medical resources: To ensure adequacy of medical resources, including professional skill-setting among the psychiatric experts, along with proper working conditions, is required. Such requirements include separate recruitment of trained teaching assistants and adequate space for both medical professionals and patients at each healthcare setting and emergency care facilities; apart from these, clear rules and regulations on duty hours, leaves, benefits, and so on should be indicated, and there should be an effective monitoring mechanism for the due enforcement of the same. At present, the strength of psychiatrists in India is 3,500, and the present ratio is 1:200,000 patients in India, while the ideal ratio is 1:8000/10,000 patients, and the Ministry of Health and Family Welfare has reported that the country is in need of 13,000 psychiatrists.[32] In so far as other supportive medical professionals for the mental healthcare services like clinical psychologists, psychiatric social workers, and psychiatric nurses are concerned, their availability is also much below the standard ratio;[33] in other words, the demand is eight times more than what is available in the mental healthcare services. Hence introduction of necessary specialized academic programs and the enlargement of the scopes for sufficient seats are the need of the hour. In addition, to dismantle the social stigma, regular and periodic awareness programs on psychological disorders and the biological basis of mental disorders with sensitivity vis-à-vis the curative measures are required to be conducted.
b. Lack of adequate infrastructure: The quality of healthy life requires leading a functional independence in day-to-day activities of life. The specificity of mental health is that, apart from the medicinal dependency, it requires recalibration, that is, to shift the self-perception within the frame of reference for independence; re-prioritization of goals, through constructive guidance and encouraging directions that would enhance quality of life, which would help and support of team and peers. Hence, it is not at all a short-term and temporary goal; rather, mental healthcare services involve acute treatment tailored to long-term rehabilitation, where more financial resources and time, and often the support of high-end technological equipment are required for assessing the improvement scale. There is an extremely low allocation of beds for mental health patients in India, that is, 2.04 beds/100,000 population,[34] whereas according to the WHO Report in the United States, it is 30.6/100,000, in France 125.55/100,000, in Australia 41.08/100,000, in Malaysia 24.85/100,000, in Thailand 8.32/100,000, and in China 24.29/100,000.[35] In pursuance of the objectives of the National Health Policy, 2017, to ensure the accessible,

available, affordable, and uniform quality healthcare services, the establishment of convalescent centers: day-care centers, vocational training centers, sheltered workshop centers, community living centers, and so on are primary requirement to provide the rehabilitation services. What is more significant is to review and analyze the policy framework with respect to the utility and necessity of a screen-based education framework for children that is contributing to so many mental disorders.

c. Lack of institutional welfare schemes for the myriad: In terms of heterogeneity of concentration of people suffering from mental disorders, the household income of the citizens like in India is not sufficient to sustain the financial (both indirect and direct costs) and other medical resources to avail adequate mental healthcare services. This is particularly difficult for outpatient care services, like ambulatory consultations with psychiatrists, psychologists, or social workers. The extant social health insurance schemes are not sufficient to mitigate the expenditures required for mental healthcare services. Therefore, in the absence of institutional welfare schemes from the government, this could pose a real challenge in the days to come. Institutional policies on day-to-day administration and monitoring of due enforcement are also necessary. The uniform application of the Clinical Establishment Act, 2018, should be implemented in every healthcare setting in a more comprehensive manner. The establishment of the prescribed institutions in view of the Mental Health Care Act, 2017, is also necessary to expand the outreach of the facilities and provisions to the care recipients.

d. Lack of insurance products in the market: No insurance product in this regard has been introduced where a contributory premium (partly by the government) could be sustained by the family members of the person suffering from a mental disorder to provide healthcare services coverage. The Insurance Regulatory and Development Authority and the government should design the necessary policies to fill this gap and make provisions for mental healthcare services as well.

e. Low in mental healthcare services: The budgetary allocation of the government is appreciably negligible in India for mental healthcare, although by dint of the National Health Policy 2017, the introduction of private capital has been prioritized. The policy is not comprehensive as it is devoid of evidence-based considerations on the mental health conditions of the citizens, and a community-based networking mechanism has not been prioritized. The demand in the healthcare market in India has underscored the dire necessity of primary healthcare services to achieve the accessibility, availability, affordability, and quality healthcare services. Any investment for providing mental healthcare services is a long-term consequence with no direct and immediate return; hence, considering the opportunity cost of capital, the private entities stay away from undertaking the risks.

> However, there has to be a rethink on the lines of mental healthcare due to the sheer prevalence of it among citizens, especially children in India.

The current reality of phone addiction has a domino effect on a child's overall well-being, especially on the mind. As per a survey by the National Institute of Mental Health and Neurosciences, the craziness among children to be present virtually, particularly on social media, has been assessed to be around 27%. The rippling effect engulfing the concentration to studies in studies, irregularity in normal sleeping patterns.[36] Anxiety, stress, and depression among children nowadays are caused by excessive use of digital media, which brings pressure to maintain an image on social media. They are exposed to cyberbullying, which negatively impacts self-esteem and emotional state of being and forces those little minds to become shy, introverted; constant comparison takes place in the mind, feeling left out, irritability, mood swings, and anger issues, which all turn into depression. These factors further contribute to a lack of focus and concentration in studies, which leads to poor academic performance.[37]

Conclusion and Suggestions

Post-COVID-19 has significantly appreciated the online transactions across the globe, whereby e-learning has gained currency as well. What is more important, as recommended by OECD, is to customize and regulate the contents and access of the same, considering the users' status. Digital 5 A Day – the digital platform introduced by England for the mental well-being of children. The easy accessibility to interact and share the emotional support and bridge the distance with friends and relatives, vis-à-vis the Resilience Revolution scheme, has also been introduced by the Centre for Resilience for Social Justice.[38] Similarly, in South Korea, it is being introduced by the National Centre for Youth Internet Addiction Treatment by pushing forward the children toward outdoor play for some 12 days.

Ineffective and fragmented schematic arrangements in the policy frameworks by the government in promoting elementary education on the indicators of mental ill-health and lack of awareness programs regarding the adverse effects of such psychological disorders have been very detrimental. In addition, much promotion of private capital has appreciated the cost of treatment as the curative measures for mental ailments require long-term and consistent pursuits. Hence, "governments must ensure that sufficient human and financial resources and institutional support and capacity are available to promote and protect children, adolescents', teachers' and caregivers' mental health and psycho-social well-being in every school and learning environment from early childhood to adolescence."[39]

Socio-economic changes, progressive trends of urbanization, and digitization have induced various vocations in our daily life in the present social context, requiring inclination to adopt on-screen activities, for example, procedural administrative compliance within the ecosystem of e-governance, payment and settlement of economic transactions, for various academic programs, e-commerce, and other activities. These daily practices have made ample scope for the users (including children and adolescents) to be accustomed to on-screen activities gradually.

The positive correlations between online presence of children and disorders in the natural mental health of the children have been established in various exploratory studies. On the contrary, the positive correlations between outdoor sports and physical activities of the children have been proven to be more beneficial and contributory to strengthening their careers and personalities have also been established.

The suggestions that should be taken into consideration by the states, governments, schools, and families are:

i. To create a positive learning ambience that boosts children's mental and physical health and well-being, through the implementation of school-based mental health and psycho-social support policies and embedding mental health literacy and social and emotional learning in the curriculum, from the early childhood to adolescence period.
ii. To provide early psycho-social services on identification of the context-variances and address the mental health services through devoted professionals and curative measures. Monitoring and auditing the reasons for early school dropouts would be another supportive tool to identify the mental health of the children at an earlier stage and to take necessary measures to continue their education.
iii. Extra-curricular programs on mental health, coupled with the school academic programs, required to be framed on all fronts – national, regional, and local levels that encompass participation of children and their families. In addition, efforts have to be taken to inculcate and reorganize the socio-cultural values and behavioral patterns and impart those mental health services that engage community engagement as well.
iv. To empower parents and family members to create a screen-free zone or have a digital detox period daily and provide healthier alternatives where the child can get engaged.
v. School should also take this very seriously and provide proper guidelines about the usage of smartphones inside the premises. They should also conduct awareness programs for the youngsters about the social media appropriate usage. Therapy sessions should also be available in schools for children who are dealing with social media addiction, anxiety, and depression.

Notes

1 Hossain, M. M., Tasnim, S., Sultana, A. *et al.* (2020). Epidemiology of Mental Health Problems in COVID-19: A Review. *F1000Research*, *9*, 636. https://doi.org/10.12688/f1000research.24457.1
2 Conway, A., Han, W. J., Brooks-Gunn, J., & Waldfogel, J. (2017). First-Year Maternal Employment and Adolescent Externalizing Behavior. *Journal of Child and Family Studies*, *26*(8), 2237–2251. https://doi.org/10.1007/s10826-017-0730-8.
3 *World Mental Health Report: Transforming Mental Health for All.* Geneva: World Health Organization. (2022). ISBN 978-92-4-004933-8.
4 *World Mental Health Report: Transforming Mental Health for All.* Geneva: World Health Organization. (2022). ISBN 978-92-4-004933-8.
5 Gull, M., & Ruth Sravani, B. (2024). Do Screen Time and Social Media Use Affect Sleep Patterns, Psychological Health, and Academic Performance among Adolescents? Evidence from Bibliometric Analysis. *Children and Youth Services Review*, *164*, 1–9. https://doi.org/10.1016/j.childyouth.2024.107886.
6 Burdette, H. L., & Whitaker, R. C. (2005). Resurrecting Free Play in Young Children: Looking Beyond Fitness and Fatness to Attention, Affiliation, and Affect. *Archives of Pediatrics & Adolescent Medicine, 159*(1), 46–50. doi:10.1001/archpedi.159.1.46.
7 Global, Regional, and National Burden of 12 Mental Disorders in 204 Countries and Territories, 1990–2019: A Systematic Analysis for the Global Burden of Disease Study 2019. *The Lancet Psychiatry*, *9*(2), 137–150. https://doi.org/10.1016/S2215-0366(21)00395-3.
8 Klass, P. (March 2, 2020). The Benefits of Exercise for Children's Mental Health. *The New York Times*. https://www.nytimes.com/2020/03/02/well/family/the-benefits-of-exercise-for-childrens-mental-health.html#:~:text=Even%20light%20physical%20activity%20among,got%20older%2C%20new%20research%20shows.&text=By%20Perri%20Klass%2C%20M.D.&text=Recent%20research%20on%20the%20link,the%20genetic%20tendency%20toward%20depression.
9 Bucklin, Mary A. *et al.* (2024). Depression Predicts Decreased Lumbar Bone Mineral Density: A Scoping Review of Chronic Psychological Stress and Spinal Tissue Pathology. *Osteoarthritis and Cartilage Open*, *6*(4), 100529. https://doi.org/10.1016/j.ocarto.2024.100529
10 Sedgwick-Müller, J. A., Müller-Sedgwick, U., Adamou, M. *et al.* (2022). University Students with Attention Deficit Hyperactivity Disorder (ADHD): A Consensus Statement from the UK Adult ADHD Network (UKAAN). *BMC Psychiatry, 22*, 292. https://doi.org/10.1186/s12888-022-03898-z.
11 Biddle, S. J. H., & Asare, M. (2011). Physical Activity and Mental Health in Children and Adolescents: A Review of Reviews. *British Journal of Sports Medicine, 45*, 886–895. https://doi.org/10.1136/bjsports-2011-090185.
12 Tatyana Bidopia, T. *et al.* (2023). Screen Media Technology and ADHD in Children and Adolescents: Potential Perils and Emerging Opportunities. In Ed. Bonnie Halpern-Felsher. *Encyclopedia of Child and Adolescent Health* (1st Edition), Academic Press, 260–274; ISBN 9780128188736. https://doi.org/10.1016/B978-0-12-818872-9.00126-6.
13 Kathleen Mikkelsen, K. *et al.* (2017). Exercise and Mental Health. *Maturitas*, *106*, 48—56. ISSN 0378-5122. https://doi.org/10.1016/j.maturitas.2017.09.003.
14 Chaput, J. P., Willumsen, J., Bull, F. *et al.* (2020). WHO Guidelines on Physical Activity and Sedentary Behaviour for Children and Adolescents Aged 5–17 Years: Summary of the Evidence. *International Journal of Behavioral Nutrition and Physical Activity*, *17*, 141. https://doi.org/10.1186/s12966-020-01037-z.

15 Lepe-Salazar, F., & Salgado-Torres, S. (2022). Multiple Composite Scenarios: A Game-Based Methodology for the Prevention of Mental Disorders. Entertainment Computing, *44*, 100519. https://doi.org/10.1016/j.entcom.2022.100519.
16 White, R. L., Vella, S., Biddle, S. *et al.* (2024). Physical Activity and Mental Health: A Systematic Review and Best-Evidence Synthesis of Mediation and Moderation Studies. *International Journal of Behavioral Nutrition and Physical Activity*, *21*, 134. https://doi.org/10.1186/s12966-024-01676-6.
17 Singh, S. *et al.* (2022). Decision Analysis of E-Learning in Bridging Digital Divide for Education Dissemination. *Procedia Computer Science*, *207*, 1970–1980. ISSN 1877-0509. https://doi.org/10.1016/j.procs.2022.09.256.
18 https://www.unicef.org/india/press-releases/unicef-report-spotlights-mental-health-impact-covid-19-children-and-young-people.
19 National Institute of Mental Health and Neurosciences: (2021) UNICEF Report.
20 Kaur, N. (2023). Unveiling Human Rights Issues in Mental Health Care: A Call for Reform and Empowerment. *IJHRLR*, *2*, 251–264. www.humanrightlawreview.in/vol-2-issue-3/.
21 Global, Regional, and National Burden of 12 Mental Disorders in 204 Countries and Territories, 1990–2019: A Systematic Analysis for the Global Burden of Disease Study 2019. *The Lancet Psychiatry*, *9*(2), 137–150.
22 National Adolescent Health Programme (Rasthriya Kishor Swasthya Karyakram).
23 Mehra, D. *et al.* (2022). Mental Health Interventions among Adolescents in India: A Scoping Review. *Healthcare*, *10*(2), 337. https://doi.org/10.3390/healthcare10020337.
24 Gonsalves, P. *et al.* (2023). Pilot Randomised Controlled Trial of a Remotely Delivered Online Intervention for Adolescent Mental Health Problems in India: Lessons Learned about Low Acceptability and Feasibility during the COVID-19 Pandemic. *BJPsych Open*, *9*(1), e7. doi:10.1192/bjo.2022.624.
25 WHO Global Action Plan on Physical Activity (GAPPA 2018–1030),
26 Tikka, S. K., Garg, S., & Siddiqui, M. A. (2021). Prescribing Physical Activity in Mental Health: A Focused Review on the Latest Evidence, Recommendations, Challenges, and Relevance to India. *Indian Journal of Psychological Medicine*, *43*(6), 535–541. https://https://doi.org/10.1177/0253717620972330.
27 Ranade, Ketki, *et al.* (2022). Mental Health Law, Policy & Program in India – A Fragmented Narrative of Change, Contradictions and Possibilities. *SSM – Mental Health*, *2*. https://doi.org/10.1016/j.ssmmh.2022.100174.
28 U.N. Convention on the Rights of Persons with Disabilities 2006.
29 Gupta, S. (2021). The Role of Policy and Legislation in Mental Health Care. *Indian Journal of Social Psychiatry*, *37*(2), 230–234. https://doi.org/10.4103/ijsp.ijsp_160_21.
30 Gore, M. *et al.* (2022). RESPIRE Collaboration: Working as Frontline Health Facilitators, Service Providers, Program Supporters, and Social Health Activists in Indian Hilly Terrain Areas: A Qualitative Study of Accredited Social Health Activists' Experiences before and during the COVID-19 Pandemic. *Journal of Global Health*, *12*, 2022. https://doi.org/10.7189/jogh.12.05052.
31 Raman, V., & Thomas, S. (2023). School Mental Health Program in India – Issues and Possible Practical Solutions. *Indian Journal of Psychological Medicine*, *45*(3), 283–288. https://doi.org/10.1177/02537176231165033.
32 Sharma, K. (October 10, 2018). We Need More Mental Health Care Professional in India. *Times of India*. https://www.google.com/search?q=Sharma%2C+K.+WE+NEED+MORE+MENTAL+HEALTH+CARE+PROFESSIONALS+IN+INDIA%3A+TIMES+OF+INDIA+OCT10%2C+2018&rlz=1C1CHBD_enIN872IN872&oq=Sharma%2C+K.+WE+NEED+MORE+MENTAL+HEALTH+CARE+PROFESSIONALS+IN+INDIA%3A+TIMES+OF+INDIA+OCT10%2C+2018&gs_lc

rp=EgZjaHJvbWUyBggAEEUYOdIBBzM0N2owajeoAgiwAgE&sourceid=chrome&ie=UTF-8.

33 Sharma, K. (October 10, 2018). We Need More Mental Health Care Professional in India. *Times of India*. https://www.google.com/search?q=Sharma%2C+K.+WE+NEED+MORE+MENTAL+HEALTH+CARE+PROFESSIONALS+IN+INDIA%3A+TIMES+OF+INDIA+OCT10%2C+2018&rlz=1C1CHBD_enIN872IN872&oq=Sharma%2C+K.+WE+NEED+MORE+MENTAL+HEALTH+CARE+PROFESSIONALS+IN+INDIA%3A+TIMES+OF+INDIA+OCT10%2C+2018&gs_lcrp=EgZjaHJvbWUyBggAEEUYOdIBBzM0N2owajeoAgiwAgE&sourceid=chrome&ie=UTF-8. Available Clinical Psychologists are only 1000 out of 20,000, Psychiatric Social Workers are 900 while the requirement is 35,000, Psychiatric Nurses are 1500 while 30,000 are required.

34 Gowda, Mahesh R. *et al.* (2017). Founding and Managing a Mental Health Establishment under the Mental Healthcare Act 2017. *Indian Journal of Psychiatry*, *61*(4), S735–S743. https://doi.org/10.4103/psychiatry.IndianJPsychiatry_147_19.

35 Mental Health Atlas 2017. WHO: ISBN 978-92-4-151401-9.

36 Jain, Sapna. (November 8, 2024). Social Media's Impact on Indian Students Well-Being. *India Today*. https://bestcolleges.indiatoday.in/news-detail/social-medias-impact-on-indian-students-well-being#:~:text=Reports%20indicate%20that%2027%25%20of,Health%20and%20Neurosciences%20(NIMHANS); Montag, C., & Elhai, J. D. (2020). Discussing Digital Technology Overuse in Children and Adolescents during the COVID-19 Pandemic and beyond: On the Importance of Considering Affective Neuroscience Theory. *Addictive Behaviors Reports*, *12*, 100313. ISSN 2352-8532. https://doi.org/10.1016/j.abrep.2020.100313; Hutton, J. S., Piotrowski, J. T., Bagot, K. *et al.* (2024). Digital Media and Developing Brains: Concerns and Opportunities. *Current Addiction Reports*, *11*, 287–298. https://doi.org/10.1007/s40429-024-00545-3.

37 Khalaf, A. M., Alubied, A. A., Khalaf, A. M. *et al.* (August 05, 2023). The Impact of Social Media on the Mental Health of Adolescents and Young Adults: A Systematic Review. *Cureus*, 15(8), e42990. https://doi.org/10.7759/cureus.42990; Kumar, V. L., & Goldstein, M. A. (2020). Cyberbullying and Adolescents. *Current Pediatrics Reports*, *8*, 86–92. https://doi.org/10.1007/s40124-020-00217-6.

38 Available at: OECD (2018). *Children and Young People's Mental Health in the Digital Age: Shaping the Future*, OECD Publishing, Paris, https://doi.org/10.1787/488b25e0-en.

39 Briefing Note for National Governments on UN Transforming Educational Summit. (2022): Five essential pillars of promoting and protecting mental health and psychosocial wellbeing in schools and learning environments, A briefing note of national governments. Available at: https://doi.org/10.54675/GCED9395.

12

RESPONSE OF INDIAN CRIMINAL JUSTICE SYSTEM TOWARDS CHILDREN AS VULNERABLE VICTIMS OF CYBERCRIME IN THE DIGITAL AGE

Rupashree Sahoo

Introduction

With the development of technology and the invention of the computer, human dependency on it has tremendously increased. The concept of the internet came into existence with the development of technology provided by the communication industry. For better security purposes, a variety of information began to be stored in computers. However, at the same time, a brand-new crime known as cybercrime appeared in the technological realm.[1] It facilitated the offenders to commit serious offences through computers or target computers to spread terror among mankind. In the present era it has become difficult to stay away from the use of internet and computers. It has not only made life more convenient but also brought people from many regions of the world together on a social, economic, and cultural level.[2] Life has become more comfortable at a personal and professional level by making the retrieval of information easier, sitting in one corner of the world to the other. The open access and flexibility have not just made it easier for users to take advantage of technology, but they have also put the system at risk from unavoidable risks like viruses, malware, hacking and phishing, copyright issues, identity fraud, data theft, and terrorism. The advancement of open cyberspace has not only connected the world through the internet in terms of speed and accessibility but also facilitated the offenders' rooting of their knowledge to achieve their selfish will and motive by manipulating the global network in their own way. The cyber offenders usually commit such types of offences through a computer system or the internet or target such resources to execute their mala-fide intention. Due to technical developments, it is now possible for spies to eavesdrop on people's private chats,

DOI: 10.4324/9781003607076-16

giving cybercriminals new weapons with which they are able to violate the privacy of others.[3] Nowadays, cybercrime is no longer confined to financial gain; rather, it has evolved into a vital weapon in the hands of criminals, allowing them to spread terror throughout the world without their physical presence while committing such crime. It is the easiest way to carry out high-tech crimes through cyberspace.

The internet provides a safe place for offenders to commit various types of crimes using cyberspace. Additionally, it is important to remember that the internet is not just a "piece of technology", a kind of "blank slate", or something that exists independently of the users. Instead, it should be viewed as a "set of social activities"; individuals use the internet in certain ways and for specific goals, which is why it has the structure that it has.[4] It depends on how people use the internet that provides a platform for the perpetrators to commit such crimes. For instance, there would not be any possibilities of credit card frauds that take advantage of users' account details, if individuals are not involved in online purchases. The widespread penetration of "computer as well as communication technology" in all facets of our livelihood has unavoidably resulted in illegal activities using such technologies. Such activities are labelled as "computer crime" or cybercrime. Many negative things and anomalies are thought to originate on the internet, requiring the application of criminal law.[5]

Computers nowadays permeate each facet of society, especially their rapid influence has shocked the legal and judicial systems.[6] The fundamental legal concepts are being put to the test because of technological advancements when it comes to providing justice to cyber victims. The rapid development of information technology in recent years has made the internet an unavoidable means to access information and knowledge in our day-to-day lives. Information exploration through the internet has become a parallel form of life, because of which the privacy of information is easily breached nowadays.[7]

The offence of cybercrime confronts the entire world by its magnitude of loss to society that creates a hurdle to conducting thorough investigations, acquiring sufficient evidence, and bringing cybercriminals to justice. Cybercrime would be destructive to the entire world if not checked as well as identified at an early stage. It would be futile in the technology world without effective means of identifying it.

India has made progress towards digitalization. In order to guarantee that all of its residents may access government services online, in 2015, the Government of India (GOI) started the "Digital India" initiative.[8] It wouldn't be incorrect to argue that individuals are addicted to the vast cyberspace, where a sizable section of the populace depends on computers, smartphones, and the apps they offer, as well as social media, as part of their daily lives. Due to the pandemic and lockdown, many people were forced to work from home and take classes online. The constant reliance on technology cannot currently be avoided, but there are always steps that can be taken to protect yourself against cybercrimes. Women and children are regarded as the most vulnerable groups in society, making them obvious targets for cybercrimes since they are easily abused and exploited in cyberspace by anonymous perpetrators.

Over the past few years, social media platforms have grown strongly and quickly, facilitating communication and information sharing between individuals beyond political, economic, and geographical boundaries. In the meantime, it has created new entry points for online aggression and new threats. Such actions include, for instance, "cyber bullying, revenge pornography, trolling, virtual mobbing, etc.".[9] The proliferation of sexually explicit websites, chatrooms, and so forth on the internet provides cyberspace a place for the perpetrators to sexually exploit the users.[10] The internet has become a potential platform for love endeavours. According to "Aunshul Rege", there are four things that make dating online enticing: first, people do not need to leave their residences or places of work to date; second, there is no insecurity because of the confidentiality and privacy on the web, which allows individuals to take part in dating in personal; third, persons choose to try different kinds of dating websites like online chat, chat rooms, sexually suggestive emojis, nods, and wiggles; and fourth, it provides as just a great combination because individuals can pick choose options for sex.[11] Youngsters are now using "social networking sites" more frequently to build relationships, connect with one another, and learn new skills. Though the social networking platform helps teens in building relationships but on the other hand the regular usage of "social networking sites" puts them at risk of online abuse.[12]

Cybercrimes are becoming more common because of criminals interacting directly with children through social media platforms and chat features in various applications and games. Cybercrimes against children can take many different forms, such as "online harassment, cyberstalking, morphing, cyber pornography, extortion, cheating, sexual exploitation, and ongoing harassment for voyeuristic purposes". Due to their propensity to trust predators and divulge personal information, which can result in offences like identity theft, child exploitation or abuse, children become the soft targets of these crimes. Because they are frequently unpleasant, rebellious, trusting, adventurous, and desperate for attention and affection, young children and teenagers lack the mental maturity to comprehend the serious consequences of what they may encounter on this cyber platform. Adolescents who are troubled and rebellious and want independence from their parents may be more vulnerable to online predators since emotionally fragile teenagers are more likely to become victims of such crimes. These online connections, which at first glance could seem respectable and safe, might not be in the long run. If they are misused by the offender, they could result in sexually explicit content, hurt the victim physically or psychologically, and even breach their rights. Parents find it challenging to protect their children online because they are often unaware of the potential risks, and they may also be unaware of the appropriate legal remedies.

It is a common misconception that cybercrimes do not affect victims substantially, but you might be surprised to learn how much psychological and physical harm is inflicted, especially on children who are abused. Since victims frequently believe their privacy has been violated, the emotional toll has a longer-lasting effect on them.

Where India has witnessed technological advancement in the field of cyberspace, it has also witnessed the growing trend in cyber offences against children. This study involves the content analysis of the laws, and the type of offences committed against children through cyberspace in India in the following aspects:

a. Qualitative analysis of the statutory definitions and punishment scheme to understand the meaning of the various offences inflicted on children through cyberspace and the punishment scheme provided by the statutes in India
b. Quantitative analysis of the rate of reporting and pendency of cases for investigation by police
c. Quantitative analysis of the disposals by the Court

Definitions and Punishments for Offences Against Children Through Cyberspace

Before discussing any offences, it is equally important to know the definition of a "child". Literally, "child" is a person considered as under age, physically not having attained puberty and mentally with incomplete cognitive development. The "International Convention on the Rights of the Child, 1989" under "Article-1" defines a child as "every human being below the age of eighteen years unless under the law applicable to the child, majority is attained at an earlier age".[13] In India, being a signatory to this convention, a child under the Protection of Children from Sexual Offences Act 2012 (POCSO Act) and the Bhartiya Nyaya Sanhita 2023 (BNS, which replaced the Indian Penal Code of 1860) is one below the age of 18 years.

The definition of any offence creates the boundary between the accepted and prohibited acts as expected by the state, although the internet poses a peculiar problem where moral, cultural and legal divergence makes it difficult to define "pornography" in such a global society.[14]

Every country has its unique traditions and customs, making it very difficult to define the term "pornography" and leaving no clear legal definition in place. While pornography is legal in certain countries, it is illegal and punishable in others. The act of making, exhibiting, transmitting, or uploading sexual or obscene content online is known as cyberpornography. Since the creation of cyberspace, cyber pornographic content has mostly replaced traditional pornographic content.[15]

According to Merriam-Webster's dictionary, "pornography" traditionally refers to material like books or photographs that contain depictions of erotic behaviour intended to cause sexual arousal.[16] Since there are no universally accepted standards of culture and ethics or standardized regulations that define pornography, what constitutes pornography is unclear. Obscenity and pornographic definitions fluctuate over time and between different nations. Obscenity and pornography are two distinct but related words that may be legal in some nations. The term "pornography" has not been defined under any law in India, and therefore has not been addressed. We must comprehend pornography and obscenity, especially while dealing with children in their broadest sense, to understand their seriousness and impact on society. The expression "obscene" refers to content that can be restricted or outlawed because it contains explicit depictions of sex, genitalia, or other bodily functions that are obviously offensive and have no aesthetic or scientific value.[17] The BNS 2023 addresses the topic of "obscenity" in India. Since modern technology in the field of cyberspace has developed in recent years, obscenity and pornography have taken on an electronic format, making it difficult to prosecute offenders as per the said Act. The GOI has passed the Information Technology Act 2000 (IT Act) to address this new technology. Section 67 of the IT Act covers "obscenity and sexually explicit content" electronically through cyberspace. According to Section 67 of the IT Act:

> Whoever publishes or transmits or causes to be published in the electronic form, any material which is lascivious or appeals to the prurient interest or if its effect is such as to tend to deprave and corrupt persons who are likely, having regard to all relevant circumstances, to read, see or hear the matter contained or embodied in it, shall be punished on first conviction with imprisonment of either description for a term which may extend to two to three years and with fine which may extend to five lakh rupees and in the event of a second or subsequent conviction with imprisonment of either description for a term which may extend to five years and also with fine which may extend to ten lakh rupees.[18]

The new developments in technology have enabled pornographers to create pornographic images of children who appear to be engaged in sexual activities even in their absence during the creation of such images. The images showing the depiction of children in such activities are manipulated into the image using computer graphics programs like Photoshop by the pornographers.

The first international definition of child pornography came into existence by the Optimal Protocol to the Convention on the Rights of the Child on 18 January 2002 as, "representation of a child by any means engaged in sexual activities in real or simulated form or exhibition of child genital for the purpose of sexual activity".[19]

When children themselves produce self-generated images willingly representing themselves, they are not held liable in any jurisdiction. However, when this material is created, even if with consent or coercion or pressure against the will of the child by another adult person and is disseminated, then this will be treated as a criminal offence and will be punishable.[20]

In case of child pornography, the types of perpetrators that are involved in the different stages of the offence are, firstly, the person who depicts children in sexual acts or takes simulated images of children, modifies them and, secondly, each one of such persons who disseminates or distributes such images only for monetary gain. And, thirdly, any adult who collects, stores, and watches such child pornographic materials.

The high usage of the internet has expanded the ambit of the offence of obscenity. Nowadays, pornographic material is freely available on the internet that brings such content to a common view with more ease. The term "pornography" has not been defined in any statute of India, rather the term "obscenity" is defined as an offence under certain circumstances under the two statutes, that is, the Bharatiya Nyaya Sanhita, 2023 (Sections 294–296), previously provided under sections 292–294 of the Indian Penal Code and the IT (Amendment) Act, 2008 (sections 66E, 67, 67A, 67B). "Section-294 of the Bharatiya Nyaya Sanhita" comprehensively defined the term "obscene material" as any book, writing, painting, figure or any other object that exhibits sexual acts or causes sexual excitement and which is likely to deprave the minds of those in whose hands that book or writing or painting is likely to fall. One who sells, distributes, or publicly exhibits such material is liable for the offence, except where such materials are for the purpose of learning science, literature, art or for the general concern, where it cannot be considered as an obscene act.

Although the Bharatiya Nyaya Sanhita, 2023, and the IT Act, 2000, do not define child pornography, Section 67(B) of the latter law forbids publishing or transmitting any visual depiction of children engaging in sexual acts through electronic means (incorporated by the IT (Amendment) Act, 2008). It is forbidden to even create, gather, browse, download, or distribute electronically any sexually explicit content that features children. The maximum sentence under this act for a first conviction is five years in prison and a fine of up to ten lakh rupees. The maximum sentence for a second or subsequent conviction is seven years in prison and a fine of up to ten lakh rupees.[21]

The expression "cyber stalking/cyber bullying" has not been defined in any statute in India. In general, stalking refers to actions that harass or threaten the other person. Cyberstalking is an extension of physical stalking that takes place online while utilizing digital technology. Cyberstalking is the practice of stalking someone online using tools like email and chat forums.

> According to Professor Lamber Royakkers – Cyber stalking is the repeatedly harassing or threatening of an individual via the internet or other electronic means of communication. A cyber stalker is someone with amorous and/or sexual motives who constantly harasses someone else electronically: via the bulletin board, chats box, e-mail, spam, fax, buzzer or voice-mail. Stalking generally involves the constant harassment or threatening of someone else: following a person, appearing at someone's house or workplace, making harassing phone calls, leaving written messages or objects, or vandalizing someone's property. Because the stalking activities are so diverse and have to be seen in their connection it is difficult to give a precise description of stalking.[22]

Section 78 of the Bharatiya Nyaya Sanhita, 2023, addresses "stalking" and defines it as following a woman and repeatedly contacting her despite her clear disinterest or monitoring her online activities without her consent, therefore includes cyber stalking also. However, we do not find any provisions against online bullying, harassment, or stalking in the IT Act of 2000.

As the decade progressed, crimes such as video voyeurism and child pornography, sending offensive emails, releasing pornographic material, and leaking private data also caught national attention. To provide for penal provisions to deal with these laws, the amendments were very important; however, the law enforcement agencies were of the view that it was extremely difficult to punish the offender under the existing provisions of the IT Act due to a lack of enforcement machinery. In fact, it was reported that very few cases were actually prosecuted under the IT Act.[23]

A case which stunned the nation was the MMS scandals, where school-going children were depicted in illicit activities. The said case is well known as *Avnish Bajaj v. State (N.C.T) of Delhi* or *Baazee.com case*,[24] where the said website was a wholly owned subsidiary of eBay and was in the news for permitting on its website the sale of obscene material in MMS involving school children. A student from the Indian Institute of Technology (IIT) Kharagpur posted the video clip for sale on the internet, which was provided in the option "Books and Magazines" and sub-option "e-books", and he used the seller's name as "Alice Electronics". Eight copies of the MMS clip were sold. Through Community Watch (which is basically an initiative to prevent crime that encourages residents to actively participate in law enforcement efforts to reduce crime in their communities), alert information was sent to the concerned people at Baazee.com, reporting that the video was illegal in India. The item on the website was closed, although not immediately. The IIT student was tracked down and taken into custody, charges were filed against the student, the Managing Director of Bazee and the Senior Manager, Trust and Safety.[25]

Ritu Kohli's case[26] in 2001, the country's first cyber stalking case, brought the seriousness of the practice into sharp relief. Manish Kathuria, the offender in the case, was taken into custody by the Delhi Police. In the aforementioned instance, Manish was illegally using "Ritu Kohli's" name for interacting using the website "www.mirc.com" while stalking Ritu Kohli online. Manish would frequently use vulgar and offensive language while conversing on the aforementioned website as Ritu Kohli, giving out her home phone number and urging other users to chat with her over the phone. Ritu Kohli, consequently, began to receive vulgar calls from chatters in both India and other countries. The Delhi Police initiated an investigation when Ritu Kohli called the police to report the incident. The police registered the case under Section 509 of the Indian Penal Code, 1860, for outraging modesty. Cyberstalking is not covered by any of the requirements listed in this section. The case of Ritu Kohli served as a warning to the government to enact legislation outlawing the aforementioned crime and providing for the protection of the victim.[27]

Therefore, stalking is not clearly addressed under the Information Technology Amendment Act of 2008. However, the issue is handled like "intrusion on the privacy of the individual" rather than as a typical "cybercrime", mentioned in "the IT Act". Sections 72 and 72A are the popular sections of the Amendment Act, 2008, "regulating cyber stalking in India". However, following the "Delhi gang rape incident in December 2012", the Indian government passed or revised a number of new legislations. The law against stalking was also passed. Section 78(1)(2) of the BNS and Section 354D of the IPC both define and punish stalking, including cyberstalking.

The POCSO Act, 2012, was passed by the Indian parliament as a special law to prevent sexual offences against minors. It forbade the use of minors in pornography and the storage of pornographic materials featuring minors for commercial gain (Sections 13, 14, and 15 of the POCSO Act). Nevertheless, the 2012 Act did not include a definition for the term "child pornography". The term "any visual depiction of sexually explicit conduct involving a child" was ultimately defined by the POCSO (Amendment) Act, 2019, under Section 2(da) as "any photograph, video, digital or computer-generated image indistinguishable from an actual child, and image created, adapted".

In addition, child pornography in India is governed by a number of laws, most notably the POCSO Act and the IT Act. Sections 13, 14, and 15 of the POCSO Act, as well as the provisions of the IT Act, address various forms of exploitation, including online and digital offences. In terms of cyber child pornography, the provisions of the POCSO Act (Sections 13, 14, and 15) and the IT Act (Sections 66E and 67B) overlap significantly.

However, Section 67B of the IT Act expressly makes it illegal to publish, transmit, or distribute content depicting children in a sexually explicit act. This section intersects with Section 13 of the POCSO Act when contents such as pictures or videos of child sexual abuse are created, saved, and distributed through digital platforms. The offender may face charges both under Section 13 of the POCSO Act (for generating or deploying a child in a sexually explicit act) and under Section 67B of the IT Act (for transmitting and disseminating illicit contents depicting children).

Section 14 of the POCSO Act specifically prohibits possession, procurement, and viewing of child pornography. Since the IT Act addresses the electronic element and the POCSO Act focuses specifically on child pornography, anyone who downloads, stores, or distributes material involving sexually explicit acts involving children may be charged under both the legal frameworks, that is, under Section 14 of the POCSO Act and Section 67B of the IT Act.

Section 15 of the POCSO Act also makes storing and transmission of material of child sexual abuse an offence. The combination of Sections 13, 14, and 15 of the POCSO Act with the IT Act provides a thorough legal framework that deals with cyber child pornography. The IT Act focuses on cybercrimes involving the publication, transmission, and possession of child pornography electronically, whereas the POCSO Act protects children against sexual offences, including pornography. Since these legal provisions overlap, they ensure that offenders can be prosecuted through a number of avenues for both the act of making and disseminating sexually explicit material depicting children and associated acts relating to cyber offences.

Responses of the Criminal Justice System Towards Cybercrime Against Children

Controlling this explosive cybercrime against children under the specific statutes in each jurisdiction is the goal of the various stakeholders in the criminal justice process, including police officers, prosecutors, courts, and technological agencies at different phases of the process. In this section, the criminal justice system's response is examined at the different stages, namely, reporting, investigation, prosecution, and court case disposal in India.

Reporting and Investigation

The consumption of child pornography has risen by 95% since the statewide lockdown in March 2020, according to research work released in April 2020 by the India Child Protection Fund. This increase in usage is a sign that perpetrators have shifted to online, making the internet a very dangerous place for children.[28]

TABLE 12.1 Punishment for offences against children for the purpose of pornography under POCSO Act in India

Sl. no.	*Statutory provision*	*Punishable act*	*Punishment*
1.	Section 14 (1)	Using a child for the purpose of pornography	First conviction – maximum five years imprisonment with a fine Second conviction – seven years with a fine
2.	Section 14 read with Section 4 (2)	Child pornography involving penetrative sexual assault	Ten years to life imprisonment with fine, but if the child is below 16 years, minimum imprisonment of 20 years and maximum life imprisonment with fine
3.	Section 14 read with Section 6 (1)	Child pornography involving penetrative sexual assault in an aggravated form	20 years to life imprisonment with a fine, which may extend to a death sentence in extreme cases
4.	Section 14 read with Section 8	Child pornography that tends to sexual abuse	Six to eight years imprisonment with a fine
5.	Section 14 read with Section 10	Aggravated sexual violence against children	Eight to ten years imprisonment with a fine
6.	Section 15 (1)	Intentionally storing pornographic content of a child without deleting or destroying to transmit the same	Fine of 5,000 rupees, which may extend to 10,000 rupees in case of a second conviction
7.	Section 15 (2)	Storing or possessing pornographic content of a child for the purpose of transmitting, displaying, or distributing	Maximum imprisonment of three years or fine or both
8.	Section 15 (3)	Possessing pornographic material depicting a child for commercial purposes	Three to five years imprisonment with a fine For repeat offenders – five to ten years imprisonment with a fine

As per Section 174 of the BNSS (previously provided under Section 154 of the CrPC), incidents of cyber child pornography or online child sexual abuse in India may be filed online through the National Cyber Offence Reporting Portal or at any police station, regardless of the location of the offence.[29] The National Crime Records Bureau has provided the types of cybercrimes committed against children, among which cyber pornography and cyber stalking or cyberbullying are the highest in number. The number of cases reported relating to hosting or creation, storage of child pornography materials, and cyber stalking or bullying[30] are shown in Table 12.2 (in ascending order).

According to Section 78 of the Information Technology (Amendment) Act of 2008, only police personnel in the inspector cadre in India are authorized to look into allegations of child pornography. Regarding India's general pattern of rising crime, Table 12.3 illustrates how few cases in which an investigation gets completed within the specified time frame result in a high pendency percentage:

Table 12.3 indicates that the pendency percentage in the disposal of cybercrime cases by police has increased in the country; that is, from the year 2017 to 2021, the percentage has increased from 37% to 57%, which is alarming.

TABLE 12.2 Number of child pornography cases and cyber stalking/bullying reported in India since 2017 to 2021

Year	*Number of child pornography cases reported*	*Number of cases reported in cyber stalking/bullying*	*Total number of cases reported in India*
2017	7	7	14
2018	44	40	84
2019	102	45	147
2020	738	140	878
2021	969	123	1092

TABLE 12.3 Status of cases investigated from 2017 to 2021 under the POCSO Act, 2013, and the IT Act, 2000, provided by the National Crime Records Bureau[31]

Year	*Total cases for investigation in that year*	*Total case disposals by the police*	*No. of investigations at the end of the year*	*Percentage of cases pending*
2017	553	343	209	37.79
2018	1061	647	414	39.01
2019	1683	920	763	45.33
2020	831	391	440	52.90
2021	1417	597	820	57.90

BNSS has integrated digital technologies in the criminal procedure and made audio-video communications and electronic communications mandatory in a number of court proceedings to cut down delays in criminal proceedings. The purpose of this modification is to increase case information accessible for all parties, reduce paperwork, and minimize errors. Under the BNSS, summons can be sent to witnesses and the accused person electronically, investigating officers can use audio-video equipment to record statements, search and seizure operations can be recorded using audio-video equipment, and other proceedings like trials, inquiries, appeals, and related proceedings can all be conducted electronically. By using electronic communications, investigations can be expedited in all types of offences, including cybercrimes.[32]

Section 57 of the BSA represents a major change in how cybercrimes are addressed in India. This section acknowledges electronic records as key evidence in court proceedings, including emails, social media posts, digital documents, and more. Compared to earlier times, when such evidence had a secondary position and needed further verification, this marks a significant advancement. Investigation and prosecution processes used to be greatly slowed down by the need to rely on hard copies of digital evidence. However, by designating electronic documents as primary evidence, Section 57 removes this obstacle. In cybercrime situations, where digital photos, videos, and other multimedia evidence are frequently pieces of evidence and play a crucial role in many cybercrime investigations, this enables courts to easily take electronic records into consideration, which could result in a quicker and more effective resolution of cases.[33]

To bring proper coordination in responding to all cybercrimes, the Indian government's "Ministry of Home Affairs" established the Indian "Cyber Crime Coordination Centre (I4C)" in 2018. The Centre is divided into seven branches: the Training Centre, the Forensic Laboratory Ecosystem, the National Cyber Crime Reporting Portal, the Threat Analytics Unit, the Research and Innovation Centre, and the Platform for Joint Cyber Crime Investigation Team.[34]

The Central Bureau of Investigation began an operation known as "Megh Chakra" (translates to cloud circle) in September 2022. During this operation, they conducted searches in 21 States and Union Territories (UT), arrested roughly 50 people, and seized their electronic devices in connection with cyber child pornography cases. This operation, known as Megh Chakra (Megh meaning cloud), targeted cloud storage services that the criminals exploited to spread illegal videos of children engaging in sexual activity.[35]

At many phases of the legal process, child-friendly protocols are established for reporting crimes, gathering evidence, conducting investigations, and trying offenders under the POCSO Act. Additionally, the idea of creating Special Courts to try legal offences has been included, and such Special

Courts are mandated to complete the trial of cases involving sexual offences against children within a year. Disclosing the child's name in the media is a crime that carries a maximum one-year sentence.[36]

The Government of India established "Central Emergency Response Team India (CERT-IN)", a nodal body that forecasts and warns of cybersecurity incidents, stops them from happening, and secures Indian cyberspace. It serves as an agency in cyber child pornography cases, accepting and reviewing complaints to restrict particular websites that feature pornography against children.[37]

Because crime against children is a serious concern for the Indian government, it encourages state governments and UT administrations to take action to effectively prevent, discover, register, investigate, and prosecute any crimes against children that fall under their purview. On 10 May 2013, the Hon'ble Supreme Court issued an advisory on missing children in *Bachpan Bachao Andolan v. Union of India*.[38]

A document titled "Child Victims of Cyber Crime – Legal Tool Kit" was released by the National Commission for Protection of Child Rights (NCPCR) to help investigating officers understand the laws pertaining to cybercrime in simple terms.[39] Also, in 2020, World Vision India released a survey titled "Child Sexual Abuse: Awareness and Attitudes", which aimed to determine the level of awareness of child sexual abuse and the willingness to report it. 32.13% of the 4500 parents or caregivers and 35% of the 4500 youngsters between the ages of 12 and 18 knew about the POCSO Act. Furthermore, just 65% of children expressed confidence that adequate action would be taken in a case of child sexual abuse, compared to 75% of caregivers. This creates a significant reporting obstacle.[40]

The issue of poor reporting and the challenge of looking into reported cases are two sides of the same coin. Reports from newspapers indicate that a relatively small percentage of cybercrime instances are being turned into formal complaints. This is one of the main reasons that paedophiles do not fear the laws that are in place to combat cybercrimes. Therefore, there is much work to be done in this area to enhance the reporting of cybercrimes, particularly those that target minors.[41]

Court Disposals of Cyber Crime Cases Against Children

In India, the pendency of cases for trial has increased in the last few years which directly impacts the conviction rate. In the year 2017, under the POCSO Act, a total of 1152 cases were pending for trial, out of which none of them could be tried. Under the IT Act, 2000, in 2014, 13 cases were pending for trial, out of which only one trial was completed, and, in 2019, 169 cases were sent for trial, out of which in only two cases trials were completed, and that ended up in a conviction. Similarly, under the POCSO Act, a total

TABLE 12.4 Court disposal in child pornography cases under the POCSO Act

Year	*Total cases for trial*	*Cases in which trials were completed*	*At the end of the year cases pending for trial*	*Cases convicted*	*Rate of conviction (in %)*	*Rate of pendency (in %)*
2017	1152	106	1046	27	25.50	90.80
2018	1614	68	1546	46	67.60	95.80
2019	2328	91	2224	34	37.40	95.50
2020	89	1	88	0	0.0	98.90
2021	104	3	98	1	33.3	94.20

TABLE 12.5 Court disposal in child pornography cases under the IT Act

Year	*Total cases for trial*	*Cases in which trials were completed*	*At the end of the year cases pending for trial*	*Cases convicted*	*Rate of conviction (in %)*	*Rate of pendency (in %)*
2017	30	0	30	0	0	100
2018	68	1	67	1	100	98.5
2019	168	2	166	2	100	98.8
2020	438	1	436	0	0.0	99.5
2021	888	13	873	7	53.8	98.3

of 2328 cases were sent for trial, out of which only in 91 cases trials were completed with a conviction rate of 37.4% and the pendency percentage is 95.5% ("Crime in India", 2019). The following two tables portray the conviction rate and pendency rate of trials in Courts under the POCSO Act and the IT Act.

Prior to 2008, the term "child pornography" was not recognized in India. Although the Act created the offences of using a child for pornography and storing the same in 2012, the POCSO Amendment Bill of 2019 introduced the definition, outlawing the act of depicting children in sexual acts through electronic means for publication and transmission. It was challenging for the Indian Criminal Justice System to classify cyber child pornography as a violation until a precise definition was established.

In addition to penalties under the IT Act, the POCSO Act's punishment scheme for using a child in pornography includes enhancements based on aggravating circumstances. The penalties range from a minimum of 20 years to life in prison, and, in extreme cases, they include the death penalty for using a child in pornography that results in both penetrative and aggravated penetrative sexual assault.

On 23 September 2024, a Division Bench of the Supreme Court of India ruled that the POCSO Act makes it illegal to merely view, possess, or store content that shows children having sex. The ruling resolves a long-running dispute among High Courts on whether "mere storage" of "child pornography" is punishable by Section 67B of the IT Act and Section 15 of the POCSO Act. In particular, it reversed the Madras High Court's ruling in *S Harish v. Inspector of Police and Others*[42] (2024), which had dismissed criminal charges against an offender after concluding that viewing or downloading "child pornography" was not, in and of itself, illegal under the IT Act or the POCSO Act.[43]

Conclusion

The rapid development of digital technologies and widespread availability of internet access, vulnerability of children to cybercrimes has significantly increased particularly child sexual abuse and child pornography. The POCSO Act, 2012, and the IT Act, 2000, are two Indian statutes that handle this intricate and gravely concerning issue. Taken together, they create a comprehensive but continuously evolving legal framework. The Bharatiya Nyaya Sanhita, 2023, which took the place of the IPC, makes additional efforts to update and simplify laws pertaining to stalking, obscenity, and other associated online offences.

Despite these efforts, challenges remain. Indian law lacks clear statutory definitions for terms like "pornography" and "cyberstalking", which frequently makes them difficult to interpret and enforce. Although the production, possession, and dissemination of child pornographic material are illegal under laws such as Section 67B of the IT Act and Sections 13, 14, and 15 of the POCSO Act, implementation of these laws is inconsistent because of technological difficulties, lack of knowledge, and investigative limits.

Landmark cases such as the Ritu Kohli case and *Avnish Bajaj v. State* (NCT of Delhi) show the inadequacies and the pressing need for strong enforcement measures. In addition to being strict, the legal structure needs to be flexible enough to accommodate emerging forms of online exploitation, such as computer-generated or manipulated content. In a nutshell, even though India has established the legal framework necessary to prevent cybercrimes against minors, the criminal justice system still urgently needs capacity-building, cross-border collaboration, specialized cybercrime units, clear statutory definitions, and ongoing legal reform. Only by taking a comprehensive and coordinated approach that includes technological, legal, and social initiatives can we successfully protect kids from the threats that lie online.

High investigation and prosecution pendency rates, along with the concerning increase in child pornography and cyberbullying cases, are indicative of structural flaws that impede prompt justice. The recent legal reform in the Indian Criminal Justice System such as BNSS and BSA, which acknowledge electronic evidence and encourage digital communication in legal proceedings, provides a potential mechanism to enhance case resolution. Special operations such as "Megh Chakra" and initiatives like CERT-IN and the I4C demonstrate growing institutional response. But poor reporting because of awareness, fear, and mistrust remains a significant obstacle, exacerbated by insufficient enforcement and prolonged judicial proceedings. Therefore, stronger interagency coordination, quick investigations, child-friendly judicial mechanisms, and increased awareness among children, parents, and law enforcement agencies are all necessary to effectively prevent cybercrimes against children. A multi-stakeholder, technology-driven, victim-centric strategy must continue to be the cornerstone of India's defence against cybercrimes that target its children, who are its most vulnerable group.

The disposal of cybercrime cases against children by Indian courts reflects an alarming trend of judicial delay and low conviction rates, particularly under the POCSO Act and IT Act. Despite an increase in the number of cases sent for trial, an overwhelming majority remain pending, with pendency rates consistently exceeding 90% and convictions often falling below 40%. This significant backlog delays justice for child victims and undermines the deterrent effect of the law.

While substantial legislative measures exist, including the possibility of life imprisonment or even the death penalty in extreme cases, their effectiveness is undermined by procedural inefficiencies and chronic delays in the judiciary. To successfully safeguard children from cyber exploitation, it is imperative to prioritize faster trials, build judicial infrastructure, train judicial officials on cyber-related offences, and ensure proper implementation of recent legal developments. In the digital era, swift and guaranteed punishment is essential for restoring trust in the judicial system and deterring potential criminals. Therefore, India must strengthen investigation and trial processes, enhance legal clarity, and adopt a coordinated, tech-driven, and child-centric approach that assures timely justice and significant deterrence.

Notes

1 Karnika Seth, Computers, Internet and New Technology Laws (1st ed. 2012).
2 Vakul Sharma and Seema Sharma, Information Technology Law and Practice (6th ed. 2019).
3 R K Chaubey, An Introduction to Cyber Crime and Cyber Law (2021).
4 Yar Majid and Kevin F. Steinmetz, Cyber Crime and society (2019).
5 Ulrich Sieber, Legal Aspects of Computer-Related Crime in the Information Society-COMCRIME-Study, 1 (1998), https://www.law.tuwien.ac.at/sieber.pdf.
6 K Jaishankar, Cyber Criminology: Exploring Internet Crimes and Criminal Behavior (2011).
7 Cameron S.D. Brown, *Investigating and Prosecuting Cyber Crime: Forensic Dependencies and Barriers to Justice*, 9 Int. J. Cyber Criminol. 55–119 (2015).

8 *Digital India | MyGov.in*, https://www.mygov.in/group/digital-india.
9 Hamid Jahankhani, Cyber Criminology (Hamid Jahankhani ed. 2018).
10 K Jaishankar, Cyber Criminology: Exploring Internet Crimes and Criminal Behavior (2011).
11 Aunshul Rege, *What 's Love Got to Do With It? Exploring Online Dating Scams and Identity Fraud*, 3 Int. J. Cyber Criminol. 494–512 (2009), https://www.researchgate.net/publication/228373590_What's_Love_Got_to_Do_with_It_Exploring_Online_Dating_Scams_and_Identity_Fraud/link/556758a408aefcb861d387ba/download.
12 June Ahn, *The Effect of Social Network Sites on Adolscents Social and Academic Development: Current Theories and Controversies*, 64 J. Am. Soc. Inf. Sci. Technol. 1435–1445 (2013), http://onlinelibrary.wiley.com/doi/10.1002/asi.22883/abstract.
13 *Convention on the Rights of the Child*, (1989), https://www.ohchr.org/en/professionalinterest/pages/crc.aspx%0D.
14 Yaman Akdeniz, *The Regulation of Pornography and Child Pornography on the Internet*, Soc. Sci. Res. Netw. 1–47 (1997), https://www.researchgate.net/publication/220667856_The_Regulation_Of_Pornography_And_Child_Pornography_On_The_Internet.
15 Vakul Sharma and Seema Sharma, Information Technology Law and Practice (6th ed. 2019).
16 *Definition of Pornography*, 1–9, https://www.merriam-webster.com/dictionary/pornography.
17 Sushila Devi Chauhan, *Combating Cyber Obscenity in India and United States of America: A Comparative Analysis*, 3 Jamia Law J. 77–90 (2018).
18 Government of India, *The Information Technology Act*, 1–36 (2000), https://www.indiacode.nic.in/bitstream/123456789/1999/3/A2000-21.pdf.
19 Ethel Quayle, *Child Pornography and Sexual Exploitation of Children Online* (2008).
20 ECPAT, *Online Child Sexual Exploitation* (2020), https://ecpat.org/wp-content/uploads/2021/05/ECPAT-Summary-paper-on-Online-Child-Sexual-Exploitation-2020.pdf.
21 Government of India, *The Information Technology Act*, 1–36 (2000), https://www.indiacode.nic.in/bitstream/123456789/1999/3/A2000-21.pdf.
22 K Jaishankar, Cyber Criminology: Exploring Internet Crimes and Criminal Behavior (2011).
23 Aparna Viswanathan, Cyber Law Indian & International Perspectives (1st ed. 2012).
24 (2005) 3 Comp LJ 364 Del (India).
25 Vakul Sharma and Seema Sharma, Information Technology Law and Practice (6th ed. 2019).
26 Amit Kumar and Dr. Dalip Kumar, *Crimes of Stalking and Harassment against Women in Cyberspace*, 5 Int. J. Multidiscip. Res. 1–7 (2023), https://www.ijfmr.com/papers/2023/6/9006.pdf.
27 Sapna Sukrut Deo, *Cyberstalking and Online Harassment: A New Challenge for Law Enforcement*, Bharati Law Rev. 86–93 (2013), https://docs.manupatra.in/newsline/articles/Upload/FDF5EB3E-2BB1–44BB-8F1D-9CA06D965AA9.pdf.
28 Kailash Satyarthi, *Entangled in the Web: Cybercrimes against Children in India* (2023), https://satyarthi.org.in/wp-content/uploads/2023/04/Cyber-Crime-Report_F.pdf.
29 Soumic Ghosh, *How to report a cyber crime in India* (2020), https://www.csoonline.com/article/3564601/how-to-report-cybercrime-in-india.html.
30 Crime in India, 1 National Crime Records Bureau (Ministry of Home Affairs) (2019), https://ncrb.gov.in/sites/default/files/CII 2019 Volume 1.pdf.

31 Crime in India, National Crime Records Bureau (Ministry of Home Affairs), https://ncrb.gov.in/en/crime-india.
32 *Stringent Measures against Cybercrimes in India's New Criminal Justice System*, 1–5 (2024), https://www.jsalaw.com/newsletters-and-updates/stringent-measures-against-cybercrimes-in-indias-new-criminal-justice-system/.
33 *Stringent Measures against Cybercrimes in India's New Criminal Justice System*, 1–5.
34 PIB, *Shri Amit Shah Inagurates Indian Cyber Crime Coordination Centre I4C) in New Delhi: Dedicates National Cyber Crime Reporting Portal to the Nation*, 1–2 (2020), https://www.pib.gov.in/PressReleasePage.aspx?PRID=1599067.
35 Devesh K. Pandey, *Operation Megh Chakra: 50 under CBI Scanner over Child Pornography*, 1–2 (2022, September 25), https://www.thehindu.com/news/national/sharing-of-child-sexual-abuse-material-cbi-raids-56-places-in-19-states-and-1-ut/article65930142.ece.
36 *Child Line India*, 1–4, https://childlineindia.org/a/issues/sexual-abuse (last visited February 2, 2025).
37 CERT-IN, 1, https://www.cert-in.org.in/.
38 AIR 2011 SC 3361 (India).
39 Child Abuse on Internet, Government of India, Ministry of Electronics and Information Technology 1–4 (2020), https://sansad.in/getFile/loksabhaquestions/annex/173/AS248.pdf?source=pqals.
40 Kailash Satyarthi, *Entangled in the Web: Cybercrimes against Children in India* (2023), https://satyarthi.org.in/wp-content/uploads/2023/04/Cyber-Crime-Report_F.pdf.
41 Kailash Satyarthi, *Entangled in the Web: Cybercrimes against Children in India* (2023), https://satyarthi.org.in/wp-content/uploads/2023/04/Cyber-Crime-Report_F.pdf.
42 CRL.O.P No.37 of 2024 (India).
43 Sushovan Patnaik, *Supreme Court Holds That Viewing, Storing and Possessing "Child Pornography" Is Punishable under the POCSO Act; Overturns Madras HC Decision*, Supreme Court Obs. 1–13 (2024), https://www.scobserver.in/journal/supreme-court-holds-that-viewing-storing-and-possessing-child-pornography-is-punishable-under-pocso-act-overturns-madras-hc-decision/.

PART 4

Response to Sexual Offences

13

IMPLEMENTATION OF THE VICTIM-FRIENDLY TRIAL PROCEDURES IN CASES OF SEXUAL OFFENCES AGAINST CHILDREN

Sonali Swetapadma

Introduction

The incidence of sexual violence has been closely linked to societal norms surrounding the use of violence as a tool to accomplish goals. Sexual violence is the most common form of oppression of women in patriarchal societies with strong male superiority ideologies that emphasize power, physical prowess, and masculine honour. The issue of child sexual abuse is so widespread that it may be compared to an iceberg floating in water. Explaining sexual violence against children is complicated by the multiple forms it takes and the contexts in which it occurs. The law relating to children in India has undergone a sea of change in the past few decades. The implementation of the Protection of Children against Sexual Offences Act 2012 (hereinafter, the POCSO Act) strengthens the legal provisions for the Protection of Children against sexual abuse. It ensures speedy justice by establishing special procedures for reporting and instituting Special Courts to try such cases. Apart from these, it is a gender-neutral legislation which recognizes sexual abuse against minor boys too.

Nevertheless, the issue of child sexual abuse and rights violations is widespread around the world, especially in India. In addition to being a strict criminal law, the POCSO Act was designed as a piece of legislation for social welfare that would give the child victim justice. Because of their vulnerability, victims of sexual abuse require sensitive handling by all parties involved, ensuring that their distinctive requirements are met throughout the criminal justice process. There is a relentless requirement for building a reassuring ambience in the Special Courts for child victims and guaranteeing the unfailing accessibility of support. The complexities of abuse should be taken into

DOI: 10.4324/9781003607076-18

account throughout POCSO case trials, and the child victim should feel supported while their testimony is being taken, their evidence is being carefully considered, and their privacy is maintained at all times. The otherwise falling conviction rate in cases of child sexual abuse might be significantly improved by these pro-victim laws. It is just as important to ease the suffering of victims of sexual offences as it is to try the guilty. Sensitization of the many organs involved is crucial, nevertheless, if the judicial system is to adequately punish the guilty.

In India, the National Mission for Empowerment of Women, which was founded on April 1, 2015, is an umbrella organization for the Indira Gandhi Matritva Sahayog Yojana (translates to Indira Gandhi motherhood cooperation scheme) and the One-Stop Centre Scheme, also referred to as Sakhi[1] (translates to a female friend). The Ministry of Women and Child Development (MWCD) created the centrally funded initiative. The MWCD seeks to create one-stop centres (OSCs) across the country to offer women and children all-encompassing support and break the cycle of violence, whether it takes place in a public or private environment. Irrespective of their age, class, level of education, culture, and so on, the OSCs aim to support women and children who have experienced physical, emotional, psychological, or sexual abuse. These centres have been established at every District Headquarter Hospital of the state of Odisha to accompany the victim during the process of medical examination and criminal justice administration.

Special Courts – The Idea Behind Their Establishment and Their Efficacy

A popular solution for the Indian courts when handling special categories of cases based on the nature of the offence, public interest, national security, or victim vulnerability is the creation of Special Courts or courts authorized to handle only one type of case. These courts are frequently used to expedite the resolution of cases that fall under their purview and to assist in lowering the total number of cases that are pending. Second, conventional courts do not have the facilities that some legislation, like the POCSO Act of 2012, demands.

The POCSO Act of 2012 articulates the provision for the establishment of Special Courts as delineated in Section 28 of Chapter VII of the legislation[2] for the purpose of ensuring speedy trial. The state bears the obligation to assign a Court of Sessions (courts that try criminal cases) in every district as the Special Court, following a consultation with the Chief Justice of the relevant High Court. The distinctive characteristic of Special Courts resides in the manner in which the trial processes are designed to unfold. It is imperative that the trial is carried out in a manner that is considerate of the victim, ensuring that their statement is documented either in a private setting, through audio-visual methods, or behind barriers that create a separation between the victim and the accused. Section 366 of the Bhartiya Nagarik Suraksha Sanhita (BNSS) (previously Section 327 under the Criminal Procedure Code, 1973/CrPC) enumerates the aforementioned principles and emphasizes conducting an in-camera trial, maintaining the anonymity of the victim. This approach aims to safeguard the child's identity and mitigate the risk of further trauma. It is essential to implement measures and protocols that enhance the accessibility and comfort of evidence-recording and trial processes for children.

Inadequate physical requirements for Special Court operations are mentioned in the POCSO Act. The main requirements include designating courts to serve as Special Courts, designating prosecutors as Special Public Prosecutors, and taking appropriate precautions to keep the accused and victim apart while evidence is being recorded.[3] Although the Act assigns Special Courts the duty to maintain a child-friendly environment, it does not go into detail about what that means, or what structural changes are necessary to make an environment 'child-friendly'.

Despite the fact that the terms 'set up' and 'designate' have different meanings, laws and regulations frequently use them interchangeably with 'Special Courts', according to a study conducted by the Vidhi Centre for Legal Policy on the operation of Special Courts under legislations from 1950 to 2015. Establishing a court requires building a new facility with specialized staff and new infrastructure, but designating a court meant giving judges more cases in different categories to handle on top of their regular caseload. The ambiguous and unequal establishment of Special Courts, as well as the tendency to 'designate' rather than construct new facilities, have hindered the objectives of Special Courts.

The Supreme Court mandated in 2019 that a centrally funded Specialized Court be established in every district of the country having more than 100 POCSO Act First Information Reports to try solely sexual offences against children. But over three years have gone by since the Supreme Court's decision, and many districts still do not have these courts.

Most people agree that the Special Courts have not been successful in achieving their goals, and a number of reasons could be blamed for their failure to fulfil the original intent. Since Special Courts are frequently labelled or designated rather than created or set up, they actually have concerns that are at par with, if not more significant than, those of regular courts. Judges who already have too much on their plates are given more types of cases to manage without any more help or resources. The overall case disposal rate would drop in this scenario. Furthermore, it is impossible to expect speedier case resolution without relaxing procedural constraints or simplifying Special Courts.

Results From Data Collection From Special Courts of Odisha

The Special Courts established in the state of Odisha to try instances involving child sexual abuse are functional. Sessions Courts, which are courts that try criminal matters at the district level, were designated as Special Courts under the POCSO Act of 2012, although they were not exclusive courts that could try POCSO cases only. The period of data collection lasted from 2018 to 2020. For the purpose of this research, the primary data was collected from a total of eight Special Courts from eight districts in the state of Odisha by way of face-to-face interview techniques of judges empowered to try POCSO cases. Similarly, responses were also collected from 61 Investigating Officers from those police stations across 8 police districts in Odisha, in order of the rate of incidence of crimes as denoted by the Crime in India statistics. The secondary data was collected from Crime in India statistics published by the National Crime Records Bureau and the respective Courts in the state of Odisha.

Indicators of Victim-Friendly Provisions

A popular remedy for a number of issues facing the Indian judiciary is the creation of Special Courts, which are courts with the authority to try only a particular class of cases. Because there are backlogs and delays in Indian courts, lawmakers frequently use these courts to expedite the resolution of the case types under their purview and assist in reducing the total number of cases pending. However, the rhetoric surrounding Special Courts leaves out any explanation of how they operate. The goal of establishing Special Courts is undermined by their inconsistent constitutions under various statutes. Instead of offering a solution, Special Courts frequently function similarly to ordinary courts and conceal judicial issues. The data so collected reflect the responses of the Special Court Judges on similar lines.

This section presents the descriptive results from the data collected on the basis of the following indicators of victim-friendly provisions that have been mandated by the POCSO Act:

1. Trials to be presided over by a female judge
2. Principal factors a judge takes into account when deciding a case under the POCSO Act
3. Conducting the trial in-camera to make the child victim feel comfortable
4. Number of times the child victim is called to testify
5. Manner of questioning of the Advocates
6. Presence of parents during trial
7. Allowing breaks to the child during the trial

Trials to Be Presided Over by a Female Judge

It was pertinent to note that in 75% of the cases the judges admitted the trials in POCSO Courts were not being presided over by female judges. In Odisha, there are 30 designated Additional District Judges' courts functioning as POCSO Courts (one per district). According to Section 366 of the BNSS[4] (previously Section 327 of the CRPC), in certain circumstances, a female judge must preside over the trial to the greatest extent feasible and practicable to give the victim enough opportunity to give her version of events and offer support. Nevertheless, these measures were created especially to help female victims of rape under the IPC. Given that girl child victims make up the victims in 99% of POCSO instances,[5] these regulations also apply to girls who are victims of sexual offences.

Principal Factors a Judge Takes Into Account When Deciding a Case Under the POCSO Act

The judge, under the adversarial system of criminal justice administration, is envisioned as an unbiased arbiter who determines which side the truth lies on following a confrontation between adversaries and the dialectical struggle between the prosecution and defence. On that note, it is imperative to understand what the primary consideration of a judge is while he undertakes the trial of a case under the POCSO Act (see Figure 13.1).

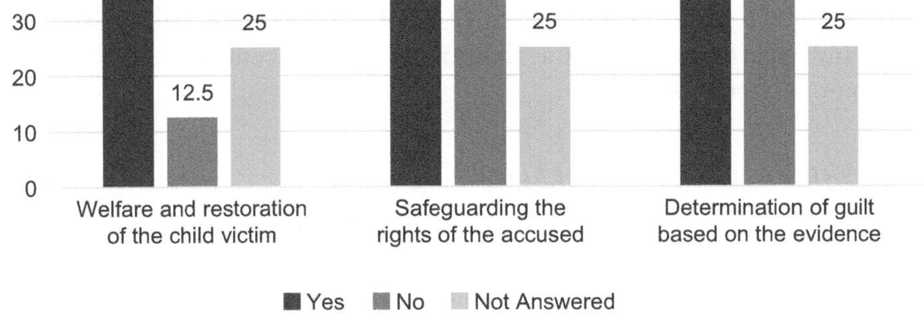

FIGURE 13.1 Principal Factors a Judge Takes into Account When Deciding a Case under the POCSO Act

The responses reflect that the primary consideration of a judge while trying a POCSO case is to restore the condition of the child and think about the child's welfare. While safeguarding the rights of the accused and determining the guilt on the basis of the evidence adduced is equally important, the matter that holds the most importance is the restoration of the child victim's condition. The Government recognizes that the impact of victimization is life-long and, for many victims, life changing. If the experience of victims in the criminal justice process is to be improved, there must be a better understanding of the impact of victimization and of the need to treat victims of crime with courtesy, compassion, dignity, and sensitivity.[6]

Speaking of a judge's responsibility under the POCSO Act, a judge of a Special Court hearing a case involving sexual offence against children is also responsible for ensuring a child-friendly environment during the trial. Section 25 of the POCSO Act[7] mandates the responsibility of the Magistrate to ensure that the child victim's statement is recorded as deposed by the child victim. According to Section 26 of the POCSO Act,[8] the judge must provide certain procedural safeguards during the trial, such as the presence of guardians when needed, the Magistrate's assistance in finding an interpreter, and, if at all feasible, the use of audio-video recording to capture the statement. Section 33[9] also restates that the Special Court must hold the trial in a way that is welcoming to child victims by allowing the victim to take breaks at regular intervals and making sure the defence attorneys do not threaten the child victim, among other things.

Conducting the Trial In-Camera to Make the Child Victim Feel Comfortable

The responses of the judges in the state of Odisha show that 75% of the sample judges emphasize conducting in-camera trials for such victims. The trials of child sexual abuse under the POCSO Act are usually held in the judge's chamber with access to limited people, thereby helping to maintain the spirit of Section 327 CrPC. Twenty-five percent of the judges interviewed did not have any experience of a trial at the time of data collection, thereby leading to a 'not answered' response.

Child Victim as a Witness in the Court

The purpose of the Witness Protection Scheme, which the Apex Court approved on December 5, 2018, was to allow a witness to testify honestly and without fear. The Supreme Court has mandated that the plan be implemented immediately in every state and become the rule of law, even though it has not yet been approved by Parliament. The goal of this approach was to adequately and appropriately protect witnesses. Helping endangered and vulnerable witnesses and fostering confidence in their capacity to testify in court are the goals of this programme. Among the facilities that attempt to better protect witnesses are in-camera trials, close physical protection, anonymized testimony, and references to witnesses in the records. Section 37 of the POCSO Act mandates in-camera trials in front of parents or any other person the child has confidence in. Where necessary, Section 38 addresses the appointment of interpreters or translators.

The Supreme Court of India in *Smruti Tukaram Badade v. State of Maharashtra & Anr.*[10] issued directions 'for the immediate establishment of at least two vulnerable witness deposition centres under every High Court's jurisdiction'. In criminal proceedings, protecting vulnerable witnesses has grown more crucial. Survivors of sexual assault, children, and others often find the trial environment upsetting. They are constantly in danger emotionally, even if not physically. Vulnerable witnesses become secondary victims as a result of the psychological stress that victims experience from other organizations or individuals after the crime has been committed, particularly when sexual abuse has occurred.

The POCSO Act's Section 26 discusses the additional steps involved in a judge's recording of the child's statement. When the child victim's statement is being recorded, the judge must make sure that the parents are present. If necessary, the interpreter must be consulted, and the statement must be recorded using audio-video wherever feasible. Additionally, Chapter VIII of the POCSO Act addresses the authority and processes of Special Courts for gathering evidence from child victims (see Table 13.1). Section 33 provides that, firstly,

> the Special Court can take cognizance of any offence under this Act without the accused being committed to it for trial (Section 33(1)). Secondly, special care must be taken by the courts to ensure that during examination of the child during cross-examination, examination-in-chief or re-examination, the questions are to be put to the child via the Court (Section 33(2)); thirdly, frequent breaks are to be allowed during trial to the child when necessary (Sec. 33(3)); fourthly, the child is not repeatedly called to the court to testify (Sec. 33(5)). And finally, aggressive questioning or character assassination of the child shall not be allowed and the court must make sure that the dignity of the child is maintained at all times during the trial (Sec. 33(6)).

The obligation on the Special Public Prosecutor and the defence counsel to communicate the questions to the child victim through the Special Court judge shows compliance of 62.5% in Odisha. Clearly, the responses show that the judges did not allow all questions submitted to them, and the advocates were also not allowed to directly question the child, bringing us to infer

TABLE 13.1 Recording of the statement of the child in the Special Court

Name of the state		*Odisha (n = 8)*	
Questions framed by the Advocates for child victim – role of the judge			
		(In figs.)	*(In %)*
Ensuring that they do not intimidate the child	Yes	5	62.5
	No	1	12.5
	Not answered	2	25
Ensuring that the questions could be understood by the child	Yes	1	12.5
	No	5	62.5
	Not answered	2	25
Allows all questions submitted to him	Yes	1	12.5
	No	5	62.5
	Not answered	2	25
The advocates directly question the child	Yes	–	–
	No	6	75
	Not answered	2	25
Steps taken to make the child victim feel comfortable during the trial	In-camera trial is mostly emphasized on	6	75
	No infrastructure available	–	–
	Not answered	2	25
Number of times the child is called to the court to testify	Once	5	62.5
	Two to three times	–	–
	As many times the Court requires	–	–
	Not answered	3	37.5
Presence of parents during trial	Mostly	5	62.5
	Sometimes	–	–
	Never	–	–
	Not answered	3	37.5
Allowing breaks for the child	Yes	4	50
	Sometimes	1	12.5
	Not answered	3	37.5

that the Special Judges stand as a protective barrier between the overzealous defence counsels and the victim to ensure that the child is not intimidated by the questioning. In certain jurisdictions where data collection was done, the Additional District Judges assigned to adjudicate POCSO cases were newly appointed. Consequently, these judges possessed limited experience in handling POCSO trials, leading to 'not answered' responses.

Like the police, the Special Courts are also obligated to create an environment that is child-friendly by allowing the parent of the child or any other person in whom the child reposes confidence to be present during the trial. Most of the judges agreed to allow breaks to the victim. In most of the cases, the victims were not repeatedly called to the court to testify.

Problems Encountered in Accomplishing the Objectives of the POCSO Act

A key feature of the POCSO Act is the establishment of the Special Courts to ensure expeditious and sensitive handling of such cases. While the intent behind these Courts is commendable, they face several challenges that hinder their effective functioning. These challenges can be identified as follows:

a. ***Ambiguity regarding the understanding of 'child friendly'***
   One of the main obstacles to the POCSO Act's successful implementation is the lack of consistency in the definition and meaning of 'child-friendly'. According to one of the judge's interviews, the POCSO Act's actual goal has not yet been accomplished as a result of this misunderstanding. Without a consistent set of guidelines, it is difficult to comprehend how to make a court child-friendly and what exactly the features of such courts are.
b. ***Inadequate infrastructure***
   Many Special Courts lack the basic facilities required for a child-friendly environment, such as separate waiting areas, video conferencing facilities, or partitions to prevent direct confrontation between the child and the accused. Overcrowding in courtrooms and a lack of designated spaces for child survivors often exacerbate their distress.
c. ***Shortage of Special Courts***
   Despite the POCSO Act mandating the establishment of Special Courts in every district, the idea of 'designating courts' instead of 'setting up' new courts adds to the existing caseload of the judges. Existing courts are often overburdened with other cases, leading to delays in the disposal of POCSO cases.
d. ***Usage of the audio-video-recorded statements of the victims***
   Section 26(4) of the POCSO Act states that, wherever possible, the statement of the child should be recorded by audio-video electronic means. The intent of the Legislature behind bringing this provision is to protect the

victim from repeated depositions in the course of criminal justice administration. The data collected from the police officers showed that a good majority of 87% of the officers agreed to be doing an audio-visual recording of the statement of the victim in the police station. On the contrary, when the Special Judges were asked if they admitted such audio-videographed statements collected by the police during trial, the results were surprising.

The fact that half of the judges stated that the police had never submitted such statements in court was unexpected. The reasons for not submitting such statements to the courts by the police could not be ascertained during the data collection. However, this implies that the trial judges are forced to call the victim to court, often more than once, as a result of the police failing to produce the recorded statement, which dilutes the objective of the POCSO Act of relieving the child witness (see Figure 13.2).

e. ***Bringing parity to the time within which the trial under POCSO is completed***

It is pertinent to mention that regarding the duration for completion of trial of sexual offence cases, the general law under Section 346 of the BNSS provides the period of two months that was introduced in the Criminal Law Amendment Act of 2018; however, the special law u/s 35 of POCSO Act remains unchanged and provides that the trial of child sexual abuse cases to be completed within one year from taking of cognizance of the offence. While the charges are framed in the POCSO Act, if the victim happens to be a girl child, then the general laws of land, that is, the Bhartiya Nyaya Sanhita (BNS), get attracted as the provision of rape is a gendered offence in India. In such situations, the procedure provided

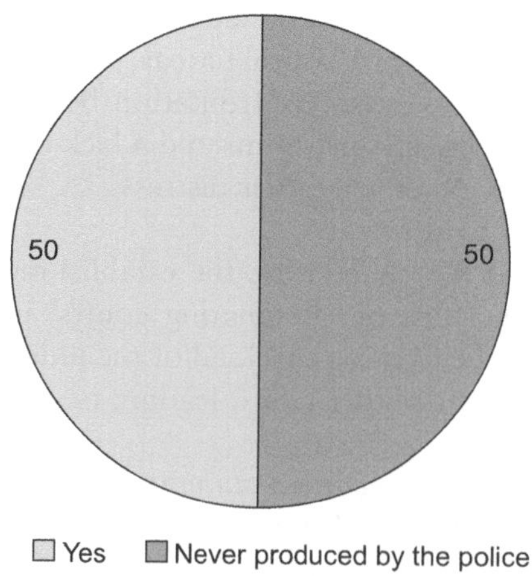

FIGURE 13.2 Admissibility of Audio-Videographed Statements in Trials

under BNSS is followed, which means that the trial of a girl child victim has to be completed within a period of two months. On the other hand, if the victim is a boy child, the BNS and BNSS do not get attracted. This means that the time period for completing the trial of a boy child is one year from the date of taking cognizance. This disparity in law is a gross injustice, which indeed is a problem in achieving the true objectives of the POCSO Act.

f. ***Lack of Victim Support Services***
The POCSO Act provides for the appointment of support persons to assist the child throughout the judicial process. In Odisha, when the data collection took place during 2019–20, the victim support services are functional as one-stop Sakhi centres across all District Headquarters Hospitals. The responses of the judges also emphasized the same finding that the OSCs should support the victims' right from their reporting of the case to the final disposal. But that does not happen in reality. In most of the situations, these centres are seen to be more functional on pen and paper than in reality.

g. ***Budgetary Constraints***
Insufficient allocation of funds for setting up Special Courts affects their ability to function effectively. Lack of resources for training, infrastructure, and victim support services further exacerbates these challenges. Since none of the Special Courts on the sample list from which the data was gathered were exclusive POCSO Courts, this challenge is consistent with the researcher's findings. The judges stated that the victim's deposition is being recorded in their rooms as well. They emphasized how crucial it is to have 'child-friendly' areas in courts to ensure that victims feel at ease throughout the criminal justice administration process and to fully accomplish the objectives of the POCSO Act. However, the same have not been put into place, citing budgetary constraints as the primary reason.

Best Practices of Support Services for Victims of Child Sexual Abuse

Child sexual abuse is a serious problem with significant legal, societal, and psychological repercussions. Strong legislative frameworks and considerate judicial procedures that put the wellbeing of the child first are necessary to ensure justice for victims. Seventy percent of the world's children live in the 40 nations that make up the index report titled 'Out of the Shadows', conducted by the Economist Intelligence Unit and World Childhood Foundation. The countries were ranked based on their legal framework to protect children, their commitment and ability to invest in appropriate responses, the environment in which child sexual violence occurs and is addressed, and the involvement of the media, civil society, and industry in the fight against the issue. With a score of 100 representing the best environment for children, the top ten countries on the index were all high-income: United Kingdom (UK) (82.7), Sweden (81.5), Canada (75.3), Australia (74.9), United States (73.7), Germany (73.1), South Korea (71.6), Italy (69.7), France (65.2), and Japan (63.8).[11] In the said index, India stands in the 15th position and was among the top-five countries in terms of protective legislation. Therefore, this segment of the research focusses on the best practices, followed by the UK, Sweden, and Canada and analyses the potential for cross-learning.

United Kingdom

To handle CSA instances, India and the UK have each created unique procedures that take into account their respective legal systems, social settings, and resource capacities. The UK's Sexual Offences Act 2003 places more emphasis on multidisciplinary cooperation and safeguarding protocols than India's POCSO Act 2012, which mandates mandatory reporting and child-friendly courtrooms. To properly address the treatment of victims under the UK's Trial Courts, this section examines the systems' advantages, disadvantages, and the potential for cross-learning. A study of the judicial systems of the UK reveals that the local Rape Crisis Centres (RCCs) have specialist workers called advocates or Independent Sexual Violence Advocates (ISVAs) who can give the reporter information and support throughout the process of criminal justice administration. Then, if the reporter wishes to proceed with the case, the ISVAs assist the reporter in registering the information with the police and, at the same time, provide support and assistance to the victims and their families.[12]

In the UK, child victims and their parents, to become accustomed to the ambience of the court, are also offered a pre-trial court visit. To provide the best evidence, the court may hold the hearings of sexual offence cases against minors in private or without the presence of the media or the general public. The right to a closed hearing is not guaranteed, though, and each case will be considered separately. After a defendant enters a guilty plea or is found guilty after a trial, the Magistrate or Judge will decide on the appropriate sentence based on predetermined standards.

Along with that, the UK has also implemented several victim-friendly trial procedures to support child sexual abuse victims during legal proceedings.[13] These measures aim to reduce trauma and facilitate effective participation in the justice system, which includes the following.

Special Measures for Vulnerable Witnesses

The Sexual Offences Act of 2003 recognizes the unique vulnerabilities of child victims, thereby making the UK courts offer 'special measures' to help them provide evidence more comfortably. These measures, as outlined by the Crown Prosecution Service (CPS), include the following:

- Screens/physical barriers: The judges ensure the presence of physical barriers in the courtroom to prevent the witness from seeing the defendant, thereby reducing intimidation.
- Live link/video conferencing: The judges also allow the witnesses to give evidence from a separate room within the court or a different location, thus minimizing courtroom stress.
- Evidence given in private: The witnesses are given an opportunity to give the evidence in private (in-camera) to create a more secure environment.
- Assistance of the interpreter: The interpreters assist the child witnesses in understanding questions and conveying their answers accurately, ensuring clarity during testimony.

These measures are designed to help child victims provide their best evidence while minimizing the emotional impact of the trial process. These measures, if examined properly, are at par with the provisions of the POCSO Act in India.

Trauma-Informed Court Practices

The CPS emphasizes the importance of understanding the impact of trauma on child victims. The prosecutors are encouraged to challenge myths and stereotypes where they actively address and dispel common misconceptions about child sexual abuse during trials. The prosecutors often resort to using expert testimonies in the courtroom to provide context on victim behaviour and the effects of trauma.

These practices aim to create a more informed and sensitive trial environment for child victims.

Multidisciplinary Support and Collaboration

The UK has a strong system in place for protecting children, which includes rules and standards from groups like the National Society for the Prevention of Cruelty to Children and the Child Exploitation and Online Protection Center. These groups are essential in spreading knowledge, offering assistance, and giving advice on matters pertaining to child protection, particularly sexual abuse. The UK employs a multidisciplinary approach to support child victims, involving collaboration between law enforcement, social services, healthcare providers, and legal professionals. This coordinated effort ensures that the child's welfare is prioritized throughout the legal process. By implementing these victim-friendly trial procedures, the UK strives to create a supportive legal environment that acknowledges the needs of child sexual abuse victims, facilitating their participation in the justice system while minimizing additional trauma.

Sweden

There is no single law pertaining to crime victims in Sweden. Rather, rights for victims of crime are dispersed throughout many laws pertaining to social justice and criminal justice. The study found that the existence of a single, comprehensive statute known as the statute of social services (Socialtjänstlagen) is one of the advantages for victims' capacity to exercise their rights when interacting with the social services.[14] Sweden has implemented several victim-friendly trial procedures to support child victims of sexual offences, aiming to minimize trauma and ensure effective participation in the justice system, wherein the best practices include the following:

Barnahus (Children's Houses)

Sweden pioneered the Barnahus model, which provides a child-friendly, multidisciplinary environment for handling cases of child abuse, including sexual offences.[15] In these centres, professionals from social services, law enforcement, healthcare, and the judiciary collaborate under one roof to:

- Conduct forensic interviews in a setting designed to be comfortable and non-intimidating for children
- Offer medical examinations and psychological support on-site
- Facilitate coordination among agencies to streamline the investigative and judicial processes, reducing the need for the child to recount their experience multiple times

This approach minimizes the child's exposure to the formal justice system and provides comprehensive support throughout the legal process.

Special Measures in Court Proceedings

To further protect child victims during trials, Swedish courts implement special measures such as:

- Screens/physical barriers: The judges ensure the presence of physical barriers in the courtroom to prevent the witness from seeing the defendant, thereby reducing intimidation.
- Live link/video conferencing: The judges also allow the witnesses to give evidence from a separate room within the court or a different location, thus minimizing courtroom stress.

- Evidence given in private: The witnesses are given an opportunity to give the evidence in private (in-camera) to create a more secure environment.

Just like the UK, Sweden also emphasizes providing a conducive environment for the child victims during the trial process.

Canada

Canada has implemented several victim-friendly trial procedures to support child victims of sexual offences, aiming to minimize trauma and facilitate effective participation in the justice system. Closed-circuit television, witness screens, a support person who might be present when the evidence is being given, and hiring an attorney to conduct cross-examination of witnesses when the accused is self-represented are examples of testimonial aids. Other parts of the Criminal Code that protect vulnerable witnesses provide the judge with the authority to bar the public from entering the courtroom, prohibit the publication of identifying information, and permit the use of videotaped evidence.[16]

The Canadian Framework for Collaborative Police Response on Sexual Violence was introduced by the Canadian Association of Chiefs of Police in December 2019 with the goal of giving Canadian police departments guidelines for victim-centred, trauma-informed, and evidence-based investigations. This framework aims to provide a coordinated, efficient, and victim-centred police response to claims of sexual violence. Facilitating the victim's interview process is a crucial component of this trauma-informed approach, as it helps them build trust with the police and remove any barriers brought on by the delicate nature of their victimization and/or past bad experiences they may have had with them. The victim's decision to cooperate and continue the investigation will be influenced by the interviewer's positive treatment.

With the exception of the availability of support personnel, a thorough analysis of best practices in the UK, Sweden, and Canada shows that the POCSO Act's requirements are essentially the same as those being followed in these nations. Despite being operational on paper, the Sakhi centres in the state of Odisha currently appear to be non-existent in practice, which prevents them from achieving the POCSO Act's genuine goals.

Role of Non-Governmental Organizations (NGOs) and the National Commission for Protection of Child Rights (NCPCR) in Providing Victim Support Services in India

Established in 2007 by the Parliament's Commissions for Protection of Child Rights (CPCR) Act, 2005, the NCPCR is a judicial authority.[17] The NCPCR, which is housed within the Central Government's MWCD, is designated by the POCSO Act as the oversight body responsible for ensuring the Act is properly implemented. Protecting, advancing, and defending children's rights nationwide is the NCPCR's primary goal. The State Commission for Protection of Child Rights' constitution is discussed in Section 17 of the CPCR. Similar to the NCPCR, the SCPCR operates at the state level. Section 44 of the POCSO Act[18] assigns the NCPCR or SCPCR, as applicable, the duty of overseeing the Act's implementation. Consequently, it is the responsibility of the NCPCR/SCPCR to guarantee that the POCSO Act is properly implemented at the federal and state levels.

On July 17, 2022, Hon. Mr. Justice Uday Umesh Lalit, the Former Chief Justice at the Supreme Court of India, introduced the POCSO tracking webpage, which has been conceptualized by the NCPCR and the National Legal Services Authority to develop the tracking portal. The need for a specialized site was recognized to fulfil its responsibility of overseeing the Act's implementation, as stated in Section 44 of the POCSO Act of 2012,[19] and to comprehend the necessity of a system that is specifically designed to facilitate services for POCSO victims. In addition to facilitating the provision of services like victim compensation and rehabilitation for their care and protection, it is intended to track child sexual abuse incidents in real time.

Section 39 of the POCSO Act 2012 outlines the crucial role of support persons in ensuring justice and support for child victims throughout legal proceedings.[20] In this light the Model Guidelines with respect to support persons under Section 39 of the POCSO Act, 2012, have been drafted by the NCPCR. These guidelines also come as a way of compliance of the order of the Hon'ble Supreme Court of India in the case titled *We the Women of India vs. Union of India & Ors*[21] and in the case titled *Bachpan Bachao Andolan*[22] *vs. Union of India*[23] where the Hon'ble Court emphasized on the importance of victim support persons and their assistance to the victims and their families throughout the justice administration process.

With a survivor-centric approach, an NGO, the Council to Secure Justice (CSJ), started its work in response to the large number of child sexual abuse cases in Delhi.[24] Over the past ten years of assisting child survivors, CSJ has created a comprehensive model of Survivor Support that provides assistance to children by attending to their two main needs – legal and psychosocial support – as they move through the criminal justice system. From reporting the offence to the police to providing need-based support referrals to the victims, CSJ assistance helps the victims to recover from the trauma of the assault, as well as becoming empowered by speaking out about their abuse without fear.

The Rape Victim's Survivor Programme by the Telengana-based NGO Prajwala[25] is particularly path breaking in this regard because it aims to provide:

- Emergency trauma care support to the minor victim and their family
- Providing safe homes for victims facing a threat perception
- Facilitating the victims for an effective prosecution and compensation

Similarly, another NGO, the HAQ: the Center for Child Rights, aspires to make a world in which social, psychological, and legal support shield children against sexual assault.[26] Their strategy, which offers survivors legal assistance, therapy, and rehabilitation, is focused on prevention, intervention, and justice. To ensure that legislation such as the POCSO Act is properly enforced, HAQ actively seeks to strengthen child protection measures through advocacy, research, and awareness campaigns. It advocates for prompt legal action to ensure victims receive justice while teaching educators, the judiciary, and law enforcement how to handle situations delicately.

Conclusion

Without a doubt, the POCSO Act has a few unique features and is rather comprehensive. The culmination of the POCSO Act in India is an outcome of putting into effect the international instruments into action. Progressive laws are only a good beginning; they are not sufficient. This is validated by the 'Out of the Shadows' report, conducted by the Economist Intelligence Unit and World Childhood Foundation, wherein the said index, India stands in the 15th position and was among the top-five countries in terms of protective legislation.

Delivering justice in cases of child sexual abuse requires not only adherence to legal mandates but also an unwavering commitment to the principles of sensitivity and child welfare. Odisha's Special Courts provide a microcosm through which the applicability of the Act's victim-friendly provisions can be assessed, reflecting both the progress achieved and the challenges that remain. Odisha's implementation of the POCSO Act demonstrates significant strides in making the judicial process more accessible and less traumatic for children.

An analysis of the functioning of the trial courts in the UK and Sweden reveals valuable insights and practices. Sweden's Barnahus model and the UK's local RCCs and ISVAs exemplify a multidisciplinary and trauma-informed approach. These centres integrate medical, psychological, and legal services in one location, minimizing the need for children to navigate multiple systems. Such models emphasize the importance of collaboration among law enforcement, social services, and mental health professionals to create a child-centred process.

In contrast, India's approach, while legally robust, often lacks the resources and systemic integration necessary for optimal implementation. Unlike the UK, Sweden, and Canada, where having specialized facilities and professionals is the norm for handling CSA victims, many Special Courts in Odisha and across India struggle with limited infrastructure, untrained personnel, and a lack of specificity of the term 'child friendly'. This has been constantly emphasized by the respondent judges, too. The response that the presence of one-stop Sakhi centres only on pen and paper is a stark eye-opener. This disparity points to a pressing need for greater investment in resources and training, as well as the development of multidisciplinary frameworks that align with India's unique socio-cultural context.

In conclusion, while the Special Courts have made commendable efforts to uphold the victim-friendly provisions of the POCSO Act, there is ample scope for improvement. Learning from international models and addressing systemic challenges within India's judicial framework can ensure that the justice delivery system truly serves the best interests of child survivors. The ultimate goal must be a system that not only delivers justice swiftly but also protects and empowers children, allowing them to heal and rebuild their lives with dignity.

Notes

1 *One Stop Centre Scheme.* n.d. "Vikaspedia." https://vikaspedia.in/social-welfare/women-and-child-development/women-development-1/one-stop-centre-scheme (Last visited June 13, 2023).
2 Section 28 POCSO Act 2012-Designation of Special Courts.
3 Section 36 of the POCSO Act-Child not to see the accused at the time of testifying.
4 Section 366 BNSS-Court to be open.
5 Crime in India statistics, National Crime Records Bureau.
6 Swetapadma, S., Subudhi, R. N., and Chattoraj, P. 2024. "Are Reporting and Investigation of Rape Cases Victim Friendly? Responses of the Police from a Cross-Sectional Study Conducted in Three States of Eastern India." *International Review of Victimology*, 30(3), 576–595. https://doi.org/10.1177/02697580231185156
7 Section 25 of the POCSO Act 2012-Recording of the statement by the Magistrate.
8 Section 26 of the POCSO Act 2012-Additional provisions regarding statement to be recorded.
9 Section 33 of the POCSO Act-Procedure and powers of the Special Court.
10 *M.A. No. 1852 of 2019 in Crl.* App. No. 1101.
11 Lu, J. 2019. "Global Child Abuse, Violence, Safety-Rankings by Country." https://undispatch.com/here-is-how-every-country-ranks-on-child-safety/ (Last visited January 28, 2025) at 17:45.
12 Reporting to the Police, Rape Crisis England and Wales. https://rapecrisis.org.uk/get-help/reporting-to-the-police/ (Last visited May 17, 2024) at 16:08.
13 Reporting to the Police, Rape Crisis England and Wales. https://rapecrisis.org.uk/get-help/reporting-to-the-police/ (Last visited May 17, 2024) at 16:08.
14 Wheldon, F. 2019. "Victims of Crime Implementation Analysis of Rights in Europe." https://victim-support.eu/wp-content/files_mf/1568031364VOCIARE_National_Report_Sweden_interactive.pdf?
15 About Barnahus. 2022. https://barnahus.eu/barnahus/about-barnahus/.
16 Northcott, M. n.d. "Facilitating Testimony for Child Victims and Witnesses." https://www.justice.gc.ca/eng/rp-pr/cj-jp/victim/rd09_2-rr09_2/p3.html? (Last visited January 29, 2025).
17 National Commission for Protection of Child Rights (NCPCR), Government of India. https://ncpcr.gov.in/pocso-act (Last visited February 4, 2015).
18 Sec. 44 of the POCSO Act – Monitoring of implementation of Act and inquiring into any matter relating to any offence under this Act.
19 Section 44 POCSO Act 2012 – Monitoring of implementation of the Act.

20 Section 39 POCSO Act 2012 – Guidelines for child to take assistance of experts, etc.
21 Writ Petition(s) (Civil) No(s) 1156/2021.
22 Translates to "save the childhood movement".
23 Writ Petition No. 427 of 2022.
24 CSJ-Council to Secure Justice. https://csjindia.org/survivor-support-program/ (Last visited February 5, 2025).
25 Prajwala. https://www.prajwalaindia.com/supportprogram (Last visited January 29, 2025) at 20:45.
26 HAQ: Centre for Child Rights. https://www.haqcrc.org (Last visited January 29, 2025) at 17:20.

14

DISSECTING THE CONUNDRUM OF MANDATORY REPORTING AND POCSO, 2012, IN THE REALM OF CHILD SEXUAL ABUSE

Anonza Priyadarshini

During the 20th century, there was a significant shift in the perception and treatment of children, formerly regarded as recipients of benevolence, children underwent a transformation in their societal standing. The United Nations Convention on the Rights of the Child (CRC), the most widely ratified human rights convention in history, marked the pinnacle of this evolution in 1989. The CRC posits the family as the fundamental societal unit, representing the natural milieu for the holistic development and well-being of all its constituents, with particular emphasis on children. Moreover, it affirms the parity of fundamental rights between children and adults, acknowledging the latter as full-fledged citizens. In essence, this international agreement underscores the significance of recognizing children not merely as recipients of care but as individuals possessing inherent rights akin to their adult counterparts.[1]

India is a signatory to the CRC and has enshrined children's rights in its Constitution. However, child sexual abuse in India is a prevalent and devastating issue, with a shocking 28.9% of children experiencing some form of sexual crime.[2] Since many cases of child sexual abuse go unreported because of fear, stigma, and misinformation, the true rate is probably much higher.[3]

Sexual abuse of children is a horrible offence that can affect victims for the rest of their lives. Emotional and bodily problems like anxiety, sadness, and post-traumatic stress disorder are the usual associated consequences. In addition, it can undermine the victims' self-worth and relationships and hinder their ability to excel in the workplace and at school. Raising awareness, teaching adults and children about their rights, and fortifying the criminal justice system to bring offenders to justice and safeguard victims are all

DOI: 10.4324/9781003607076-19

necessary components for addressing these issues, especially in India with such high prevalence.[4]

However, the following sources offer information on the subject:

Worldwide:

- World Health Organization: According to a 2022 report, one in four girls and one in ten boys under the age of 18 were believed to have experienced sexual violence.[5]
- United Nations Children's Fund (UNICEF): One in ten girls under the age of 20 (or 120 million) have had forced sexual intercourse, according to a 2017 UNICEF report.[6]
- End Child Prostitution in Asian Tourism International: ECPAT is an international network of groups aiming to end the sexual exploitation of children for commercial purposes. Over 2 million kids are allegedly victimized in the commercial sex trade annually.[7]

It is essential to remember that many incidences of sexual abuse against children go unreported, thus these data are probably underestimated. Furthermore, the COVID-19 pandemic's effect on child sexual assault is still being evaluated; however, there is evidence that the pandemic has made the situation worse.[8]

According to the latest reports in 2023, child sexual abuse continues to be a major issue in India, with a significant number of cases going unreported. Here are some updated statistics based on the search results:

- The National Crime Records Bureau (NCRB) has documented a 16.2% surge in child-related crimes in India between 2020 and 2021. Across all states and Union Territories, there were fewer than 1.5 lakh recorded cases of child-related crimes.[9]
- As to a report from 2023, it is estimated that 74% of Indian children report experiencing physical abuse, 72% report emotional abuse, and 69% report sexual assault.[10]
- 54.4% of the children who reported experiencing sexual assault – defined as penetration of the vaginal, anal, or oral sex – were boys.[11] Child Line India Foundation (a non-governmental organization (NGO)), with a 24-hour nationwide helpline for children needing care and protection, reports that only one out of ten instances of child sexual abuse are recorded, indicating that the actual number of incidents is likely to be substantially higher.[12]
- A 2018 Ministry of Women and Child Development report found that more than 53% of Indian youngsters have been sexually abused at some point.[13]

- Both boys and girls are equally impacted by the epidemic-level child sexual abuse in India. According to additional research, up to 95% of children who experience sexual abuse are victimized by someone they know.[14]

These updated statistics highlight the urgent need for continued efforts to address child sexual abuse in India, including increased awareness, prevention, and support for victims. Legal aid services and access to justice are crucial components of these efforts, as they ensure that all citizens have equal access to legal representation and protection under the law.

Decoding Child Sexual Abuse

It is indeed crucial to remember that child sexual abuse can happen in a multitude of settings, such as the home, school, and community. It can be perpetrated by anyone with authority or trust over a child, including family members, teachers, coaches, and religious leaders. Understanding the meaning of the term is essential to comprehending the size and significance of the problem. Additionally, it's critical to make sure that offenders are brought to justice and that survivors get the help and compensation they need.

The United Nations and the Standing Committee on Sexually Abused Children define child sexual abuse as a situation where a child is subjected to sexual acts or exploitation by an older child or adult, including those who hold a position of power and authority, like a parent or caretaker. The Standing Committee expands this definition to include any child under the age of consent used for sexual pleasure by a mature individual, whether the mature individual approved the act or not.[15]

A form of abuse known as child sexual abuse occurs when a juvenile or adult perpetrates sexual abuse or exploitation of a child. Depending on the source, the term "child sexual abuse" can mean several things, but typically it means:

- Sexual assault: This term broadly refers to any form of molestation, fondling, or sexual contact.
- Rape: This entails forcing a body part or object by a man into the girl child's body.
- Sexual exploitation: This includes a wide range of violations engaging a minor in prostitution or creating, owning, or disseminating child pornography.
- Grooming: This process entails gaining a child's trust and emotional support to obtain access to them for sex.[16]

Before POCSO, the IPC (now *Bharatiya Nyaya Sanhita*) was unaware of the various facets and situations that could lead to child sexual exploitation at home or in society. Any of these instances fell within Section 354 of the IPC's definition of outraging a woman's modesty or Section 377's definition of unnatural offences. The IPC concentrated on cases of girl-specific child sexual exploitation. Boys who had experienced sexual abuse were not included, and it was not gender neutral.

The POCSO, 2012, was created with consideration for international requirements included in both the Convention on the Elimination of All Forms of Discrimination Against Women and the United Nations CRC. Since the POCSO Act was passed in 2012, various sexual offences, including their forms and execution techniques, are now included to protect the child victim. The Act systematically addresses the exceedingly complicated subject of sexual harassment or assault in the criminal justice system. It acknowledges that, regardless of their sex, social status, race, or religion, children are susceptible to assault and harassment from known people and strangers.

No matter what gender a person is POCSO Act provides protections for those under the age of 18. It acknowledges that minors can be victims of any gender, and it guarantees that the law will act appropriately to hold the offender accountable. The broad provisions of the Act encompass a wide range of sexual offences, including penetrative and non-penetrative sexual assaults, sexual harassment, and child pornography.

The definition of sexual harassment under the POCSO Act has been extended beyond that of the IPC. It encompasses all sexually motivated unwanted touching of a child's body. The Act acknowledges situations in which a child becomes more exposed, or a crime of penetrative sexual abuse or even sexual assault is committed, it is classified as aggravated penetrative sexual assault[17] and aggravated sexual assault,[18] and the punishment is severe in these cases.

According to the NCRB statistics from 2018, 94.8% of rape cases involving minors were committed by someone known to the child rather than a stranger.[19] The perpetrators familiar to the child include friends, educators, caretakers, or someone who knows the child well. In 10% of cases, members of their own immediate family or relatives raped children.[20] Neighbors were the worst offenders among these acquaintances, with 3,149 cases (35.8%).[21] These statistics highlight the importance of addressing rape in India, as it affects a significant portion of the population, particularly minors. The government has been working to increase the willingness to report rapes and improve the reporting system.

Therefore, the POCSO Act, enacted in 2012, stands as a robust and all-encompassing legal framework within the Indian context, specifically addressing the grave issue of child sexual abuse and exploitation. This comprehensive legislation serves as a shield against various forms of sexual offences that children may encounter, aiming to ensure their safety, well-being, and protection.

This comprehensive statute safeguards children's interests at all stages of the judicial system by incorporating child-friendly procedures for reporting, recording evidence, conducting investigations, and accelerating the trial of offenders through specially designated Special Courts. The Law Commission of India has cautioned against lowering the age of consent under the POCSO Act, highlighting the potential negative impact on the fight against child marriage, child trafficking, and the increased risk of child sexual abuse. The Act also places a strong emphasis on the requirement that reports of child sexual abuse be made to ensure that these cases are discovered and dealt with; nevertheless, the Act also addresses the possibility of false accusations. Therefore, the POCSO Act represents a significant step forward in addressing and combating the terrible crimes of sexual exploitation and abuse of minors, providing a more comprehensive and protective legal framework for children in India.

Provisions of Mandatory Reporting and the Silence

Moving to the legal framework, the POCSO, in the children's best interest, provides for mandatory reporting of sexual offences. Mandatory reporting of child sexual abuse refers to reporting suspected incidents of child abuse to the relevant authorities by several professionals, including teachers, medical personnel, and social workers. This is to ensure that children will be shielded from continued abuse and neglect, and that responsible will be made to answer for their acts.

The POCSO Act's emphasis on mandatory reporting is a crucial step in addressing and combating the terrible crimes of sexual exploitation and abuse of minors, providing a more comprehensive and protective legal framework for children in India.[22] Anyone who is apprehended or has knowledge of crimes against children must notify the police about any of the sexual offences against children as enumerated, according to Section 19 of the Act. Failure to report may result in a penalty such as a fine, a jail sentence of up to six months, or both. It imposes a requirement on everyone who is aware of or concerned about performing such an act.

Media representatives and employees of any lodgings, hotels, clubs, clinics, studios, or picture facilities must report on the case. The police are now required to file the First Information Report in every case of child abuse. A female police officer not below the rank of sub-inspector is authorized to obtain a child's statement in any location, including the child's home or another preferred location.[23]

The legislature's primary goal in requiring mandatory reporting of sexual abuse cases is to reduce the number of children who are sexually exploited by family members, very close relatives, or other people in whom the child's family places their trust. In these situations, sexual abuse may persist over time while remaining unreported. There is also a potential fear among child victims that family members will not believe them, or even if they do, they will not take the perpetrator to task to protect the family member's reputation. Therefore, one of the strong justifications for not reporting is fear of social stigma. This fear of social stigma can be expressed in two situations: firstly, when the perpetrator is a family member, and, secondly, even when the perpetrator is an outsider and the reporting will expose such an incident in the family, tarnishing its so-called reputation in the community.[24]

Therefore, the POCSO Act recognizes that children who have been subjected to such serious abuses are not able to report their situations and require advocacy. They require an adult who can listen to them and respond appropriately because being the target of abuse is traumatic in and of itself. By requiring reporting, the clause aims to shield the child from further harm.

The Supreme Court ruled in *Shankar Kisanrao Khade v. State of Maharashtra*[25] that violations of POCSO must be notified by:

- Those in charge of schools and colleges, shelter homes, foster care, correctional facilities, hostels, detention homes, and prisons, among other items.
- Staff from the media, as well as those in charge of hotels, lodges, hospitals, clubs, galleries, and photography centers.
- Children with developmental disabilities or people needing treatment and protection are kept in facilities.
- Children's hospitals that are medical facilities that treat children, whether they are private or state hospitals. More research may be conducted on reports that are received by the NCPCR, women's groups, NGOs, SCPCR Child Welfare Committee and Child Helpline, and so on.
- In case the offender of the crime is a family member, extreme caution should be exercised, and further intervention should be done with the child's mother and perhaps other female relatives, keeping in mind that the best interests of the child are imperative.

According to Section 21 of the Act, a person may face up to six months in prison, a fine, or both if they wilfully ignore a breach of Sections 19(1) or 20 or fail to disclose a violation of Section 19(2). Anyone in charge of a company or organization who neglects to report the illegal act under Section 19(1) in regard to a subordinate under their control faces a fine and a maximum of one-year sentence in jail.

However, including a mandatory reporting clause in the Act is insufficient in some instances of child abuse where the abuser is a close relative. To supplement mandatory reporting, well-framed legal requirements, appropriate teaching practices and training, effective reporting procedures, and adequate enforcement and oversight bodies with adequate investigation techniques are required.[26] Just imposing a legal duty with punishments and punitive measures will be ineffective unless and until the process for enforcing the rule is in place. There is indeed a risk that the statute will only be uniformly enforced to prosecute offenders rather than ensuring that competent authorities also receive the report of alleged child sexual exploitation in every situation.

Only a small percentage of sexual harassment and abuse cases are reported to the authorities.[27] This is due to various factors, including police coercion, stressful and unpleasant medical exams, and threatening demands by the accused to drop the charges.[28] People believe that society, the police, and the Court will mistreat the child during the trial when their actual situation is in public.[29] Another major reason is the confusion and dilemma among the people with different responsibilities for the same offence in various special laws. The following are discussed in the sub-chapters.

Obligations of Possible Mandatory Reporters

Intermediaries and Increasing Online Child Sexual Abuse

Illicit material exchange, which includes the use of the dark web, has become quite prevalent in the digital age. As a result, combating cyber child pornography and protecting children from online sexual exploitation needs a coordinated approach and worldwide uniformity of national laws. The internet has made the world a small place where everything is at a distance. This has also led to a rise in the sharing of illegal materials and the usage of the dark web. On Facebook, there were 16.8 million images of child sexual abuse, according to the National Centre for Missing and Exploited Children. According to the most recent Internet & Mobile Association of India Digital in India study, around 71 million Indian children between the ages of 5 and 11 use family members' devices to access the internet, accounting for nearly 14% of the country's 500 million+ active internet users.[30]

However, in India, intermediaries are not responsible for any information uploaded by a third party on the website. They have been provided with a safe harbor under the Information Technology Act, 2000. In the case of *Avnish Bajaj v NCT of Delhi*,[31] the Court highlighted intermediaries could not be exposed to such liability as it would create obstacles in the e-commerce arena. Section 79 of the Information Technology Act (IT Act 2000) talks about the safe harbour given to the intermediaries.

To combat the rising rate of child cybercrime, the Central Bureau of Investigation launched the "Online Child Sexual Abuse and Exploitation Centre" in 2019. In just three months, 63 incidents of online sexual assaults were reported to the Online Child Sexual Abuse & Exploitation Centre's cyber unit, per a 2019 report.[32] Data from Child Line India (an NGO) indicates that during the lockdown in 2020, there were approximately 3 lakhs cases and 92,000 SOS calls.[33]

In the case of *Avnish Bajaj* it was decided that the spectrum of security provided to intermediaries needed to be extended, so the IT Act was amended in 2008 to provide a safe harbour mechanism under Section 79 of the IT Act, as well as to change the concept of intermediaries. In the landmark decision of *Shreya Singhal v. Union of India*,[34] the Supreme Court observed that it would be extremely challenging for intermediaries like Google, Facebook, and others to operate if they were required to handle many complaints. The burden would then fall on these intermediaries to decide which complaints are valid and which are not. To prevent such an obligation from being imposed on intermediaries, the Court ruled that only complaints specifically directed by a Court's order would be binding on them.

The Supreme Court of India issued orders to intermediaries in the case of *Kamlesh Vaswani v Union of India*,[35] requiring them to disable relevant content on websites that were running child pornography. In the case of *My Space Inc. v Super Cassettes Industries Ltd*,[36] however, the Court slightly shifted from the earlier position, and the Court described the term "actual or specific knowledge of intermediaries". The Court held that intermediaries could be held responsible when they have actual or specific knowledge of illegal materials on their website from content producers yet do not remove it after being notified. In these situations, a Court order is not needed.

The Central Government, using the powers granted to it by Sections 69A (2), 79(2)(c), and 87 of the IT Act, worked closely with the Ministries of Electronics and Information Technology and Information and Broadcasting to enact the Information Technology (Guidelines for Intermediaries and Digital Media Ethics Code) Rules of 2021. Rule 4 mandates that all intermediaries take down or limit access to content related to electronic impersonation and non-consensual sexually explicit material (such as revenge pornography) within 24 hours after being notified by users or their representatives.

However, intermediaries still do not have direct liability to remove any content in the absence of complaints or Suo moto report to the police regarding such content, even if it relates to child pornography. This contradicts the mandatory reporting of POCSO. There must be an exception in sensitive cases like child sexual abuse, where intermediaries must be strictly liable with respect to the contents uploaded by third parties. They must not be provided with any protection in case child pornography is uploaded on their website, whether they know it or not.

Doctors and Their Dilemma

While analyzing the doctors' responsibility under POCSO to mandatorily report abuse cases, we find various inconsistencies and conflicts among different provisions. After the Criminal Law Amendment 2013, under Section 357C (497 of BNS), it is now the hospital's duty, whether private or public to provide first-aids to victims of sexual offences and to inform the police immediately if the offences fall under Section 326A, 376, 376A, 376B, 376C, 376D, or 376E of the Indian Penal Code (corresponding sections 198, 63, 64, 65, 66, 67, or 68 of BNS). If this mandate is violated, the penalty can be either a fine or up to a year in jail or both. In addition, medical professionals are required by Section 19 of the POCSO Act to report any abuse that they witness or come across.

Mandatory reporting conflicts with the other laws that prevent doctors from breaching patient confidentiality and violating informed consent. Section 164A of the CrPC (Section 312 of BNSS) makes it compulsory for medical practitioners to obtain informed consent for the medico-legal examination. The idea of informed consent has been derived from the Principle of Autonomy, by which the doctor is bound to inform the patient (victim) about every aspect of injury and treatment for such injuries so that the evidence can be collected. This information helps the victim to form and give consent and is informed in nature. The information is essential to make a consent or to reject the medico-legal examination.[37]

However, this contradicts the aims and objectives of the POCSO Act, which puts a mandatory obligation to report the crime. This puts the doctor and other medical practitioners in a dilemma of whether to go by informed consent when the patient does not want the police to be informed and only consented to treatment. The main intention in clarifying the position of access to treatment is to provide adequate treatment to the victims and protect their identity.[38] Mandatory reporting is against this intention and can prevent the victim from reaching out for treatment and refuting the whole idea of providing access to healthcare.

Even the Medical Termination of Pregnancy (Amendment) Act 2021 puts doctors obligated to maintain confidentiality about abortions. The conflict between the Medical Termination of Pregnancy (Amendment) Act, 2021, which mandates confidentiality, and the POCSO Act, which requires mandatory reporting of cases involving minors, was highlighted in *State of Maharashtra vs. Dr. Maroti s/o Kashinath Pimpalkar*.[39] The Supreme Court emphasized the statutory duty to report under POCSO while recognizing the need for legislative clarity to balance this with confidentiality. Similarly, in *X vs. Principal Secretary, Health and Family Welfare Department, Govt. of NCT of Delhi*,[40] the Court expanded the scope of the MTP Act to safeguard privacy, emphasizing the need for legal alignment to protect victims' rights.

However, the POCSO Act does not differentiate between consensual sex and rape. The doctor is under a statutory obligation to report it; on the other hand, the confidentiality clause also binds him. This results in the case either being underreported or keeping the victim from opting for the treatment. Here, Article 21, under which the right to privacy has been recognized as a fundamental right in *Justice K.S. Puttaswamy vs. Union of India case is*,[41] also comes into conflict. Even if the child is unwilling to report or parents are adamant not to report, to what extent does the doctor's responsibility lie? It seems that by mandatory reporting, the legislation wants to reduce crime but fails to consider the victim's priorities.

Educational Counsellors, Schools, and Child Care Organizations and Faith

Sexual offences against children in schools are a matter of intense concern for parents and school administrators, who are subjected to intense oversight by parents, the state, law enforcement, and the community. As a result, schools must be mindful of the existing legislative system and its consequences to enforce effective policies to prevent such events from happening in the future, as well as the adequate procedures to be followed within the scope of the law in the event of such an unfortunate incident occurring in their schools.[42]

The effect on school counsellors who want to develop and preserve a mutually trusting relationship with the children is that the breach of confidentiality resulting from reporting to the police will jeopardize the child's recovery and development. This will also lead children, courageous enough to speak up in the first place, to withdraw in the future. The child's age and maturity are important factors to consider, as older teenagers may better understand the need for confidentiality breaches in certain situations and may not be as deterred from seeking help again. The challenge lies in balancing the child's need for support with the legal obligation to report.[43]

The POCSO Act of 2012 stipulates that when people commit sexual crimes in positions of control or ownership of educational facilities or positions of trust and authority over children, those persons are subject to stricter penalties than other citizens.[44] However, the students are not that open to their teachers and are hesitant to talk about the abuse. In addition, the lack of sex education among the children prevents them from reporting the abuse, as they cannot figure out what is happening to them is a violation under the law.

Global Scenario

Mandatory reporting regulations are the main mechanism for child sexual abuse by ensuring quick intervention and justice. As per these laws, individuals, especially professionals, are held responsible for the occurrence of any kind of abuse to alert authorities. In India, the POCSO Act makes it obligatory for each person who knows about the incident of abuse to report it. In cases of non-compliance, individuals may be subject to legal penalties that may lead to incarceration. Even though such an approach mirrors India's strict policy against child sexual abuse, it is still an issue to be dealt with due to difficulties in the aspect of implementation, especially in a society where caste differences, monetary disparities, and habitual prejudices prevail.[45]

Community groups that are marginalized in India frequently opt not to report crimes committed against them because they fear that the authorities might ostracize or discriminate against them. What makes it more complicated is the legal omission of a clear line of distinction between consensual and non-consensual sex involving minors.[46] The mandatory report requirement is a difficult choice for professionals like doctors and counsellors who are obliged to report but also have an ethical mandate to keep things private. This conflict makes the victims reluctant to the ones who must come forward because they fear exposure and social hostility, thus rendering the law does not achieve its aim.

On the other hand, various US courts have more discreet measures of mandatory reporting. California, for example, requires only some professionals, such as teachers and healthcare workers, to be designated as mandatory reporters. The law like Marsy's Law and also known as the Victims' Bill of Rights, on the one hand, lays emphasis on the privacy and rights of the victims who report the abuse while mandating reporting.[47] The California system, by doing so, understands the intricacies of such cases and primarily focuses on personnel through education to ensure the victims' trauma is not intensified by reporting. This approach puts the victim in the first place and therefore motivates reporting and builds trust in not giving away the victim's well-being.[48]

Australia similarly implements state-specific mandatory reporting laws that integrate support services for victims. In states like New South Wales and Victoria, professionals are required to report suspected abuse to child protection services.[49] However, the focus extends beyond legal compliance to include robust counselling and support mechanisms. Professionals are extensively trained to handle sensitive cases, prioritizing the child's psychological recovery and well-being. Unlike India, where penalties for non-reporting are emphasized, Australia's model highlights prevention and victim support as fundamental goals.[50]

Canada's mandatory reporting laws, harmonized across provinces, adopt a balanced approach. Any individual with reasonable grounds to suspect abuse is obligated to report it to child protection services. However, Canadian laws emphasize the child's best interests and allow discretion in cases where reporting might cause further harm.[51] The Canadian framework also focuses on community engagement and public awareness, aiming to reduce stigma and encourage reporting. Clear guidelines and resources are provided to mandatory reporters, ensuring that they fulfil their obligations effectively while prioritizing the victim's welfare.[52]

Comparative analysis shows that, in India, the POCSO Act provides an absolute and universal mandate in contrast to the more flexible and victim-centric legal frameworks in countries such as United States, Australia, and Canada. The non-availability of the training for the mandatory reporters and integrated support systems in India are the main reasons for the hindrance in the application of the law. Moreover, the societal stigma and the prevailing systemic blockades single out the necessity of public awareness campaigns and cultural sensitization along the line with Canada. The Californian Marsy's Law presents the need for the protection of the minor, as well as the fight alongside mandatory reporting and the concern for private information. This is the path that India may choose to follow.

India, through the POCSO Act, shows its dedication to eliminating child sexual abuse. Nonetheless, the setbacks in its effective practicality indicate the necessity for reconsideration. By absorbing other countries' experiences, India could renovate its structure by employing professional training measures, combining victim assistance services, and improving the general perception of the issue. The achievement of the goal through compulsory reporting and consideration of ethical standards and children's welfare will bring a perfect balance. Consequently, the methodology that recognizes the children's best interest is the primary archetype of lawful mandatory reporting.

Conclusion and Recommendations

It is undisputed that mandatory reporting is an effective response to cases of child sexual abuse because it puts an obligation on the family, community and the government to ensure that reporting is completed.[53] According to a study, people are more willing to report abuse when strong evidential marks of abuse are visible and severe enough to warrant sanctions. Mandatory reporting, on the other hand, covers all forms of abuse in India without making any distinctions in degree, scope, or even relationship between the victim and the complainant.[54]

In the case of *Gaurav Jain v Union of India*,[55] the Supreme Court stated that the government and non-governmental organizations must take the appropriate steps to protect children who have been sexually abused so that they can live a life of dignity. However, no government organization could alone treat the case sensitively and preserve and protect the privacy of both the child and the individual who reported the case to prevent future abuse and ultimately ensure justice.

Most cases are not reported for many reasons, to protect the child from the additional trauma that can be caused due to the investigation, to protect the honour of the family and maybe to protect the abuser when he is a close family member. The lack of awareness regarding the act and normalization (at times acceptance) of abuse against children stems from fear of social stigma. Underreporting of child sexual abuse in India can be attributed to several interconnected factors, such as caste discrimination, economic disadvantage, lack of awareness, and institutional failures. Victims from marginalized caste groups often fear social stigma and discrimination, leading them to hesitate in reporting abuse, believing their cases will not be taken seriously. Children from economically disadvantaged backgrounds may lack the resources or support systems to seek help, further silencing their voices. Additionally, many families in rural or undereducated areas are unaware of the legal processes or may not even recognize signs of abuse. Further, the image of the police and the legal system is one of the complications, insensitivity and troubles that might deter people.

The primary reason for the underreporting by individuals could be inadequate punishment. The punishment of six months is not adequate for the heinous crime. The idea is that since the POCSO Act has already acknowledged that the severity of the punishment for penetrative and aggravated penetrative sexual assault varies depending on the relationship between the child and the abuser, however, the same cannot be said for the requirements pertaining to mandatory reporting. The provision is ineffective in cases where the abuser is someone inside the family. It is because family members do not report to prevent their family from breaking apart. Putting the same liability on strangers and family members will not serve the purpose. The responsibility of care for the parents can never be the same as the responsibility of care for the neighbors. There is a need to put some strict liabilities on the people closely related to the child so that they cannot hide their child's suffering under the honor of the family.[56]

If we go by the strict interpretation of Section 21 of the POCSO Act, it means that there is no discretion on the part of the prospective reporters (doctors, teachers, reporters, etc.). NCPCR recommended that the reporting should be optional and not mandatory;[57] along with this, the Standing Committee on the POCSO Act in 2011, while indicating the counter-productivity of this obligation, said that there must be a limitation to a particular professional dealing directly with the children and not mandatory for everyone.[58] The duty and responsibility must be based on the degree of care, protection and relationship with the child.

Once the child presents the issue to them, even professionals like doctors, teachers, nurses, and counsellors do not know how to handle it. These professionals' lack of training exposes the shortcomings of the system. Schools are more concerned with protecting their own reputation than they are with reporting abuse in most cases. By placing the onus of accountability on the child's parents, they escape responsibility. There are significant flaws in the existing education system's compliance with legislative requirements, and therefore the mandatory reporting framework fails. Most people who work with children are required by law to disclose alleged child abuse and neglect and those who do not comply face civil and criminal penalties.[59]

Since intermediaries have the power to stop child sexual abuse online, it is important to acknowledge their role in the process. When it comes to child pornography, intermediaries should be held strictly liable and expected to fulfil two roles. Firstly, it must be their duty not to let any third party post any materials related to child sexual abuse on their websites and, secondly, to inform the police about the postings by such person immediately under the POCSO Act, 2012. This will ensure that any individual from the internet access no child pornography.

The provision itself needs to be changed, and the primary focus ought to be placed on the requirement for professionals to disclose abuse and report it to the police rather than making it equally applicable to everyone, as this could result in harassment by the public, as the mandated reporting provision can be based on mere apprehension. There must be more stringent punishment for the known people around the child experiencing harassment. The reporting of real instances is impacted by an increase in false cases because it becomes impossible to locate the evidence in cases when reporting is delayed. False reporting or reporting based only on suspicion by all parties will make things more complicated. As there is a fine line between apprehension and false reporting, clear goals must be set to protect the reporter when cases are reported while under arrest. In these situations, it becomes challenging to demonstrate the reporter's motive. The POCSO Act, 2012, must have precedence over all other laws in situations where reporting is required of professionals, and the government must create specific rules to classify those situations.[60]

The prevailing conservative stance in Indian society not only hampers but also actively obstructs discussions around sexual abuse. This reluctance not only empowers abusers but fosters an environment where they can operate with impunity. The pervasive silence, fueled by parental apprehension and institutional indifference, serves as an inadvertent endorsement of abuse.

Safeguarding children from violence and abuse demands a resolute and comprehensive strategy. Immediate intervention is imperative when child sexual abuse occurs. In cases where the perpetrator is a parent or guardian, the current lack of a system to monitor the well-being of victims during legal proceedings is a glaring gap. The urgency lies in empowering children with knowledge about their rights. Special standardized protocols for police, NGOs, counsellors, and so on as first responders must be devised to respond to cases of child sexual abuse. This will foster a robust, child-friendly reporting system that ensures swift and effective action under the law. It's time to confront these issues head-on and create a society where the protection of our children is non-negotiable.

Notes

1 Katrina Dade et al., *A Comparative Analysis of the Laws and Procedures Dealing with Sexual Offences Against Children in Four Common Law Countries* (HAQ: Centre for Child Rights & Macquarie Univ., Nov. 2015), available at: https://haqcrc.org/wp-content/uploads/2016/06/comparative-analysis-of-laws-on-child-sexual-abuse-in-4-common-law-countries.pdf

2 Megha Chaturvedi, *Child Sexual Abuse in India: Alarming statistics, Lifelong Impact, How to Heal*, India Today, Aug. 4, 2023, https://www.indiatoday.in/education-today/featurephilia/story/child-sexual-abuse-in-india-alarming-statistics-lifelong-impact-how-to-heal-2416285-2023-08-04 (last visited Dec. 26, 2024).
3 Shwetha Prabhu, Savitha Prabhu & Flavia Sharlet Noronha, *Knowledge of Child Sexual Abuse and Attitudes Towards Reporting It among Teachers and Parents of Children Studying in Selected Primary Schools of Udupi Taluk, India*, 13 Egyptian Journal of Forensic Sciences (2023).
4 Arun B. Mattamana & Anchayil Anjali, *Intermediary Liability and Child Pornography: A Comparative Analysis*, 5 Journal of International Commercial Law and Technology (2010), https://www.researchgate.net/publication/40765450_Intermediary_Liability_and_Child_Pornography_A_Comparative_Analysis (last visited Dec. 27, 2024).
5 World Health Organization, *Violence against Children*, Who.int (2020), https://www.who.int/news-room/fact-sheets/detail/violence-against-children (last visited Dec. 3, 2023).
6 UNICEF, *Sexual Violence against Children*, UNICEF (2022), https://www.unicef.org/protection/sexual-violence-against-children (last visited Dec. 3, 2023).
7 Trends in Online Child Sexual Abuse Material, ECPAT (2018), https://ecpat.org/resource/trends-in-online-child-sexual-abuse-material (last visited Dec. 3, 2023).
8 Jyoti Belur & Brijesh Bahadur Singh, *Child Sexual Abuse and the Law in India: A Commentary*, 4 Crime Science (2015).
9 Taabinda Jameel, *Crimes against Children Increases by 16.2%, Child Sexual Abuse Cases Go Up*, The News Minute (2022), https://www.thenewsminute.com/news/crimes-against-children-increases-162-child-sexual-abuse-cases-go-167363 (last visited Dec. 3, 2023).
10 Gwen Fernandes, *Seen but Not Heard: Addressing the Silent Epidemic of Child Maltreatment in India | Policy Bristol | University of Bristol*, Policy Bristol (2021), https://www.bristol.ac.uk/policybristol/policy-briefings/child-maltreatment-india/ (last visited Dec. 3, 2023).
11 Aarambh India, *Alarming: Stats Reveal Widespread Sexual Abuse of Boys in India*, Youth Ki Awaaz (2017), https://www.youthkiawaaz.com/2017/11/even-boys-need-protection-from-abuse-heres-what-the-data-shows/ (last visited Dec. 3, 2023).
12 Meghna Chaturvedi, *Child Sexual Abuse in India: Alarming Statistics, Lifelong Impact, How to Heal*, India Today (2023), https://www.indiatoday.in/education-today/featurephilia/story/child-sexual-abuse-in-india-alarming-statistics-lifelong-impact-how-to-heal-2416285-2023-08-04 (last visited Oct. 7, 2023).
13 S. Tyagi & S. Karande, *Child Sexual Abuse in India: A Wake-Up Call*, 67 Journal of Postgraduate Medicine 125 (2021).
14 Christianez Ratna Kiruba, *Silent Suffering | Think Global Health*, Think Global Health (2023), https://www.thinkglobalhealth.org/article/silent-suffering (last visited Dec. 3, 2023).
15 Bruce Laflen & William R. Sturm, *Understanding and Working with Denial in Sexual Offenders*, 3 Journal of Child Sexual Abuse 19 (1995).
16 Dr Shekhar Seshadri, *CSA Is about Power and Domination*, The Asian Age (2018), https://www.asianage.com/discourse/070518/csa-is-about-power-and-domination.html (last visited Jul. 10, 2023).
17 Section 3, POCSO Act, 2012.
18 Section 6, POCSO Act, 2012.

19 Global Annual Results Report 2022 (2022), https://www.unicef.org/media/143226/file/Global%20Annual%20Results%20Report%202022%20:%20Goal%20area%203.pdf (last visited Dec. 3, 2023).
20 Global Annual Results Report 2022 (2022), https://www.unicef.org/media/143226/file/Global%20Annual%20Results%20Report%202022%20:%20Goal%20area%203.pdf (last visited Dec. 3, 2023).
21 Global Annual Results Report 2022 (2022), https://www.unicef.org/media/143226/file/Global%20Annual%20Results%20Report%202022%20:%20Goal%20area%203.pdf (last visited Dec. 3, 2023).
22 Understanding the Pocso Act: Safeguarding Children Against Sexual Offences, LinkedIn (2023), https://www.linkedin.com/pulse/understanding-pocso-act-safeguarding-children-against-sexual (last visited Dec. 3, 2023).
23 Section 24 of POCSO Act, 2012.
24 Lisa Aronson Fontes & Carol Plummer, *Cultural Issues in Disclosures of Child Sexual Abuse*, 19 Journal of Child Sexual Abuse 491 (2010).
25 2013 CriLJ 2595.
26 Ben Mathews & Delphine Collin-Vézina, *Child Sexual Abuse: Toward a Conceptual Model and Definition*, 20 Trauma, Violence, & Abuse 131 (2017), https://journals.sagepub.com/doi/pdf/10.1177/1524838017738726 (last visited Dec. 3, 2023).
27 Arman Chacko et al., *A Study on Child Sexual Abuse Reported by Urban Indian College Students*, 11 Journal of Family Medicine & Primary Care 5072 (2022), https://web.p.ebscohost.com/ehost/pdfviewer/pdfviewer?vid=4&sid=fef92b50–039f-472a-a703-debd6328672e%40redis (last visited Dec. 26, 2024).
28 Chloe Haderlie, *Sexual Assault against Women in India*, Ballard Brief (2017), https://ballardbrief.byu.edu/issue-briefs/sexual-assault-against-women-in-india (last visited Dec. 26, 2024).
29 Chloe Haderlie, *Sexual Assault against Women in India*, Ballard Brief (2017), https://ballardbrief.byu.edu/issue-briefs/sexual-assault-against-women-in-india (last visited Dec. 26, 2024).
30 India: Internet Subscribers by Region 2022, Statista (2022), https://www.statista.com/statistics/638548/internet-subscribers-by-region-india/ (last visited Dec. 3, 2023).
31 (2005) 116 DLT 427: (2005) 79 DRJ 576.
32 B. Chauhan, *CID Gets 63 Cases of Online Child Sex Abuse in 3 Months*, The New Indian Express (2020), https://www.newindianexpress.com/states/karnataka/2020/jan/03/cid-gets-63-cases-of-online-child-sex-abuse-in-3-months–2084352.html (last visited Dec. 3, 2023).
33 Shreya Pothula, *This Delhi-Based NGO Aims to Prevent Child Sexual Abuse in India with the Rakshin Project*, Youth Story (2020), https://yourstory.com/socialstory/2020/05/sakshi-ngo-child-sexual-abuse-awareness-campaign (last visited Dec. 3, 2023).
34 (2013) 12 SCC 73.
35 (2014) 6 SCC 705.
36 C.M. APPL.20174/2011
37 Shobhit Jain & Harjeet Jain, *Mandatory Reporting of Sexual Offences in Indian Legislation: An Ethical Dilemma for Medical Professionals*, 31 The National Medical Journal of India 125 (2018), https://doi.org/10.4103/0970-258x.253159 (last visited Dec. 27, 2024). Jairo Werner & Maria Cristina Milanez Werner, *Child Sexual Abuse in Clinical and Forensic Psychiatry: A Review of Recent Literature*, 21 Current Opinion in Psychiatry 499 (2008), https://doi.org/10.1097/yco.0b013e328305e4b0 (last visited Dec. 27, 2024).

38 State of Karnataka v Manjana Appeal (crl.) 1911 of 1996.
39 Crl. Appeal No. 1874 of 2022.
40 *C.A. 5802 of 2022.*
41 AIR 2017 SC 4161.
42 Sibnath Deb & Kerryann Walsh, *Impact of Physical, Psychological, and Sexual Violence on Social Adjustment of School Children in India*, 33 School Psychology International 391 (2012).
43 B. Venkatesulu & M. Abdul Khalid, *Study of Cases Booked under POCSO (Protection of Children from Sexual Offences) Act in Chittoor*, 13 Indian Journal of Forensic Medicine & Toxicology 91 (2019).
44 Sections 4 and 6 of POCSO Act, 2012.
45 Panchami Manjunatha, *Mandatory Reporting of Child Sexual Abuse offences: Call for Reform in the POCSO Act*, The Leaflet (2023), https://theleaflet.in/criminal-justice/mandatory-reporting-of-child-sexual-abuse-offences-call-for-reform-in-the-pocso-act (last visited Dec. 27, 2024).
46 Sheila Ramaswamy et al., *Balancing the Law with Children's Rights to Participation and Decision-Making: Practice Guidelines for Mandatory Reporting Processes in Child Sexual Abuse*, 81 Asian Journal of Psychiatry 103464 (2023).
47 Marsy's Law, Office of Victim and Survivor Rights and Services (OVSRS) (2008), https://www.cdcr.ca.gov/victim-services/marsys-law/ (last visited Dec. 27, 2024).
48 Rob Bonta, *Victims' Bill of Rights*, State of California – Department of Justice – Office of the Attorney General (2019), https://oag.ca.gov/victim-services/content/bill_of_rights (last visited Dec. 27, 2024).
49 Australian Institute of Family Studies, *Mandatory Reporting of Child Abuse and Neglect*, Mandatory Reporting of Child Abuse and Neglect (2023), https://aifs.gov.au/resources/resource-sheets/mandatory-reporting-child-abuse-and-neglect (last visited Dec. 27, 2024).
50 Ben Mathews, Mandatory Reporting Laws for Child Sexual Abuse in Australia: a Legislative History – Report for the Royal Commission into Institutional Responses to Child Sexual Abuse (2014), https://eprints.qut.edu.au/82522/ (last visited Dec. 27, 2024).
51 Lea Tufford & Barbara Lee, *Decision-Making Factors in the Mandatory Reporting of Child Maltreatment*, 12 Journal of Child & Adolescent Trauma 233 (2018).
52 Public Health Agency of Canada, *A Pathfinding Country – Canada's Road Map to End Violence against Children*, Government of Canada (2019), https://www.canada.ca/en/public-health/services/publications/healthy-living/road-map-end-violence-against-children.html (last visited Dec. 27, 2024).
53 Ben Mathews, *Mandatory Reporting Laws and Identification of Child Abuse and Neglect: Consideration of Differential Maltreatment Types, and a Cross-Jurisdictional Analysis of Child Sexual Abuse Reports*, 3 Social Sciences 460 (2014), https://eprints.qut.edu.au/75835/ (last visited Dec. 3, 2023).
54 Jill Bryant & Amy Milsom, *Child Abuse Reporting by School Counselors*, 9 Professional School Counseling 63 (2005), https://www.jstor.org/stable/42732645.
55 AIR 1997 SC 3021.
56 Rajeev Seth & R. N. Srivastava, *Child Sexual Abuse: Management and Prevention, and Protection of Children from Sexual Offences (POCSO) Act*, 54 Indian Pediatrics 949 (2017), https://doi.org/10.1007/s13312-017-1189-9 (last visited Dec. 27, 2024).
57 An Analysis of Mandatory Reporting under the POCSO Act and its Implications on the Rights of Children, Centre for Child and the Law, National Law School of India University, Bangalore, 2018.

58 National Informatics Centre, *Digital Sansad*, Digital Sansad (2011), https://rajyasabha.nic.in/rsnew/Committee_site/Committee_File/ReportFile/16/16/240_2016_6_16.pdf (last visited Dec 3, 2023).
59 Douglas J. Besharov, *Child Abuse Realities: Over-Reporting and Poverty*, 8 VIRGINIA JOURNAL OF SOCIAL POLICY & THE LAW 165 (2000).
60 Jill E. Korbin, *Child Sexual Abuse: Implications from the Cross-Cultural Record*, 11 CHILD SURVIVAL 247 (1987).

15

THE MODEL FOR JUVENILE SEXUAL OFFENDERS IN INDIA

A Need for a Relook?

Saumya Tripathi

Introduction

Children in conflict with the law (hereinafter referred to as 'CCL') represent one of the most significant challenges to both the child care and protection systems and the legal system in India, like in many parts of the world. On the one hand, their behaviours may be seen as part of the norm during adolescence, but, on the other hand, there is an apprehension about whether these children will persist in their deviant behaviour into adulthood, yet many of them may eventually cease to show such behaviours. Consequently, numerous mental health professionals and legal authorities recognize the importance of tackling the issue of identifying which CCLs can have their deviant behaviours treated and managed through rehabilitation programmes, and which of these may be less responsive to such treatments. Such considerations become even more sensitive when the child is accused of committing a sexual offence that attracts the wrath of the community as we saw in case of the juvenile involved in the Delhi gang rape case of 2012 (commonly known as the 'Nirbhaya Case'), but at the same time paying attention to the overarching principle of liberal and reformative treatment of such a child. This insight plays a vital role in deciding whether a child exhibiting antisocial behaviour should be handled under the juvenile justice framework or be moved to the 'adult criminal justice system' (CJS) – a shift introduced in India through the enactment of the Juvenile Justice Act of 2015 (hereinafter referred to as the 'JJ Act') as an aftermath to the public outrage on account of the liberal treatment of the juvenile offender in the Nirbhaya case (discussed elaborately in the subsequent section).

DOI: 10.4324/9781003607076-20

In this backdrop, the present chapter intends to look at the model, both legal and institutional, as it currently exists for the juvenile sexual offenders. The scope of this chapter covers the intersectionality aspect of the JJ Act and the POCSO Act 2012 (hereinafter referred to as 'POCSO Act'). The cases involving adolescents aged between 16 and 18 years who engage in a consensual sexual act, thereby attracting the JJ Act and the stringent provisions of the POCSO Act, have been specially focused on in this chapter. Though such acts are non-exploitative and consensual in nature, the application of Section 15[1] and Section 18[2] of the JJ Act and Section 4[3] and Section 6[4] of the POCSO Act comes into play in such instances. Under Section 15 read with Section 18 of the JJ Act, the accused juvenile stands the risk of trial as an adult, whereas Sections 4 and 6 of the POCSO Act, which fall under the category of 'heinous' offence, provide a minimum mandatory sentence of up to 10/20 years (depending on the age of the victim). Data show that 89.2% of those accused in 'romantic' cases are charged under Section 4 or 6 of the POCSO Act or Section 376 of the Indian Penal Code (IPC) (provision providing punishment for rape).[5]

Another grey area exists in the law. Unlike the IPC that only punishes sexual offence by a male perpetrator on a female victim, though POCSO Act is a gender-neutral legislation where both the girl and the boy, by law, can be the aggressor and the victim in adolescent sexual relationship cases, it has been observed that, in most cases, the boy is identified as the offender, while the girl, a victim.[6] The author would also highlight certain key judgements towards the end of this chapter to observe the response of the courts toward such juveniles.

This chapter, therefore, aims to look at the existing framework and its response towards CCL, in particular, juvenile sexual offenders in the age bracket of 16–18 years who, on account of being in a consensual adolescent sexual relationship, become perpetrators due to the stringent POCSO legislation. The author will also examine certain specific elements of the 'preliminary assessment' outlined in Section 15 of the JJ Act, which is a step to decide whether such a juvenile should be responded to within the juvenile justice system (JJS) or be tried as an adult, to have a better understanding of the framework as it currently exists for juvenile sexual offenders.

Dissonance Between Statutory Law and Social Reality

The POCSO Bill of 2011 (hereinafter, referred to as 'the Bill'), introduced by the Ministry of Women & Child Development, acknowledged that children aged 16 to 18 could give consent. Clause 2(d) of the Bill defined a 'child' as anyone under 18 years of age, unless stated otherwise. Although the definition of a child included all individuals below 18, the Bill set the age of consent at 16, thereby recognizing the capacity of those aged 16 to 18 to consent to sexual activities.

The Bill, in its original form, when introduced in the 'Rajya Sabha'(the upper house of the Indian parliament) in 2011, in clauses 3 and 7 that dealt with the offences of penetrative sexual assault, and sexual assault had an exception clause based on consent for persons between the ages of 16 and 18.[7] However, when the Bill was referred to the Parliamentary Standing Committee, they recommended deletion of the consent-based exception clause. They observed as follows:

> *The Committee is of the view that once the age of child has been specified as 18 years, the element of consent should be treated as irrelevant upto this age. Therefore, the provisos to clauses 3 and 7 of the Bill should be deleted to protect the rights of child and for the sake of protecting children against abuse.*[8] The rationale was that repeatedly questioning a child during the trial about whether they had actually given consent could have a deeply distressing and traumatic impact on them.

During the parliamentary discussions on the introduction of the POCSO Bill, 2011, in the Rajya Sabha, some members expressed the view that consensual acts between two young individuals should not be treated as criminal, and the boy involved should not be penalized. It was further suggested that if there is an age gap of five years or more between the man and the minor girl, then only the man could be held accountable.[9]

Even subsequently post the legislation of 2012[10] came into force which defined a child as 'any person below the age of 18'[11] and the age of consent was also kept the same, repeated calls were made to lower the 'age of consent' for sexual relations to 16 years owing to the rise in adolescent consensual sexual relationship between 16 and 18 age group and their automatic criminalization under the current scheme of the POCSO Act and the Bharatiya Nyaya Sanhita (BNS) (erstwhile IPC), and furthering the same line of thought, it was also recommended by the 283rd Law Commission that the age of consent would stand as 18 years and would not be reduced to 16 as was the situation prior to the enactment of the POCSO legislation although there should be discretion on the courts to deal cases on consensual sexual interactions between adolescence with less stringency, at the sentencing.[12] This meant that the consent in adolescent sexual relationships would continue to hold no value in the eyes of the law, and such relationships would be automatically criminalized.

With this arose an anomalous situation which was blatantly ignored by the legislature. As a result of the POCSO legislation being gender-neutral, in instances of consensual sexual relationships between adolescents, both the male and the female could be an offender as well as the victim under the scheme of the POCSO Act. However, the neutrality of the legislation is not reflected in the implementation of the legislation, as the treatment and response become gendered. In most instances, the male is identified as the accused while the female is regarded as the victim.[13] Adolescent boys are discriminatorily treated as CCL and can even be tried as adults.[14] As in *Ajithkumar v state*[15] the victim was aged 17 years, and CCL was 15 years of age. The Juvenile Justice Board (JJB) convicted the CCL for the offence under Section 5, read with Section 6, for a period of 3 years. The HC of Madras ruled that the infatuation of two adolescents had been given a criminal colour, resulting in one of them facing punishment. Since the girl's age was not conclusively established and the matter appeared to involve a romantic relationship, the order of detention by the JJB was set aside. If this case is looked at from a gender-neutral lens, the victim child in this case was older than the petitioner. Ideally, a determination should have been made to come to the conclusion as to who the aggressor was.

'Heinous' POCSO Offence and Trial as an Adult

Certain legislative amendments acquired pertinence in the context of addressing juvenile sexual offenders. The 2012 Delhi gang rape incident prompted substantial deliberation on the appropriateness of prosecuting a minor as an adult. In that case, one of the accused, being a minor, was adjudicated under the then prevailing JJ (Care and Protection of Children) Act, 2000. The sentence awarded (up to three years of detention in a Special Home), in accordance with the provisions applicable to juveniles, was widely perceived as disproportionate to the gravity of the offence committed.

Consequently, Section 15 of the JJ Act, introduced in 2015, allowed for juveniles to be tried as adults in cases involving heinous crimes. Section 15 (1) read as

> In case of a heinous offence alleged to have been committed by a child, who has completed or is above the age of 16 years, the Board shall conduct a preliminary assessment with regard to his mental and physical capacity to commit such offence, ability to understand the consequences of the offence and the circumstances in which he allegedly committed the offence, and may pass an order in accordance with the provisions of sub-section (3) of section 18.

Heinous offences are defined under Section 2(33) of the JJ Act, 2015, as 'those for which the minimum punishment under the IPC or any other law for the time being in force is imprisonment for 7 years or more'. Section 4 of the POCSO Act prescribes the punishment for penetrative sexual assault, which has been enhanced[16] to a 'minimum term of ten years rigorous imprisonment, extendable to life imprisonment'. Moreover, in those instances where the victim is below the age of 16 years, the law mandates a threshold of a minimum sentence of 20 years' imprisonment, which can be extended to life.

Thus, in situations involving a romantic relationship between two children aged 16 to 18, there exists a risk that one of them could be prosecuted as an adult and face a punishment as severe as that which could have been meted out to an adult upon conviction. Juvenile in such a relationship is mostly charged under Sections 4 and 6 of the POCSO Act, and offences under these two sections are 'heinous' without any exception for consensual sexual relationship.

Additionally, the frequent application of the strict provisions of the POCSO Act against boys has raised concerns, which have been highlighted by several High Courts over time.

According to the 'Crime in India Report 2022' published by the National Crime Records Bureau (NCRB),[17] the 16- to 18-year age bracket accounts for the highest proportion of victims under the POCSO Act, and they are mostly girls.[18] And when examining juveniles apprehended under the POCSO Act, it becomes evident that most of the accused are boys,[19] highlighting a gendered trend. Furthermore, the data does not distinguish cases involving consensual romantic relationships, as all such incidents are recorded uniformly as criminal offences.[20]

Additionally, the gender-specific wording in certain sections of the POCSO Act, like Section 3, disproportionately targets male adolescents, thereby undermining the entitlement to equal treatment as ensured by Article 14 of the Constitution.[21]

TABLE 15.1 Adolescents as victims of sexual offences

	Victims under Section 4 and Section 6 of the POCSO Act or Section 4 and 6 read with Section 376 of the IPC		
	Against boys	*Against girls*	*Total*
States	407	36,696	37,103
UTs	7	1334	1341
Total	414	38,030	38,444

TABLE 15.2 Adolescents apprehended being accused of sexual offences

Crime head	*Juveniles apprehended (16 years and above and below 18 years)*		
POCSO Act	*Boys*	*Girls*	*Total*
	1878	4	1882

Juvenile Justice vis-à-vis Criminal Justice Framework for Adolescents

The phrase 'juvenile justice' originates from the Latin word 'juvenis', which means 'young', and signifies a legal system designed specifically for young individuals. Historically, the idea of juvenile justice developed from the understanding that issues involving juvenile delinquency and at-risk youth require specialized approaches and cannot be resolved through traditional criminal law processes. JJS, therefore, is concerned with administering justice to minors who have allegedly broken the law by tempering the adult CJS to accommodate the unique needs and situations of children and young people.

An adolescent who is the alleged accused, in the age group of 16–18 years, can be tried by the JJB or the Children's Court based on the preliminary assessment under Section 15[22] read with Section 18(3).[23] If the evaluation determines that the juvenile should be moved to the Children's Court for trial, they will subsequently be tried as an adult. Under the current legal framework in India, the adult CJS differs significantly from the JJS. The adult system primarily focuses on retribution, deterrence, and the incapacitation of offenders through imprisonment. In contrast, the JJS operates under the belief that adolescents and youth lack the maturity and criminal intent of adults, and, being at an impressionable age, their behaviour and personality traits can be modulated with nuanced treatment with rehabilitative interventions. Therefore, the JJ (Care and Protection of Children) Act, 2015, is fundamentally guided by the principles of reform and rehabilitation rather than punishment.[24] This distinction is explained in more detail in the following section.

Differences in the JJS and the CJS Working in India

It was highlighted in *Subramanian Swamy and Ors vs. Raju through Member Juvenile Justice*[25] (2014) that there exists a substantial difference in the functioning of the systems which exists for juveniles and the ones in place for adults. This case emerged following the infamous Nirbhaya incident, where a woman was brutally raped by five men, leading to her death. Among the accused, one was a minor and his trial was brought before the JJB. In interpreting the concerned legislation (JJ Act, 2000), the Supreme Court noted that the language of the law left no room for ambiguity, demonstrating a definite legislative intent to rehabilitate and reintegrate juveniles. The law specifically classified individuals under the age of 18 as juveniles, thereby subjecting them to a different investigative and criminal justice process than adults. Furthermore, the Constitution permits such classification, as it is based on reasonable distinctions that align with the law's objectives. Consequently, the Supreme Court affirmed the validity of treating individuals

TABLE 15.3 Comparison of criminal justice process u/CJS and JJS

Criminal justice process	*BNSS/CrPC*	*JJ Act 2015*
Investigation and Inquiry	Sections 175 [156 of Cr. P.C.] and 176 of the BNSS [157 Cr. P.C.] details the authority and process for the police to investigate cognizable offences, which are crimes where police can make arrests without a warrant. Under the applicable statutory framework, the investigating authority is vested with the power to interrogate witnesses and duly record their statements. Upon culmination of the investigative process, it becomes incumbent upon the officer-in-charge to furnish a final report of the findings before the Magistrate, in accordance with the mandate prescribed under sub-section (3) of Section 193 BNSS [Section 173(2) Cr. P.C.]	The procedure requires that the juvenile taken into custody be produced before the JJ Board with promptness, which means there is little police investigation that is possible. Prior to the first hearing, the police shall prepare a report entailing the juvenile's social background, manner of taking the child into custody, and nature of the alleged act.[26] Additionally, FIR is to be registered only when a heinous offence has been committed by a juvenile. In cases that are less serious, or when taking the child into custody is not considered to be in their best interest, the police must send the information regarding the alleged offence, along with the juvenile's social background, to the Board, and notify the parents or guardian about the date and time the child will appear before the Board for the hearing.[27]
Arrest	The arrest of accused individuals is governed by Chapter V of the BNSS [Chapter V of Cr. P. C.] Law enforcement officers have the authority to detain a person suspected of a cognizable crime if any such act was witnessed by an officer or if they have sufficient reason to believe the individual was involved in committing it. Furthermore, an arrest may be necessary to stop the individual from engaging in further criminal activity, tampering with evidence, or interfering with the investigation.[28] For non-cognizable offences, an arrest can only be made with a warrant issued by a Magistrate.[29]	Once a CCL is apprehended, the police are required to notify the designated 'Child/Juvenile Welfare Officer', the juvenile's parents or guardian, and the relevant Probation Officer (for the social background report).[30] The apprehended juvenile is then placed in an Observation home (if not released on bail) under the care of the Welfare Officer, who is responsible for presenting the juvenile before the Board within 24 hours.[31] The police are strictly prohibited from placing a juvenile in a lockup or jail under any circumstances and must promptly hand over responsibility to the Welfare Officer without delay.[32]

TABLE 15.3 (Continued)

Bail	Chapter XXXV of the BNSS [Chapter XXXIII in CrPC] addresses bail and bonds. Bail can be granted for both bailable and non-bailable offences under Sections 479 [Sec. 436 Cr. P.C.] and 482 of BNSS [Sec. 437 Cr. P.C]. However, bail in cases of non-bailable offences may be denied if there is sufficient reason to believe that the individual is involved in a crime 'punishable with death or life imprisonment', or if the person has a previous record of criminal activity.[33]	A juvenile charged with either a 'bailable' or 'non-bailable' offence must be granted bail or entrusted to the supervision of an appropriate individual or organization, with three exceptions which highlight the circumstances in which bail can be denied: (i) if releasing the juvenile would associate them with known criminals, (ii) if releasing the juvenile could subject them to 'moral, physical, or psychological harm', or (iii) if their release might interfere with the course of justice.[34] Even when the juvenile's case falls within the three exceptions and the bail is being refused, the juvenile must be housed in an 'observation home' or a designated secure facility, rather than being confined in a jail.
Trial and Adjudication	The criminal justice system follows a defined procedure for the trial of an accused, which emphasizes clarity in the charges against the individual, prosecution's duty to establish those charges using credible and lawful evidence, while the accused is presumed to be innocent. Guilt is determined based on proof beyond a reasonable doubt, and if convicted, the prescribed punishment must be imposed with minimal or no exceptions.	As per the mandate of Section 14, when an accused juvenile is brought before the Juvenile Justice Board, the Board is required to conduct an 'inquiry'. Juveniles cannot be tried along with adults.[35] The entire process should be carried out in a manner that is sensitive to the needs and rights of the child, with the juvenile being given the right to be heard.[36] The inquiry should not follow an adversarial approach, and the Board must keep this in mind when examining witnesses.[37] Rule 13(4) of the 'Model Rules, 2016' states that the Board should ensure that the juvenile feels comfortable and relaxed during questioning and while their statement is being recorded, encouraging open discussion about the offence as well as their home and social circumstances. As the primary aim of the JJ Act is that rehabilitation of the juvenile is of key importance, the Board should address not only the offence but also the social factors underlying it. Prior to assessing the juvenile's involvement, the Board is required to examine the social investigation report prepared by the Welfare Officer.[38]

under 18 separately under the JJ Act, 2000. In this light, the case provided a distinction between the adult system and the JJS.

Some other key differences between the JJ System and the CJS include:

1. The JJ Act 2015 has replaced the term 'juvenile' with 'child'. Ironically, the title of the Act retains the term 'juvenile'.
2. A CCL is not 'arrested' but rather 'apprehended'.
3. Upon apprehension, the police are required to immediately transfer the juvenile to a Welfare Officer, who is responsible for presenting the juvenile before the JJB. Consequently, the police do not keep the juvenile in custody prior to the trial.
4. At no time – whether prior to, during, or following the Board's inquiry – should CCL be detained in jail or a police lockup.
5. Granting bail to CCL is the usual practice.
6. The JJB conducts a child-friendly 'inquiry', not an adversarial trial. While both prosecution and defence present their cases, the proceedings are designed to be child-sensitive rather than adversarial.
7. In criminal trials, the focus is on determining guilt or innocence and punishing offenders if guilty. In juvenile 'inquiry', the primary goal is to establish guilt or innocence while also investigating the social or family circumstances that may have influenced the alleged offence. The purpose of juvenile sentencing is to focus on reforming and rehabilitating the child rather than just punishing them.

Understanding of Adolescence and the Effect of Rehabilitation Measures

The unpredictability of adolescent behaviours is explained by the continuing changes in the prefrontal cortex of the brain. Imperative functions such as reason are controlled by this part of the brain.[39] Ample scientific evidence shows that brain development and the child's growth continue at least till the child attains the age of 18 years.[40] Childhood and adolescence are periods of transition. In particular, the transiency in adolescent development is associated with an increased likelihood of responding appropriately to treatment services.[41]

In this period of transiency, adolescents often engage in a sexual relationship. But such cases are dealt with in equivalence to the cases of child sexual abuse under the POCSO Act. It also disregards the fact that the mostly adolescent juvenile stands the risk of trial as adults, as the POCSO offence with which the juvenile is charged in such situations is 'heinous' in nature. While there may be an acquittal later on in such cases in the interest of justice, the trauma and oppression which such a child goes through, throughout the trial process, is unparalleled.

Although teenagers today often appear to reach physical maturity earlier than their parents did and may display behaviour resembling that of adults, such outward maturity does not necessarily equate to a comprehensive understanding of the consequences and implications of their actions. While this can be argued in favour of the fact that such children deserve higher protection of law under the POCSO Act as adolescents aged 16 to 18 years are still considered children, the very same children the legislation sought to protect are being labelled as perpetrators under the Act, with the chances of being tried under the framework meant for adults.

Consensual Romantic Relationship Between Adolescents in the Age Frame of 16–18 Years

Consensual romantic relationships among adolescents are covered by the POCSO Act. When two consenting adolescents, both aged between 16 and 18, engage in such a sexual relationship, it is treated as a criminal act under the POCSO Act. In these cases, technically, both adolescents are victims as well as CCL, as the POCSO Act is a gender-neutral legislation. However, in most cases, the male is identified as the offender, while the female is regarded as the victim. Ideally, the accused juvenile should be prosecuted under the JJ Act, which provides more flexibility in terms of punishment and sentencing. However, the JJ Act also allows a child to be prosecuted as an adult for heinous offences. Since offences under Sections 3 and 7 of the POCSO Act are classified as heinous – carrying minimum sentences of 10 to 20 years – there is a possibility that a child may be tried as an adult, even when the sexual act was consensual. Hence, it is essential to amend the JJ Act to ensure that children involved in romantic relationships are responded to under the JJ Act rather than being treated as adults.[42]

In lieu of this, the 283rd Law Commission Report has also proposed adding a proviso to Section 18 of the JJ Act, 2015. It suggests that if a CCL is found to have committed a sexual offence under the POCSO Act, 2012, against a child aged 16 or older, the JJB or the Children's Court may, considering the specific facts and circumstances of the case and providing special and adequate reasons, issue an appropriate dispositional order under Section 18. This amendment would help ensure that the accused child stays under the jurisdiction of the JJS.

In the case of *State of U.P. v. Sonu Kushwaha*,[43] the Supreme Court observed that the POCSO Act lays down a strict legal regime that mandates minimum sentencing requirements, and that judicial discretion to impose a lesser sentence is not permissible once it is confirmed that an offence under the Act has been committed. Therefore, the introduction of such a proviso to Section 18 would provide some respite to male adolescents who, by law, are victims too under the POCSO Act but are in reality, are being punished as perpetrators under the same legislation which is meant to provide protection to them. This amendment would ensure that the juveniles get the advantage of being tried under the provisions of the JJ Act. It would also ensure that young adolescents do not receive mandatory minimum punishment such as those of 10/20 years as prescribed under Section 4 and Section 6 of the POCSO Act.

Additionally, in cases involving two children, age and psychological development should be the key factors in determining who is the victim and who is the CCL.[44] In situations such as love affairs, child marriage, or elopement, both children can be treated either as CCL or as victims.[45]

The 283rd Law Commission

By the Dharwad Bench of the Hon'ble High Court of Karnataka, the Law Commission[46] on November 9, 2022, received a reference, seeking a reconsideration of the legal age of consent due to the rising instances of adolescent girls, aged above 16, entering into romantic relationships, eloping, and engaging in sexual activity with boys[47] – conduct that often constitutes an offence under the provisions of the POCSO Act, 2012 and/or the IPC, 1860. A similar reference was also made by the Hon'ble Madhya Pradesh High Court (Gwalior Bench), urging the Commission to suggest amendments to the POCSO Act, enabling the Special Judge to exercise discretion in waiving the mandatory minimum sentence in cases where the girl's de facto consent is evident or if the relationship has led to marriage, with or without children.

Following a detailed review, the Commission arrived at the conclusion that changes to the POCSO Act are required to address situations where children aged 16 to 18 years may offer tacit approval, even though it does not constitute legal consent. The Commission argued that these cases should not be handled with the same level of severity as those originally intended under the POCSO Act. As a result, the Commission proposed the introduction of judicial discretion in sentencing, ensuring a fairer approach that prioritizes the child's best interests.

The Commission stated that there should not be an automatic decriminalization of sexual acts involving individuals aged 16 to 18 years, as consent is something which can be manufactured due to the vulnerable age of the victim. A more reasonable approach would be to allow limited judicial discretion during the sentencing phase. This discretion, given to the Special Court, should apply in cases where there is apparent factual consent from a child over the age of 16 for the alleged act.

There was a general consensus that the POCSO Act is being counterproductive to the very children it is meant to protect. The criminalization of sexual activities involving children in a blanket manner under the very Act (POCSO Act), which intended to safeguard them, has led to the incarceration of young boys and girls engaging in such behaviour out of sexual curiosity or the need for exploration. This creates a social cost, with negative physical and mental health impacts on children and added burdens on investigative agencies and courts. This diverts attention from genuine child sexual abuse cases that require urgent consideration. Despite the recommendation of the Law Commission to introduce limited judicial discretion at the stage of sentencing under Sections 4 and 6 of the POCSO Act in cases of consensual adolescent relationships, no such amendment has been introduced till now, and the position stands unclear for the courts as to how to go about dealing with such cases.

In addition, the recommendation to introduce a proviso under Section 18 of the JJ Act, 2015, has also not been acted upon till now. The same would mean that dispositional orders under Section 18 for juveniles accused of a heinous offence cannot be passed, and such juveniles would stand the risk of trial into the adult system, with the possibility of the imposition of mandatory minimum punishment. Though the conviction rate in cases of adolescent consensual sexual relationship till the case reaches the appellate stage is not very high, the trial courts take a harsh approach, bail is often denied, and conviction is commonplace due to the stringency of the POCSO Act. Also, the accused undergoes a substantial term of detention while the case is still ongoing.

Dilemma Faced by the Judiciary in Deciding Cases on Consensual Sexual Relationships

In the case of *Ranjit Rajbanshi v State of West Bengal*,[48] the victim girl was admittedly 16½ years old and the accused was 22 years old. The court held that, while the consent of a minor is not legally recognized and cannot be construed as valid 'consent' under the law, the term 'penetration' under the POCSO Act must be interpreted as implying a positive, unilateral act by the accused. In cases where the sexual act is evidently participatory in nature, it would be, however, inappropriate to impose criminal liability solely on the male participant, based merely on anatomical differences between genders. It was also opined that the psyche of the parties and the maturity level of the victim must also be considered in determining whether the act constituted unilateral penetration attributable solely to the accused. It was held that in light of the established history of prior consensual physical relations between the parties and the demonstrated maturity of the victim, the alleged act, even if proven, did not amount to the kind of penetration contemplated under Section 3 of the POCSO Act. Accordingly, the court emphasized that 'in adjudicating charges of penetrative sexual assault, the psyche, maturity level, and prior conduct of the victim in relation to the accused are pertinent' and must be factored into the judicial determination.

In *Vijaylakshmi v State*,[49] it was a case where the petitioner and the respondent ran away in order to get married and consummated their marriage. *The court noted that in such cases, 'when the parents or family of the victim lodge an FIR, as a result of such an FIR being registered, invariably the boy gets arrested and thereafter, his youthful life comes to an abrupt standstill'.*

The court reiterated that, given the strict stipulations of the POCSO Act, the actions of the adolescent boy would technically amount to an offence under the existing legal framework of the Act. However, it also observed that the intent of the legislature was never to criminalize adolescent boys engaged in consensual relationships with minor girls by branding them as offenders. The court expressed concern that subjecting such a boy to imprisonment would result in long-term stigma and hardship. It accordingly urged the legislature to consider the unique circumstances of adolescent relationships and to introduce appropriate amendments to the POCSO Act to address such cases with nuance and sensitivity. In view of this discussion, the criminal proceedings were quashed.

The court, in *Sabari v Inspector of Police*,[50] opined that 'in case a boy and girl below 18 years elope, only the boy is punished which is detrimental against the natural justice for the boy'. The court observed that once it is established that the girl in such a relationship is under 18 years of age, it is almost certain that the boy involved would face a sentence of at least 7 or 10 years of imprisonment, depending on the circumstances. The court also proposed that 'the definition of "Child" as given in Section 2(d) of the POCSO Act could be revised to mean 16 years instead of 18'. It is recommended that any consensual sexual acts involving individuals aged 16 and above should be addressed under more lenient provisions, which could be incorporated into the Act. This would serve to distinguish cases involving teenage relationships after 16 from those of sexual assault on children below 16. The court proposed an amendment to the POCSO Act, stating that the offender's age should generally not exceed that of the consenting girl aged 16 or above by more than approximately five years offender's age should generally not exceed that of the consenting girl aged 16 or above by more than approximately five years, to prevent exploitation of the victim's impressionable age by someone significantly older and beyond the presumed stage of youthful infatuation or innocence.

In *Probhat Purkait @ Provat v State of West Bengal*,[51] the appellant was convicted for kidnapping under Section 363 and 366 of IPC and, Section 6 of the POCSO Act. The trial court pronounced 20 years of rigorous imprisonment. The High Court of Calcutta, however, opined that it was a case of 'non-exploitative consensual relationship between two adolescents'. While recognizing that the consent of the victim is immaterial, the court recognized that the two adolescents had started a conjugal life and even a female child was born to them. The court eventually invoked its inherent authority under Section 482 of the Cr. P. C. to quash the conviction by the trial court. It was also observed that the failure to acknowledge consensual sexual activity between older adolescents has resulted in their automatic criminalization, blurring the distinction between consensual and non-consensual acts.

Again, in the case of *Shri Silvestar Khonglah v State of Meghalaya*,[52] two teenagers were involved in a romantic relationship of their own free will and unaware of the legal consequences of such a relationship. Under Section 5(1)/6 of the POCSO Act, a case was registered and the accused was in custody for about ten months. The court held that, 'considering the unique facts and circumstances – such as the relationship between a young boyfriend and girlfriend – the term 'Sexual assault' under the POCSO Act could not be applied to an act characterized by mutual love and affection'. Using its inherent powers under Section 482 of the Cr. P. C., the First Information Report was quashed by the High Court.

It was held in the case of *Ravi @Virumandi v state*,[53] that the language of consent is unknown to the POCSO Act. The Madras High Court opined that it cannot traverse beyond the statute as the victim was a child aged around 17 years. The court expressed its anticipation for a legislative amendment. In the present case, it found the appellant guilty of penetrative sexual assault, concluding that the offence falls under Section 5(l) and is liable for punishment in accordance with Section 6 of the POCSO Act.

It is expected that the legislature would address this grey area of adolescent consensual sexual relationships and courts would be considerate in dealing with such juveniles in light of the cases discussed before and also in the following judgements.

- *Ashik Ramjan Ansari v. State of Maharashtra*:[54] The conviction of a 25-year-old man under the POCSO Act was set aside by the Bombay High Court in this case. It was opined that the sexual relationship with the girl who was 17 years old was consensual.
- *Mahesh Kumar v. NCT Delhi*:[55] In its judgement, the Delhi High Court ruled that the case appeared to arise from a teenage romantic relationship, where the couple, not fully understanding the consequences of their actions, decided to run away and live together. It further noted that while the law does not recognize the consent of a minor, given the unique facts and circumstances of this case, it would be inappropriate to treat the applicant as a criminal.
- *Olius Mawiong v. State of Meghalaya*:[56] In this case, the complainant was a 17-year and 7-month-old girl who was married to the accused and they stayed together as husband and wife. When she got pregnant from her marriage, she was compelled to lodge an FIR against her wishes as the POCSO Act requires such matter to be reported to the police.

  In this case, the court opined that, notwithstanding the stringent provisions of the POCSO Act, it is imperative to consider the practical and contextual nuances of each case. The Act criminalizes 'penetrative sexual assault' and 'aggravated penetrative sexual assault', thereby mandating punishment where sexual penetration involves a minor. However, where mitigating circumstances exist – such as consensual sexual relations or marital intimacy involving minors – failing to consider these factors in their proper context may result in a mere formal application of the law, rather than the actual advancement of justice.

Summarizing the present deadlock in cases of consensual relations, the court observed in *Anoop v. State of Kerala*[57] that 'although conviction in "romantic" cases is an exception, the majority of accused individuals – both men and boys – are generally charged with serious non-bailable offences like rape and penetrative sexual assault' The court further observed that cases involving consensual adolescent relationships have become increasingly prevalent in the judicial system, with courts adopting a range of stances. Nevertheless, a discernible trend emerged with High Courts tending to grant bail in such cases, whereas trial courts, due to the severity of the offences, often deny bail despite pleas that the relationship between the victim and the accused was based on mutual consent. In relation to sentencing, the court noted that the trial courts lack discretion under the POCSO Act, as it mandates a fixed approach.[58] It was also observed that the High Court, in suitable cases, has quashed proceedings where continuing the case would ultimately harm the welfare and future of the children involved, especially if the proceedings are deemed to constitute an abuse of the judicial process.[59]

Institutional Framework for Juveniles Tried as an Adult: An Analysis of Its Robustness

Section 15 requires the JJB to conduct an inquiry in the form of a preliminary assessment to decide whether a juvenile is to be transferred into the adult system. This provision is applicable only if a heinous offence is committed by a juvenile under Section 2(33) of the JJ Act. POCSO offences, such as those punishable under Sections 4 and 6, with which adolescents in consensual relationships are charged, fall under this category.

Once the inquiry concludes and it is decided that the juvenile should be tried as an adult, the JJB is required to pass an order under Section 18(3) to transfer the trial of the case to the Children's Court. The case may be forwarded to the Children's Court only after such an order is issued. Upon receiving the case, the Children's Court must independently evaluate the necessity of conducting an adult trial, in accordance with Section 19(1) of the JJ Act.

In *Ajeet Gurjar v. State of Madhya Pradesh*,[60] it was emphasized that the steps provided under Sections 15 and 19 are compulsory. Moreover, as per Section 19(1)(ii), if the Children's Court concludes that an adult trial is not appropriate, it is permitted to assume the role of the JJB and deliver appropriate dispositional directions under Section 18.

Section 15 of the JJ Act provides for three criteria of assessment for the transfer of a juvenile into the adult system, that is, 'the physical and mental capacity to commit the offence, the ability to understand the consequences of the offence and the circumstances in which the offence was committed'. According to a report by UNICEF,[61] preliminary assessments are challenging due to the shortage of professionals/experts and the absence of reliable scientific tools to assess mental capacity. Additionally, the infrastructure for CCL is inadequate, with many districts lacking essential facilities like Observation Homes and Places of Safety. Several states are yet to officially designate such Places of Safety, and those that exist frequently operate without properly trained personnel. Additionally, the shortage of female police officers to investigate POCSO cases involving girls presents another challenge.[62] Given these issues, it would be incorrect to claim that there is a strong system in place for juveniles, who are the perpetrators in a consensual sexual relationship or are being tried as adults.

Is the Transfer System a Deterrent in Sexual Offence Prevention?

The NCRB, functioning under the Home Affairs Ministry, is responsible for collecting data on crime and recidivism. However, a significant gap exists in that it does not track juvenile recidivism, creating a barrier to appropriately address the needs of these children and thereby assess the effectiveness of the JJS.[63]

Juveniles are a highly vulnerable group that requires careful handling to prevent repeat offences, foster reform and reintegration, and challenge the outdated notion that children who commit adult crimes should face adult punishments. In this context, it is essential to highlight the shortcomings of the JJ Act 2015, which include the following:

- The Act wrongly assumes that children are capable of standing trial as adults.
- Heinous offences are defined as those carrying a minimum sentence of seven years or more, and juveniles who fall in the age group of 16 to 18 could potentially face an adult trial for 46 different offences, not just murder and rape, but also under laws like the NDPS Act.[64]
- Most offences committed by juveniles are property-related crimes, such as theft, criminal trespass, and housebreaking, with rape and murder being relatively rare.[65] However, the transfer policy was introduced in the law as a reaction to the apparently liberal treatment of the juvenile in the Nirbhaya case where he committed rape as a part of a gang.
- Under the JJ Act of 2015, following conviction after being tried as an adult, a juvenile will the same legal disqualifications as adults.[66]

Also, the crime trend does not justify the need for such exclusion, as there has been no significant rise in crimes committed by juveniles. In 2022, a total of 30,555 cases were registered against juveniles, marking a 2.0% decline compared to 31,170 cases in 2021.[67]

The 'Subramanian Swamy' ruling was against introducing an amendment in the JJ Act, 2000 which allowed for a transfer provision to the adult system. Even when it was not a hidden fact that there are stark differences between the adult and juvenile CJS, the JJ Act, 2015 was introduced which provided a special categorization for juveniles aged between 16 and 18 years who are accused of heinous offence to be transferred into the CJS.

Empirical studies have repeatedly shown the negative effect of formal justice system involvement to treat juvenile offenders. For example, research has shown that criminal justice intervention can have a negative impact, leading to an increased likelihood of serious delinquency in the future.[68] Youth who engage with the legal system often report heightened involvement in subsequent criminal behaviour because being officially labelled creates a cycle of cumulative disadvantage, which propels the juvenile to future crime and delinquency.[69] The stigma associated with any involvement in the justice system can hinder access to education, employment, housing, and other services.[70]

It is also important to note that when children who commit heinous offences are transferred to the adult system, the concern is not just the harsher punishments and stricter sentences, but adult criminal trials differ significantly from 'child-friendly' trials. Such adult trials could undermine the child's rights to be heard, be informed, and receive legal aid.[71]

Challenges for Rehabilitation

- Lack of counsellors, psychologists, probation officers, special educators, and others: A major gap exists in the availability of qualified professionals who can assess the psychological and emotional condition of CCL for the purpose of formulating care plans, particularly in district regions. Furthermore, effective counselling services are often unavailable in Special Homes and Observation Homes because of a lack of adequately trained counsellors. Furthermore, there is a lack of scientific tools for conducting psycho-social assessments of CCLs, which are essential for the process of transferring cases to the Children's Court.[72]
- Societal barriers: The social stigma associated with CCL, especially those involved in sexual offences, creates significant barriers to their reintegration into society. Biases from institutional stakeholders, community members, and even family members often hinder their progress. In some cases, children are not allowed to re-enrol in school due to the shame linked to their offences. Institutional stakeholders are hesitant to include CCLs in

training programmes, and the disclosure of a CCL's identity in certain cases further complicates their rehabilitation process.[73]

- Challenges related to preliminary assessment: There is a shortage of experts to assist the JJB in conducting the preliminary assessment. Furthermore, there is an absence of a standardized and scientifically reliable framework for psychiatric assessment of CCLs between 16 and 18 years who are involved in heinous offences.[74] There is also ambiguity regarding the procedure for such assessments when a child is apprehended after crossing the age of 18.[75]

Conclusion

The preamble to the POCSO Act underscores that the legislation is to be implemented with the paramount consideration of the child's best interests and overall well-being at all stages. However, by penalizing consensual relationships between adolescents in the same manner as cases of child sexual abuse, the Act diverges from its intended purpose, thereby subjecting to criminal liability those very individuals it was designed to protect and safeguard. The accused juvenile in a consensual sexual relationship case is bound to face prosecution due to the stringency of the POCSO legislation.

Additionally, as far as the expression of sexual autonomy is concerned, juveniles who fall in the age bracket of 16–18 years are considered not to possess adequate developmental and maturity levels so that their consent can be legally recognized. However, the same age group can become subject to trial as an adult on the basis of assessment under Section15 of the JJ Act, 2015. Such a distinct and dual standard in the treatment of a particular class of children requires attention from the legal scholars.

The risk of trial as an adult in cases of adolescent consensual sexual relationships can have a deep impact on the adolescent as a result of their engagement in the criminal justice process. The male adolescent stands at an even greater risk. The trauma and oppression in such cases can remain with them for years. Also, the trial courts do not take a lenient stand as far as such adolescents are concerned. The decisions mostly result in conviction, and bails are denied. As it has been seen that male adolescents are routinely accused in consensual relationships, appropriate mechanisms have to be adopted to determine who the aggressor is. This would buttress the gendered discrimination which male adolescents are currently facing till the time an amendment is introduced in the concerned legislation with respect to consensual sexual relationships. The psyche, maturity levels, and the previous conduct of the victim vis-à-vis the male adolescent should be appropriately looked into in this regard (*Ranjit Rajbanshi Case*).

It has been observed that to bring respite to the adolescents in general and male adolescents in particular, the expression 'penetration' under the

POCSO Act has been interpreted to mean a unilateral positive act. The courts have noted that there is no need to indict only the male when the union is participatory in nature (*Ranjit Rajbanshi Case*). The appellate courts are also exercising their inherent power to quash the conviction or FIR in such cases (*Probhat Purkait Case*). Henceforth, though it is an established and acknowledged fact that consent of a child is not legally recognized, courts are cognizant that adopting a strict approach may not serve the cause of justice in such cases. However, there still exists precariousness to an extent as to how such cases should be dealt with. In some instances, strict letters of the POCSO legislation have been abided, which does not grant much scope for exercise of discretion, in matters of trial and punishment.

Also, the trial as an adult of such juveniles is a real scenario. Henceforth, both the POCSO Act and the JJ Acts need to be amended to bring respite to the concerned section of adolescents. As adolescent consensual sexual relationships are on the rise, the sooner an intervention is done, the better the cause of child rights and procedural justice will be served.

Notes

1 Juvenile Justice (Care and Protection of Children) Act, No. 2 of 2016, § 15.
2 Juvenile Justice (Care and Protection of Children) Act, No. 2 of 2016, § 18(3).
3 Protection of Children from Sexual Offences Act, No. 32 of 2012, § 4.
4 Protection of Children from Sexual Offences Act, No. 32 of 2012, § 6.
5 Anoop v. State of Kerala, Bail Appl. No. 3273 of 2022 decided by the Kerala High Court on 08.06.2022.
6 Law Commission of India, Report No. 283, *Age of Consent under the Protection of Children from Sexual Offences Act* (2023), p. 107, https://cdnbbsr.s3waas.gov.in/s3ca0daec69b5adc880fb464895726dbdf/uploads/2023/09/2023092946619 4485.pdf (last visited Dec. 20, 2024).
7 Gitanjali Ghosh & Shishir Tiwari, Decoding the Conundrum in Indian Legal Framework Governing Age of Consent and Age of Marriage, 14 RMLNLU L.J. 198 (2022), https://papers.ssrn.com/sol3/papers.cfm?abstract_id=4461135 (last visited Apr. 29, 2025).
8 Parliament of India, 240th Report of the Parliamentary Standing Committee on Human Resource Development on the Protection of Children from Sexual Offences Bill, 2011, at 27, 31–33 (Rajya Sabha, Dec. 2011).
9 Statement of Dr. T.N. Seema, Rajya Sabha Debates, May 10, 2012, at 373, https://rsdebate.nic.in/birsrream/123456789t603084/1/ID2251005201_p361_p39129.pdf (last visited Apr. 29, 2025).
10 Protection of Children from Sexual Offences Act, No. 32 of 2012.
11 Protection of Children from Sexual Offences Act, No. 32 of 2012, § 2(d).
12 Law Commission of India, Report No. 283, *Age of Consent under the Protection of Children from Sexual Offences Act* (2023), p. 107, https://cdnbbsr.s3waas.gov.in/s3ca0daec69b5adc880fb464895726dbdf/uploads/2023/09/20230929466194485.pdf (last visited Dec. 20, 2024).
13 Law Commission of India, Report No. 283, *Age of Consent under the Protection of Children from Sexual Offences Act* (2023), https://cdnbbsr.s3waas.gov.in/s3ca0daec69b5adc880fb464895726dbdf/uploads/2023/09/20230929466194485.pdf (last visited Dec. 20, 2024).

14 UNICEF, *Implicationof the POCSO Act in India on Adolescent Sexuality: A Policy Brief*, https://www.girlsnotbrides.org/documents/1960/POSCO-Act-Policy-Brief_wUlR95W.pdf (last visited Apr. 28, 2025).
15 Ajithkumar v state, 2022 SCC OnLine Mad 1961.
16 Protection of Children from Sexual Offences (Amendment) Act, No. 22 of 2019.
17 Ministry of Home Affairs, National Crime Records Bureau, *Crime in India 2022, STATISTICS* (Vol. 1, 2022), at table 4A.2(ii), p. 327, https://www.ncrb.gov.in/uploads/nationalcrimerecordsbureau/custom/1701607577CrimeinIndia2022Book1.pdf.
18 Ministry of Home Affairs, National Crime Records Bureau, *Crime in India 2022, STATISTICS* (Vol. 1, 2022), p. 86, https://www.ncrb.gov.in/uploads/nationalcrimerecordsbureau/custom/1701607577CrimeinIndia2022Book1.pdf.
19 Ministry of Home Affairs, National Crime Records Bureau, *Crime in India 2022, STATISTICS* (Vol. 1, 2022), p. 86, https://www.ncrb.gov.in/uploads/nationalcrimerecordsbureau/custom/1701607577CrimeinIndia2022Book1.pdf.
20 Ministry of Home Affairs, National Crime Records Bureau, *Crime in India 2022, STATISTICS* (Vol. 1, 2022), p. 86, https://www.ncrb.gov.in/uploads/nationalcrimerecordsbureau/custom/1701607577CrimeinIndia2022Book1.pdf.
21 Vishal Vaibhav Singh, Adolescent Relationships and the Indian Legal Framework: Urgent Need for Reform, *Cls NLUO Blog* (Mar. 27, 2025), https://clsnluo.com/2025/03/27/adolescent-relationships-and-the-indian-legal-framework-the-urgent-need-for-reform/.
22 Juvenile Justice (Care and Protection of Children) Act, No. 2 of 2016, § 15.
23 Juvenile Justice (Care and Protection of Children) Act, No. 2 of 2016, § 18(3).
24 Ajithkumar v. State Rep. by the Inspector of Police, 2022 SCC OnLine Mad 1961.
25 Subramanian Swamy and Ors vs. Raju Thr. Member Juvenile Justice, 2014 (8) SCC 390.
26 Juvenile Justice (Care and Protection of Children) Model Rules, 2016, r. 8(1).
27 Juvenile Justice (Care and Protection of Children) Model Rules, 2016, r. 8(1) proviso.
28 Bharatiya Nagrik Suraksha Sanhita, 2023, § 34; Code of Criminal Procedure, 1973, § 41.
29 Bharatiya Nagrik Suraksha Sanhita, 2023, § 35(2); Code of Criminal Procedure, 1973, § 41(2).
30 Juvenile Justice (Care and Protection of Children) Act, No. 2 of 2016, § 13; Juvenile Justice (Care and Protection of Children) Model Rules, 2016, r. 8(2).
31 Juvenile Justice (Care and Protection of Children) Act, No. 2 of 2016, § 10; Juvenile Justice (Care and Protection of Children) Model Rules, 2016, r. 8(2).
32 Juvenile Justice (Care and Protection of Children) Act, No. 2 of 2016, § 10 proviso; Juvenile Justice (Care and Protection of Children) Model Rules, 2016, r. 8(3).
33 Bharatiya Nyaya Sanhita, No. 45 of 2023, § 327; Indian Penal Code, No. 45 of 1860, § 437(1).
34 Juvenile Justice (Care and Protection of Children) Act, No. 2 of 2016, § 12.
35 Juvenile Justice (Care and Protection of Children) Act, No. 2 of 2016, § 23.
36 Juvenile Justice (Care and Protection of Children) Act, No. 2 of 2016, § 14(5) (b) & (c).
37 Juvenile Justice (Care and Protection of Children) Model Rules, 2016, r. 10(7).
38 Juvenile Justice (Care and Protection of Children) Model Rules, 2016, r. 10(8) & 10 (9).
39 Anshul Rahul Dalmia & Stuti S. Kokkalera, Re-Examining India's Juvenile Justice Framework: A Call to Recognize a Juvenile's Mitigated Culpability and Potential for Reform, 12 J. Indian L. & Soc'y 1 (2021), https://heinonline.org/HOL/Page?handle=hein.journals/jindlas12&collection=journals&id=19&startid=&endid=40.

40 Salil Bali v. Union of India, (2013) 7 SCC 705; (2013) 3 SCC (Cri) 686 (India).
41 Salil Bali v. Union of India, (2013) 7 SCC 705; (2013) 3 SCC (Cri) 686 (India).
42 Law Commission of India, Report No. 283, *Age of Consent under the Protection of Children from Sexual Offences Act* (2023), p. 107, https://cdnbbsr.s3waas.gov.in/s3ca0daec69b5adc880fb464895726dbdf/uploads/2023/09/2023092946619448 5.pdf (last visited Dec. 20, 2024).
43 U.P. v. Sonu Kushwaha, criminal appeal No. 1633 of 2023.
44 *Ranjit Rajbanshi v State of West Bengal*, 2021 SCC OnLine Cal 2470.
45 Law Commission of India, Report No. 283, *Age of Consent under the Protection of Children from Sexual Offences Act* (2023), p. 107, https://cdnbbsr.s3waas.gov.in/s3ca0daec69b5adc880fb464895726dbdf/uploads/2023/09/20230929466194485.pdf (last visited Dec. 20, 2024).
46 Law Commission of India, Report No. 283, *Age of Consent under the Protection of Children from Sexual Offences Act* (2023), p. 107, https://cdnbbsr.s3waas.gov.in/s3ca0daec69b5adc880fb464895726dbdf/uploads/2023/09/20230929466194485.pdf (last visited Dec. 20, 2024).
47 Law Commission of India, Report No. 283, *Age of Consent under the Protection of Children from Sexual Offences Act* (2023), p. 107, https://cdnbbsr.s3waas.gov.in/s3ca0daec69b5adc880fb464895726dbdf/uploads/2023/09/20230929466194485.pdf (last visited Dec. 20, 2024).
48 *Ranjit Rajbanshi v State of West Bengal*, 2021 SCC OnLine Cal 2470.
49 *Vijaylakshmi v State*, 2021 SCC OnLine Mad 317.
50 *Sabari v Inspector of Police*, 2019 SCC OnLine Mad 18850.
51 Probhat Purkait @ Provat v State of West Bengal, (2023) 1 HCC (Cal) 626.
52 Shri Silvestar Khonglah v state of Meghalaya, 2022 SCC OnLine Megh 575.
53 Ravi @ Virumandi v. State represented by the Assistant Commissioner of Police & Anr. Madras High Court CRL.A. No. 627 of 2021 dated 18.11.2022.
54 *Ashik Ramjan Ansari v. State of Maharashtra*, 2023 Cri LJ 3633.
55 *Mahesh Kumar v NCT Delhi*, 2023 SCC OnLine Del 2634.
56 *Olius Mawiong v. State of Meghalaya*, 2022 SCC OnLine Megh 332.
57 *Anoop v. State of Kerala*, Bail Appl. No. 3273 of 2022 decided by the Kerala High Court on 08.06.2022.
58 Law Commission of India, Report No. 283, *Age of Consent under the Protection of Children from Sexual Offences Act* (2023), p. 107, https://cdnbbsr.s3waas.gov.in/s3ca0daec69b5adc880fb464895726dbdf/uploads/2023/09/20230929466194485.pdf (last visited Dec. 20, 2024).
59 *Kajendran J. v. Superintendent of Police*, H.C.P. No. 2182 of 2022 (Madras H.C. Mar. 14, 2025).
60 *Ajeet Gurjar v. State of Madhya Pradesh*, 2023 SCC OnLine SC 1255.
61 UNICEF, Effective Implementation of the Juvenile Justice (Care and Protection of Children) Act, 2015: Focus on Rehabilitation Services and Linkages with the POCSO Act, 2012, Third Round of Regional Level Round Table Consultations Report, New Delhi (August 2017), https://www.orissahighcourt.nic.in/uploads/ac/national_report/1565340016.pdf (last visited Dec. 24, 2024).
62 UNICEF, Effective Implementation of the Juvenile Justice (Care and Protection of Children) Act, 2015: Focus on Rehabilitation Services and Linkages with the POCSO Act, 2012, Third Round of Regional Level Round Table Consultations Report, New Delhi (August 2017), https://www.orissahighcourt.nic.in/uploads/ac/national_report/1565340016.pdf (last visited Dec. 24, 2024).
63 UNICEF, Effective Implementation of the Juvenile Justice (Care and Protection of Children) Act, 2015: Focus on Rehabilitation Services and Linkages with the POCSO Act, 2012, Third Round of Regional Level Round Table Consultations Report, New Delhi (August 2017), https://www.orissahighcourt.nic.in/uploads/ac/national_report/1565340016.pdf (last visited Dec. 24, 2024).

64 Atul S. Jaybhay, Critical Analysis of Juvenile Justice System in India, 2017 Bharati L.R. 103–111, http://docs.manupatra.in/newsline/articles/Upload/85D28740-6B71-4969-970D-18EDDC7E245B.pdf.
65 Atul S. Jaybhay, Critical Analysis of Juvenile Justice System in India, 2017 Bharati L.R. 103–111, http://docs.manupatra.in/newsline/articles/Upload/85D28740-6B71-4969-970D-18EDDC7E245B.pdf.
66 Juvenile Justice (Care and Protection of Children) Act, No. 2 of 2016, § 24.
67 Ministry of Home Affairs, National Crime Records Bureau, Crime in India 2022, STATISTICS (Volume 1, 2022), at 13, https://www.ncrb.gov.in/sites/default/files/CII%202022%20Volume%201.pdf.
68 Jon Gunnar Bernburg, Marvin D. Krohn & Craig J. Rivera, Official Labeling, Criminal Embeddedness, and Subsequent Delinquency: A Longitudinal Test of Labeling Theory, 43 J. Res. Crime & Delinq. 67 (2006), https://journals.sagepub.com/doi/abs/10.1177/0022427805280068 (last visited Dec. 6, 2024).
69 Eric A. Stewart, Ronald L. Simons, Rand D. Conger & Laura V. Scaramella, Beyond the Interactional Relationship between Delinquency and Parenting Practices: The Contribution of Legal Sanctions, 39 J. Res. Crime & Delinq. 36 (2002), https://doi.org/10.1177/002242780203900102.
70 Eric Rasmusen, Stigma and Self-Fulfilling Expectations of Criminality, 39 J. L. & Econ. 519 (1996), https://doi.org/10.1086/467358.
71 Arlene Manoharan & Swagata Raha, The Juvenile Justice System in India and Children Who Commit Serious Offences: Reflections on the Way Forward, in International Colloquium on Juvenile Justice: A Report 16 (HAQ: Centre for Child Rights, 2013), https://haqcrc.org/wp-content/uploads/2016/07/international-colloquium-on-juvenile-justice-a-report-16-18-march-2013-new-delhi-india.pdf.
72 UNICEF, Effective Implementation of the Juvenile Justice (Care and Protection of Children) Act, 2015: Focus on Rehabilitation Services and Linkages with the POCSO Act, 2012, Third Round of Regional Level Round Table Consultations Report, New Delhi (August 2017), https://www.orissahighcourt.nic.in/uploads/ac/national_report/1565340016.pdf (last visited Dec. 24, 2024), p. 47.
73 UNICEF, Effective Implementation of the Juvenile Justice (Care and Protection of Children) Act, 2015: Focus on Rehabilitation Services and Linkages with the POCSO Act, 2012, Third Round of Regional Level Round Table Consultations Report, New Delhi (August 2017), https://www.orissahighcourt.nic.in/uploads/ac/national_report/1565340016.pdf (last visited Dec. 24, 2024), p. 47.
74 UNICEF, Effective Implementation of the Juvenile Justice (Care and Protection of Children) Act, 2015: Focus on Rehabilitation Services and Linkages with the POCSO Act, 2012, Third Round of Regional Level Round Table Consultations Report, New Delhi (August 2017), https://www.orissahighcourt.nic.in/uploads/ac/national_report/1565340016.pdf (last visited Dec. 24, 2024), p. 47.
75 UNICEF, Effective Implementation of the Juvenile Justice (Care and Protection of Children) Act, 2015: Focus on Rehabilitation Services and Linkages with the POCSO Act, 2012, Third Round of Regional Level Round Table Consultations Report, New Delhi (August 2017), https://www.orissahighcourt.nic.in/uploads/ac/national_report/1565340016.pdf (last visited Dec. 24, 2024), p. 47.

CONCLUSION

Paromita Chattoraj

Conclusion

It has been more than three decades since India ratified the United Nations Convention on the Rights of the Child (UNCRC). By ratifying the Convention, India wanted to establish and implement laws, regulations, and policies to secure the rights of children and protect them from various forms of violence and exploitation.

There has never been a more critical time to focus on the rights of children. The resolution adopted by the UN General Assembly on 25 September 2015 titled "Transforming Our World: The 2030 Agenda for Sustainable Development" provides a plan of action with 17 Sustainable Development Goals for people, planet, and prosperity with the aim of strengthening universal peace. Also, while India celebrated 30 years of having ratified to UNCRC, it is still far from achieving its goal of ensuring the rights accorded to every child in the country. India has a host of legislations directly impacting children for providing basic rights and protection from various forms of vulnerabilities, especially, protection from violence and exploitation. Some of the legislations directly impacting the children's well-being and protection are the Juvenile Justice (Care and Protection of Children) Act, 2015; Commissions for Protection of Child Rights Act, 2005; the Rights to Education Act, 2009; Protection of Children from Sexual Offences Act, 2012; Child Labour (Prohibition and Regulation) Act, 1986; Prohibition of Child Marriage Act, 2006; and Right to Education Act, 2009, while few others indirectly affecting the lives of children are the National Food Securities Act, 2013; Mental Healthcare Act, 2017; Rights of Persons with Disabilities Act, 2016; Information Technology Act, 2000; and so on. It is, therefore, imperative to understand

DOI: 10.4324/9781003607076-21

the current concerns surrounding the different facets of child rights. It is also important to deduce evidence by analyzing the effectiveness of the laws and policies formulated for children and finding ways to address the underlying challenges that are acting as a hindrance in achieving children's welfare and well-being.

In India, the notion of juvenile Justice was introduced by the enactment of the first legislation, namely, the Apprentices Act in 1850, providing for the diversion of young vagrants and petty offenders below the age of 15 years from the criminal justice system to impart them skills to prepare them for some job or occupation. Next came the segregation of children who were accused of committing offenses from the criminal justice system with the passage of the Madras Children Act, 1920, making way for subsequent legislation to provide for the production of children before a special children's court and the use of prisons only in exceptional cases. The first central legislation for children in India, namely, the Children Act 1960, applicable only to Union Territories, set the norm of prohibiting the use of police stations and prisons for children under any circumstances. The Juvenile Justice Act, 1986, was yet another landmark that began the period of uniform law for the whole country for treating juveniles who committed any offence and also children who were neglected. With India becoming a signatory to the UNCRC in 1992, all children below the age of 18 years were brought within the purview of the Juvenile Justice Act, 2000. The gradual progression of juvenile justice in India was from the selective exclusion of children to complete coverage of all children under the age of 18 years within the umbrella of juvenile justice. The direction was toward bringing more and more children within the purview of juvenile justice, extending the scope of care, protection, and rehabilitation opportunities for children. The Juvenile Justice Act 2015, however, has taken the norms of the last century by providing for the exclusion of some children from juvenile justice to the criminal justice system (which was only for adults). It is important at this juncture to analyze, protect, preserve, and expand the spaces this legislation still provides for the protection of children in difficult circumstances.

The Children in Need of Care and Protection (CNCP) can be explained literally as denoted or within the definition of such children under Section 2(14) of the Juvenile Justice (Care and Protection of Children) Act (JJ Act) 2015, as amended in 2021. The JJ Act encompasses all types of children who are required to be dealt with under the legal processes and myriad situations. Although the JJ Act, which represents the Juvenile Justice System of India, broadly covers two separate categories of children, namely, the CNCP and the Children in Conflict with Law (CCLs), periodical analysis carried out by the National Crime Records Bureau indicates that most of the CCLs also happen to be falling in the category of CNCP as well. The types of CNCP as defined under the law may range from being those found without home, settled abode, or ostensible means of subsistence or working, begging, and living on streets; residing with someone (even parents and guardians) threatening to kill, causing or creating likelihood of injury, exploitation, abuse, or neglect; who do not have parents and none to take care or protect; and abandoned or surrendered.

In this book chapters have been brought under four broad themes. The first theme is on "Child in Need of Care and Protection and in Conflict with Law". Under this theme there are four chapters where the authors have come to some key findings that may be summarized as follows:

In the chapter entitled "Child in Need of Care and Protection – Their Rights Deserve the First Call", the author observes that the CNCP need to be prioritized by effective implementation of the JJ Act. However, it is often hindered by friction from bureaucratic red tape, resource constraints, and inadequate training of personnel. The author impresses upon innovative approaches for rehabilitation and support, focusing on the best practices from around the globe. Also, advocacy strategies play a pivotal role in enhancing awareness and implementation of laws pertaining to CNCP and engaging dialogues with stakeholders and fostering collaboration is essential to drive systemic changes and ensure the rights of CNCP are upheld. Organizations like Prayas (the author is the founder of Prayas) must evolve their role in line with emerging realities, leveraging opportunities for research, advocacy, and policy interventions. Embracing technological advancements and evolving societal norms will be key in shaping the future of juvenile justice. The author concludes with the observation that the resources available to serve millions of CNCP in India are extremely inadequate, considering their huge numbers, which are not enumerated in any form beyond the 2011 Census in India. The authors call for collective action to prioritize the rights of CNCP and cultivate a society where every child is valued, protected, and empowered.

In the next chapter, "Role of Higher Judiciary in Monitoring Juvenile Care Through Juvenile Justice Committees – An Insider's Perspective", the author who was a former judge of the Supreme Court of India and appointed as the first one-man Juvenile Justice Committee (JJC) shares firsthand experience regarding the evolution and coming into being of the JJC the challenges faced by it and how the various stakeholders were integrated toward the common goal of providing care and rehabilitation of the children. The impact of the efforts made by the JJCs in the High Courts and the Supreme Court is difficult to assess, but there has definitely been a perceptible change for the better, in terms of attitudinal changes focusing more toward children. The author concludes by observing that while a lot has otherwise been achieved through sustained efforts by JJCs and all those associated with them across the country, there is still a long way to go before we can confidently say that we have achieved the objectives of the JJ (Care and Protection of Children)

Act and allied laws including those relating to child sexual abuse, trafficking, child marriage, child labor, and so on. The author stressed the fact that the JJCs must widen their activities to include mental trauma that children suffer from, due to adverse circumstances and events, the rights of children with disabilities, meaningful education to children, and proper nutrition, which are part of the Directive Principles of State Policy mandated under the Constitution of India.

In the chapter "Comparing the Role of Child Care Institutions in Rehabilitation of Children in Conflict with Law in India With Global Best Practices", through an examination of the circumstances found in juvenile prison facilities in India and other developed countries, the author highlights the support systems and rehabilitation services open to young offenders, assessing how well they work to help them reintegrate into the community and avoid repeat offenses. The author observes that all three countries highlighted in this chapter, the US, the UK, and Germany, recognize the importance of rehabilitation, education, and protection of juvenile rights through family involvement and community-based approaches for successful reintegration. India might adopt the restorative justice approaches as in the US, which emphasize rehabilitation over punishment. Children's psychological well-being would be enhanced by improving mental health and trauma-informed care, as provided in Germany and the UK. The author concludes by observing that reintegrating young people into society would be facilitated by offering more comprehensive educational and career training and by ensuring long-term funding and improving social and legal support systems. These changes would create a more effective and therapeutic environment for the CCLs in India.

In the final chapter under this theme, "Procedural Aspects Concerning Child in Conflict with Law in the Indian Legislative Framework", the author focused on handling of CCL under the JJ Act due to the apparent gaps between the legally prescribed procedure and the practical implementation thereof. The chapter highlights the dilemmas faced by the courts in determining the juvenility to procedures for the transfer of cases in cases of children falling in the borderline age of 16–18 accused of heinous or serious offences. The author's analyses show that there are procedural deficiencies in the management of CCL, including delays in age verification, uneven enforcement of bail regulations, and insufficient psychiatric and social evaluations. The procedural elements, as examined through the judicial rulings, disclose variations in age assessment, initial evaluations, and trial procedures. The author concludes that enhancing the functions of JJBs, Children's Courts, and child welfare institutions is essential for guaranteeing that juveniles obtain equitable, rehabilitative, and reintegrative justice instead of punitive actions that obstruct their future opportunities with involvement of NGOs and children care organizations from the beginning of the police response.

The second theme is on "Addressing Specific Child Vulnerabilities". Under this theme, specific situations have been discussed under four chapters that highlight the findings in relation to addressing the child vulnerabilities as follows:

The first chapter under this theme focuses on the aspect of child marriage in the chapter entitled "A Socio-Legal Examination of Child Marriage and Its Societal Ramifications". This chapter highlights that the Indian government is trying to curb child marriages through certain policies; however, the author admits that these policies and plans can work only with effective enforcement and implementation of the Prohibition of Child Marriage Act of 2006. These policies focus on a child's right to nutrition, education and development, protection, and participation. The authors observe that the law enforcement authorities like the Police, Child Marriage Prohibition Officer, District Magistrate, and District Women and Child Development Office need to be more active, particularly in rural areas, to unearth instances of child marriage, and imposing the punishments on the wrong-doers may instill a sense of deterrence. However, child marriages have been historically practiced in India, and they continue to be practiced due to customary beliefs and economic hardships; therefore, deterrence alone is not adequate to eradicate child marriage. The author concludes by observing that it has to be supplemented with measures to spread awareness, educating children and families about its long-term repercussions, providing financial support and vocational training to combat the causes of child marriages.

In the next chapter, "Legal Rights of the Children Born Out of Live-In Relationships", the vulnerabilities associated with children in a live-in relationship are explored. In this chapter the author argues that though judicial pronouncements have progressively recognized the legitimacy of live-in relationships; however, a critical gap still remains due to the absence of a comprehensive legal framework explicitly addressing the rights and responsibilities of live-in partners and their children. After analyzing the various legislative framework or the lack of it in relation to protecting the children in live-in relationship, the author, to ensure legal clarity and protection for live-in relationships in India, empresses on a distinct legislative framework to differentiate them from traditional marriage while providing safeguards through registration, succession laws recognizing inheritance rights for children, and a functional parenthood model to uphold caregiving roles, joint custody, and child welfare. The author concludes that the judiciary and executive bodies should adapt to evolving family structures, and public awareness campaigns should reduce stigma.

In the chapter "Myriads of Vulnerabilities of Distressed Child Migrants: A Case study From Odisha" the vulnerabilities associated with child migrants have been highlighted by the authors as they observe that there is a gap in the law in question with respect to child migrant workers. This chapter explores on the socio-economic protections, specifically, focusing on four safeguards – education, working hours, employment wages, and stable living arrangements. The authors present findings from the data collected as part of a social mapping exercise of inter-state migrant workers in four districts of in the State of Odisha (India) through a household survey, in the context of gaps existing in the law and policy framework. The authors come to the conclusion that a holistic approach must be taken while framing policies to arrest migration among children that not only focus on improving access to education as a strategy but must take note of all causative factors.

In the last chapter under this theme, "Are the Children Lacking an Exclusive Green Safeguard in India?", the author explores the vulnerable conditions of children when they lack the green safeguards. In this chapter the author comprehensively discusses the different child rights, aligned to the environmental rights of the children, with special focus on the UN Committee on the Rights of the Child that has brought out the General Comment No. 26 (GC26) on the Rights of the Child and the Environment, prioritizing the climate disaster threat to the youth. The author concludes that India still lacks protection of the ecological interest of the children, though India ratified the sustainable goal, but there must be more emphasis on the child rights-based approach. The author concludes that unless the absence and requirement of the core right are realized, the policy framers fail to give it a proper legal shape.

The third theme revolves around "Protection of Children in the Online Platforms". There are four chapters under this theme exploring the vulnerabilities of children in the online platform and the response mechanisms for protecting children in the digital platforms. The key findings of each of the chapters are given here:

The first chapter under this theme is "Balancing Protection and Participation: Children's Data, Online Privacy, and Age of Digital Consent". In this chapter the author discusses two central premises: differential age of consent based on the capacity of each child and the disadvantageous position of parents or guardians in giving digital consent on behalf of their children. This chapter highlights that in the realm of the concept of "evolving capacities of the child", children being digital natives often have a refined understanding of the potential risks and rewards involved in the online world than the older generation. The author argues that it is crucial to move beyond chronological age as the sole determinant of the "capacity to consent" in the digital arena and recommends the adoption of a differential age of consent that recognizes children's ability to understand and make informed decisions about digital interactions since it is influenced by various factors, including social, economic, political, and demographic conditions. This could be done by creating an all-encompassing, nuanced, and context-specific rubric that should factor in a child's gender, age, family background, social standing, financial health, educational level, cultural context, and national environment to determine the quality of capacities the said child evolves or may evolve. The author concludes by observing that it is imperative to enhance digital literacy education for both children and parents.

In the second chapter on "Safeguarding the Vulnerabilities of Children Relating to Cyberbullying From the Socio-Legal-Technical Dimensions in India" the authors in this chapter highlight the vulnerabilities specifically in the cyberspace with a special focus on the issue of cyberbullying of children and the social, legal and technological (cyber-security technology) measures, which can be adopted for securing the interests of the children in cyberspace. The authors emphasize that since there is no law on this issue and no definition of cyberbullying, this gap must be addressed by the lawmakers, and the Indian government must deploy enough funds toward creating a strong infrastructure for innovating new technological measures to ensure data privacy in the digital world, especially when children are being victimized. The authors conclude by saying that strategies for awareness campaigns in schools and colleges, highlighting the importance of ensuring privacy of personal data in cyberspace, should be built to protect children from any form of cyberbullying.

In this chapter of "Protection of Mental Health of Children in Digital Ecosystem: A Socio-Legal Study", the author discusses the *New Normal* due to social distancing mandates during post-COVID 19 period and prolonged on-screen activities through various electronic devices, leading to sedentary behaviors and mental health issues. The author gives illustrations from other countries to neutralize the ill effects of such prolonged online exposures of children, like Digital 5 A Day – introduced by England and South Korea, pushing for children outdoors playing for some 12 days. The author concludes with recommendations to create positive learning ambience that boost child mental physical health and well-being; provide early psycho-social services on the identification of the context variances; address the mental health services through devoted professionals and curative measures; and empower parents and family members to create screen-free zone or have digital detox period daily and schools to conduct awareness programs for the youngsters about the social media appropriate usage and therapy session for children who are dealing with social media addiction, anxiety, and depression.

The last chapter under this theme is "Response of Indian Criminal Justice System Toward Children as Vulnerable Victims of Cybercrime in the Digital Age". In this chapter the author focuses on the offenses committed against children through cyberspace in India and analyzes the laws prevailing in India relating to cybercrime against children. The author highlights the lacunae in the responses of the criminal justice system and emphasizes that law enforcement agencies should update themselves with emerging technological advancements to effectively handle such cases.

The fourth theme in this book is on "Response to Sexual Offences". There are three chapters under this theme. Two of the chapters deal with two different aspects of responding to sexual offence victimization, whereas the last chapter deals with adolescents involved in sexual relations but treated as offenders under the law applicable to them. The key findings of these chapters under this theme are as follows:

In this chapter of "Implementation of the Victim-Friendly Trial Procedures in Cases of Sexual Offences Against Children", the author sheds light on the Protection of Children from Sexual Offences (POCSO) Act, 2012, designed to protect children from sexual abuse. The author presents the data on the implementation of child-friendly procedures from eight Special Courts and 61 police stations and comes to the conclusion that Odisha's implementation of the POCSO Act demonstrates significant strides in making the judicial process more accessible and less traumatic for children. The author also analyzes the functioning of the trial courts in the United Kingdom and Sweden, which reveals a multidisciplinary and trauma-informed approach achieved by collaboration among law enforcement, social services, and mental health professionals to create a child-centered process in contrast to India's approach, which often lacks the resources and systemic integration necessary for optimal implementation. The author concludes by observing that learning from international models and addressing systemic challenges within India's judicial framework can ensure a system that not only delivers justice swiftly but also protects and empowers children, allowing them to heal and rebuild their lives with dignity.

The chapter "Dissecting the Conundrum of Mandatory Reporting and POCSO, 2012, in the Realm of Child Sexual Abuse" critically explores the mandatory reporting provisions under the POCSO Act in cases of child sexual abuse, which mandates professionals like teachers, medical personnel, and social workers to promptly report suspected cases of child sexual abuse to relevant authorities. The author observes that, despite its gravity, individuals, organizations, and entire communities choose to overlook or conceal the issue. Through this chapter, the author emphasizes the societal responsibility to break this silent pact, advocating for the crucial role of reporting child sexual abuse, on the one hand, and the rights of the child and guardians, urging a conservative approach to prevent unwarranted accusations, on the other hand. The author concludes that the provision of mandatory reporting needs to be modified in a manner where the primary focus should be placed on professionals to disclose abuse and report it to the police, rather than making it equally applicable to everyone, as this could result in harassment by the public, as the mandated reporting provision can be based on mere apprehension. Also, the author emphasizes making the punishment more severe for non-reporting of sexual offences, but such a punitive approach may be counterproductive to the very notion of collaborative law enforcement with the involvement of the community for handling cases of child sexual abuse, which is aimed at by such provisions of mandatory reporting.

The final chapter under this theme and also the book is on "The Model for Juvenile Sexual Offenders in India: A Need for a Relook?". In this chapter the author focuses on the dichotomous situation presented by cases of sexual offences involving adolescents (within the age frame of 16–18 years) within the present legal framework where the dual laws of POCSO Act and JJ Act intersect, treating the girl as a victim and the boy as the perpetrator under the JJ Act even when the POCSO Act is a gender-neutral legislation. The chapter looks at the model, both legal and institutional, and highlights the dilemmas faced by the courts in dealing with such cases and the lack of institutional mechanisms to handle such juvenile sexual offenders, proving counterproductive to the very ideal of rehabilitation that is central to the JJ Act. The author concludes by recommending that both the POCSO Act and the JJ Act need to be amended to bring respite to the adolescents within 16–18 years, as adolescent consensual sexual relationships are on the rise, and the sooner the law is amended, the better the cause of child rights and procedural justice will be served.

Through this book on "Child Protection: Assessing Multi-Disciplinary Response Mechanisms in the Indian Perspective", an attempt was made by the authors in the chapters under four different themes to highlight the vulnerabilities of children in various contexts and how the stakeholders through various laws and policies are responding to such children with the sole aim of protecting them to give them a safe and secure childhood.

INDEX

Note: Numbers in **bold** indicate a table. Numbers in *italics* indicate a figure.

For Product Safety Concerns and Information please contact our EU representative GPSR@taylorandfrancis.com Taylor & Francis Verlag GmbH, Kaufingerstraße 24, 80331 München, Germany